The Transition in
Eastern Europe

A National Bureau
of Economic Research
Project Report

The Transition in Eastern Europe

Volume
1

Country Studies

Edited by Olivier Jean Blanchard, Kenneth A. Froot, and Jeffrey D. Sachs

The University of Chicago Press

Chicago and London

OLIVIER JEAN BLANCHARD is professor of economics at the Massachusetts Institute of Technology. KENNETH A. FROOT is professor of business administration at the Graduate School of Business, Harvard University. JEFFREY D. SACHS is the Galen L. Stone Professor of International Trade at Harvard University. All are research associates of the National Bureau of Economic Research.

The University of Chicago Press, Chicago 60637
The University of Chicago Press, Ltd., London
© 1994 by the National Bureau of Economic Research
All rights reserved. Published 1994
Printed in the United States of America
03 02 01 00 99 98 97 96 95 94   1 2 3 4 5
ISBN: 0-226-05660-0 (cloth)

Library of Congress Cataloging-in-Publication Data

The Transition in Eastern Europe / edited by Olivier Jean Blanchard,
    Kenneth A. Froot, and Jeffrey D. Sachs.
        p.   cm.—(A National Bureau of Economic Research Project
Report)
    Includes bibliographical references and index.
    Contents: v. 1. Country studies—v. 2. Restructuring.
    1. Europe, Eastern—Economic conditions—1989– —Congresses.
    2. Europe, Eastern—Economic policy—1989– —Congresses.
    3. Economic stabilization—Europe, Eastern—Congresses.
    4. Privatization—Europe, Eastern—Congresses.   I. Blanchard, Olivier
(Olivier J.)   II. Froot, Kenneth.   III. Sachs, Jeffrey.   IV. Series.
HC244.T6989   1994
338.947—dc20   93-36585
                                                                          CIP

Relation of the Directors to the
Work and Publications of the
National Bureau of Economic Research

1. The object of the National Bureau of Economic Research is to ascertain and to present to the public important economic facts and their interpretation in a scientific and impartial manner. The Board of Directors is charged with the responsibility of ensuring that the work of the National Bureau is carried on in strict conformity with this object.

2. The President of the National Bureau shall submit to the Board of Directors, or to its Executive Committee, for their formal adoption all specific proposals for research to be instituted.

3. No research report shall be published by the National Bureau until the President has sent each member of the Board a notice that a manuscript is recommended for publication and that in the President's opinion it is suitable for publication in accordance with the principles of the National Bureau. Such notification will include an abstract or summary of the manuscript's content and a response form for use by those Directors who desire a copy of the manuscript for review. Each manuscript shall contain a summary drawing attention to the nature and treatment of the problem studied, the character of the data and their utilization in the report, and the main conclusions reached.

4. For each manuscript so submitted, a special committee of the Directors (including Directors Emeriti) shall be appointed by majority agreement of the President and Vice Presidents (or by the Executive Committee in case of inability to decide on the part of the President and Vice Presidents), consisting of three Directors selected as nearly as may be one from each general division of the Board. The names of the special manuscript committee shall be stated to each Director when notice of the proposed publication is submitted to him. It shall be the duty of each member of the special manuscript committee to read the manuscript. If each member of the manuscript committee signifies his approval within thirty days of the transmittal of the manuscript, the report may be published. If at the end of that period any member of the manuscript committee withholds his approval, the President shall then notify each member of the Board, requesting approval or disapproval of publication, and thirty days additional shall be granted for this purpose. The manuscript shall then not be published unless at least a majority of the entire Board who shall have voted on the proposal within the time fixed for the receipt of votes shall have approved.

5. No manuscript may be published, though approved by each member of the special manuscript committee, until forty-five days have elapsed from the transmittal of the report in manuscript form. The interval is allowed for the receipt of any memorandum of dissent or reservation, together with a brief statement of his reasons, that any member may wish to express; and such memorandum of dissent or reservation shall be published with the manuscript if he so desires. Publication does not, however, imply that each member of the Board has read the manuscript, or that either members of the Board in general or the special committee have passed on its validity in every detail.

6. Publications of the National Bureau issued for informational purposes concerning the work of the Bureau and its staff, or issued to inform the public of activities of Bureau staff, and volumes issued as a result of various conferences involving the National Bureau shall contain a specific disclaimer noting that such publication has not passed through the normal review procedures required in this resolution. The Executive Committee of the Board is charged with review of all such publications from time to time to ensure that they do not take on the character of formal research reports of the National Bureau, requiring formal Board approval.

7. Unless otherwise determined by the Board or exempted by the terms of paragraph 6, a copy of this resolution shall be printed in each National Bureau publication.

(Resolution adopted October 25, 1926, as revised through September 30, 1974)

Contents

Preface

This volume contains seven papers that were prepared as part of a research project by the National Bureau of Economic Research on the Transition in Eastern Europe. These papers examine the experience of specific countries, including Poland, Czechoslovakia, Hungary, Germany, Slovenia, and the former Soviet Union, with emphasis on macroeconomic policies and performance.

In addition to the papers in this volume, the project also includes studies of the problems of restructuring, from fiscal reform, to labor market structure, to the design of privatization and bankruptcy mechanisms, to the role of foreign direct investment. These studies are included in the second volume of this two-volume set.

The findings of the NBER's Eastern Europe project were presented at a conference for economists, journalists, and policymakers from the United States and Europe. The conference was held in Cambridge, Massachusetts, 26–29 February 1992.

We would like to thank the Pew Charitable Trusts for financial support of this work.

Olivier Jean Blanchard, Kenneth A. Froot, and Jeffrey D. Sachs

Introduction

Olivier Jean Blanchard, Kenneth A. Froot,
and Jeffrey D. Sachs

When communism fell in Eastern Europe in 1989, the issue in most countries was not whether to go to a market economy but how to get there. Arguments ranged from the timing of stabilization, to the speed of price liberalization, to the design of privatization.

The debate was extraordinarily compressed in time, for several reasons. First, and most important, the new governments came into power with little preparation and had to formulate programs quickly in the face of worsening economic conditions. During the late 1980s, the anti-Communist reformers certainly had little premonition that they would be in office (some of the new leaders came almost directly from jail), and the oppressive political milieu of the Communist period had prevented a full and open debate over economic options. As a result, the policy debate had typically been about long-term and philosophical issues rather than short-term and programmatic issues. Also, microeconomic issues, such as privatization and demonopolization, rather than macroeconomic issues, tended to dominate the debate, and many basic macroeconomic issues had hardly been discussed. The prevailing view among reformers at the end of the Communist period was that macroeconomic reforms, such as price liberalization and convertibility of the currency, would be gradual.

Much of this changed with the emergence of the Solidarity-led government in Poland in September 1989. In view of the rapidly deteriorating macroeconomic conditions in Poland at the end of 1989, the debate shifted quickly to macroeconomic stabilization and exchange rate management. And, with widespread public support for fundamental change, the policy debate shifted in favor of radical reforms. This shift of focus and emphasis culminated in the Balcerowicz Plan, introduced on 1 January 1990, which called for rapid price liberalization, sharp cutbacks in the budgetary deficit, tight monetary policy, and a quick opening of the economy, all this without waiting for privatization.

Czechoslovakia, Bulgaria, and Romania subsequently followed Poland's lead, while East Germany had a "shock" program of its own resulting from the economic and monetary union with West Germany in the summer of 1990. The situation was different in Hungary, where both the political and the economic transformations were less abrupt than elsewhere. Market reforms in Hungary had been under way gradually since 1968, and the macroeconomic situation was adverse but not collapsing. Under these circumstances, the new government opted for a more gradual course, although also one that was based on stabilization and liberalization first, to be followed only later by privatization.

Most of those countries have now taken the key steps of substantial price liberalization and macroeconomic stabilization, or at least enough stabilization to arrest the slide to hyperinflation. The process has been controversial from the start and has raised many questions. Can orthodox stabilization measures work in an economy dominated by state ownership? Can the lessons of stabilization in other parts of the world be transferred to the socialist economies? Can successful stabilization precede privatization and demonopolization of industry? These questions remain controversial. But they largely concern the past. East European governments are now turning their attention to the problems of privatization and restructuring. Here, the very scope of systemic transformation is such that there are few historical experiences on which to rely. Some apparent guideposts, such as privatization in Western countries, can be more misleading than helpful. Other historical cases, such as postwar reconstruction in Western Europe, provide at best fuzzy guides. The problem in Eastern Europe is not just to rebuild but to transform. Resources locked up in heavy industry must be reoriented toward light industry, housing construction, and services. Enterprises organized for a planned economy must be restructured in order to be responsive to market signals. Governments must also create the right incentives for economic actors during the transition period. This is proving difficult.

The purpose of this NBER conference, held in Cambridge, Massachusetts, in the spring of 1992, was to take stock, to identify common progress, common difficulties, and tentative solutions. The conference was divided into two parts, which correspond to volumes 1 and 2, respectively: (1) looking at the experience of specific countries (Poland, Czechoslovakia, Hungary, Germany, Slovenia, and the former Soviet Union), with an emphasis on macroeconomic policies and performance, and (2) looking at the problems of restructuring, from fiscal reform, to labor market structure, to the design of privatization and of bankruptcy mechanisms, to the role of foreign direct investment.

One of the aims of the conference was to draw on both the experience of those who have shaped or closely followed events in Eastern Europe and the expertise of those who, while not having been involved in the process of transition, were familiar with the particular issues at hand. This mix is reflected in the set of papers presented here.

A theme clearly emerges from the two volumes. The private sector is growing fast and filling many of the holes left by the previous Soviet-type economies. By contrast, the transformation of the large state firms is proving slow and difficult. This is not so much because they were in worse shape than expected as because privatization has been slower than expected, leaving those firms with neither the incentives nor the tools to restructure. The future of reform depends on the success of the delicate balancing act between growth of the private sector and rationalization of the state sector that governments have to perform. The newly emerging private sector is not yet large enough or wide enough to bring success alone. The state sector must be cut down to size, made more efficient through privatization and restructuring, before its inertia bankrupts the process of transition.

Volume 1: Country Studies

The countries of Eastern Europe can, for our purposes, be roughly divided into three groups. The first includes the major countries of Central Europe, in which there has been generally strong support for reform and, until recently, few redefinitions of borders. Those countries have already gone through stabilization and price liberalization and are now proceeding with privatization and restructuring. The second group includes just one country, the former East Germany, where the resources and the role of West Germany are so overwhelming as to lead to a radically different adjustment process. The third group includes those countries that have to struggle with both less support for reform and the redefinition of borders. This includes the states born out of both the former Yugoslavia and the former Soviet Union. The conference focused on both the experience of Slovenia, a new state born out of Yugoslavia, and the start of the reform process in the former Soviet Union.

Reform in Central Europe

Reform in Central Europe is the topic of the first four papers. The first is by Michael Bruno, who identifies both similarities and differences in the reform experience of Hungary, Poland, Czechoslovakia, Bulgaria, and Romania. Except for Hungary, which has pursued a stop-and-go limited reform process for most of the past twenty years, reform in those countries is a recent process. The first one to implement a full-fledged stabilization and liberalization plan was Poland, in January 1990. The others followed in early 1991. The experience of Poland is then reviewed in detail by Andrew Berg and Olivier Blanchard, that of Czechoslovakia by Karel Dyba and Jan Svejnar, and that of Hungary by Kemal Derviş and Timothy Condon. From these four papers, one can draw the following lessons:

1. In all countries, stabilization has been associated with a sharp initial decrease in measured output. While there are serious problems of measurement, the sign of the movement is unambiguous, although the scale is not. An important issue is how to allocate the causes of the measured output decline

among possible causes, including mismeasurement (especially underreporting of the new private sector), the decline of previously subsidized and protected sectors, the cyclical effects of monetary stabilization, and the collapse of trade arrangements within the CMEA (Council for Mutual Economic Assistance), especially between the East European countries and the Soviet Union. For Czechoslovakia, Bulgaria, and Romania, stabilization and the collapse of the CMEA coincide, making it difficult to allocate blame. But the decline of output in Poland in 1990, before the major collapse of the CMEA, suggests an important role of stabilization and also mismeasurement. Contrary to some expectations and fears, the decline in output appears to be due not to supply disruptions but rather to a demand contraction.

2. In all countries, stabilization and price liberalization have led to a large price adjustment. In Poland and Czechoslovakia, there was a large jump in the price level at the point of price liberalization. In some countries, inflation has since tapered off; in others, it is still running at 2–5 percent a month. The initial price adjustment was higher than initially forecast, but it is not clear that much more has been at work than the passthrough of cost increases that were also larger than expected. Berg and Blanchard argue that, in the case of Poland, the price increase can be more than fully attributed to cost increases, counter to the idea that price liberalization allowed monopolistic enterprises to raise their markups over costs. Bruno raises the possibility that, in some countries, the large initial devaluation may have contributed to the initial inflation.

3. In all countries, there has been some shift of export markets from the East to the West. One of the most controversial elements of the "big bang" in Poland and elsewhere has been the rapid opening of the economy. This trade liberalization typically embodied several steps, including a steep devaluation, followed by convertibility of the currency on current account; an elimination of most quantitative trade restrictions; and the imposition of relatively low tariff rates. One of the goals of the rapid liberalization was to end the "anti-export" bias of the old regime, in which exporters were subject to a hugely overvalued exchange rate as well as many other restrictions. The second goal was to introduce international competition into domestic markets that were typically oligopolistic in market structure. One wide fear in Eastern Europe was that quality of production was so low that "there would be nothing to sell in the West." These fears have not materialized. In fact, exports to the West have grown rapidly and have helped compensate for the very sharp decline in trade with the Soviet Union.

4. Implementing privatization has proved harder than expected. In most countries, substantial progress has been made in privatizing small- and medium-scale firms. But privatization of large firms is still largely in the future, for many reasons. Parliaments have insisted on extensive involvement, making the process more democratic but also cumbersome. Various stakeholders have had strong incentives to oppose or sabotage particular schemes. Initial schemes, often modeled on Western ones, have proved unworkable, or work-

able only at very low speeds. Countries are now experimenting with a variety of more radical schemes. Poland is preparing for mass privatization, through the creation of investment funds as financial intermediaries. Hungary has shifted to a system with more reliance on individual initiative and only ex post control by the state. Czechoslovakia has embarked on the most ambitious plan, a voucher system with auctions, for about one-fourth of all large state firms. Dyba and Svejnar give an insightful discussion of the benefits and dangers of the voucher plan.

5. Largely as a result of slow privatization, there has been less restructuring than was expected and than is needed. In many countries, and particularly in Poland, workers have gained substantial rights of governance within the enterprise and in many cases have operated with shorter and shorter horizons. Firms have decreased employment by less than output, leading to declines in labor productivity. Despite the presence of government incomes policies in all countries, wages have increasingly appropriated revenues, and profits have declined. In the presence of constraints on credit to state firms, firms in difficulty have often relied on forced interenterprise credit. Bankruptcy laws have been little used for several reasons: many creditors are now hostages to borrowers; banks are state owned, with few incentives to press bankruptcy proceedings; the bankruptcy laws are difficult to apply; and creditors, debtors, and the courts have little experience. The credibility of the hard budget constraint is and will be tested for some time to come. Reading the papers in these two volumes, one senses different degrees of pessimism among the authors, with somewhat more pessimism regarding Poland than Hungary. Nonetheless, given the sketchy information available, it is difficult to judge whether the different nuances add up to real variations among countries. Data comparisons between Hungary and Poland, for example, do not suggest any notable differences in macroeconomic performance.

6. In all countries, the private sector has done very well. In the nonagricultural economy, Poland's private sector now represents around 30 percent of total employment, up from 13 percent at the start of reform. Including agriculture, almost half of Polish GNP is already produced in the private sector. Most of the growth has been in services and trade, two sectors repressed under the previous system. Some of it has been in industry, and some signs are very encouraging. At the end of 1991, private exports accounted for 20 percent of total exports in Poland; in Hungary, 50 percent of exports was accounted for by firms with fewer than fifty workers. Nevertheless, because of lack of knowhow, of entrepreneurs, and of a competent banking system, new private firms remain for the most part very small businesses; it is clear that the new private sector cannot by itself be counted on to replace the state sector. The papers point to interesting differences in private-sector growth. In Czechoslovakia, private-sector growth appears to have been much faster in the Czech lands than in Slovakia, leading to much higher unemployment in Slovakia. Variations are also evident in Poland, with low unemployment rates in the largest cities (ex-

cept for high-unemployment Lodz) and higher unemployment in the rural areas.

7. Two years into reform, most governments face similar short-run issues. Reform fatigue tends to set in, making it harder to pass legislation with large redistributive implications. Most governments are faced with chronic deficit problems, coming primarily from the declining revenues from the profit tax on state enterprises. In the short run, they must deal with the fiscal crisis, until revenues from the new taxes come on line. But, more fundamentally, they must change the behavior of state firms. Even if the current privatization schemes proceed on schedule, it is not clear that the decentralized ownership that they may generate will be sufficient to bring about restructuring. Clarification of bankruptcy rules is essential. So is the reform of the banking system, an issue discussed at some length by Bruno. And so is maintaining the credibility of the hard budget constraint: even profit-maximizing owners have an incentive not to pay taxes or not to repay loans if they think that there are no risks in doing so.

The Absorption of the Former East Germany

The experience of the former East Germany, which is reviewed by Rudiger Dornbusch and Holger Wolf, differs in two major ways from that of other Central European countries. First, firms in the former East Germany have been pressed to pay wages close to those current in West Germany. Second, the former East Germany is benefiting from an infusion of West German know-how, finance, and transfers on a scale unavailable to other countries.

The first issue taken up by Dornbusch and Wolf is that of conversion of the ostmark into the deutsche mark, at a one-to-one exchange rate. Even though most observers concur that the conversion took place at a hugely overvalued exchange rate for the ostmark, Dornbusch and Wolf argue that the rate of conversion probably made little difference to the macroeconomic outcome. In particular, given the implicit commitment of the German government and the privatization agency, the Treuhand, to absorb losses of firms for some time to come, the drive for wage parity was probably unavoidable and not very much affected by the official rate of conversion. In fact, East Germany wages rose sharply in nominal terms after the conversion of ostmark wage rates into deutsche mark wage rates, suggesting that the conversion itself was not the source of the wage pressures in East Germany.

Dornbusch and Wolf then document the extent of the drop in production in East Germany. Industrial production was down by 54 percent in 1990 and by another 20 percent in 1991. In effect, very few products are competitive at the existing wages. At the same time, transfers from the West to the East amounted to 73 percent of East Germany GDP in 1991. The high transfer payments therefore are supporting the high wages and consumption levels, despite the lack of competitiveness at those wage rates.

Dornbusch and Wolf then turn to the actions of the Treuhand, which at the beginning assumed 95 percent of the enterprise sector and was given the task of privatization. Its strategy has been to look for single buyers, preferably with expertise in the given sector, and to put weight not only on price but also on employment and investment commitments. This has led the Treuhand to dismantle some of the larger *Kombinate,* in order to make the pieces more attractive, and to be more discretionary in its choice of buyer than auction systems would have been. Progress has been fast, but, as is documented in the paper, tax breaks and debt relief have made some of these sales very costly for German taxpayers. Earlier studies have suggested that East Germany could address its lack of competitiveness by putting in place wage subsidies that would phase out automatically over time. Alternatively, Dornbusch and Wolf suggest announcing an end to subsidies for jobs and the enforcement of bankruptcy rules thereafter, saying that what is important is to "protect people, not jobs." It is, however, an open question whether the German government can actually commit to a fixed timetable for removing subsidies, especially in cases of large firms in regions with high unemployment.

Dornbusch and Wolf conclude that the reform is likely to prove a success, albeit a very costly one. In view of the size of the transfers from West to East Germany, they wonder whether Central European countries will be able to succeed, whether the much more depreciated exchange rate (and lower wages) will be sufficient to offset the lack of transfers.

Creating New States: Slovenia and the Former Soviet Union

According to the paper by Boris Pleskovic and Jeffrey Sachs, Slovenia's recent experience in achieving political and economic independence offers lessons for the nineteen other new countries that have emerged out of the former Yugoslavia and the former Soviet Union. Slovene independence from Yugoslavia was achieved in steps during the period January 1991–October 1991. By the end of this process, on 8 October 1991, Slovenia introduced its own currency, the Slovene tolar, thereby becoming the first of the new states to achieve monetary independence. Subsequently, it stabilized the economy and carried out fundamental economic and institutional reforms. This progress was accomplished despite difficult circumstances, including the Yugoslav civil war and the nearly complete loss of the former Yugoslav market.

The basic idea of the monetary reform was straightforward. All bank accounts and domestic wages, prices, and other contracts were to be converted automatically from dinars to the new currency, the tolar, on a one-to-one basis. The currency in circulation was to be physically converted during a short period of time. The new currency was to be the sole legal tender after conversion and was to trade freely with international currencies on a convertible basis and also to float freely against the Yugoslav dinar. The implementation of the monetary reform was carried out during 7–10 October 1991, according to plan, although some vestiges of the old multiple exchange rate system remained for a few months.

The most urgent motivation for the monetary reform was to protect the Slovene economy from hyperinflation, a fate expected for the Yugoslav dinar. As it turned out, these expectations were correct. Yugoslav inflation has grown very rapidly since October 1991, reaching 100 percent per month in June 1992. In contrast, in Slovenia, monthly inflation peaked at 21.5 percent in the month of conversion and since then has fallen gradually, to 5.1 percent in April 1992 and to 1.2 percent in August 1992.

Slovenia has also been successful in other areas of macroeconomic stabilization and trade liberalization. It carried out a tax reform and achieved a slight budget surplus in 1991. Exports to the West increased, and the economy experienced a trade and balance-of-payments surplus both in 1991 and in the first half of 1992. The decline in industrial output continued in 1992, but at a slower rate than in the last quarter of 1991. The unemployment rate reached around 11 percent in early 1992. As elsewhere, progress on privatization and financial restructuring has been very slow.

According to Pleskovic and Sachs, there are several lessons to be gained from Slovenia's experience. First, the experience shows that it is possible to move quickly on macroeconomic stabilization with the help of a well-conceived monetary reform. Second, convertibility (at least trade transactions) can and should be introduced from the beginning of the monetary reform. Third, technical work on the conversion can be done quickly. Fourth, trade will reorient itself to new markets, as soon as sufficient opening of the economy occurs. Fifth, as in Central Europe and the former Soviet Union, Slovenia's experience also shows the risk of becoming bogged down in a protracted privatization debate.

At the time of the conference, reform had barely started in the former Soviet Union (FSU) and was taking place within the context of a collapse not only of the relations between republics but also of the central structure within each republic. After reviewing the past, in particular the New Economic Policy (NEP), Stanley Fischer focuses on the two issues that are making reform in the FSU harder than elsewhere.

Macroeconomic stabilization requires a firm grip on the budget and on money creation, but that firm grip is present in neither case. Taxes collected at the local level are often not being transferred to the center. The central bank, sometimes under pressure from the Parliament or the government, is willing to let credit to state firms increase rather rapidly, making stabilization more difficult. Thus, as of the time of this writing, the budget deficit is large and inflation high.

Privatization is nevertheless proceeding. The collapse of the center has left managers de facto in charge of firms (unlike in Poland, workers in the FSU have little authority within the enterprises). Fischer argues that Russia has learned from the problems of privatization in other East European countries. Current privatization plans recognize the de facto stakeholders, so as to enroll their support. He suggests a two-track privatization plan, one for small firms and one for larger firms, the latter encouraging self-privatization with approval by the privatization agency.

Fischer then turns to the relations between republics. He argues that, to understand current developments, one must understand the role of Russia as the leader and the sheer difficulty the other republics have taking steps on their own, such as creating their own currencies. He discusses the pros and cons and the ways of introducing different currencies. He argues for the creation of a payments union, whether or not republics move to the adoption of convertibility and their own currency.

Volume 2: Restructuring

With the country papers in volume 1 having provided the context, the papers in volume 2 then turn to the particular issues. These include labor market institutions, public finance, privatization, bankruptcy reform, and foreign trade. We discuss them in turn.

Organizing Labor Market Relations

Should East European countries move toward a system of centralized or decentralized bargaining? Should institutions be different during the process of transition? These are the questions taken up by Richard Freeman. Given that we do not have the answers to those questions even for Western countries, Freeman emphatically refuses to make specific recommendations. But his paper nevertheless provides a useful framework within which to think about the issues.

Freeman first looks at existing institutions and points out that the old Communist unions are doing well. In Czechoslovakia, the old unions have been taken over by new leaders. In Poland, Bulgaria, and Albania, old and new unions coexist; in Hungary and Romania, new unions coexist with breakaways from the old ones. Old unions are doing well because of the advantages of incumbency, the large resources that they have been able to keep, the organizational weakness of the new unions, and the benign neglect of the government. Thus, the initial situation in labor relations as well as in most other places is not one of a tabula rasa.

Freeman then looks at changes in the labor market. Wage dispersion is increasing, usually in a way related to differences in profitability across enterprises. Unemployment is increasing but is not yet felt to be a major hardship by the population as a whole. The private sector is growing and the state sector contracting. Freeman argues, both informally and with the help of a simple model, that the main risk to reform from the labor market is that an increasingly large group of workers will feel that they will lose from reform and at the same time be sufficiently powerful to stop it. Thus, he argues, structures of negotiation and organization that reduce this risk, for example, unions that cover both the contracting and the expanding sectors, will increase the chances of success of reform.

Achieving Fiscal Reform

Three papers deal with fiscal reform. Roger Gordon looks at fiscal policy in the transition and the design of a new fiscal structure. Peter Diamond looks at the setting up of pension funds. Alain de Combrugghe and David Lipton look at the concrete problems faced by Polish fiscal policymakers today, as a case study of the budget in transition economies.

Roger Gordon emphasizes two aspects of prereform fiscal policy. The first is that the structure of taxes differs considerably from that of Western counterparts, in particular, with the large role played by profit taxes. The second is that, as soon as the transition process starts and prices start playing a role, all the distortions implicit in the tax system are activated. If not changed, the heavy emphasis on enterprise profits, together with the steady decline in the profits of state firms in the transition, is a recipe for fiscal crisis, as has indeed occurred in a number of countries. This problem, together with the many distortions of the tax system, implies that fiscal reform should be high on the reform agenda; distortions can derail the reform process.

After looking at the institutional constraints, including the lack of a reliable accounting system, the difficulty of taxing much of the private sector, and the difficulties in enforcing tax collection, Gordon recommends the replacement of both turnover and profit taxes by a value-added tax. Given the relatively small dispersion of most incomes, he even suggests that a value-added tax may for a while be an acceptable substitute for an income tax. Gordon suggests first changing from the turnover tax to a value-added tax on state firms, a change that can be achieved rapidly, and then introducing a value-added tax on private firms, a move that will take longer.

The transition economies of Eastern Europe are surely not first-best economies. Thus, many proposals have suggested offsetting the various externalities and distortions by taxes and subsidies. In the last part of his paper, Gordon discusses a number of such proposals, from tax holidays to the design of unemployment benefit systems. There is no simple punchline here, but an informed and useful discussion.

One of the largest components of the fiscal reform is the pension and disability system. Peter Diamond's paper examines pension reform proposals in Poland, the country that has gone the furthest toward developing a new system. As with the overall fiscal situation, the status of the pension system as the Communist regime collapsed was highly problematic. The Polish system was a defined-benefit system, with benefits based on years of service and earnings in the last twelve months of work. As Diamond argues, this structure presents a number of incentive and compliance problems and is likely to be inappropriate for a capitalist economy with voluntary (and variable) employment. (To complicate transitional matters, no records are currently being kept for earnings prior to each employee's last year of work.) Furthermore, the current structure provides for only a very low level of income for many current and prospective retirees, and there is little operating room in the overall fiscal position.

It is in this environment that the Poles are considering revamping their pension system. Diamond explores various implications of the current proposal, which has three critical features: first, it would provide for a *social* pension system with initial benefits of up to 120 percent of the national average wage; second, it would mandate a ceiling on *total* (social plus private) benefits of 250 percent of the national average wage; and, third, it would create a privately funded system for benefits in between 120 percent and 250 percent of the national average wage.

As both the United States and Chile provide models for advanced, privately funded, defined-contribution pension systems, Diamond draws lessons from these cases. He considers in detail some of the key differences between privately run, defined-contribution plans and publicly run plans. The most important of these include the effects that changes in pension expenditures have on nonpension parts of the government budget, the pros and cons of having a competitive group of privately managed pension funds (as opposed to a centralized fund), and the transition difficulties involved in establishing fully funded plans.

Diamond also discusses the particular difficulties of finding channels for pension savings in a country with poorly developed capital markets. In some respects, forced pension saving mandated by the government may be considerably less efficient than private savings, which may not need the same degree of financial intermediation. Diamond explores many other considerations, such as implications for corporate governance and management oversight and the feasibility of regulating privately sponsored retirement plans.

De Crombrugghe and Lipton look at the difficulties of managing the fiscal budget before, during, and after the transition to a decentralized economy. Their specific focus is on Poland, but it is striking how widely relevant the discussion is for any country in transition. The paper begins with a description of the pressures on Poland's budget as the Communist regime collapsed. Despite sharp decreases in revenues, the budget still averaged a 3 percent surplus in 1990. De Crombrugghe and Lipton argue that this was the result of four factors: a one-time paper profit windfall, leading to temporarily high measured profit; the sharp cut in subsidies associated with the price liberalization facet of the reform program; the reduction in external debt service; and a reduced level of government investment spending.

However, new budgetary pressures emerged. Over time, the immediate improvement in enterprise tax revenues vanished, as some of the capital stock became useless at market prices and with the collapse of the CMEA, as further wage increases in the state-owned sector reduced profits, and as many new private-sector businesses were able to escape taxes on profits. A new tax system is being put together, but it will take time to eliminate loopholes and improve compliance. On the expenditure side, spending on unemployment insurance and social security benefits has begun to rise rapidly.

De Crombrugghe and Lipton emphasize that these budgetary pressures will continue in the years ahead. Public investment is badly needed to clean up severe environmental degradation and to shore up an infrastructure that is inadequate for a growing economy. Recapitalization of the banks (whose assets include a sizable proportion of bad loans) will also create demands on the budget. Deficit financing for these needs may be desirable if bond finance (domestic or foreign) rather than monetary finance can be tapped.

The authors emphasize the magnitude of the short-run dangers. Demands on the budget will grow much more rapidly than either financing or tax-revenue-raising programs. There will be a strong near-term temptation to monetize deficits, which must be resisted if inflation targets are to be achieved. Existing taxes, such as "dividends" (a tax on enterprise assets), should be used actively until more flexibility is developed. The task of reinventing fiscal expenditure and revenue programs is immense and is one that every East European economy currently faces.

Accelerating Privatization

Three papers in volume 2 address what is probably the single most formidable obstacle facing Eastern Europe in its transition to capitalism—privatization. As the privatization process unfolds across Eastern Europe, it is clear that the experience across countries will be highly varied. In general, privatization will take place amid prolonged confusion about the identity of owners (including past owners), the rights of managers and workers, and the role of the government. While, in Germany, the Treuhand rapidly sells thousands of East German enterprises to West German firms, the other countries will necessarily confront a period of conflicting claims among various stakeholders in state property. Large state-owned firms will certainly pose the greatest challenges, as they present a complex web of overlapping claims for residual control rights and no easy answers.

This diversity of claims is well illustrated by Russia, where existing control rights are among the most poorly defined in Eastern Europe. Andrei Shleifer and Robert Vishny argue that the first hurdle in accomplishing Russian privatization will be to resolve ambiguous and conflicting ownership claims among various enterprise stakeholders. The state and (what is left of) the central ministries, local governments and bureaucrats, managers, and workers all have some powers of residual control and therefore some bargaining strength. Each of these groups must somehow be either accommodated or disenfranchised if privatization is to go forward. The paper gives a sense of the power positions of these groups by tracing the evolution of de facto ownership claims since the collapse of central planning. Until the 1988 reforms, central bureaucrats had a good deal of bargaining power, and the workers had none (in spite of ideological assertions to the contrary). Since that time, the situation has been nearly completely reversed.

Shleifer and Vishny point out that the presence of such imprecisely defined control rights leads to the failure of the Coase theorem. That is, under current circumstances, there is no reason to think that negotiations among interested parties will produce an efficient allocation and end use of enterprise assets. Interest groups may have an incentive to undertake destructive actions, block moves away from the status quo, or roll their own brand of "spontaneous" privatization, in which management and workers "buy" enterprises by bribing local officials and ignoring control claims of the center. Such spontaneous privatizations are technically illegal but can often be accomplished quickly because they respect the claims of most stakeholder groups. The resulting concentrated management buyout (MBO)–type ownership structure may produce relatively efficient, if inequitable, economic outcomes (although Shleifer and Vishny question whether such structures give too much control to workers). However, the main disadvantage of spontaneous privatization is the political dangers that it brings. Spontaneous transactions are likely to be perceived as unfair because they occur at very low prices and primarily benefit the old-guard incumbent managers and *nomenklatura.*

Shleifer and Vishny suggest that a Russian program of rapid, broad-scale commercialization could help shut down spontaneous privatizations and set the stage for a smoother privatization process. Commercialization entails the conversion of a state enterprise into a state-owned joint-stock company, subject to the normal commercial law for joint-stock companies and governed by a normal supervisory board (or board of directors) rather than by a ministry or a workers' council. The charter of the new joint-stock companies would spell out the rights and responsibilities of management and the supervisory board and would put legal constraints on self-dealing and conflicts of interest of the managers.

A program of comprehensive commercialization could also reduce corruption by stripping local governments and bureaucrats of their ability to dictate privatization outcomes. However, commercialization may be difficult to accomplish as it is likely to be opposed by managers to the extent that it reduces their bargaining power. A successful commercialization program is therefore likely to require the immediate transfer of some of the enterprises' shares to management and workers. It remains to be seen whether the center has sufficient power to mandate and execute a large-scale commercialization program, although it will try to do so. Of course, for large, capital intensive firms, spontaneous privatization is not really an option; for these enterprises some form of top-down process that begins with commercialization will be necessary.

As Andrew Berg's paper points out, a policy of mandatory commercialization from above was briefly attempted by the first post-Communist government in Poland in early 1990 but soon abandoned. Workers' councils, which gained de facto and de jure prominence in Poland during the 1980s, strongly resisted the approach. As a consequence, Poland's post-Communist governments have so far treated commercialization as a voluntary measure, to be carried out on an enterprise-by-enterprise basis, as each firm is prepared for privatization. Subsequent to commercializing, some firms have been sold to investors through IPOs (initial public offerings) and through trade sales to other businesses, both domestic and foreign. Some firms have been corporatized in preparation for Poland's Mass Privatization Program, described below.

An alternative privatization track, known in Poland as "liquidation," has been far more extensively used, having already been selected by firms representing about 10 percent of the work force. Under the liquidation approach, the firm ends its existence as a state enterprise, and the assets of the enterprise are then made available to the workers and management in a lease-buyback arrangement. Liquidation has been particularly popular for small- and medium-sized firms with relatively low capital intensity. There is as yet no established privatization track that has been widely used by the large Polish enterprises.

Liquidation, which is a bottom-up process that respects most enterprise stakeholders, has similarities with the spontaneous privatizations in Russia and Poland, in that assets end up with the "insiders" (workers and management). The difference is that liquidation is a legal process that is monitored and regulated, with the result that a wide cross section of workers and management, rather than a few *nomenklatura* managers, ends up with ownership rights. In this way, the liquidation track also seems to have solved the potential political problems posed by spontaneous privatizations. Significantly, it appears that firms that undertake these liquidation privatizations often engage in significant and beneficial restructuring.

This is not to say, however, that privatization through liquidation is moving quickly enough. Berg's paper explores many of the reasons why privatization generally has been difficult and delayed in Poland. For liquidations in particular, the approvals process (which includes the Ministry of Privatization and the responsible branch ministry) can be painstakingly slow. Individual bureaucrats, concerned with the criminal liabilities that arise if there is impropriety or the appearance of impropriety anywhere in a transaction, have little incentive to push privatization forward. This is, of course, an inevitable cost of the extra transparency compared with spontaneous privatizations.

The progress on mass privatization schemes for large firms has also moved slowly in Poland. Although Poland was the first country to begin grappling with the problems of mass privatization of large industry, it has been hampered by political disputes as well as the complexities of coordinating wide-scale distribution and management of ownership claims on large enterprises. Czechoslovakia, by comparison, experienced less internal dispute within the federal government in the formulation of a mass privatization program and as a consequence has already succeeded in promulgating a mass privatization program and in issuing vouchers. Delays in initiating mass privatization in Poland almost surely have given vested interests time to dig in further and to oppose a wide distribution of enterprise shares.

The privatization of business and the growth of the private sector have occurred most rapidly in East Germany. The Treuhandanstalt (the agency charged with accomplishing the privatization and restructuring of East German enterprises) has aggressively sold Eastern firms to West German companies. Wendy Carlin and Colin Mayer examine the activities and goals of the Treuhand. They articulate five functions that the Treuhand actually performs: valuation of enterprises; liquidation and closure of uneconomic activities; creation of supervisory boards for ongoing concerns; selection and evaluation of prospective buyers; and negotiation of purchase terms. In many cases, the price a buyer is willing to pay for a firm is less important to the Treuhand than are other non-price terms. Acquiring firms will often guarantee minimum levels of employment and investment spending over time. In doing this, the Treuhand attempts to create freestanding enterprises that can obtain external financing without giving up control to foreigners.

Carlin and Mayer also discuss what other East European countries might learn from the German experience. East Germany's rapid privatization is of course made possible by its close links with the West German commercial and financial infrastructure and made so pressing by the high level of East German wages established during unification. Carlin and Mayer argue that the Treuhand's interventionist approach to privatization, which includes investment and corporate control, has some advantages over standard arm's-length auctions of enterprises. Even before the enterprise is sold, the board of directors becomes active in establishing policies that keep the value of the enterprise from needlessly declining.

In the conference discussion of the Carlin and Mayer paper, several participants stressed the important differences between East Germany and the rest of Eastern Europe, which limit the direct relevance to other countries of the Treuhand's experience. Most important, the Treuhand has relied on sales at low prices to West German enterprises. This is both politically and economically possible because, in such sales, the enterprise stays "within the family," that is, in Germany. In the rest of Eastern Europe, there is no corresponding network of private firms willing and able to buy up the state industrial enterprises. Moreover, as Carlin and Mayer make clear, the Treuhand approach has been enormously costly in many cases, with large subsidies promised to prospective buyers. Once again, such largesse would be crippling in the financially strapped countries elsewhere in Eastern Europe.

Designing Bankruptcy Rules

One strength of the Treuhand's interventionism is that it involves restructuring *both* sides of an enterprise's balance sheet so that all financial claims are rationalized in the privatization process. Outside Germany, it will be common for enterprises to enter into commercialization and privatization with large debt burdens. It is likely that there will be a lot of financial restructuring to do in the aftermath of privatization. And, as in the West, this will need to be accomplished through some form of bankruptcy proceeding.

Philippe Aghion, Oliver Hart, and John Moore examine the options that East European countries face in choosing bankruptcy rules. They argue that there are important flaws in currently used bankruptcy procedures such as Chapters 7 and 11 in the United States or the receivership system in the United Kingdom. They propose a new bankruptcy procedure that avoids some of the main pitfalls of the existing procedures. In it, a bankruptcy judge allocates shares (and perhaps options to purchase shares) to enterprise claimants according to absolute priority. Next, shares are traded in an open market among claimants. The judge then solicits bids to purchase the enterprise, which the final shareholders vote on. Once the shareholders' decision is made (they may choose not to sell the firm at all), the firm exits from bankruptcy.

This kind of procedure has several advantages over standard bankruptcy proceedings. First, unlike existing procedures in the West, implementing it would not require a large number of experienced and specialized bankruptcy judges and lawyers. Judges and lawyers do not need to get involved with how the firm is run during bankruptcy as long as creditors and shareholders follow the procedure. Second, the bids to purchase the firm can be evaluated by outside or inside consultants engaged by the ultimate shareholders. Third, there is some leeway in how the equity-allocation rules are designed. One *dis*advantage of this approach is that creditors would need to understand the enterprise's business well enough to act intelligently. This may be a problem in Eastern Europe, where the largest creditor is often a national bank with little or no expertise in industrial oversight or in making valuations of enterprises (and, perhaps, without the proper incentives to carry out these tasks). Nevertheless, the lack of financial and bankruptcy expertise in Eastern Europe will hinder *any* bankruptcy policy.

Nurturing the Growth of the Private Sector

Of crucial importance to the success of reform is the emergence of a new private sector. Simon Johnson's paper looks at the growth of private-sector activity in Poland, Czechoslovakia, and Hungary. The growth of private-sector activities is probably the most rapid in Poland, and in some sectors privately owned activities are already the dominant ownership form. Even though there are relatively few remaining barriers (e.g., tax, export-import, foreign exchange) to private activity, private businesses remain small in size. One problem may be a lack of bank-borrowing opportunities, on which small Western firms are highly dependent for growth. East European firms can often grow only as fast as they can retain earnings.

Johnson also points to some country-specific differences in the growth of private business. Poland's private sector has developed more quickly than Hungary's, which has developed more rapidly than Czechoslovakia's. While private activity has been growing steadily in Hungary over the past decade, in Poland the liberalization of 1990 generated a surge of activity so large that Poland has surpassed Hungary in total small-firm private activity. This suggests that a poorly developed private sector does not constitute a valid argument against rapid transition.

Fostering Foreign Investment and Foreign Trade

With the radical transformation of these economies has come a wave of interest by both countries and companies in inward foreign direct investment (FDI). But relatively few large deals have been finalized, and today it looks unlikely that foreign direct investment will provide substantial net capital inflows. The major problem confronting countries is to find a way to lower the costs of involving foreigners in the privatization process.

Kenneth Froot's paper looks at the costs of getting foreigners involved in the privatization process and in how countries have attempted to lower these costs. In many cases, complex rules and changing tax laws and property rights make it extremely time consuming and costly for foreign firms to consider investment seriously. Froot traces out developments in Poland's treatment of FDI that are the result of the authorities' attempts to cut down on these costs of exploration and establishment.

The paper also looks more theoretically at how entry costs to FDI can seriously impair the ability of countries to obtain competitive prices for enterprises being privatized. Froot then explores a number of ways that countries can improve their bargaining power. He finds that it is probably much better for countries to invoke a kind of two-step process, in which assets are first privatized to dispersed groups of domestic investors and then sold to foreigners later.

The reforms in Eastern Europe brought with them two major changes for trade. First, the macroeconomic stabilization and liberalization programs in the East led to radically different price structures, to large exchange rate devaluations, and to an opening of borders. Second, trade among Eastern bloc countries institutionalized in the CMEA collapsed. Both these shocks had major effects on both East European terms of trade and the level of trade.

Dani Rodrik's paper investigates the effects of the transition on Eastern Europe's foreign trade. He looks at Czechoslovakia, Hungary, and Poland and finds that all three have achieved a substantial degree of openness to foreign trade. In all three countries, trade is now demonopolized, and licensing and quotas play a very small role. Exchange controls have virtually disappeared for current account transactions. Judging by partner statistics, export performance has been impressive in all three countries, and import booms are under way in at least Hungary and Poland as well. Rodrik finds that the export growth in the West is not simply a shift from the Soviet market to the West European market. On the whole, it seems that, in the first stages of adjustment, former exporters to the Soviet market have not had much success in finding new sales in the West. Rather, the increased exports seem to come from firms that were already exporting in the West or that are shifting from domestic markets to Western markets.

The collapse of the CMEA represents a significant shock, amounting to a loss of real income of 3–4 percent of GDP in Poland and 7–8 percent of GDP in both Hungary and Czechoslovakia. Export performance can be attributed to exchange rate policy in part, but the collapse of domestic demand has possibly played an even more important role. Finally, Rodrik suggests that trade liberalization in the first year or two after the start of reforms appears to have had little effect on internal price discipline, in large part because of the substantial devaluations that have accompanied it. This will likely change, however, as currencies appreciate in real terms following the initial large devaluations.

1 Stabilization and Reform in Eastern Europe: A Preliminary Evaluation

Michael Bruno

The transformation of Eastern Europe from centrally planned to market economies provides an unprecedented challenge for policymakers in these countries
as well as for the international community involved in financing and monitoring their economic programs. It also poses an unusual challenge for the economics profession because there is little prior experience on which to draw for
lessons that could be applied to the present context.[1]

According to the customary classification, the East European countries be-
long to the group of middle-income countries. Their relative income levels
(with suitable correction of relative prices), past growth rates, levels of education, and health all put them in this class. Their political and economic crisis
came in the wake of increasing maladjustment of the whole ex-Soviet bloc to
the changing world growth and trade environment. In that superficial respect,
the adjustment and structural reform problems of Eastern Europe would seem
to be akin to those of other middle-income countries, such as Brazil, Mexico,
or Israel; these countries had enjoyed long periods of growth and relative price
stability in the past, but in the course of the 1970s and 1980s they underwent
severe structural crises that were either exacerbated or caused by poor response
to external shocks such as the oil and debt crises. The delayed effects of some

Reprinted with permission from *IMF Staff Papers* 39:4 (December 1992), © 1992 International
Monetary Fund.

This paper was written while the author was a visiting professor at the Massachusetts Institute
of Technology and a visiting scholar in the International Monetary Fund's Research Department.
He wishes to thank Massimo Russo and Michael Deppler for initiating this study and many members of both the European I and the Research departments for helpful discussions and comments
on earlier drafts. He is likewise grateful to Olivier Blanchard, Mario Blejer, Kemal Derviş, David
Lipton, Stanley Fischer, and Hans Schmitt.

1. Hungary started its reform process at an earlier stage, and some of the lessons from this
experience are of considerable importance. However, the scope of the reform in the other four
countries and the speed with which it was initiated have no precedent in a command economy.

of these same shocks (e.g., energy and raw material prices) are only now being felt in Eastern Europe. The difference, however, is not only one of timing or of degree. Here, it is the whole political and economic framework that has collapsed. Far-reaching political reform was followed by the adoption of an economic reform the desired end product of which was similar to that of other middle-income countries, but the distance between the initial point and the desired goal is not only wider but also substantially deeper.

The present discussion is confined mainly to the lessons that can be learned from the aftermath of stabilization and price reform programs adopted in five East European countries—Hungary, Poland, the Czech and Slovak Republics, Bulgaria, and Romania—in 1990 and 1991. By this stage, some institutional reforms had already begun to take effect, such as the breakup of the monobank into separate central bank and commercial banking systems. Privatization, however, was only in the early legislation stage.

How similar are the aims of the reform in Eastern Europe to other recent efforts? One similarity is the attempt to reform and adapt the economic structure for integration into the world economy, which involves opening up the economy and moving from a completely controlled and distorted set of relative prices to relative world prices (for tradable goods). Another similar aim is macroeconomic stabilization, which has to do with the price level as well as internal and external balances. Stabilization, in turn, implies the elimination of high inflation or hyperinflation, which either already exists or is repressed (by open budget deficits, or soft budget constraints, or monetary overhang) and is bound to erupt once prices are decontrolled. Thus far, the objectives (and even the means of attaining them) are quite similar to those in other reforms (consider, e.g., the recent Mexican reform comprising simultaneous stabilization and opening up).

The chief novelty in the East European experience is the revolutionary change that is required in the institutional infrastructure—the financial system (such as the breakup of a monobank system), the fiscal structure, social safety nets, the establishment of private property rights, and the mass privatization effort. One could easily point to many noncentrally planned economies that have either soft budget constraints, a financially repressed business sector, or highly subsidized state enterprises, or some combination of all three. However, their underlying structure is nonetheless market oriented, and private property rights are reasonably well defined. Although a lot can be learned from the reforms that have been applied to the distorted subsystems in these other countries, there is a sea of difference between them and those countries where the whole economy is one centrally controlled, nonmarket, publicly owned and financed system, with no other normative internal reference point, and a market economy has to be created where none had existed before. These circumstances have dictated a more comprehensive approach to the reform process than has ever been adopted to date.

All the reform plans, which were part of International Monetary Fund (IMF) programs, recognized that a simultaneous assault on macroeconomic stabilization, prices, and property rights was necessary from the inception stage of these programs.[2] The programs have been largely "heterodox" in their approach to price stabilization, although they have differed from their predecessors (e.g., Israel and Mexico) in several respects, such as the way in which wages were controlled. But the programs have been much more far reaching and ambitious in their attempt to move at great speed from the initial production equilibrium of the old system to the desired new market-based structure.

The initial stabilization results have been impressive by and large, even though the initial price shock in all countries was larger than expected, leading, in most cases, to persistent inflation. Likewise, the observed balance-of-payments improvements may in some cases turn out to be transitory. The main surprise for policymakers, and the major departure from the IMF's initial forecasts, was the speed with which the old productive system responded to the new price and incentive signals. The collapse of the Council for Mutual Economic Assistance (CMEA), which, in a sense, was an exogenous event from the point of view of each country, had disastrous consequences on output in almost all countries; but this is probably not the whole story. While a private, small enterprise sector was developing, both demand and supply factors played a much larger than expected role in sharply contracting the output of the large state-owned enterprises (SOEs). Although some of this contraction may be endemic to the process of stabilization, in virtually all cases the more problematic issues were the slow tempo of structural adjustment and the sluggishness of the privatization effort.

Although this paper addresses issues common to all the countries involved, one should not ignore differences in performance, some of which originate from the considerable diversity in initial conditions that the countries faced at the start of the present reform process. Section 1.1 begins with a brief survey of these initial conditions as well as a general outline of the IMF-supported programs.[3] Section 1.2 follows with a general discussion of the concept of economic reform, based on previous experience with relative speeds of adjustment in different markets and spheres of economic behavior. A distinction is drawn between stabilization of prices and exchange rates, which can be achieved fairly rapidly, and the responses of production structure, investment, and ownership patterns to sharp changes in *relative* prices, all of which tend to be extremely slow. Market failure may indeed persist for a long time, which

2. It is important to point out that, unlike many past cases, IMF programs in East European economies thus far have typically been self-imposed, drastic adjustment programs, to which the IMF has given its blessing rather than having been the primary initiator. (For comparative details of IMF programs in Eastern Europe, see table 1.2 below).

3. A more detailed discussion of developments in each country can be found in individual country surveys published by the Organization for Economic Cooperation and Development (OECD) and the IMF (Demekas and Khan 1991; and Aghevli, Borensztein, and van der Willigen 1992). See also the papers by Derviş and Condon (on Hungary), Berg and Blanchard (on Poland), and Dyba and Svejnar (on Czechoslovakia) in this volume.

raises the vexing issues of sequencing and the need for, or extent of, residual government involvement in the transition stage.

Price overshooting and the output collapse, and their relation to the choice of policies, are taken up in sections 1.3 and 1.4, respectively. Section 1.5 discusses the fiscal balance and, in particular, its sustainability in view of the inevitable erosion of the state enterprise tax base and persistent pressures for additional social expenditures (replacing the old subsidies). Section 1.6 addresses the problems of financial reform, bad loan portfolios, interenterprise credit arrears, and the need for a major cleanup and capitalization of the weak commercial banking sector. Section 1.7 raises the question of interim production, trade, and financial regimes for the state enterprise sector during the uncertain ownership and control period. Section 1.8 offers concluding remarks.

1.1   Initial Conditions and Country Programs

Although almost all the countries in question had embarked on partial structural reform in the 1960s, only in Hungary did these reforms not subsequently grind to a halt. Although the reform process in Hungary was gradual and beset by many setbacks, it persisted over a period of twenty years, and, even though the objective of that reform was not a market-based economy, Hungary emerged better prepared on the institutional economic front than the other countries for the dramatic political liberalizations of 1989–90. Reforms had already led to price and trade liberalizations[4] and developments in the small-scale private ownership sector, and Hungary had also introduced a two-tier banking system, a tax reform, and a corporate law before 1989.

In Poland, which has always had a private agricultural sector,[5] there were also some private-sector developments prior to 1989. Both countries, however, suffered from an initial external debt overhang (see table 1.1, which details initial preprogram conditions), and both showed practically no growth in the 1980s. Unlike Hungary, Poland's imbalance prior to 1989 was also internal, the result of a large monetary overhang that the partial price liberalizations and ensuing hyperinflation of 1989 helped eliminate, or at least reduce substantially, before the January 1990 program.

In the absence of an explicit measure of the monetary overhang, the estimate of the ratio of money to gross domestic product (GDP) (row 6 in table 1.1) gives a rough indication. If 0.4 can be considered the norm, there was no over-

4. By 1982, over 50 percent of consumer goods were free of control, the percentage gradually increasing to 80 percent by 1990 and to over 90 percent in 1991. Trade liberalization proceeded more slowly. On the Hungarian economic reform process since 1968, see Boote and Somogyi (1991). For a good account of the more recent economic developments, see the OECD survey on Hungary (OECD 1992).

5. Also, in Poland the weakening of state control had already started in 1981, with two Solidarity-induced laws that gave a measure of autonomy to firms and induced the beginning of a private sector outside agriculture. Poland's other institutional reforms, however, lagged behind Hungary's (see Lipton and Sachs 1991).

Table 1.1   **Eastern Europe: Initial Conditions**

Indicator	Hungary	Poland	Czechoslovakia	Bulgaria	Romania
Population (in millions, mid-1989)[a]	10.6	37.9	15.6	9.0	23.2
GNP per capita (in 1989 US $)[a]	2,590	1,790	3,450	2,320	2,290
GNP growth (average annual rate, in %, at constant prices):[b]					
1970s	4.5	5.5	4.6	7.0	9.3
1980s	.5	−.7	1.4	2.0	1.8
Administered prices (% of total)	15	100[c]	100	100	80
State ownership (%)	90	70	100[d]	100[e]	100[d]
Money (M2)/GDP (1990)	.4	.9	.7	1.3	.6
External debt/GDP (1990, %)	65	80	19	50	3
External debt-service ratio (1990)	57[f]	56	23	116	...
Exports to CMEA, 1990:[g]					
% of total exports	43	41	60	69	...
% of GDP	16	14	25	34	...

[a]World Bank (1991); IMF staff estimate for Romanian GNP per capita. All these data are highly sensitive to the choice of exchange rates.

[b]Net material product (ICES 1990).

[c]Excluding food prices.

[d]Economy-wide.

[e]Economy-wide, except 15 percent of agriculture.

[f]In percentage of merchandise exports.

[g]Estimates are tentative since they are very sensitive to distortions in intra-CMEA prices and exchange rates. Data for exports are based on estimated world market prices (considerably above the official traded prices); however, the GDP data are based on actual official prices. For Romania, export data are available only at official prices, which tend to underestimate the weight of CMEA trade; on this basis, CMEA exports were 39 percent of total exports and equivalent to 6 percent of GDP.

hang in Hungary at the start of the reform process; it was large in Poland (in 1989 and probably even larger before 1989) and Bulgaria and smaller in Czechoslovakia and Romania.

It is interesting that, during the twenty years following the spring of 1968, Czechoslovakia reverted to the most orthodox centrally planned economy (see table 1.1) and was thus, in a structural sense, much less prepared for the big change. Yet, on the eve of the January 1991 reform, not only did Czechoslovakia enjoy the most favorable initial internal and external macroeconomic balance, but it also had only a small monetary overhang and an extremely low ratio of external debt to gross national product (GNP).[6]

6. In an interesting recounting of economic developments in these countries in the pre-Communist era (Solimano 1991), Czechoslovakia stands out as having had a prudent macroeconomic tradition. It also had the most developed industrial structure by the time communism took over. Major subsequent development took place in Slovakia, which has undoubtedly had repercussions on Czechoslovakia's present structural reform process and interrepublican political and social problems.

Bulgaria had the most extensive industrial development in relation to its starting point (with some 60 percent of the labor force in that sector, compared to a mere 20 percent in the 1930s), much of it confined to exports to the former Soviet Union (see row 9 in table 1.1). In the years since 1985, Bulgaria incurred a sizable external debt as its foreign finances faltered, and the country faced a severe foreign exchange constraint by the time the reform started as well as a substantial monetary overhang. Romania, which had no external debt at all and was less dependent on CMEA trade, was nonetheless plagued by severe internal economic, social, and political problems, on top of specific supply problems in the oil market.

At the beginning of 1991, three of the countries—Czechoslovakia, Bulgaria, and Romania—adopted programs that essentially resembled the Polish program of 1990. (For a comparison of programs, see table 1.2.) The main breakaway from their past was an almost complete price liberalization and a substantial elimination of price subsidies, with the aim of achieving fiscal balance, coupled with the establishment of strict monetary targets and wage ceilings. The choice of exchange rate regime differed, with Czechoslovakia, like Poland in 1990, adopting a peg as a nominal anchor (after several devaluations in the preceding months, which almost doubled the exchange rate). Lacking foreign exchange reserves, Bulgaria and Romania both floated and let the interbank market determine a considerably depreciated exchange rate, thereby tripling the previous official rate (fig. 1.1), although the phasing in of the exchange rate reform was more gradual in Romania. In all four countries, the external reform program included substantial trade liberalization with current account convertibility and other measures and institutional changes pertaining to structural adjustment and privatization.

Hungary adopted a gradualist program in January 1991, involving a much smaller devaluation (15 percent), a further liberalization of prices (up to 90 percent of the consumer basket by the end of 1991, a considerable stepping up of the previous gradual move from 56 percent in 1985), and restrictive fiscal, monetary, and incomes policies. The program, which was more ambitious than previous programs, also included a substantial further liberalization of imports and another set of structural adjustment and privatization measures.[7]

The programs for Poland, Czechoslovakia, Bulgaria, and Romania were obviously conceived as "big bang" moves. The underlying theme was that, with few exceptions, the price and trade systems had to be liberalized all at once under the umbrella of fiscal, monetary, and incomes restraint. At the same time, new financial institutions were being put in place, and the productive systems were slated for rapid privatization so as to minimize the uncertainties of operation under public ownership and controls.

---

7. The average tariff dropped from 18 percent in 1985 to 16 percent during 1986–89 and to 13 percent in 1991. The share of imports liberalized rose from 0 to 16 percent in 1989 and 37 percent in 1990, to reach 72 percent in 1991 (see Derviş and Condon, in this volume).

gradualist

Big bang
Shock Therapy

Table 1.2   Eastern Europe: Comparison of Fund Programs

Indicator	Hungary	Poland	Czechoslovakia	Bulgaria	Romania
Date	20 February 1991	5 February 1990	7 January 1991	15 March 1991	11 April 1991
Length	36 months	13 months	14 months	12 months	12 months
Exchange system	15% devaluation in January, then managed	Initial sizable devaluations, then fixed	35% devaluation in October, 1990; 15% devaluation and unification with tourist rate in December 1990; then fixed	Floating interbank	Official rate fixed; floating interbank. Convergence of official and interbank
Wages	Tax-based incomes policy	Tax-based incomes policy	Tax-based incomes policy	Real wage cut by 35%, implemented by ceilings on wage bills	Tax-based incomes policy
Interest rates	With abolition of interest rate ceilings will be market based	Establish positive real interest rates	Increase before program and flexible management thereafter	Very large increase before program; flexible adjustment thereafter	Complete liberalization; CDs with flexible rates
Privatization	Continue in 1991	Continue in 1991	Start in 1991	Start in 1991	Start in 1991
Two-tier banking system[a]	1987	1990	1990	1989	1990

[a]The establishment of a two-tier banking system ended direct central bank involvement in commercial banking.

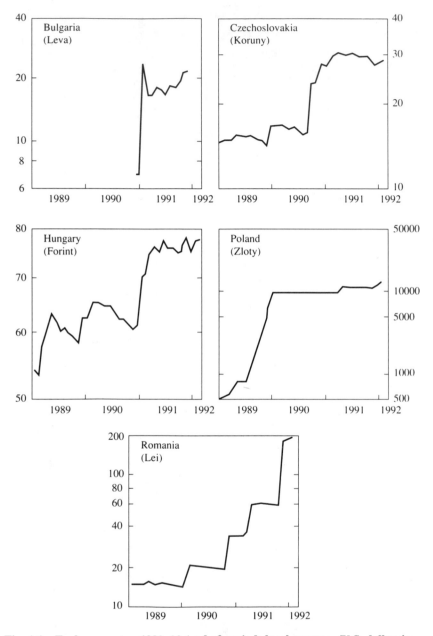

Fig. 1.1   Exchange rates, 1989–92 (end of period: local currency/U.S. dollar, in log scale)

Sources: National authorities and IMF staff estimates.

In all five countries, the initial price liberalization was expected to involve a substantial price shock, to be followed a few months later by relative price stability. The actual results are discussed in section 1.3.

1.2   Concepts of Economic Reform—Big Bang and Gradualism

The key question that has to be asked at the outset of any major reform process is whether to adopt the big bang approach or gradualism in the move from the distorted equilibrium of the prereform period to the desired new quasi equilibrium. The answer to this question is not at all clear. Cumulative experience from hyperinflation and high-inflation episodes (say, at least three-digit annual inflation rates) points only to the clear advantage of the big bang approach at the inflation stabilization stage (recent successes have been Bolivia, Mexico, and Israel).[8]

In the recent successful stabilizations in Israel and Mexico, credibility, expectation signaling, and the problem of nominal synchronization (i.e., avoiding sharp changes in relative prices) dictated a multiple anchor or "heterodox" approach. The initial hyperinflation outburst prompted Poland and Yugoslavia to follow this approach in the 1989–90 stabilizations. Czechoslovakia, Bulgaria, and Romania also chose a big bang approach in 1991, even though their inflation rates were relatively low.[9] Given the repressed prereform system, the potential for inflationary outburst may have justified their choice, which enabled them to avoid the hyperinflation that would have erupted in the price liberalization stage in the absence of tight macro policies.

These choices, however, apply only to price stabilization and the achievement of initial internal and external balance. There still remains the question of how much and how fast one should go on a broader reform front. For example, do trade liberalization and a move to convertibility, let alone privatization, necessarily require a big bang approach? The answer is much less clear ex ante and is even less clear given the results. Trade liberalization, for example, can give the right long-term signal from the start, but its execution could, in principle, be gradual. (This question will be taken up in the discussion of output collapse in sec. 1.3.) Similar examples in either direction can be cited, such as the opening up of internal and external financial and capital markets. The United Kingdom opted to go cold turkey, while other European countries chose to move more gradually and nonetheless achieved their targets. Israel applied shock therapy to inflation but opened up its financial, capital, and for-

8. Chile's 1970 stabilization is the only successful example of the gradualist approach (the trade liberalization, interestingly enough, was done relatively quickly). The social cost, however, was extremely high, and the strategy would probably not be feasible in an open democracy. For a comparative analysis of the stabilization and reform experience in Latin America and Israel, see Bruno (1993). Fischer and Gelb (1990) were among the first to discuss the phases of reform for Eastern Europe.

9. Hungary could afford gradualism because, as noted earlier, its opening up and structural reform process had been going on for much longer—in a sense, since 1968.

eign exchange markets gradually (as it successfully did with trade liberalization in the 1960s).

A closely related issue is the speed of adjustment of markets to changes in
signals and the credibility that agents attach to announced signals of future
market environments that are not yet evident in today's markets. It is well
known that the speed of adjustment in asset markets is extremely high; the
response is often instantaneous because the adjustment costs are low. However,
adjustment in commodity and labor markets, let alone the production response
that follows from new investment, is considerably slower, often lasting three
or four years. Any reform such as privatization of large-scale enterprises or the
introduction for the first time of a value-added or income tax that requires
complicated legislation, the introduction of new accounting procedures, and
new implementation or monitoring mechanisms may take at least as long as
that.

It is important to stress that these long adjustment lags do not occur solely
in hitherto centrally planned economies. Structural adjustment is a slow process even in the most advanced market-based economy—even when the reform is credible. This was true of the reconstruction effort in Europe after
World War II and of structural adjustment efforts following on a successful
major stabilization (such as in Israel in the wake of the 1985 stabilization).
Even in a country like Finland, the collapse of the CMEA caused a substantial
drop in GDP. In all these cases, adjustment was or will be prolonged, even
though the underlying structure is market based.

Therefore, the advocate of a big bang has to make clear which particular
portion of the policy package is implied. Also, the argument for a big bang
beginning may rest on a special political opportunity, as in Poland. But there
may also be an intertemporal political trade-off: overly costly programs might
lead to political reversal at a later stage, as "adjustment fatigue" sets in or
social aspirations, such as employment opportunities and living standards, are
frustrated. Have policymakers sufficiently considered these questions at the
inception stage of the program?

It is not clear whether there were any illusions about the length of time
it would take the East European economies to attain the competitive market
structure, private ownership, and properly functioning financial system of a
typical Western economy. But there seems to have been overoptimism at the
onset of the programs about the speed of the supply response and other behavioral responses that could come in the wake of a drastic change in the economic environment.

1.3   Stabilization: Was the Initial Price Shock Necessary?

In all cases except Hungary, the initial price shock turned out to be substantially larger than expected, but, within six months of the program, inflation
came down to less than 2–3 percent a month in Poland, Czechoslovakia, and

Hungary. Inflation edged up, after a temporary drop, to an average monthly rate of 4–5 percent in Bulgaria and 10 percent in Romania (see averages in table 1.3 and monthly data in table 1.4 and fig. 1.2). However, by the end of 1991, only Czechoslovakia and Hungary were running annual rates of inflation below 20 percent,[10] or a monthly rate of less than 1.5 percent, while Poland's rate has been running at least twice as high (about 3.0–3.5 percent a month, or 40 percent a year). The Czechoslovak stabilization was virtually a textbook case—the initial price shock was followed by price stability throughout most of the second half of 1991 (fig. 1.2 and table 1.4).

Differences in initial conditions no doubt played an important role. Poland started its program in the midst of a hyperinflation caused by a series of price hikes that may or may not have eliminated the monetary overhang by January 1990 (this issue is in dispute). At any rate, a 45 percent price shock was forecast for January 1990, but the actual outcome was 80 percent (for January and February together; the respective figures are 67 percent forecast and 122 percent actual). During the whole of 1990, inflation was expected to be less than 100 percent and ended up at about 250 percent; thus, even the residual inflation, after the initial shock, turned out to be higher than planned.

For Czechoslovakia, which started from a stable price level and a considerably smaller monetary overhang, a price increase of only 25 percent was forecast. The actual increase was 40 percent in the first quarter of 1991, a smaller relative discrepancy than Poland's. Moreover, the residual inflation in Czechoslovakia during the first year was only 10 percentage points higher than expected, after allowing for the first quarter's shock.

Both Bulgaria and Romania started off from a much worse initial position and made a number of additional price corrections during the year, so it is probably too early to pass judgment on the success of the initial move, particularly for Romania. The sharp foreign exchange shortage in these two countries, which necessitated the adoption of a different exchange rate regime at the start and a considerably larger initial exchange rate hike, may also account for the worse subsequent inflation profile. As in other aspects, Hungary was an outlier. Its initial price shock was small, 10 percent, as expected, and its residual inflation also hit the target (table 1.3).

Three questions arise in the face of these initial price developments, after due consideration is taken of the fact that price comparisons between a postliberalization system and a distorted and rationed preliberalization stage impart a considerable upward bias to the data.[11] Why was the price shock in most cases so much higher than expected? What are the implications of the initial shock for the subsequent inflation profile (the implications for the real system will be discussed later)? Was an initial price shock as large as Poland's necessary?

10. This is a convenient reference point because it corresponds to recent inflation rates in the successful stabilizers of high inflation—Bolivia, Chile, Israel, and Mexico (see Bruno 1993).

11. An interesting question is whether different initial conditions in the various countries might have led to different relative biases in these price shock estimates.

Table 1.3   Eastern Europe: Selected Indicators, 1990–91

Program/Actual	GDP[a,b]	Consumer Prices[c]	Nominal Wage[c]	Broad Money[c]	Budget Balance[d,e]	Convertible Current Account[e]	Convertible Current Account[f]	Total Exports[f,g]
Hungary								
1990 actual	−4	33	23	29	−.1	.4	.1	8.9
1991 program	−3	31	...	23	−1.5	−3.6	−1.2	12.6
1991 actual	−8	32	20	29	−4.1	1.0	.3	9.6
	(−8)							
Poland								
1989 actual	...	640	472	236	−7.4	−2.7	−1.8	8.1
1990 program	−5	94	...	87	−.1	...	−3.0	...
1990 actual	−12	249	160	122	3.5	1.3	.7	15.0
1991 program	3	36	...	43	−.6	−2.7	−2.7	...
1991 actual	−8	60	54	49	−7.2	−2.9	−2.2	13.2
	(−4)							
Czechoslovakia								
1990 actual	...	18	8	1	−.3	−2.4	−1.1	11.6
1991 program	−5	30	17	6	.8	−7.1	−2.5	12.6
1991 actual	−16	54	14	27	−2.1	.7	.2	10.9
	(−9)							
Bulgaria								
1990 actual	−12	64	32	12	−9.2	−16.1	−1.2	5.7
1991 program	−11	234	146	24	.1	...	−2.0	6.6
1991 actual	−23	339	142	25	−3.7	−11.8	−.9	3.7
	(−16)							
Romania								
1990 actual	−7	5	11	17	−.5	−8.0	−1.7	5.8
1991 program	...	104	...	15	−1.5	...	−1.7	5.4
1991 estimate	−12	223	124	66	−3.0	−6.6	−1.3	3.5
	(−10)							

[a]Figures in parentheses provide an estimate of the fall of GDP owing to the fall in exports; percentage point contribution of the change in total exports to the percentage change in GDP.

[b]Figures given in terms of percentage change.

[c]Figures given in terms of year-end percentage change.

[d]For Poland, general government balance; for Czechoslovakia, central and local government, extrabudgetary funds, excluding takeover of export credits, and transfers to the banks and foreign trade organizations on account of devaluation profits and losses; for Bulgaria, based on actual external debt service payments; for 1991, after external debt rescheduling and debt referral.

[e]Figures given in terms of percentage of GDP.

[f]Including transactions in nonconvertible currencies.

[g]Figures given in billions of U.S. dollars.

Table 1.4   **Eastern Europe: Monthly CPI Inflation Rates, 1989–91 (%)**

	Bulgaria	Czechoslovakia[a]	Hungary	Poland	Romania
1989					
Jan.	...	...	4.5	11.0	...
Feb.	...	...	3.4	7.9	...
Mar.	...	...	1.0	8.1	...
Apr.	...	...	1.7	9.8	...
May	...	...	.5	7.2	...
Jun.	...	...	.4	6.1	...
July	...	...	2.1	9.5	...
Aug.	...	...	.3	39.5	...
Sep.	...	...	1.0	34.3	...
Oct.	...	...	1.1	54.8	...
Nov.	...	...	.7	22.4	...
Dec.	...	...	.8	17.7	...
1990					
Jan.	...	...	7.7	79.6	...
Feb.	...	...	5.3	23.8	...
Mar.	...	...	2.7	4.3	...
Apr.	...	...	2.5	7.5	...
May	...	...	.8	4.6	...
Jun.	3.5	...	.4	3.4	...
July	3.6	10.0	2.6	3.6	...
Aug.	16.3	...	2.9	1.8	...
Sep.	4.5	...	1.5	4.5	...
Oct.	4.2	3.4	1.5	5.7	...
Nov.	5.3	.8	2.1	5.0	23.4
Dec.	10.2	.8	1.7	5.9	11.6
1991					
Jan.	13.6	25.8	7.5	12.7	14.8
Feb.	105.2	7.0	4.9	6.7	7.0
Mar.	32.7	4.7	3.7	4.5	6.6
Apr.	1.8	2.0	2.4	2.7	26.5
May	1.6	1.9	2.2	2.7	5.1
Jun.	5.0	1.8	2.1	4.9	2.0
July	7.9	−.1	.9	.1	9.4
Aug.	5.1	...	.2	.6	11.2
Sep.	4.7	.3	1.5	4.3	7.3
Oct.	3.1	−.1	1.3	3.2	10.4
Nov.	3.5	1.6	1.4	3.2	10.4
Dec.	3.1	1.2	1.7	3.1	13.7

Sources: National authorities and IMF staff estimates.

[a]Rates from July–December 1990 are estimates from quarterly data.

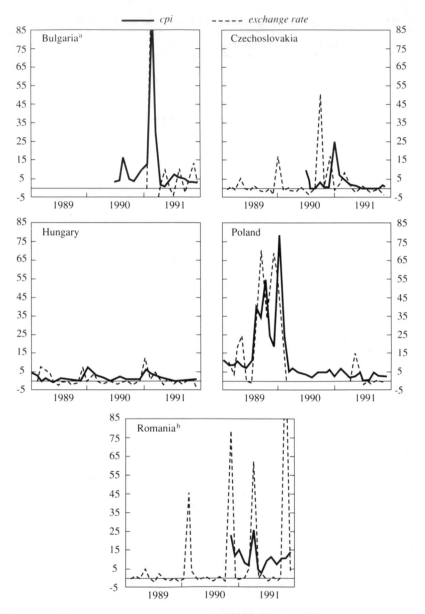

Fig. 1.2   CPI inflation and exchange rates, 1989–91 (monthly percentage change)

Sources: National authorities and IMF staff estimates.
[a]CPI: February 1991 = 105.2. Exchange rate: February 1991 = 247.1, March 1991 = 30.5.
[b]Exchange rate: November 1991 = 204.84.

Possible sources of the unexpectedly high price level shocks include the existence of a larger unabsorbed monetary overhang, underprediction of the effects of a large initial devaluation, and monopolistic behavior on the part of state enterprises in anticipation of the imposition of price controls. In Bulgaria, and partly in Poland, the initial monetary overhang may have played a sizable role, whereas, in the other countries (in particular, Poland), the price response to the exchange rate devaluation alone or combined with other factors may have been responsible. Inflationary experience elsewhere has shown that the exchange rate, in the absence of another reliable measuring rod, often serves as the indicator to which pricing agents attach themselves, even when their product is not tradable.[12]

The answer to the second question about the relation of the initial shock to the subsequent inflation profile depends on whether the source of the shock is indeed confined to an existing monetary overhang. It would then follow that a higher initial price jump would "save" the system from additional inflationary adjustments later on, and there would thus be a positive trade-off between the initial shock and subsequent price stability.

If a monetary overhang is not the cause of the price shock, and if there is also a tendency for other nominal magnitudes in the system (money, credit, and wages) to "catch up" in line with their initial "planned" positions relative to the price level, then an initial price level discrepancy will also lead, through inertia, to higher than expected inflation. This may have been what happened in Poland and Bulgaria, but probably not, or less so, in Czechoslovakia. In the second half of 1990, money, credit, and wage ceilings were adjusted upward in Poland, and a similar correction was made in the second half of 1991 in Czechoslovakia and Bulgaria. In Poland, the difference between the actual wage and the wage ceiling in the earlier phase could be made up later, and enterprise managers availed themselves of this option, paying substantial additional taxes while doing so.

Hence, the third question: Was there an option of a smaller planned, or a smaller actual, price shock at the beginning? Technically, the answer is yes. Compare these programs to one successful heterodox predecessor: Israel in July 1985. With the substantial elimination of subsidies, Israel limited its initial price shock to 27 percent by opting for an attenuated devaluation (relative to what the fundamentals seemed to dictate) and introduced temporary price controls that were then gradually removed. However, there was obviously no monetary overhang, and the relative price levels were certainly not as distorted as those in the East European economies.

Yet it may be argued that Poland could have chosen a smaller devaluation up front and left price controls at a higher level for three months, say, and only

---

12. In Israel, this is called the *dentist effect* (because dentists raise their fees by the same rate at which the price of their material inputs rises, even though these inputs constitute only a small portion of the cost of treatment).

then decontrolled completely, either all at once or gradually.[13] But it could also be argued that, with distortions as big as they were and the new government's initial high credibility, it may have been just as well to "chop off the dog's tail all at once."

It is interesting that Czechoslovakia retained some control over its initial price shock through moral suasion and by stipulating maximum prices or trade margins on some key commodities and by requiring prior notification of price increases in some monopolistic sectors. Also, in Czechoslovakia and Bulgaria, certain price increases, such as for energy and housing, were delayed.

Do the initial benefits of a big price bang outweigh the subsequent costs of higher inertial inflation as well as other social costs? In pursuit of its devaluation and price liberalization goals, Poland was probably right in choosing to abolish price controls at the beginning, but it could have devalued by less and thus reduced the initial shock. The exchange rate may then have had to be realigned earlier than mid-1991, but the cumulative price increase over the two-year period could nonetheless have been smaller. For Bulgaria and Romania, the question arises whether they could afford to opt for a far-reaching relaxation of foreign exchange restrictions when the foreign exchange shortage was (and is) so extreme. One counterargument is that the administration of such restrictions would be ineffective.

Ending on a positive note—with all the quibbles afforded by hindsight duly noted—the overriding fact remains that in most of the cases far-reaching liberalization has been achieved, together with a reasonable measure of macroeconomic stability, in spite of a highly distorted starting point and immense economic and political risks. Finally, from the consumer's perspective, the qualitative change that has taken place in the market environment probably outweighs the statistical measure of price increase.

1.4   Was the Output Collapse Unavoidable?

There are several reasons for the large output fall. First of all, the anticipation of a sharp price increase stimulates hoarding, which is immediately followed by a substantial reduction in demand. Next, when prices rise by more than was planned while money, credit, and wages are kept within their specified nominal ceilings, the obvious result is a considerably larger than expected reduction in real money and credit as well as in real wages. This happened in Poland in 1990 and was repeated in the other countries that experienced shocks.

13. In the Polish case, in the initial absence of alternative inflation-immune financial assets, the free market exchange rate reflected a stock demand and far exceeded the relevant purchasing power parity exchange rate. This was the reason the authorities chose a smaller devaluation than initially planned. Ex post it may still have been too high—note that it took a year and a half of substantial inflation until the real appreciation of the exchange rate began to "bite" from a competitive point of view.

How much of the output reduction, which was considerably larger than expected, can be directly linked to this price shock discrepancy? The results for the Polish program of 1990 show a considerable reduction in measured output, of around 12 percent, compared to a considerably lower forecast.[14] Both the real wage squeeze and the real monetary squeeze certainly affected consumer demand and thus depressed output on the demand side.

The credit squeeze can also operate on the firm supply side if the financing of working capital is considered to be one of the factors of production (see Calvo and Coricelli 1992). Another channel through which the credit squeeze operates is the real interest rate if nominal interest rates are initially set at a level that is too high relative to the inflation rate that is expected after the initial price level shock. There is some evidence that the high initial real interest rate has in fact constrained firms more than the quantity of credit[15] (to which they can and, in fact, did adjust through interfirm credit arrears). However, how much of the output decline, even in 1990, could be ascribed to this factor alone remains an open question.

1.4.1 Supply-Side Shock

In Poland, as well as in some of the other countries, there was a general shock on the supply-side, which can be termed a comprehensive *management shock*. Enterprise managers who were used to operating in a command environment where their "market" was assured and their financing accommodative suddenly had to make their own decisions in a completely transformed environment characterized by tremendous uncertainty. In these circumstances, the first natural impulse is to adopt a "wait and see" attitude, or to continue producing the old stuff for inventory, as long as there is working capital. Evidence points to unfulfilled credit ceilings in the first few months of the Polish, Czechoslovak, and Bulgarian programs, followed by a period in which credit ceilings were effective but wage ceilings were not reached. This situation was repeated during much of 1991 in the Bulgarian and Romanian programs. In Bulgaria and Romania (and, earlier, Czechoslovakia), the nominal interest rate was set at a level corresponding to the estimated postshock rate of inflation, rather than at a level that would ensure a positive real rate of interest in the first month. It is important to remember, however, that, in these three countries, unlike the Polish case, there was no preceding hyperinflation to contend with. Therefore, that a more moderate interest rate policy did not lead to an inflationary outburst is no proof that this policy should have been pursued in a hyperinflationary situation (such as Russia's).

It is important to remember that a credit crunch and high real interest rates

14. There is some doubt about the relevance of the -5 percent projected output drop. According to participants in the planning stage, this estimate had been arbitrary and was not based directly on any of the plan parameters.

15. This information comes from an unpublished World Bank report based on interviews in seventy-five state-owned enterprises in September 1991.

are a universal problem in the immediate aftermath of sharp stabilizations (as was true for Bolivia, Mexico, and Israel). It could also be argued that the uncertainty about the outcome of stabilization justifies a highly contractionary monetary policy as a support for the exchange rate or wage anchors. Of the mistakes that can be made, it is better to err on the side of an overly restrictive stance. However, once initial success is achieved, a gradual, although careful, relaxation is called for.

1.4.2   CMEA Collapse

The collapse of the CMEA was another major contributor to the fall in output. Table 1.2 provides rough IMF staff estimates of that part of the output drop in 1991 that can be ascribed to the fall in exports caused by the demise of the CMEA. This estimate was based on the demand side, under the assumption of no short-run market substitutability (which obviously did not hold for Hungary or Czechoslovakia; see sec. 1.7). It did not explicitly take into account the very sharp terms of trade effect of the collapse, which was a substantial exogenous supply shock, much like the effect of the relative rise of energy and raw materials prices on the industrial countries in the 1970s and 1980s. It is interesting that, with the exception of Hungary, the implied unaccountable drop in output shown in table 1.3 seems to be correlated with the degree of prior dependence of the country on CMEA trade (table 1.1, row 9), which may be a proxy for the relative size of the potential terms of trade shock.[16]

The CMEA collapse caused the most damage in Bulgaria, the bulk of whose exports had gone to the CMEA. Bulgaria and also Romania, saddled by their foreign currency restraint, suffered severely from a lack of raw materials.[17] The relatively larger fall in Poland's output in 1991 than seems warranted by its dependence on CMEA trade may have to do with the degree of rigidity in wages. In Poland, the real product wage did not continue to fall in 1991 but rather increased by 15 percent, thus exacerbating the effect on the terms of trade. At any rate, more detailed country studies of the components of the output collapse are needed before we can assess how big a margin needs to be explained over and above the effects of the CMEA collapse in 1991.

To what extent was this unprecedented output drop unavoidable? Even if it could not have been avoided, it is not clear whether other policies—such as structural adjustment policies and privatization—can facilitate a rebound in

16. A recent estimate by Rodrik (1992) of the trade shock in the former Soviet Union, which includes the effect on the terms of trade for Hungary, Poland, and Czechoslovakia, is remarkably close to the numbers appearing in the brackets in table 1.3, so they may include terms of trade effects after all. In any case, neither the IMF's nor Rodrik's estimates include Keynesian multiplier effects or the effect of aggregate supply curve shifts under wage rigidity (see Bruno and Sachs 1985).

17. This is a clear case in which the short-run marginal product of additional infusion of foreign capital inflow is very high. Given excess capacity in complementary factors of production, the marginal GDP product of foreign exchange equals the reciprocal of the ratio of raw materials to GDP.

output in the near future. A substitute for the CMEA in the form of a payments union or trade arrangement would certainly help. Given the financial and political problems of the former Soviet Union, it is not clear how well such an arrangement could have worked during 1991, but even maintaining some of the distorted bilateral arrangements during the transition could probably have softened the blow.

Given the magnitude of the output shock and the long time it takes for the productive system to respond to the new market signals, ways should be found to soften the blow to output and employment in the interim period, even if they may seem distorted from the long-run point of view. Government intervention in other forms is the likely alternative—extending credit and granting subsidies to ailing enterprises in a particular region or assigning larger budgetary allotments to unemployment relief.

1.4.3   Exchange and Trade Policies

The wisdom of applying the cold turkey solution to trade liberalization can be questioned, and moving in stages to current account convertibility through gradual reduction of tariff barriers may be a sensible policy (see Greene and Isard 1991; Tanzi 1991; and McKinnon 1991). There are strong arguments in favor of eliminating import licensing and quotas at one go, but there is no good inherent reason to move all at once to a zero, or very low, tariff. It is true that a gradualist strategy may lend itself to discretionary reversals by governments with low credibility. But, when it is credible, the strategy can mitigate the immediate output and employment costs while continuing to send the right price signals for long-term investment. If the strategy is to be credible, a commitment has to be made to a well-defined time path from a differentiated tariff structure toward a common low tariff within a few years (no more than, say, five). Examples of successful liberalizations that followed a preannounced gradualist path include the European Common Market, whose members agreed to a gradual mutual removal of tariffs in the 1950s and 1960s,[18] and individual countries, such as Israel, whose trade liberalization in the 1960s followed a gradualist path.

Even when the gradual path is chosen, the question remains whether initial tariffs should be differentiated across goods. To avoid political pressures, the policymaker may choose, for example, to differentiate only by general category of goods (raw materials, investment, and consumption goods) rather than by individual commodity or producer. In the next section, which takes up the fiscal balance, I argue in favor of a flat across-the-board tariff for purely fiscal reasons, until a value-added tax (VAT) is introduced.

A country that has opted for an ambitious trade reform from the start may not want to backtrack at a later stage because of loss of credibility, but it is a

---

18. In the case of the Common Market, it has taken quite a few years to phase out declining industries—e.g., coal and steel.

lesson to bear in mind for future reference (e.g., in the states of the former Soviet Union), and, in fact, Poland eventually introduced a new and higher tariff structure in the second half of 1991. For some countries, however, the introduction of customs duties or tariffs may not be feasible, either because of the complete openness of their borders or because of the lack of necessary administrative capabilities. Unfortunately, that argument could also hold for any taxation, such as the VAT.

1.4.4   Future Prospects

Even when the output downturn is reversed, the experience of past reform and structural change (elsewhere as well as in Eastern Europe) shows evidence of substantial labor shedding and increasing unemployment, even as output rebounds.

Although public-sector output is collapsing, the small-scale private sector, especially in trade and services, seems to be thriving. However, given this sector's small initial base, even large increases at an early stage cannot affect the overall result unless the country starts off with a larger private sector to begin with. Poland may have been in this situation by 1992, when aggregate GDP started rising; at the time of writing, one can rely only on partial evidence and varying interpretations of the meaning of some numbers—for example, on unemployment. Although unemployment in Bulgaria had reached 10 percent, some have argued that there can be no serious unemployment problem if one cannot even find domestic help willing to work at the minimum wage; other observers have claimed that serious unemployment problems were emerging among the young. Both allegations may be correct, just as zero unemployment in Budapest or Prague can be entirely consistent with very serious unemployment in other heavily industrialized regions. It has also been argued that the Bulgarian state sector could sustain a major reduction in employment with minimum social upheaval because many of these workers could return to family farms or work on their own privately owned plots. For a country with excessive industrialization (60 percent of the labor force!), a shift to small-scale services, trade, and agriculture could be considered a move toward the correct long-run equilibrium composition of output.

For policy planners, the most relevant issue is the likelihood of immediate reversals in output and, especially, in the employment downturn because this outcome will determine the economic and, especially, the political sustainability of the initial set of stabilization policies.

1.5   Can the Fiscal Balance Be Sustained?

A key feature of the initial stabilization phase in all cases has been the balancing of the budget, primarily through a substantial, permanent cut in subsidies on goods and services, on the one hand, and an increase in expenditure on the social safety net, on the other. Given the existing tax revenue base, budget balance was assumed to be assured, as the figures for the respective programs show (see table 1.3). Keeping the budget in balance always requires careful scrutiny so that transitory changes can be isolated from permanent changes. Although the initial budget outcome seemed satisfactory in most countries, subsequent developments (usually starting in the second half of the first year) point to the emergence of serious problems for the second and third years of the programs. Let us consider the various causes and implications of these developments, starting with the experience of Poland.

At first glance, the Polish fiscal performance in 1990 turned out to be a surprising success, switching from a deficit of about 7 percent of GDP in 1989 to a surplus of about 3.5 percent. As Lane (1991) showed in detail, it was initially expected that the budget would follow a U-shaped profile over the year, with a shortfall in revenue in the first part of the year and an approximate balance over the year as a whole. In actual fact, the balance followed an inverted U shape, with an increasing surplus in the first two quarters of 1990, turning into a drop in the surplus in the third quarter and a deficit in the fourth quarter of 1990. The estimates for 1991 showed a deficit of 7.2 percent for the year (compared to a planned approximate balance), with the prospect of an even larger deficit for 1992 if no corrective action were taken.[19]

The reasons for this outcome are important for future reference. The price surprise led to an unexpected deep fall in real wages resulting in larger-than-expected profits and higher tax revenues. To these revenues was added a tax on capital gains on inventories and foreign currency deposits. Revenue from the latter was an entirely fortuitous one-time effect, resulting from an improper accounting for inflation. Once real wages rebounded and profits were squeezed, returns on the profit tax fell substantially. The profit squeeze has persisted into 1991 and is the more permanent effect of the liberalization process (see McKinnon 1991).

Czechoslovakia has gone through a similar process: a temporary surplus in the first few months of 1991 and an increasing deficit toward the end of the year. Similar problems are also emerging in Bulgaria, which differs from the others by not having had its enterprises' initial capital gains taxed away. Bulgaria showed a large increase in its deficit along with the output and import collapse. Romania's budget has stayed close to balance. In Hungary's budget, a deficit of close to 4 percent has emerged, despite the new VAT and income tax.

As was shown by Tanzi (1991), the East European countries typically enjoyed a profit tax revenue of about 15–20 percent of GDP, compared to a 3 percent average for the OECD. Table 1.5, based on Kopits (1991), gives an average breakdown of general government revenues and expenditures for 1985 in the five East European countries, compared with the former Soviet Union and the European Community. Although the cut in subsidies may account for

---

19. The deficit includes arrears to the nonbank public and unpaid obligations of the government to the domestic banking system. The cash deficit for 1991 is estimated at 5.7 percent.

Table 1.5   **Comparative Structure of General Government Budget, 1985 (% of GDP/GNP)**

Budget Item	Five East European Countries[a]	Former Soviet Union	European Community
Total revenue:	56	46	44
Enterprise taxes	17	18	4
Personal income tax	4	4	9
Social security	11	4	13
Trade taxes	2	6	. . .
Expenditure taxes	16	12	11
Other	6	2	7
Total expenditures:	55	56	46
Current goods and services	20	21	16
Investment goods	3	8[b]	3
Subsidies and transfers to enterprises	19	18	4
Transfers to households	12	8	15
Interest payments	1	. . .	5
Other	. . .	1	3

Source: Based on Kopits (1991, table 2).
[a]Unweighted average.
[b]Includes some investment transfers to enterprises.

a savings of 8–10 percent of GDP on the expenditure side, additional safety net expenditures and unemployment benefits are likely to expand as the process of structural change and labor shedding deepens. Further, the drop in enterprise profit taxes is likely to continue to exceed the net drop in expenditures.

A critical problem in all five countries is the transition from a relatively egalitarian and well-endowed social welfare network to a market system in which all the income and wealth distribution problems, unemployment risks, and other adverse social side effects of free capitalism suddenly emerge. Policymakers will face strong social and political pressures to continue the existing generous social security services and to correct for their recent erosion brought about by the sharp price increases. A large percentage of voters in these countries are pensioners. In Hungary, where 25 percent of the population are pensioners, male employees retire at 60 and females at 55. In Bulgaria pensioners are estimated to account for 35 percent of the voters, and the relative number of people receiving pensions in Poland has recently exceeded 40 percent. In Czechoslovakia, pressure may also come from the higher-than-average unemployment rate in the Slovak Republic (over 11 percent by the end of 1991 and rising, compared with a rate in the Czech Republic that was only 4 percent in 1991 and virtually zero a year earlier). Despite these pressures, there is room for streamlining the social welfare framework—for example, through privatization of some of the health services, charging for medication, and progressively taxing child allowance.

One way or another, the net budget outcome is likely to be a permanent imbalance, unless output, sales, and the profit base rebound quickly or new taxes are imposed. Past experience shows that the introduction of a VAT takes at least three years in a country with reasonably organized enterprise accounts, and it is unlikely that this period can be effectively shortened. In the first year in which a VAT is introduced and existing taxes are replaced, there tends to be a reduction in revenues anyway. There is thus an urgent need to plan for temporary substitutes. For example, if trade liberalization were coupled from the beginning with a considerably larger tax on imports (even at a flat rate, say), the revenue from this source could have temporarily closed the gap, at least in part.

In the absence of a tax alternative, the pressure to balance the budget usually leads to expenditure cuts in areas where political opposition is light but the long-term economic cost is high, namely, investment in infrastructure (roads, communications). This is the one area where government intervention is usually essential and the positive externalities for the long-term growth of the private enterprise sector may be highest. There may be gradations in the urgency of the problem in the different countries (probably less crucial in Hungary and Czechoslovakia, more so in the other economies), but there is a minimum requirement in all of them, quite apart from the common need to cope with the inherited environmental damage.

This discussion leads to two important policy considerations. First, should some fiscal deficit be allowed for the interim period (until the tax reform is fully in place)? Second, should infrastructure investment be treated as part of regular government expenditure?

The answers to both questions should be considered in the context of each economy. The first and most important point is that, given the time-phasing nature of the problem, it is important that the annual budget plan should be embedded within a well-specified medium-term framework (of three years, at least). Ideally, the country should precommit itself to a budget trajectory for each of the coming years, with full budget balance to be regained within, at most, three years and the deficit in no year exceeding a certain percentage of GDP, say, 4 or 5 percent. The financing of this deficit should not come from the central bank[20] but should be the responsibility of the ministry of finance, which must finance it from foreign or domestic private-sector borrowing, depending on the country's initial internal and external debt situation. A clear signal of precommitment along these lines may help prevent the adverse infla-

---

20. In theory, once there is positive real growth of GDP, the money supply could be increased, assuming stable velocity, at the rate of real growth. However, this decision had best be left to the discretion of monetary policy and an independent central bank and should not be built in as a potential source of deficit financing. Otherwise, political pressures on the central bank to accommodate a deficit may become ruinous. Recent developments in several of the countries in question bear out the importance of this caveat.

tionary or crowding-out effects that a protracted deficit would otherwise engender.

Should infrastructure investment be treated differently? A textbook solution is to distinguish between the total deficit and the concept of government (dis)-saving. The latter is more relevant for gauging the internal balance (although the former will still be important for financial planning). In this case, infrastructure investment could appear "below the line" as part of a separate capital budget that need not be financed by taxes. The objection to this "pure" solution is that it leaves the way open for potential abuse. Anything, so practical wisdom says, can be called *investment,* be it teachers' salaries, defense expenditures, or retraining for the unemployed. These loopholes can be closed, however, by adopting strict definitions of what constitutes direct government investment, limiting the percentage of GDP allowed (say, no more than an extra 3–5 percent), or not allowing for separation of budgets but raising the allowable total deficit by 1 percent, for example, for each 2 percent of planned additional infrastructure, with a total ceiling of no more than 5–6 percent. Earmarking specific foreign lending (e.g., by the World Bank) does, of course, ease matters.

There are no universal rules governing these considerations; they must of necessity be geared to each economy's specific risks or past record.

1.6   What to Do with Bad Loan Portfolios and Enterprise Arrears?

In all the East European countries, the previous economic and financial regimes left a legacy of bad enterprise debts that have continued to mount and have been stacked in the portfolios of the commercial banking system. The stringent stabilization programs, the credit crunch, and the collapse of the ruble zone export market have exacerbated the problem, as has the mounting interenterprise debt. In the early stages of stabilization, this problem was in most cases put off to one side. Unfortunately, the problem usually does not go away while waiting to be attended to but, on the contrary, gets worse and may interfere with the process of stabilization and structural adjustment. The existence of a large bad loan portfolio on banks' balance sheets is one of the causes of the persistent large gap between deposit and lending interest rates. It may also distort the relative creditworthiness of enterprises in a way that is not necessarily correlated with their potential profitability or long-run solvency in the new market environment.

In theory, the issue of bad loan portfolios is best dealt with up front in the context of a broader currency reform. When loan cleanups are included in the initial package, there is a better chance of avoiding the severe moral hazard problems that any such cleanups entail. In practice, no such provisions were included in the original packages. Even if they had been, the problem would have lingered on because much of the outstanding bad debt continued to accumulate in the poststabilization phase. When the problem is confronted, experience has shown that extreme solutions should be avoided. One extreme is to leave the issue out of the central government's budgeting perspective altogether by "letting the banks deal with the problem," which seems to have been the prevailing view in Czechoslovakia at one point. If this approach is followed, quite apart from sending out the wrong price signals in the credit markets, it would eventually lead to a banking crisis, and the government would have to step in, and on a much larger scale than would be required otherwise. The other extreme solution is to yield to the cumulative political pressures from the debt-ridden enterprise sector and pass blanket debt-cancellation laws, which was the approach taken in Romania. Besides being indiscriminate, this solution invites serious moral hazard, reinforcing bad borrowing behavior by setting up the expectation that next time around enterprises will be bailed out again.

Outstanding bad debt is estimated at 15–20 percent of total bank debt in Hungary and Czechoslovakia and about 30–40 percent in Poland and Bulgaria. The ideal solution would be a credible, one-time cleanup of the books, with the government buying up debt through the commercial banks on a case-by-case basis, cleaning an enterprise only on the basis of a clear recovery plan, with strict conditionality and a strictly enforced budget constraint.[21] However, this solution is probably unworkable for most of the countries and enterprises and banks in question, unless it were introduced during privatization as part of a sale bargain. In any event, those enterprises that can be identified as total failures should be phased out as quickly as possible. In Hungary, this procedure was recently used for the coal mining industry.

A major problem is the large number of enterprises whose future is uncertain but that have some potential for restructuring. Some policymakers in these countries are resisting across-the-board cleanups, citing an inherited lack of credibility with which the new governments have to contend. In their view, announcing in advance that something is to be done once and for all amounts to threatening with an unloaded gun. Only a slow process of rejections and tough bargaining will, according to this argument, instill the right discipline.

In general, the problem has been tackled through a gradual institutional and political bargaining process. In Hungary, for example, the government recently guaranteed 50 percent (Ft 10 billion) of the bad debts inherited by the banks from the previous regime. The remaining bad debt that has accumulated, mainly as a result of the CMEA collapse, will be provisioned by the banks over a three-year period, with the implicit understanding that it will be deducted from the annual profits for tax purposes (this implies an implicit participation

---

21. This procedure was followed in Israel in recent major debt-rescheduling schemes for the Histadrut-owned (trade union federation) industrial conglomerate (Koor) and in the settlements belonging to the Kibbutz movement. Both groups were in severe financial straits in the aftermath of the 1985 stabilization programs. The Kibbutz movement's cumulative debt had reached some 15 percent of total GDP before the financial restructuring plan was implemented. In another group, the Moshav (cooperative) movement, an earlier scheme had to be shelved because of noncompliance and political pressure, and a new one has yet to be instituted.

of the state budget of 40 percent). This solution is politically attractive because it reduces the apparent profits of the banks (which have recently been exorbitant, given the large interest rate margins) while appearing to conceal the implicit cost to the budget. In Czechoslovakia, the government decided to allow the National Property Funds, the recipients of the proceeds from privatization, to issue Kčs 50 billion in bonds to be used to write off old enterprise debt and to provide a direct capital injection to the banks. This solution actually seems to be working (see below), especially since Czechoslovakia's internal debt is small. It remains to be seen whether Czechoslovakia and Bulgaria can also introduce a bank provisioning and tax participation scheme similar to the one adopted in Hungary.

Another major problem is how to prevent enterprises from continuing to borrow to survive rather than adjusting. Recapitalizing the banks and letting them handle the problem would seem to be the best policy, provided that the banks are equipped to make the proper economic analysis and are able to take into account the interests of the bond issuers, namely, the government or the taxpayers (who implicitly cover the tax losses). Unfortunately, the financial interests of commercial banks and the long-run economic viability of the enterprise do not necessarily coincide; ideally, the existing owner of the asset, namely, the state, should participate in the process. This is part of the more general problem of enterprise control in the transition period (see the next section) and is further compounded by the fact that the commercial banking system itself is not yet financially independent of the central bank, leaving part of the quasi-fiscal deficit open ended.

How should the public financing of bank capitalization and enterprise restructuring be treated? If this type of public expenditure takes the form of a once-and-for-all stock adjustment, it should not be reckoned as part of the regular tax-financed budget. Rather, it should be included as part of the privatization accounts (as is done by the Treuhandanstalt in East Germany or, implicitly, in the recent Czechoslovak financial injection). Even if there is an initial net debt position, it could be financed by the issue of domestic bonds and/or external financial aid. Alternatively, it could be included in a broader capital account budget from which infrastructure investment could also be financed. To be credible, a one-time stock adjustment should not be perceived as a permanent rise in the money and credit growth rates.

Finally, it is essential that enterprises are given the right signal—that financial rescheduling is a one-time conditional act, not a precedent.

1.7   Privatization of Large State-Owned Enterprises—What to Do during the (Long) Transition?

In all five East European countries, the privatization of (mainly small-scale) trade and services enterprises has moved briskly, but it is at a virtual standstill for large-scale enterprises, primarily in the manufacturing sector. The reasons for the delay have been legal (restitution problems in Czechoslovakia), political (bad experiences with instant privatization in Hungary and Poland), or practical (lack of foreign or domestic investors). Even with the advanced voucher scheme being implemented in Czechoslovakia, it is not yet clear how a new, workable corporate control will emerge. It is clear that in all countries there will be a prolonged interim period during which the state will continue to own a considerable portion of the enterprise sector.

In privatization, as in loan cleanups, extreme solutions (completely discard or continue to embrace the past regime) are not workable and certainly not the optimal solution. The problem is how to instill market-oriented behavior in management and workers without unduly delaying the privatization stage. It appears that this problem has not been systematically addressed in any of the countries.

In Hungary, an attempt has been made to learn from the failure of the previous government's "spontaneous privatization" episode. The new Law on Economic Transformation moves the state-owned enterprises (SOEs) out of the jurisdiction of enterprise councils and gives them company status, under the aegis of the State Property Agency (SPA). In the transition period, the state becomes the legal owner as audited balance sheets and a board of directors are introduced. Supervision of management is partly subcontracted to approved advisory agencies, which become the agents of the SPA.

Much of the Hungarian privatization has taken the form of "self-privatization," whereby a manager looks for potential buyers, who then must be approved by the SPA or its accredited consulting firms. The process is obviously a slow one. The Czechoslovak government, in contrast, seems to have opted for speedy privatization since only the new owners will be in a position to do what is good for the firm. As a result, no systematic thought has been given to how the enterprises in the so-called no-man's land are to be controlled. Although the view is understandable, ignoring the problem does not help since pressure is mounting for subsidies or cheap credit for enterprises in depressed regions.

Giving in to these pressures could result in SOEs staying in state hands forever. Unfortunately, there seems to be no escape from these halfway policies, unless the authorities are willing to take the line that what cannot be privatized instantaneously had better be scrapped. This option, however, makes little economic sense from a medium-run point of view since a sizable amount of industrial product may be made marketable after marginal investments have been made in physical and/or human capital, especially on the marketing side. Moreover, because of the huge potential unemployment problem (with employment in SOEs anywhere between 30 and 50 percent of the labor force), wholesale scrapping is not very likely to be feasible.

In Poland, commercialization as an intermediate step was envisaged as important since it was more likely to free managers from the control of the workers' councils. Managerial compensation is important to avoid decapitalization of firms. Such compensation could be given, at least in part, by long-maturity stock options or by including a longer-term profit share in the manager's contract. A compelling alternative argument, at least for the Polish case (see Dabrowski, Federowicz, and Levitas 1991), is that the power of the workers' councils is too important a legacy from the Communist regime to be easily dissipated. According to this view, the only way to resolve the political stalemate between the workers' councils and the state is mass privatization through giveaway schemes in which the present stakeholders in the enterprise, namely, the workers' councils and the managers, will be the major beneficiaries. This would be a form of controlled spontaneous privatization.

The variety of experience across countries suggests that there may not be one best way of resolving the privatization issue and that each country must choose the one that best fits its political and social framework. But, no matter which strategy each country adopts, it is important that it be transparent, sending clear signals to investors, managers, and workers, so as to minimize uncertainty in the transition period. Also, policy framers must not forget that macroeconomic policies alone can achieve only so much and that micro management policies should be integrated into the general policy framework right from the start as well as throughout the program. Privatization is one part of the reform process where the integration of macro and micro policy is essential.

1.8   Concluding Remarks

This discussion of the recent East European experience with stabilization points to broad common denominators in the five countries considered here as well as with countries elsewhere. The sharp stabilization approach applies more or less generally, while any differences across countries originate in the varying ability to control the budget or the amount of credit or wage policy rather than in the underlying conceptual macroeconomic framework. The greatest differences across countries are also the micro foundations of each economy, such as in ownership rights and financial accountability—which have also proved most resistant to change. The general lesson to be learned here is that, from the start, the policy reform package has to put even greater emphasis on implementation of the institutions and rules of behavior for the micro units. Otherwise, the stabilization part of the reform could unravel.

Another related issue is the perceived role of government in the transition from a centrally planned to a market economy. In the old days, communism was often viewed from the outside in highly simplified terms—a minutely detailed central plan and an omnipotent government. Likewise, today, capitalism is viewed simplistically by those who would like to embrace it as a well-oiled system consisting only of private property ownership and pure laissez-faire and self-adjusting market mechanisms, requiring no government interference. However, market failures often occur in the most laissez-faire economies (e.g., in financial markets), and governments have to intervene in the microeconomy.

Thus, a hands-off policy during the transition from a centrally planned to a market economy would be most inappropriate. The temptation to resort to the old mistakes under central planning may be strong—for example, in the process of restructuring—but that possibility should not be used as an argument against any government intervention during the transition period. If the necessity for intervention is not acknowledged and guidelines regulating its application and defining its purpose are not established, there will be intervention in practice anyway, but, without an overall view of its scope, direction, and implications, intervention will be haphazard and could involve costs that would breach budget constraints and threaten macroeconomic stability.

This discussion has concentrated mainly on issues common to the five East European countries during the past two years. As time passes, the differences among these countries are likely to become more important from a policy perspective, as has usually been the experience of other countries undergoing stabilization and structural reform.

One issue on which economists cannot be of much help is the internal politics of reform. The external observer is struck by the apparent universal acceptance of the drastic changes that have taken place so far, despite the sharp real wage cuts, the fall in living standards, and the rise in unemployment. Although it can be reasonably argued that the official statistics do not really capture reality because of statistical biases, incorrect coverage, and so on, it is also true that numbers, even if inaccurate, are used in the political marketplace (e.g., the consumer price index is used in the wage bargaining process, whether formally or informally). Some recent attempted strikes in Czechoslovakia ran into public opposition, and the policy stance of the government appears to be well understood by the public at large. The government in Bulgaria, with all its difficulties, apparently seems to have public support. In Hungary, however, there seemed to be a contrast between the apparent success of macro policies and the public's negative perception of them, as if the government has been unsuccessful in selling its policy product.

The experience with reforms both elsewhere and across countries in Eastern Europe points to the paramount importance of policymakers being able not only to spell out government strategies in detail and in terms that can be widely understood but also to sell their product to the public. The impending internal social problems in all the countries will no doubt put all the reform efforts to a serious test, as political democratization proceeds and the possibility of bliss recedes. The social element is no doubt the biggest imponderable in each of the countries: what, if anything, can ensure the maintenance of the social consensus over the period of the reform program and its political sustainability in the near future? As one observer has asked, "Are they, in return for true freedom, prepared to give up bread lines for unemployment lines?"[22] The 1991–92

---

22. The quote, attributed to Susan Marie Szasz, appears in Klaus (1991).

postelection developments in Poland and the separatist movement in Czechoslovakia do not bode well, but in this area, as with many others surveyed in
this paper, it is probably much too early to tell.

References

Aghevli, Bijan G., Eduardo Borensztein, and Tessa van der Willigen. Stabilization and
    structural reform in the Czech and Slovak Federal Republic: First stage. Occasional
    Paper no. 92. Washington, D.C.: International Monetary Fund, March.
Boote, Anthony R., and Janos Somogyi. 1991. Economic reform in Hungary since
    1968. Occasional Paper no. 83. Washington, D.C.: International Monetary Fund,
    July.
Bruno, Michael. 1993. *Crisis, stabilization and economic reform: Therapy by consen-
    sus.* Oxford: Oxford University Press.
Bruno, Michael, and Jeffrey Sachs. 1985. *Economics of worldwide stagflation.* Cam-
    bridge, Mass.: Harvard University Press.
Calvo, Guillermo A., and Fabrizio Coricelli. 1992. Stabilizing a previously centrally
    planned economy: Poland 1990. *Economic Policy,* no. 14 (April): 176–226.
Dabrowski, J. M., M. Federowicz, and A. Levitas. 1991. Polish state enterprises and the
    properties of performance: Stabilization, marketization, privatization. *Politics and
    Society* 19 (December): 403–37.
Demekas, Dimitri G., and Mohsin S. Khan. 1991. The Romanian economic reform
    program. Occasional Paper no. 89. Washington, D.C.: International Monetary
    Fund, November.
Fischer, Stanley, and Alan Gelb. 1990. Issues in socialist economy reform. Working
    Paper Series Discussion Paper no. 565. Washington, D.C.: World Bank.
Greene, Joshua E., and Peter Isard. 1991. Currency convertibility and the transforma-
    tion of centrally planned economies. Occasional Paper no. 81. Washington, D.C.:
    International Monetary Fund, June.
Institute for Comparative Economic Studies (ICES). 1990. *COMECON data.* Vienna.
Klaus, Vaclav. 1991. Dismantling socialism: A preliminary report. Occasional Paper
    no. 35. Sydney: Centre for Independent Study.
Kopits, George. 1991. Fiscal reform in European economies in transition. Working
    Paper no. 91/43. Washington, D.C.: International Monetary Fund, April.
Lane, Timothy D. 1991. Inflation stabilization and economic transformation in Poland:
    The first year. Working Paper no. 91/70. Washington, D.C.: International Monetary
    Fund, July.
Lipton, David, and Jeffrey Sachs. 1991. Creating a market economy in Eastern Europe:
    The case of Poland. *Brookings Papers on Economic Activity,* no. 1:75–147.
McKinnon, Ronald I. 1991. *Taxation, money, and credit in liberalizing socialist econo-
    mies.* Washington, D.C.: Institute for Policy Reform, November.
Organization for Economic Cooperation and Development (OECD). 1992. *Economic
    survey for Hungary, 1991.* Paris.
Rodrik, Dani. 1992. Making sense of Soviet trade shock in Eastern Europe: A frame-
    work and some estimates. Working Paper no. 4112. Cambridge, Mass.: NBER, June.
Solimano, Andres. 1991. The economies of Central and Eastern Europe: An historical
    and international perspective. In *Reforming Central and Eastern European econo-*

mies, ed. Vittorio Corbo, Fabrizio Coricelli, and Jan Bossak. Washington, D.C.: World Bank.

Tanzi, Vito. 1991. Tax reform in economies in transition: A brief introduction to the main issues. Working Paper no. 91/23. Washington, D.C.: International Monetary Fund, March.

World Bank. 1991. *World development report.* Washington, D.C.

2 Stabilization and Transition: Poland, 1990–91

Andrew Berg and Olivier Jean Blanchard

Poland has had two tumultuous years. Since stabilization and price liberalization in January 1990, it has been hit by two large shocks. The first, in early 1990, was associated with stabilization. The second, in early 1991, was associated with the collapse of Soviet trade. Those shocks have shaped the process of transition. State firms, which had a lot of adjustment to do, have not done well. In contrast, the private sector has grown fast, but from a narrow and uneven base. The issues for the future are clear: how and how much of the state sector will adjust and survive and whether the private sector can grow fast and wide enough to take up the slack.

Our paper takes stock of these two years. We do not offer a detailed historical narrative as many descriptions of decisions and events have already been given elsewhere.[1] Rather, after providing a brief summary of policies and events since 1990 in section 2.1, we take up five specific issues. In sections 2.2 and 2.3, we examine the causes of the two sharp output drops of early 1990 and early 1991. In sections 2.4 and 2.5, we examine the evolution and behavior of state firms and the growth of the private sector. In section 2.6, we analyze the evolution of inflation. We end, in section 2.7, by drawing the implications of our analysis for the near and medium terms.

The authors thank Mark Schaffer for his many comments, and Mariusz Banaszuk, Pawel Dobrowolski, and Jan Rajski for their help with the data. They have also benefited from comments by conference participants.

1. A partial bibliography includes Lipton and Sachs (1990), Gomulka (1991), Coricelli and de Rezende Rocha (1991), and Lane (1991), which focus on the initial effects of the stabilization program. More recent accounts include Gomulka (1992b), Berg and Sachs (1992), and Schaffer (1992a). Schaffer also gives a useful description of the historical background and of the effects of the reforms of the 1980s. As of the time of this writing, the most up-to-date assessment is in Gomulka (1992a). Finally, the OECD economic survey on Poland is due out soon.

2.1   Policies and Events

2.1.1   The Initial Reform Package

The year 1989 had been characterized by budget deficits, high growth of domestic credit, and, in the end, hyperinflation. The macroeconomic part of the reform package, designed during the last quarter of 1989 and implemented on 1 January 1990, had four main components:

1. *Fiscal consolidation.* The budget was to move from a deficit of about 3 percent of GDP in the last quarter of 1989 to rough balance in 1990, mainly through a decrease in subsidies.

2. *Control of inflation through the control of growth of domestic credit.* This was to be achieved through high refinance rates for banks, 36 percent at a monthly rate for the month of January.

3. *A tight incomes policy aimed at limiting wage growth.* A firm-specific wage-bill norm was established and only partially indexed to inflation, with heavy penalties for payments of wages in excess of the norm. No such restrictions were put on prices, allowing firms to make the required adjustments in relative prices.

4. *Convertibility of the zloty.* In the absence of large international reserves, and without much knowledge as to how the shift to convertibility and changes in relative prices would shift exports and imports, the exchange rate was set and pegged low. At the initial exchange rate, the average Polish wage in industry was $0.40 an hour. Tariff rates were decreased to an average of 10 percent and made more uniform. And the pervasive quantitative restrictions and licensing requirements on trade were largely eliminated.[2]

The main element of reform on the microeconomic side was price liberalization. Food prices had been freed in August 1989. The proportion of controlled prices was further decreased from 50 percent to 10 percent. Most remaining regulated prices, especially energy prices, were sharply increased, although not to world levels and with further increases planned for later. The legal status of state firms remained unchanged, but with the government signaling a clear change in the rules governing relations between these firms and the state. Firms could no longer expect ad hoc transfers from the budget to make up for losses, as had been the case in the previous regime. Attempts had been made to tighten these policies during 1989, but January 1990 was a clear break from the past. Bankruptcy rules for state enterprises were clarified and strengthened, and firms widely feared that laws on the books for many years would now be enforced. The assets serving as the base for the "dividend tax" levied by the government on firms were revalued for inflation, and failure to pay the tax was made a trigger for starting bankruptcy proceedings. Definition and implemen-

---

2. For further discussion of how the exchange rate was chosen, see Gomulka (1992b). For a discussion of the role of convertibility, see Berg and Sachs (1992).

tation of the more complex and politically delicate structural reforms, such as privatization, had to be left to later.

2.1.2   1990

Together with the virtually instantaneous elimination of rationing, the effects of the January program were a sharp increase in prices and a sharp decrease in activity. (Table 2.1 gives basic macroeconomic statistics from the last quarter of 1989 to the last quarter of 1991.) The consumer price index (CPI) rise by 80 percent in January.[3] With nominal wages unchanged, measured real wages fell by 40 percent. Sales from industry were down by 20 percent in January. One happy surprise was a trade surplus, or at least a measured trade surplus, as some imports surely went unrecorded. Both exports and imports in convertible currency were up in the first quarter (over the first quarter of 1989), and for the year as a whole the trade surplus was an impressive 4 percent of GDP.

With the jump in prices, real zloty money balances fell by 33 percent in January, although they recovered to 96 percent of the December level by March. And the budget surplus was much larger than anticipated, some 2 percent of GDP in the first quarter. The source of the windfall was large reported profits by state firms and thus large revenues from the profit tax; these profits were, however, in part paper profits coming from high inflation and the use of historical costs for inputs of firms.

Political pressures from the recession, the large decrease in measured real wages, and the initial budget surplus combined to encourage a less restrictive macroeconomic policy during the second half of 1990 (see, e.g., Dabrowski 1991). The lid on government expenditures was loosened. Nominal interest rates were lowered, leading to negative ex ante real rates. The initial parity of the zloty proved, however, easy to defend, and the nominal exchange rate was maintained throughout the year.

Progress on the microeconomic front was slow. Progress on privatization in particular was uneven, both in 1990 and in 1991. Once new local governments were in place in the spring of 1990, privatization of retail shops proceeded steadily, mostly through leasing. By the end of 1991, it was largely achieved. A comprehensive privatization law was passed in July 1990, after intense political debate. And, as a result, some progress was also made in the privatization of small- and medium-sized firms, usually through lease-to-buy arrangements. But, in sharp contrast, there was in effect no progress in the privatization of large firms. The law envisaged privatization of these large firms mainly through case-by-case sales. The result was a grand total of twenty-six firms sold by the end of 1991. As a result, the Treasury has remained to this day the de jure owner of state firms.

---

3. The CPI in Poland is here and usually measured as the change of the average price level from month to month. The PPI, in contrast, is measured as the change from the beginning to the end of the month.

Table 2.1 Poland, 1990/1991: Basic Macroeconomic Statistics

	1989:4	1990:1	1990:2	1990:3	1990:4	1991:1	1991:2	1991:3	1991:4
Index of real sales	1.00	.77	.72	.74	.75	.65	.57	.57	.57
Employment	17.6				16.5				15.9
State	11.7				10.0				8.8
Private	1.8				2.3				3.0
Unemployment rate (%)	.0	1.5	3.1	5.0	6.1	7.1	8.4	10.4	11.4
CPI inflation (%)	31	32	5	3	5	8	3	2	3
Exports:									
Rubles (millions)	3,910	2,688	3,110	2,205	3,011	561	560	84	175
Dollars (millions)	2,412	2,182	2,705	3,133	4,000	2,751	3,459	3,196	4,812
Imports:									
Rubles (millions)	2,725	1,706	1,505	1,443	1,985	558	163	68	47
Dollars (millions)	2,182	1,573	1,465	1,825	3,391	3,050	3,457	3,047	4,692
Markups (%)	40	31	29	28	24	16	14	19	13
Government surplus									
(%)	−3.6	1.6	3.4	1.7	−3.9	−2.4	−3.6	−3.8	−3.1
Refinance rate	11.7	22.0	5.8	2.8	4.3	5.5	5.3	3.8	3.3

Note: The index of real sales is measured in the last month of each quarter. Employment is measured in thousands at the end of the year. Private employment does not include agriculture. Unemployment is in the last month of each quarter, expressed as the share of the labor force. CPI inflation is average monthly inflation for the quarter. Exports and imports are for the quarter, in millions of rubles and dollars. The markup is defined as (sales − costs)/costs for the quarter, for the socialized sector. Government surplus is for the quarter, as a percentage of GDP. It is computed as the surplus as a share of expenditures, multiplied by the ratio of expenditures to GDP for the year. The refinance rate of the NBP is the average monthly rate for the quarter.

Despite the less restrictive macroeconomic policy in the second half of the year, overall economic activity remained relatively flat. The main aggregate developments were a steady fall in employment in state firms and a steady increase in employment in the private sector. By the end of the year, employment in the state sector stood at 10 million, down by 1.7 million workers; employment in state firms in industry was 3.6 million, down by about 0.9 million. The proportional decrease was, however, less than the decrease in output so that, at the end of the year, labor productivity in industry was still equal to only 90 percent of its prestabilization value. Profit rates were also steadily lower throughout the year. Markups, defined as profits over accounting costs, were down from 40 percent in the last quarter of 1989 to 24 percent in the last quarter of 1990. This had direct fiscal implications through the fall in profit taxes. By the last quarter, the budget surplus had turned into deficit.

Employment decline in the state sector was partly offset by growth of private employment. Measured private nonagricultural employment grew by 31 percent to 2.3 million at the end of 1990. This was, however, insufficient to prevent a steady rise in unemployment, and the unemployment rate at the end of the year stood at 1.1 million, or about 6.5 percent of the labor force. Finally, as is often the case in stabilization episodes, inflation was down but not out. Excluding the January price adjustment, inflation remained at a relatively high average rate of about 5 percent for the rest of the year.

Thus, the first year of reform was characterized by a sharp contraction at the beginning and divergent evolutions of the state and private sectors thereafter. Because of the many statistical and conceptual problems involved, the magnitude of the fall in GDP is controversial. Official numbers put the decline at 12 percent. Estimates from Berg and Sachs (1992) suggest a number closer to 5 percent.

2.1.3   1991

At the beginning of 1991, the Polish economy was hit by a severe external shock, the collapse of the CMEA (Council for Mutual Economic Assistance) trade regime. The end of the CMEA was associated with both a large terms-of-trade shock and, more important, a large decrease in the volume of trade. The increase in import prices from former CMEA countries for the first two quarters of 1991 over the first two quarters of 1990 was 161 percent, the increase in export prices only 23 percent. Decreases in import and export volumes with former CMEA countries over the same periods were 39 percent and 40 percent, respectively.

The collapse of trade coincided with a tightening of macro policy, in response to what was perceived as too lax a stance during the second part of 1990. Refinance rates were increased to 6 percent monthly from February on. The results of the CMEA shock and tighter policy were a further sharp drop in output and another sharp increase in prices. Sales from industry were down another 25 percent over the first two quarters; inflation was equal to 12 percent in January. In May 1991, to slow down the real appreciation of the zloty, the exchange rate was moved to a slow crawling peg, implying a depreciation vis-à-vis the dollar of about 1.8 percent a month, smaller than inflation.

The rest of the year was a broad replay of 1990, with a decline in the socialized sector and rapid expansion in the private sector. There was limited action on microeconomic reforms. In particular, as we already mentioned briefly, large state enterprises remained in limbo as almost none were privatized and the state did not exert ownership rights. Employment in state firms declined by another 1.2 million, to 8.8 million. Again, the decline in employment was not enough to reestablish labor productivity, which at the end of 1991 stood at only 78 percent of its prestabilization level. In contrast, nonagricultural private employment was up another 31 percent, to about 3 million workers. Thus, by the end of the year, some 45 percent of employment (and 26 percent of nonagricultural employment) was in the private sector. By the end of the year, the unemployment rate was equal to 11.4 percent.

Profit rates declined further throughout the year. Markups in the last quarter were down to 13 percent, and net profits were −6.5 percent of sales for the economy as a whole.[4] The direct implication was a growing fiscal deficit, of 4.5 percent for the year, both because of lower accrued taxes and because of increasing tax arrears. Tax arrears at the end of the year were equal to 12 percent of total tax revenues for the year.

Official estimates are that the decrease in GDP for 1991 was roughly 8–10 percent. In contrast to 1990, real consumption was up, by 6 percent. Fixed investment was down by about 10 percent. And the trade position, which had shown a surplus of 4 percent of GDP in 1990, was roughly in balance in 1991. Total real imports (including trade with former CMEA countries) were up 39 percent; total real exports were constant. Inflation for the year was still a high 60 percent.

As a result of parliamentary elections in November 1991, Lezcek Balcerowitz, who had been the architect of the economic reform under both the Mazowiecki and the Bielecki governments, was replaced as minister of finance. One of the most urgent tasks confronting the new Olszewski government was to control the fiscal crisis triggered by the near disappearance of profits in state firms.[5]

2.1.4   Five Issues

Having sketched the landscape, we now ask five more specific sets of questions. (1) What were the causes of the output decline of early 1990? Was it primarily due to the dislocations implied by the move to a market economy or

---

4. The numbers for markups for 1990 and 1991 are not strictly comparable. In particular, "costs of financial operations" were taken out of "costs of own sales" in 1991. Thus, the numbers in table 2.1 for 1991 may overestimate markups by 2–3 percent. We thank Mark Schaffer for pointing this out to us.

5. For further details, see de Crombrugghe and Lipton (in vol. 2).

instead to a demand contraction? (2) What were the causes of the other sharp decline in output at the beginning of 1991? What was the role of the CMEA collapse? Was the effect through dislocations or through a fall in external demand? (3) How should one think of the evolution of state firms over the last two years? Have we seen the orderly decline and transformation of a sector that was too large in the first place? Or have we seen increasing paralysis, without much restructuring? (4) Where and how has the private sector grown? Is it filling some holes and not others; is it replacing or complementing the state sector? (5) Why did prices increase so much at the beginning, and why has inflation been so persistent since? To what failures of policy—incomes, micro-, or macroeconomic, if any—can it be ascribed? The answers to these questions are critical, not only in helping design reform plans for other countries, but also in assessing the issues facing Poland in the near and medium term. We take these five questions in turn.

2.2   The Initial Decline in Output

With the implementation of the reform program in January 1990, there were many reasons to expect a drop in output, surely more so than in the typical stabilization.

It was plausible to expect a large drop in aggregate demand. In addition to conventional reasons, in particular the fiscal consolidation and the decrease in money growth, there are others specific to stabilization in this unusual type of economy. Dishoarding, not only of traditionally high inventories in Soviet-type economies, but also of inventories accumulated by firms and people in anticipation of price liberalization, might lead to a fall in sales and a further fall in production given sales. Unusually high uncertainty as to what the future holds might lead workers to increase saving and firms to suspend investment plans. Despite the low exchange rate, the sudden availability of foreign goods might lead to a sharp increase in imports and a fall in domestic demand. And, in contrast with the situation in other East European countries at the time of stabilization, partial price liberalization and the high inflation of 1989 had left little if any "overhang": the ratio of financial assets to income for households was only 3.7 months in December 1989.

But there were also reasons to expect that the large reallocation of demand implied by the change in relative prices and the elimination of rationing might also lead to a decline in aggregate output: sectors facing a decrease in demand would decline; sectors facing an increase might be unable to respond. There were even good reasons to fear widespread supply constraints, as the reform program might lead, for example, to large dislocations in the distribution system, preventing inputs from going to firms or goods from getting to consumers.

In the event, there was indeed a sharp drop in output. At least in the state sector—for which reliable monthly data are available—the decrease in sales was nearly instantaneous. Sales from industry were down by 20 percent in

January, by 24 percent over the first quarter. The decrease was across the board: 93 percent of all three-digit branches had declines over the first quarter.[6] Within industry, the decrease was largest in consumer goods and smallest in heavy manufacturing and mining.

That there was also a large reallocation of demand is not in doubt. The standard deviation of sales changes across three-digit branches in industry in the first quarter of 1990 was 14 percent, a large number by normal Western standards.[7] And the standard deviation of relative price changes was 23 percent. But the evidence, to which we now turn, suggests that the output drop was mostly due to a shift in aggregate demand.

First, the perception of the firms themselves was that the proximate cause of the drop in output was a sharp drop in their demand. Surveys of several hundred state enterprises reported in Gorski, Jaszczynski, and Geryszewska (1990) show that, whereas, in November 1988, 87 percent of firms had perceived their market as being either balanced or in "excess demand," in February 1990, 97 percent perceived it as either balanced or in "excess supply," with 48 percent in the category "state of relative surplus: relative lack of demand in relation to real possibilities of production; inventories being amassed; price discounts, etc." Only 9 percent indicated any inability to meet demand.[8] Firms in a survey of about 700 industrial enterprises carried out every few weeks from 1989 to 1991 (CRETM 1990) stated that, of the "factors limiting the growth of output in the enterprise," supply and employment shortages were the limiting factors in 62 percent of firms in October 1989, 37 percent in January 1990, and 10 percent by April. Finally, in their study of nine Polish firms, Jorgensen, Gelb, and Singh (1991) summarize the managers' perceptions of the initial output drop as coming nearly entirely from demand, with dislocations, credit, and other factors as "irritants."

Had supply bottlenecks and other disruptions been prevalent, many firms would have operated along the vertical portion of their supply curve; thus, prices would have risen to clear markets, and, given incomes policy and the resulting sharp constraints on wage increases, markups of prices over costs should also have gone up. It turns out that, while prices were indeed sharply higher in January, something at which we shall look in detail in section 2.6, the increase is more than accounted for by the increase in costs, and markups of prices over costs were sharply down. The average markup of prices over accounting costs for state firms was down from 40 percent in the last quarter of 1989 to 31 percent in the first quarter of 1990. And the markup was down in sixty-six out of eighty-five branches at the three-digit level.

A cleaner test along the same lines is provided by the behavior of finished

6. This is seventy-nine out of eighty-five branches in industry. The sample of branches excludes branches with growth either below −60 percent or above 50 percent, in which case we suspect that the change reflects reclassification rather than actual change, and excludes branches with sales of less than Zl 100 billion in the last quarter of 1989.

7. The sample of branches is the same as is outlined in no. 6 above.

8. This survey was conducted once in November 1988 and once in March 1990.

goods inventories. If production bottlenecks were behind the decrease in output, one would have expected firms constrained in production to satisfy sales as much as possible out of inventories and thus inventory to be decumulated. But if demand contraction was the proximate cause of the output decline, one would have expected instead firms at the beginning both to cut production and to accumulate inventories.

Thus, in appendix A, we look at both the aggregate and the cross-sectional evidence on inventories. The examination is fraught with measurement problems, the main one being the issue of proper deflation of existing stocks. Doing our best, we reach two main conclusions.

First, while the evidence is ambiguous on the movement of inventories in trade at the beginning of the year, there was clearly a large increase in finished goods inventories in industry at the beginning of 1990, followed by decumulation later in the year. This conclusion is consistent with the evidence from data on quantities produced. Schaffer (1992a) constructs a production index for industry directly from quantity data and concludes that the decline in sales was much larger than that in production in January 1990.

Second, turning to the cross-sectional evidence, we find that 90 percent of three-digit branches in industry had an increase in finished goods inventories in the first quarter. And, in a cross-sectional regression of changes in inventories on initial inventories and changes in sales, we find a clear relation between sales declines and inventory accumulation. This suggests that decline in demand and not difficulties with production was the proximate cause of the fall in sales. The sector where the relation appears not to hold is the food-processing sector, where indeed anecdotal evidence suggests that there were serious distribution problems in early 1990.[9]

Using our cross-sectional data on three-digit branches, we explore further a hypothesis advanced by Calvo and Coricelli (1991). Examining the Polish macroeconomic evidence, they suggest that part of the output decline was indeed due to supply constraints, themselves due to the sharp fall in working credit preventing firms from buying inputs needed in production. Thus, we first add the change in working credit to our inventory regressions and estimate the relation between changes in inventories, sales, and working credit either by OLS or by using initial working credit as an instrument for changes in credit. We find a strong effect of working credit. Given sales, firms that were more credit constrained in the first quarter of 1990 satisfied those sales more from inventories than from production. We then look at the relation of sales themselves to working credit. We find only a weak relation; the evidence does not appear to support a strong effect of working credit on sales through the supply side.[10]

9. This sector is also the only one where the private sector was sufficiently developed initially to seriously encroach on the state firms within the first quarter.

10. These regressions are not the last word on this issue. Since the writing of our first draft, Calvo and Coricelli have used our data to estimate alternative specifications and have found that, if the specification is one of the rate of change of sales on the rate of change of working credit,

Turning to the causes of the decrease in demand, the evidence is clear that it was not a sudden shift toward imports or a loss of export markets, as was to be so dramatically the case in East Germany later in 1990. At the new exchange rate, exports in convertible currency were sharply up, imports in convertible currency slightly up, with a—measured—net trade surplus as a result.[11] The proximate sources of the demand contraction were decreases in both consumption and investment demand. Despite a large decrease in real wages, and thus a larger decline in disposable income than in output, personal saving was up substantially for the first half of the year. Just as for wage restraint, which we shall document in section 2.6, this was probably because of uncertainty about the future. It may have also been from the desire to rebuild real balances. Over the year, there was some recovery of consumption, in line with real wages. But this was offset by inventory decumulation and declining investment, keeping demand and output low.

The conclusion that a drop in aggregate demand rather than dislocations was in large part responsible for the initial output decline implies that one cannot avoid the question asked by Bruno (in this volume): Could this sharp contraction have been partly avoided? With the benefit of hindsight, the answer must be a qualified yes. Profit taxes, coming largely from paper profits due to the valuation by firms of inputs at historical cost and from the revaluation of foreign deposits, were larger than expected. As we shall argue later when examining inflation, and as is suggested by Schaffer in his Comment on our paper, the effect of the large profit taxes was to lead to low nominal wage increases and thus to lower disposable income of workers and lower consumption demand. In retrospect, the budget surplus was probably both too contractionary and the source of pressures for increased spending later in the year, a dangerous course as high revenues, largely due to inflation, were temporary. But we emphasize the importance of hindsight here. Guessing what would happen to aggregate demand, the trade balance, and capital flows in January 1990 was at best a difficult exercise, and credibility required erring, if anything, on the side of excess.[12]

2.3   The Collapse of the CMEA and the Second Output Decline

In January 1991, the Polish economy was shaken by another major shock, the breakdown of trade within the CMEA.[13]

---

the relation between sales and working credit is stronger than the relation that we report in app. A. We see, however, our findings of a strong positive relation between sales declines and inventory accumulation as powerful evidence against their pure hypothesis, which clearly predicts a negative relation.

11. Berg and Sachs (1992) find no positive relation between import penetration and declines in output across industries.

12. For a related discussion, see Dornbusch (1991).

13. For a detailed examination of Poland, Hungary, and Czechoslovakia, see Rodrik (in vol. 2).

Until the end of 1990, trade between most socialist countries had taken place under CMEA arrangements. Prices were set in a common unit of account, the transferable ruble, and the general principle was one of balanced trade.[14] While relative prices in rubles were supposed to reflect relative world prices, the relative price of finished goods in terms of materials was substantially higher than the relative world price. Thus, a country like Poland, for which the share of industrial goods in exports to the Soviet Union was more than 80 percent and the share of raw materials in imports from the Soviet Union was more than 55 percent, had particularly favorable terms of trade under CMEA arrangements.

Was Poland buying cheap oil from the Soviet Union—compared to world prices—and selling normally priced industrial goods, or was it instead buying oil at world prices and selling industrial goods above world prices? From an economic point of view, this is irrelevant: with balanced trade between the two countries, all that mattered was the terms of trade.[15] But the answer matters in understanding what happened to measured CMEA exports and imports when there was a shift to world—dollar—prices. What is needed is the exchange rate between the transferable ruble and the dollar. There were two such rates. The first was the official CMEA (IBEC) rate, which in 1990 was about $1.50 per ruble. At that rate, oil was priced in line with world prices, and finished goods were priced much above world prices. The second was the rate used by the National Bank of Poland (NBP), which was $0.22 per ruble in 1990. At that rate, both oil and finished goods were underpriced, oil more so than finished goods. To consolidate ruble and dollar transactions, Polish statistics used the second rate. At that rate, the share of trade with the Soviet Union in 1989 was 21 percent for exports and 18 percent for imports. At the official CMEA rate, the numbers were 46 percent and 37 percent, respectively.

It was widely understood in 1990 that the end of the year would mark the end of CMEA trade arrangements and would be associated both with a terms-of-trade shock and a decrease of trade between CMEA countries. Indeed, throughout 1990, there was already a steady shift in ruble-to-dollar trade within the CMEA, varying in degree across CMEA partners. While, in the first quarter of 1990, 20 percent of exports and 23 percent of imports with the Soviet Union were settled in dollars, the numbers were 44 percent and 76 percent at the end of the year.

At the end of 1990, a careful survey was conducted, asking Polish and Soviet importers and exporters what quantities and at what prices they thought they would import and export after the shift (Rosati 1990). The first conclusion was that, compared to preshift dollar prices using the NBP rate to convert rubles to dollars, import prices would increase by a factor of four, export prices by a factor of three, thus leading to an adverse terms-of-trade shift. The second

---

14. A detailed description of CMEA trade is given in World Bank (1989).

15. Here we differ from Rodrik's (in vol. 2) position that the "right" rate is, in any useful sense, the International Bank for Economic Cooperation (IBEC) rate.

conclusion was that the volume of Polish exports to the Soviet Union would decrease by 20 percent and that the volume of Polish imports from the Soviet Union would also decrease by 20 percent.

The shock to the economy turned out to be larger than this survey anticipated.[16]

The increase in import prices from former CMEA countries for the first two quarters of 1991 compared to the first two quarters of 1990 was 161 percent, the increase in export prices only 23 percent.[17] These smaller than expected increases in export prices probably reflect the fact that part of the adjustment had already taken place in 1990 and that firms had been overly optimistic as to the quality of their goods. The decreases in import and export volumes were 39 percent and 40 percent, respectively, thus larger than expected. The decrease in the value of exports to the Soviet Union was particularly large; in contrast, the value of trade with Hungary and Czechoslovakia was only marginally down. It appears in retrospect that much of the decrease in volume was due not so much to a shift in CMEA country demand toward non-CMEA products as to the collapse of the Soviet Union and to the payments mechanism. As a result, the overall trade balance, which had shown a surplus of about $1 billion in the first two quarters of 1990, was balanced in the first two quarters of 1991.

The result of the shock was another large drop in output. Industrial output in February was 20 percent below that of December and roughly remained there for the rest of the year. The output drop was accompanied by another large increase in the price level. Inflation for January was 12.7 percent. The increase in prices was due both to a large increase in the price of CMEA imports and to further elimination of a number of subsidies.

An important question is whether and by how much the CMEA shock was compounded by tight credit policies at the beginning of 1991. It was widely felt at the end of 1990 that the incomes policy was in danger of failing[18] and that monetary policy had been too lax in the second half of 1990. Nominal interest rates were increased from November on, reaching annual rates of 72 percent from February to April, and then decreasing again to reach 40 percent in October. In appendix B, we take a first pass at this question by examining the cross-sectional evidence on changes in sales, CMEA exports, and CMEA imports.

We look at changes in those variables for the first five months of 1991 over

16. The degree to which enterprise managers underestimated the effects of the CMEA shock is surprising in retrospect. Government efforts to provide restructuring assistance in 1990 to firms dependent on CMEA trade met with virtually no interest. Survey data from CRETM (1990) confirm that, at least through late 1990, few firms predicted major consequences from the end of the CMEA.

17. Our source here is the August 1991 issue of *Plan Econ*. We are not sure about the treatment of East Germany in those numbers. It is likely that trade with East Germany is counted in 1990. It is not counted in 1991.

18. We return to this issue when studying inflation below.

all of 1990. Building on the work in Berg and Sachs (1992), the variable for CMEA exports measures the value of direct and indirect exports of a given branch to CMEA countries transacted in rubles, where indirect effects are constructed using an input-output matrix. The export measure covers only ruble trade with CMEA countries; thus, to the extent that some trade was conducted in dollars, the measured decrease in exports overestimates the true decrease. (Aggregate exports to the former CMEA countries fell some 40 percent in value while ruble exports fell about 80 percent in the first half of 1991.) Regressions using data from both two-digit and three-digit sectors in industry yield three main findings.

First, using two-digit-level data, we find a strong effect of direct and indirect changes in CMEA exports on branch sales. The coefficient is significantly different from both zero and one. The fact that it is less than one is probably due to the fact that some of the trade was continued in dollars, rather than to the redirection of exports to the West. For the three-digit regressions, where no trade data were available for 1991, the CMEA variable measures the initial share of ruble exports in total sales. Given the overall value decline of about 40 percent, the coefficient of -0.4 is consistent with little reorientation of sales. Second, we find a negative but weak effect of CMEA imports, suggesting effects through the supply side, through the loss of crucial imports. Third, the constant term in each regression, which captures the decline in output not explained by the export and import variables, accounts for 50–75 percent of the decline. These regressions cannot, however, tell us whether it captures further multiplier effects from the loss of exports or other factors, such as a tighter macroeconomic policy.

2.4   The Evolution of State Firms

At the beginning of the reform program, there were in Poland about 8,500 state firms. Of those, 1,000 had more than 1,000 employees and accounted for 66 percent of industrial production. One of the crucial issues in the reform process was whether and how they would adapt and restructure. Two years later, at the end of 1991, the evidence was not encouraging.

1. The enormous problems that these largely dysfunctional state firms would face in restructuring were well documented before the fact by Kornai (1990) and, in the case of Poland, by Lipton and Sachs (1990). But those inherited problems were compounded by two additional factors.

The first was the lack of progress in the privatization of large state firms.[19] After a bitter debate in Parliament, a privatization law was passed in July 1990. The results, at least for large firms, have been very limited. Not before November 1990 were the first five firms sold through public offerings. At the end of

---

19. For details, see Berg (in vol. 2).

1991, five more firms had been sold in the same manner, and another sixteen had been sold through public tenders or auctions.[20]

The lack of privatization did not, however, imply that firms were under the effective control of the state. A latent structure of control, the "workers' councils," had been put in place in the reform of 1981. As long, however, as managers had the backing of the center, those councils did not play a dominant role. But, with the fall of the Communist government in the summer of 1989, the councils took on progressively more power, including the ability to hire and fire managers. This tendency was reinforced over the following two years. Elections for new councils in 1990 were often followed by referenda on the management. By the end of 1990, half of all managing directors had been confirmed by elections, 40 percent of these new. (For an excellent discussion of ownership and control of Polish state firms in the 1980s and in 1990, see Dabrowski, Federowicz, and Levitas 1991.)

Thus, the stalling of privatization did not preserve the strong role of the state in running firms. Instead, it led to an increase in the power of insiders, especially workers, in firms while at the same time making their stake in the ultimately privatized firm very uncertain.

2. Under those conditions, how would we have expected managers to behave?

Had managers acted only on behalf of the absentee owner (the state or the owner-to-be after privatization), they would have adjusted prices so as to maximize profits. They would then have decreased employment at least in line with sales. To the extent that the firms had market power, they would have passed on wage increases partly or fully through prices. And they would have started restructuring firms.

Had managers instead acted only on behalf of workers, they would have chosen prices so as to maximize revenues net of nonlabor costs. Absent any constraint on wages, they would then have chosen the wage so as to redistribute revenues to the workers. How much they would have kept in profits would have depended on the horizon of workers, thus on the stake that workers expected to have in the newly privatized firms, as well as on such factors as their degree of liquidity constraints and their attachment to the firms.

Given constraints on wages, such as were actually imposed by the incomes policy, they would have kept employment high, as high employment was the only way of increasing the wage bill and thus the share of revenues going to workers. And increases in the wage norm would not have affected the revenue-maximizing price and thus would not have been reflected in increases in prices.[21]

20. In addition, some eighty-two firms with over five hundred employees were leased to management and workers in a procedure designed for small- and medium-sized enterprises.

21. In 1990, firms generally could not vary the limit on the total wage bill by changing employment. Thus, a reduction in employment allowed an increase in the wage. In 1991, the norm on the

We read the evidence as saying that, during 1990–91, managers quickly shifted to act primarily in the interests of their workers. And, more important, we read the evidence as suggesting that the horizon of the workers, and thus of the managers' decisions, became increasingly short. At the end of 1991, the results of such behavior were excess employment, the nearly full appropriation of quasi rents in wages, and little in the way of restructuring. We now review the evidence, starting with the reaction of firms to the initial stabilization program.[22]

3. Surprisingly, wages were initially set below what was allowed by the—not very generous—increase in the norm under the incomes policy. In retrospect, the main reason was probably uncertainty as to what stabilization might bring, including the possibility of bankruptcy and thus of loss of control of the firm by workers and managers (see Dabrowski, Federowicz, and Levitas 1991). In addition, the design of the incomes policy allowed for shortfalls from the norm to be made up later in the year and thus gave another reason to err on the side of prudence at the beginning. Yet another factor, to which we return below, was that, despite high accounting profits, cash flows were low, owing to high taxes on those paper profits.

Markups, defined as revenues minus (accounting) costs over costs, had steadily increased throughout 1989. Average markups stood at 32 percent for the year as a whole and at 40 percent for the last quarter.[23] They were sharply down, at 31 percent, in the first quarter of 1990. The size of the decline is consistent with the joint hypothesis that, for lack of a more sophisticated strategy, firms initially set prices using their traditional markup over anticipated unit cost and that they underpredicted the fall in output, as the survey evidence indeed suggests (see CRETM 1990). As the decline of output was not accompanied by a proportional decrease in employment, the result was a decline in labor productivity and thus lower profits and markups.

In looking at markups or at other profit and cost measures in both 1989 and early 1990, a caveat is, however, in order. During that period, very high rates of inflation together with accounting of inputs at historical cost were the source

---

wage bill moved proportionally with employment. A formal model of a labor-managed firm in a transition environment is given by Jackman and Scott (1992).

22. An early paper on the response of state firms to the 1990 reforms in Frydman and Wellisz (1991). Other papers looking at the behavior of state firms during 1990 are Schaffer (1992b), Dabrowski, Federowicz, and Levitas (1991), and Commander, Coricelli, and Staehr (1991).

23. Depending on availability, we give in this section numbers for one of two sets of firms. The first, to which this number refers, includes all nonagricultural enterprises with fifty or more employees in industry and construction and twenty or more in other sectors. This is the sector covered as a rule in the monthly *Statistical Bulletin* published by the Polish Statistical Office (GUS). There is a break in the series in 1991, when sufficiently large private firms are added. This change is not significant for the markup as the share of the private sector in these larger firms is small (4 percent in the third quarter of 1991). The other set includes all state firms (or, more precisely, all firms subject to the dividend tax), thus excluding private-sector firms and cooperatives. This is the set that we use when we refer to three-digit branches.

of large paper profits. True profits were smaller. We have constructed a simple inflation-adjusted markup series by regressing markups monthly for 1989–91 on the average inflation rate over the current and past two months and removing the estimated effect of inflation. This crude "inflation-adjusted" series gives markups of 24 percent for the fourth quarter of 1989 and of 15 percent for the first quarter of 1990. For later quarters, as inflation is lower, the difference between markups and adjusted markups is under 3 percent. In his Comment on our paper, Schaffer shows that, despite high reported profits, after-tax cash flows were actually negative in the first quarter of 1990. This is not only because inputs had to be purchased at their current price but also because taxes, levied on accounting profits, were unusually high.

4. Soon after stabilization, it became clear to workers and managers that their worst fears had been excessive and that, while profits and sales had declined, firms were still making profits and the risk of bankruptcy was low. Thus, the rest of 1990–91 was characterized by a steady transfer of rents from profits to wages, together with a steady but insufficient decline in employment.

Employment in state firms in industry, which stood at 4.1 million at the end of 1989, stood at 3.6 million at the end of 1990 and at about 3.2 million at the end of 1991. The available evidence suggests that the decline was accomplished mostly by attrition. The proportion unemployed from group layoffs stood at only 16 percent of total unemployment at the end of 1990 and at 23 percent at the end of 1991.[24] But this decline in employment was insufficient to restore labor productivity even to its preform levels. At the end of 1990, labor productivity in industry stood at 90 percent of its December 1989 value; at the end of 1991, it was down to 77 percent.

With positive profits and, after a few months, improving cash flows as well, the initial wage restraint quickly disappeared. By June 1990, nominal wages were back to the norm. By the end of the year, they were 22 percent above the norm, the result in part of a flaw in the design of the policy, in which firms that had paid wages below the norm at the beginning of the year could use this accumulated credit to pay wages above the norm later in 1990. With the beginning of a new calendar year, firms had either to cut nominal wages to be below the new norm or to pay considerable excess wage taxes. The outcome was a partial accommodation of the pressure by an upward revision of the norm and low wage settlements, in no doubt made easier by the coincident CMEA-induced decrease in output. But, throughout 1991, firms were increasingly willing to pay the excess wage tax in order to pay wages above the norm. At the end of the first half of 1991, 38 percent of state industrial enterprises were paying some excess wage tax. In the fourth quarter of 1991, more than 36 percent of total tax revenues (excluding the turnover tax) were coming from the excess wage tax.

---

24. Since 1990, Polish law assigns special rights to those fired in "group layoffs." Since these rights impose burdens on the enterprise and may generate an incentive to disguise these layoffs, these data must be treated with caution.

Profit rates steadily declined. Measured markups, which were equal to 31 percent in the first quarter of 1990, were down to 24 percent in the last quarter of 1990 and to 13 percent in the last quarter of 1991. In the last quarter of 1991, 29 percent of two-digit branches were reporting negative gross profits (and 75 percent reported negative net profits), something no branch had done in 1990. The evidence supports the hypothesis that this came largely from incomplete passthrough of wage increases. The evidence from the last three quarters of 1990, which we give in the section on inflation below, is particularly clear. During those three quarters, relative nonlabor costs in state firms remained roughly constant, while wage costs per unit of output were up by 58 percent. The increase in the producer price index was only 26 percent, thus implying a passthrough coefficient of about half.

There is, however, an alternative interpretation of the evidence of declining profits, namely, that, because of foreign competition, firms were only partially able to pass wage increases into prices and that the low profit margins at the end of 1991 reflected instead an overappreciation of the zloty.[25] Between January and December 1990, the real appreciation of the zloty was indeed a large 250 percent and, despite the shift to a crawling peg in May, was another 15 percent in 1991. How much of the decrease in profit margins was due to the appropriation of rents in wages and how much was the result of a loss of competitiveness is crucial to assessing both the past and the options for the future, such as the desirability of a sharp devaluation. To some extent, one can test the two hypotheses by looking at the difference in the evolution of profit rates across sectors with differential exposure to foreign competition. The evidence on the distribution of profit rates across three-digit branches does not show a clear pattern. More formal but preliminary regressions of the change in profit rates as a function of import penetration in 1990 do not show a significant effect of the import variable. But the issue deserves further work.[26]

5. At the end of 1991, there were ominous signs that, with not enough profits to cover tax liabilities, many firms were now testing the credibility both of the banking system and of the government. Banking reform is another area where little progress has been made. The traditional monobank of centrally planned economies had been broken up into a central bank, six specialized banks, and nine commercial banks in February 1989.[27] But, over 1990–91, those banks had neither the incentives nor the know-how to change their lending practices,

25. A nice example of the role of foreign competition in limiting prices is given by the price of black-and-white televisions in 1990. The price was Zl 430,000 in December 1989, Zl 773,000 in January 1990, and Zl 1.3 million in February. But, from then on, it steadily went down, reaching Zl 1.1 million in July and Zl 1.0 million in December. The question is how general this constraint was.

26. Specifically, we have regressed the markup in the first five months of 1991 on the markup, energy as a share of sales, exports to the CMEA as a share of sales, and imports from the West as a share of domestic industry sales, all in 1990. The only insignificant variable ($t = 0.4$) was the import share.

27. The commercial banks were further transformed into joint-stock companies in October 1991.

so they continued to lend mostly to state firms, regardless of their financial conditions. At the end of 1991, loans to state firms still accounted for 90 percent of the portfolio of commercial banks; of those, it was estimated that about 30 percent were nonperforming. Thus, while the inflation of 1989 had largely wiped out the debt position of firms, after two years of new lending banks were again hostages to their borrowers and obviously reluctant to start bankruptcy proceedings. A similar game was played vis-à-vis the government. An increasing number of firms were in arrears in their payments of taxes, testing the credibility of the government's stated policy to trigger bankruptcy for nonpayment of taxes.

6. The evolution of profit rates over 1990–91 points to the limits of incomes policy, a point of significance beyond Poland. One of the goals of the incomes policy was to avoid a redistribution of revenues from profits toward wages. Nevertheless, by the end of 1991, after-tax profit rates were very nearly equal to zero. How did this happen? As we document in section 2.6, the incomes policy, with its limited indexation, probably slowed the straightforward transfer of revenues to workers through increases in wages given prices in 1990. But, in addition to the fact that firms seemed by the end of 1991 ready to pay or at least accrue large excess wage tax liabilities, the policy left two channels open. The first is that, in response to decreases in output, firms could increase the share of revenues going to workers by reducing employment less than output.[28] The second is that, in response to increases in the price level not due to an increase in the producer price index, such as rents and electricity, firms could increase wages according to the partial indexation of the norm without further increasing their prices. Both these channels explain why profit margins steadily decreased over those two years. There is probably a general lesson here, that incomes policy can slow down but cannot stop the transfer of revenues to workers if they are so inclined.

7. The picture of state firms that we have just painted has been gloomy. One question is whether it is uniformly gloomy or whether at least some sectors are restructuring. There are few encouraging signs. There is much qualitative evidence that, in 1990, many firms were trying to develop contacts with foreign firms and to develop new markets (Jorgensen, Gelb, and Singh 1991; Bruno, in this volume; Dabrowski, Federowicz, and Levitas 1991). But little came out of it, and most firms have given up those efforts. Quantitative data do not show signs of a shake out either. The dispersion of profit rates across three-digit branches in industry, as measured by the standard deviation of the distribution, has fallen steadily since the end of 1989. Food processing is the only two-digit industry that grew during 1991. The one positive note is given by non-CMEA

---

28. As indicated earlier, this applies to the post-1990 period, when the wage norm applied to wages rather than the wage bill.

exports, but even this is dimming. Exports to the EC were up by 65 percent in dollars in 1990 over 1989. They were up by a smaller 13 percent in 1991.[29]

2.5   The Growth of the Private Sector

1. We now turn to the brighter side of the story. Both 1990 and 1991 saw a spectacular increase in the size of the private sector. Despite obvious shortcomings in the data, the basic trends are clear.[30]

In December 1988, recorded private employment outside agriculture was 1.2 million. At the start of stabilization, it had already increased to 1.8 million jobs. By the end of 1991, it stood at 3.0 million, a cumulative increase of 67 percent over two years. Put another way, in two years, its share of total nonagricultural employment doubled, from 13 to 26 percent.[31] Including agriculture, which was already mostly private, the share of private-sector employment at the end of 1991 stood at 45 percent of total employment. Thus, as a matter of arithmetic, the increase in private-sector employment over those two years was equal to nearly half the decrease in state firm employment.

2. Not surprisingly, the growth of the private sector was stronger in those sectors that had traditionally been repressed in the Soviet-type economies.[32] In trade, the private sector accounted for 75 percent of sales at the end of 1991, compared to 10 percent at the end of 1989, the result of both privatization of shops and of high rates of firm creation: total employment growth was 16 percent in 1991. The private sector has also become dominant in construction. At the end of 1991, private-sector sales accounted for 50 percent of total sales, up from 22 percent in 1989. By contrast, in industry, the private sector accounted for only 18 percent of sales, up from 7 percent in 1989.

Also not surprisingly, given the concentration of private-sector activity in trade and services and the excessively concentrated industrial structure characteristic of centrally planned economies, most of the jobs have been created in very small businesses. Firms with fewer than 100 employees represented 1.4

29. The official increase in exports to the EC including East Germany was 21 percent. One statistical problem, however, is the inclusion of Eastern Germany in the EC from October 1990 on. The number in the text gives our estimate of the increase in exports to the EC, excluding East Germany in both 1990 and 1991.

30. The numbers below come from forms filled out by the private-sector firms and from newly instituted surveys by the Polish Central Statistical Office. Those forms are similar to those filled out by state firms. Obvious caveats as to coverage and accuracy apply. The broad trends below are consistent with the evidence from a number of surveys of private-sector firms. Johnson (in vol. 2) reports preliminary results.

31. These numbers, and the numbers below, do not include cooperatives. Cooperatives were initially counted in official data as in the state sector. They are now counted as part of the private sector. The share of private and cooperative employment in total nonagricultural employment went from 31 percent in 1989 to 38 percent in 1991; some of the increase in the private sector reflects, therefore, the privatization of cooperatives.

32. Bolton and Roland (1992) point out that the share of services in total 1989 employment was 36 percent in Poland, compared to 53 percent in a sample of eight poorer OECD countries.

percent of total 1989 industrial employment in Poland, compared to 14 percent in West Germany and 32 percent in Italy (Bolton and Roland 1992). Official statistics distinguish between three types of private businesses: joint ventures (firms with some foreign capital), domestic firms, and individual businesses. The difference between the last two is technically one of legal status (the existence of trade books) but is mostly one of size. The rate of growth of all three over 1990–91 was roughly the same. But, because individual businesses represented more than 80 percent of employment at the start, more than 80 percent of the growth of employment over 1990–91 was in individual businesses. Average employment in those businesses, at the end of 1990, was 1.7 workers.

3. That the Polish economy needed more trade, services, and construction is not at issue. But, given how little restructuring has happened in state firms, the question arises of whether this can be accomplished instead by growth of the private sector. This raises the issue of how and what private medium-sized firms, especially those in industry, have been doing.

The converse side of the statistics we just saw for individual businesses is that, while the number of private-sector jobs in larger domestic firms, with or without foreign capital, is increasing at high rates, those jobs accounted for only 500,000 workers in mid-1991, up from 250,000 prestabilization. Similarly, output of private-sector industry grew by 48 percent in 1991, but from a small base. This evidence is consistent with the small recorded flows of foreign direct investment (FDI). Again, while FDI increased from $11 million in 1990 to $100 million for the first three quarters of 1991, this still accounts for less than 0.2 percent of GNP.[33]

The picture that we can assemble of the performance of these larger private firms is fragmentary, but the pieces seem to fit. First, the larger private-sector firms that existed before stabilization (about 1,500 industrial companies, employing about 29,000 people in 1989) clearly did better than the state firms during stabilization; their real sales in particular were down only by 2 percent in 1990. Second, while the profit rates of firms with some foreign capital were affected by the output decline of 1990, their investment was stronger than that of state firms. Third, in 1990, for firms with some foreign capital, the ratios of exports and imports to sales were 39 percent and 11 percent, respectively, compared to 8 percent and 15 percent for the average state firm. Exports by the private sector have been growing more rapidly than total production, and their share of total exports was 20 percent at the end of 1991, compared to 4.9 percent at the end of 1990. Major categories include processed food (mainly milk), furniture, and industrial metal goods. Finally, real sales in private industry grew by 48 percent in 1991 after growing by 9 percent in 1990. Thus, the evidence is that, while they account for a small proportion of employment, larger private firms are doing well.

---

33. Gomulka (1992a) gives a higher number "from a government source"—$680 million from January 1989 to October 1991.

If the state sector does not adjust, the issue for the future is whether such firms can be created in time to take up the slack or whether, in the meantime, the declining state firms will be able to extract ruinous amounts of subsidies from the banking system and the government in lieu of adjustment, thereby endangering the entire reform.[34]

2.6 Wage and Price Setting and Inflation

Stabilization was associated with a sharp increase in prices: the increase in the CPI from the beginning to the end of January was 106 percent. After that, inflation declined sharply but has remained at an average rate of about 3–5 percent per month. This raises two sets of issues. What caused the initial jump in prices? Was it due to an increase in costs, to supply bottlenecks, to the exercise of monopoly power, to an overdevaluation of the zloty? And how could inflation remain high for so long in the presence of an incomes policy with low indexation of wages? In this section, we develop a simple accounting framework that allows for identification of proximate causes.[35] Having done so, we describe the inflation process over 1990–91. In the process, we return to a number of themes touched on already in previous sections.

Let w, p_c, and p_i denote the logarithms of the nominal wage, the consumer price, and the producer price at t, and let Δ denote a first-difference. Thus, as a matter of accounting, we can write:

(1) $$\Delta w = \alpha \Delta p_c + \varepsilon_w,$$

(2) $$\Delta p_c = \Delta p_i + \varepsilon_{pc},$$

(3) $$\Delta p_i = \Delta w + \varepsilon_{pi}.$$

The first equation decomposes the change in the wage into the component due to inflation through indexation and a residual. The second equation decomposes the change in the consumer price index into the change due to the producer price index and a residual. The third decomposes the change in the producer price index into the change in wages and a residual. Combining the three equations gives inflation as a function of the three ε's and the degree of indexation:

(4) $$\Delta p_c = (\varepsilon_w + \varepsilon_{pi} + \varepsilon_{pc}) / (1 - \alpha).$$

We now construct and further decompose the various ε's.

---

34. Bolton and Roland (1992) try to estimate the amount of labor reallocation that could take place without privatization. They assume that the growth in small firms and in services required to match poor OECD countries comes not through privatization but through new private firms and similarly that the required reduction in employment in large firms and in industry takes place through job loss. This leaves only 28 percent of the total 1989 labor force and 44 percent of industrial labor potentially involved in privatization.

35. This approach is developed in more detail in Blanchard and Layard (1992).

2.1.1   The Movement of Wages

The incomes policy that was put in place in December 1989 has been kept to this day. It initially covered all firms, but private firms were excluded from 1991 on. Each firm is subject to a wage norm, which was initially roughly equal to the prestabilization wage. The norm for each firm has increased through time for three reasons. First, it has been partially indexed to inflation, the effect captured in the wage equation above. The coefficient of indexation was equal to 0.3 in January 1990 and to 0.2 from February through April, and it has stayed at 0.6 thereafter, with a brief jump in June 1990 to 1.0. Second, because the wage norm applied in 1990 to the wage bill rather than the wage, it allowed for a further increase in the wage itself in proportion to the decline in employment. Since 1991, the wage norm applies to the wage so that this effect is no longer present. Third, the wage norm has increased as a result of other, ad hoc, adjustments; as we shall see, these were important at the end of 1990.

The wage norm is not an absolute constraint on firms. Rather, excesses of wages above the norm are taxed at very high rates, from 100 percent up to 500 percent. The tax applies to the excess of the total wage bill since the beginning of each year over the total wage norm since the beginning of the year. Thus, firms that paid a wage lower than the wage norm early in the year can pay a wage above the norm at the end of the year without incurring excess taxes; this aspect also turned out to be important at the end of 1990.

On the basis of this brief description, in table 2.2 we decompose quarterly changes in the logarithm of the nominal wage in industry from the last quarter

Table 2.2   **Decomposition of Wage Inflation**

Quarter	Δw	$a\Delta p_c$	ε_w			
			Total	Employment Effect	Other Norm	Other Nonnorm
1990:1	14	20	−5	3	2	−11
1990:2	14	7	7	4	0	3
1990:3	25	7	18	4	1	13
1990:4	29	10	19	5	3	11
1991:1	2	14	−12	0	8	−20
1991:2	6	6	0	0	0	0
1991:3	9	3	6	0	0	6
1991:4	22	7	15	0	0	15

Note: All data are for the wage in industry only. $\Delta w = \ln(W_t) - \ln(W_{t-1})$, where W is the nominal wage at the end of quarter t. $a\Delta p_c = a_t [\ln(P_{ct}) - \ln(P_{ct-1})]$, where a_t is the average degree of indexation during the quarter, and P_c is the CPI at the end of the quarter. The "employment" term is $- [\ln(N_t) - \ln(N_{t-1})]$ for 1990, 0 for 1991, and captures the fact that the wage bill rather than the wage was subject to the wage norm in 1990. "Other Norm" denotes adjustments of the logarithm of the norm, and "Other Nonnorm" is equal to the difference between the logarithm of the wage and the logarithm of the norm.

of 1989 on, into four components. The first is that due to inflation and index-ation. The other three correspond to ε_w, The first reflects the "employment ef-fect," the fact that in 1990 the wage norm could go up in proportion to the employment decline. The second reflects other adjustments of the norm. The third reflects deviations of the wage from the wage norm.[36]

Table 2.2 shows that the beginning of stabilization was associated with con-siderable wage restraint. Despite a large increase in prices and low indexation of the norm, wages were still 11 percent below what was allowed by the norm in March 1991.

As the last column of the table shows, this initial restraint was followed for the rest of 1990 by an increase in wages first to and then above the wage norm. This was due to two factors. The first was the progressive realization by work-ers that profits were still high and that wages could be increased to the norm without triggering immediate bankruptcy. Indeed, the realization was that wages could actually be increased *beyond* the norm without dire effects: by the end of the year, roughly two-thirds of firms in industry were willing to pay the excess wage tax in order to transfer some of the profits to their workers. The second was the result of the design of the incomes policy. As most firms had paid wages below the norm in the first three months, they could afford to pay wages above the norm for the rest of the year without paying the excess tax. As a result, by July, wages were above norm wages. And, by December, the excess of the wage over the wage norm, the cumulative value of the numbers in first four rows of the last column, was 16 percent.

At the beginning of the new year 1991, firms were thus faced with the choice of either reducing wages by more than 16 percent to get them under the norm or having to pay considerable excess wage taxes. The political outcome was of partial accommodation of wage realities by adjustments of the norm. As table 2.2 shows, the increase in the norm unrelated to inflation was 8.0 percent. The CMEA shock and the drastic decline in profit margins did the rest, and wage growth was slow enough so as to get wages back within the norm within a month. But, by midyear, the increase in wages was again in excess of the norm, with, as a result, steadily increasing excess wage tax payments, which we docu-mented earlier.

2.6.2   The Movement of Prices

Table 2.3 decomposes in turn the movement in the CPI. The first two col-umns give the change in (the logarithm of) the CPI and the change in the CPI in excess of the change in the producer price index, ε_{pc}. The next set of columns decomposes the change in the producer price. The decomposition is motivated as follows. Consider the following identity:

$$(5) \qquad P_iY = (1 + \mu)(WN + C),$$

---

36. We thank Jan Rajski for information about the norm.

where WN is the wage bill, C is nonwage costs, Y is gross output, and μ is the markup. Let α be the share of wages in total costs. Then, taking logarithms, differentiating with respect to time, and rearranging, we can write

$$(6) \qquad \Delta p_i = \Delta w + \varepsilon_{pi},$$

where

$$(7) \quad \varepsilon_{pi} = (\Delta n - \Delta y) + [(1 - \alpha) / \alpha] (\Delta c - \Delta p) + (1/\alpha) \, \Delta \, ln(1 + \mu).$$

ε_{pi} is the sum of three terms. An increase in any of these three terms increases the producer price given the wage. The first is the negative of the rate of change in labor productivity. The second is proportional to the rate of change in the relative price of nonlabor inputs; c is defined as the logarithm of C/Y.[37] The third is proportional to the rate of change of one plus the markup. The last five columns of table 2.3 give the decomposition of changes in the producer price index. Table 2.3 suggests the following conclusions.

The initial increase in prices was due neither to an increase in consumer prices over producer prices nor to an increase in markups. We think that these facts largely put to rest three common prestabilization fears: that either because of an excessive devaluation, because some firms were now in a position to exert monopoly power, or because of sharp supply bottlenecks, prices would increase far in excess of costs.[38]

The increase was due instead to an increase in the relative price of nonlabor inputs and the large decrease in labor productivity. In Blanchard and Layard (1992), we further decompose the increase in costs and find, in addition to the removal of subsidies, two surprising culprits. The first is imputed depreciation. The book value of capital was multiplied by eleven in January 1990. The other is high nominal rates at the beginning of stabilization. It is clear that neither of the economic costs associated with either capital depreciation or interest payments went up much in January 1990 (ex post rates ere large and negative in January). But one can easily believe that these were treated mostly as increases in costs by firms.

Thereafter, the evolution of prices was the result of two divergent evolutions. One was the increase of the CPI over the PPI, which was due to increases in electricity prices, rents, and gas prices as well as in retail price margins. But, while ε_{pc} increased, ε_{pi} decreased. And the main source of the decrease was the decrease in the markup. As we discussed in the section on state firms, there are two potential reasons for the decline in the markup. The first is that increasing foreign competition prevented firms from passing on costs into prices. The

37. As we indicated earlier, reported C is measured at historical cost, with the result that it underestimates true cost when inflation is high. We did not attempt to adjust for inflation, with the result that the increase in costs is probably overestimated when inflation slows down. This is probably most important for the second quarter of 1990.

38. Bruno (in this volume) argues that the large devaluation of the zloty was a cause for the initial price jump. We see no evidence in favor of this argument.

Table 2.3   **Decomposition of Price Inflation**

Quarter	Δp_c	ϵp_c	Total	Δw	Total	Relative Cost	Inverse Productivity	Markup
1990:1	84	1	82	14	68	92	29	−53
1990:2	15	11	5	14	−9	3	8	−19
1990:3	10	1	9	25	−16	−0	−7	−8
1990:4	16	4	12	29	−17	−2	−11	−5
1991:1	23	7	17	2	15	34	12	−31
1991:2	10	4	6	6	0	−4	8	−4
1991:3	5	0	5	9	−4	−26	−6	28
1991:4	12	7	5	23	−18	7	−11	−14

The Δp_i header spans the Total, Δw, Total, Relative Cost, Inverse Productivity, and Markup columns.

Note: $\Delta p_c = \ln (P_{ct}) - \ln (P_{ct-1})$, where P_{ct} is the consumption price index at the end of the quarter. $\varepsilon_{pc} = \ln (P_{ct}) - \ln(P_{ct-1}) - \ln (P_{it}) + \ln (P_{it-1})$, where P_{it} is the industrial price index at the end of the quarter. $\Delta w = \ln (W_t) - \ln (W_{t-1})$, where W_t is the wage at the end of the quarter in industry. ε_{pi} is decomposed into three components, which are constructed from industry data. The first is $[(1 - \alpha)/\alpha][\ln(C_t) - \ln (P_{it}) - \ln (C_{t-1}) + \ln (P_{it-1})]$, the weighted change in the real cost of nonlabor inputs in industry. C_t is the cost of nonlabor inputs in industry during the quarter. α is the weighted average of the share of wage costs in total costs for the current and the past quarters. The second is $\ln (N_t) - \ln (Y_t) - \ln (N_{t-1}) + \ln(Y_{t-1})$, the change in the inverse of labor productivity, where Y and N are average gross output and employment in industry at the end of the quarter. The third is equal to $(1/\alpha) [\ln(1 + \mu_t) - \ln (1 + \mu_{t-1})]$, where μ_t is the ratio of sales minus costs to costs in industry at the end of the quarter.

second is that managers have increasingly passed on revenues to workers. We argued earlier that the second was the dominant part of the story.

We can now briefly put our results together. The initial increase in prices was due primarily to an increase in nonwage costs. The persistence of inflation later in 1990 was due primarily to the catching up of wages, coming itself from the undoing of initial restraint and design flaws of the incomes policy. In 1991, new nonwage relative cost increases, increases in the consumer over the producer price index, and increases in wages beyond the norm all contributed to the persistence of inflation. Thus, there is no single cause of the persistence of inflation in Poland. There was no "stickiness" of inflation, just many shocks along the way. This conclusion is again more likely to be of general relevance than it is relevant to Poland for these two years.

2.7   Issues for the Near and Medium Term

Two years after stabilization, the two fundamental issues are the behavior of state firms and the nature and speed of private-sector growth.

1. Lack of progress on privatization has left state firms adrift. The nominal owner, the state, exerts no control, while workers have gained power over management. The magnitude of the restructuring task, together with uncertainty about their stake in the restructured firm, has led managers and workers to

act with increasingly short horizons. The incomes policy has slowed but not prevented a steady transfer of revenues to workers; profit rates have steadily decreased to the level just sufficient to avoid triggering bankruptcy.

Absent changes in incentives, most state firms are likely to stagnate or decline slowly, behaving passively until threatened with extinction, acting to avoid closure but not taking the more difficult measures needed to survive and grow. Thus, on the positive side, in response to increased foreign competition, wages are likely to adjust so as to maintain minimal profit margins. On the negative side, cheaper credit or subsidies are likely to translate into higher wages rather than into higher investment or restructuring.

Creditors, including the banking system, the government, and other enterprises, have been unwilling to take responsibility for closing or restructuring an enterprise, instead making credit available when necessary to avoid collapse. The problem is compounded by the fact that the banking system has also not been either privatized or restructured. There are ominous signs that many firms are attempting to take advantage of this unwillingness. The proportions of bad loans in banks' portfolios and of firms in tax arrears are steadily increasing.

2. Private-sector growth has been impressive, and it is leading to the development of a much needed trade and service sector. More generally, the overall pattern of adaptation in the economy is rapid and in the right direction. Heavy industries are in relative decline, trade with the West is expanding, and the small- and medium-sized firms that were missing in the Polish economy are being created. Absent privatization, however, large state firms will continue to dominate industry for the next few years, and they are increasingly extracting resources from the government and the banking system. It is clear, then, that private-sector growth cannot, in the short or medium term, substitute for the restructuring and privatization of state firms.

3. Current macroeconomic problems are mainly the manifestation of these two underlying structural developments.

The most pressing crisis is fiscal. Preliminary estimates put the budget deficit for 1991 at 4.5–6 percent of GDP.[39] The proximate source of the deficit is the decline in profit tax revenues, which is in turn due to the sharp decline in profits of state firms in 1991. Original estimates were that the tax would yield 11.7 percent of GDP in 1991; actual income taxes were only 5.1 percent for the year. It is, however, easy to see other crises in the making. If nonrepayment of loans does not trigger bankruptcy, for example, an increasing number of firms will finance higher wages through borrowing. Or, as the nontradable sector grows and the tradable sector stagnates or shrinks, the trade balance may

---

39. These numbers, as well as the numbers just below, are from Gomulka (1992a), who gives a detailed description of the budget for 1991 and of budget proposals, as of February, for 1992. See also de Crombrugghe and Lipton (in vol. 2).

turn to deficit, requiring either steady real depreciation or a further contraction of output.

Our assessment raises two types of policy issues. The first is that of the role of conventional macro tools—fiscal, monetary, exchange rate policies—in the current environment. The second is that of which measures should be put in place to enhance structural adjustment.

4. The role of macro policy in increasing activity in the current environment is sharply limited. Some instruments are simply unavailable, most obviously fiscal policy. But, more generally, the response to traditional macro policy tools may, in the current environment, be too weak to justify their use. It is true that much of the decrease in output over the last two years has come from adverse shifts in demand, from stabilization first and from the collapse of the CMEA later. But, because of the evolution of the state firms over these two years and their likely response to different policies, it does not follow that there is much room now for demand to increase output.

Consider, for example, the likely effects of a devaluation, an a priori appealing policy prescription given the sharp deterioration of the trade position from a surplus of close to 4 percent in 1990 to trade balance in 1991 and the emergence of a deficit in 1992. In those state firms that have been able to maintain employment or at least limit the decline to the rate of attrition despite the sales decline, the devaluation is more likely to translate into an increase in prices and wages than an increase in output. Our conclusions on the inefficacy of the incomes policy to limit wage increases suggest that this may take some time but will eventually take place. Only those state firms that are being forced to cut employment sharply and that would be able to sell more on Western markets at lower prices are likely to fire fewer workers and expand output; they may not be many. And, of the various constraints on the growth of the private sector in tradables, access to credit, skilled labor, or foreign capital and expertise probably play a more important role than competitiveness.

A loosening of credit policy is likely to be even more harmful, especially without quantitative limits on credit to state enterprises. Given the behavior and incentives of the enterprises, it would be likely to raise wages and perhaps increase the insolvency of the state sector. And it could easily have a perverse effect on enterprise restructuring by drawing resources into those firms that adjust least. In contrast, reestablishing some of the CMEA trade, being aimed by its nature at many of the firms that are making the largest losses and contracting employment, would be more likely to slow down the employment decline in the state sector without drawing valuable resources away from the expanding private sector.

5. More important is that measures are needed to accelerate the restructuring process. These include, not surprisingly, privatization, reform of the banking system, and a credible commitment of the government to start bankruptcy proceedings when appropriate. Similar statements could have been made—and

were made—two years ago. But the last two years have made much clearer how state firms behave in the absence of such conditions.

While this is not the place to discuss privatization strategies, there are both additional constraints and lessons from the last two years (see Berg, in vol. 2). And we see both as implying that workers must play a large role in the privatization process. First, in order to obtain the required employment and wage adjustments that are now needed to reestablish profit margins, any realistic privatization plan must give workers a large stake in the outcome. Second, whatever adjustment there has been has been undertaken by workers and managers, not by the state. Privatization plans that weaken their power without immediately providing adequate substitutes risk decreasing horizons further and slowing adjustment.[40]

At this point, delinquent tax payments by state firms amount to 12 percent of total tax revenues. Moreover, the proportion is accelerating sharply. The government thus has to reestablish the credibility of its hard budget constraint by starting bankruptcy proceedings for some of those firms that are late in their tax payments.[41]

Along with a hardening of the government budget constraint, a reform of the banking system is urgently needed. Thanks to the high inflation of 1989, enterprise debt levels were low at the beginning of the stabilization program. But many firms have increasingly followed a policy of borrowing in lieu of adjustment. While commercial banks were transformed into joint-stock companies in October 1991, privatization is still some time off. A cleanup of balance sheets is needed now. Current proposals by the Ministry of Finance and the central bank to close some of the debtor firms, replace some of the firms' debts by government debt, and transform some into equity positions by banks go in the right direction (see Gomulka 1992a). If such cleaning up is implemented some time before privatization of banks, however, quantitative restrictions on loans to state firms will be required to prevent a new runup of debt.

7. If some of these structural measures are taken, Poland will then enter the next phase of the transition. And one can already identify the next set of problems that it is likely to confront. All state firms will have to shed a large amount of labor, and many will have to close. We saw that just getting labor productivity back to its prestabilization level implied a significant further decrease in

---

40. Similarly, we fear that commercialization not quickly followed by privatization may be counterproductive as it risks removing whatever incentives are left for workers and management to start restructuring.

41. The complexity of bankruptcy proceedings in the current legal, accounting, and political environment is clearly shown in the study by Banaszuk (1992) of bankruptcy proceedings against Ursus, a giant Polish tractor enterprise. Over the course of six months in 1991, three creditors filed bankruptcy petitions (one a second time after a partial repayment by Ursus), and two groups associated with Ursus management filed for protection from creditors. The legal status of the last two petitions is unclear because, among other reasons, both groups have ceased to exist legally. The case is apparently stuck in appeal, in part because the court needs to get a statement from the Ministry of Industry about its intentions toward this sector of the economy.

employment. We suspect that, if progress is made with privatization, the central set of issues two years from now will be high unemployment, the search for a social insurance system, the effects of unemployment and state firm wages on private-sector wages, and the nature of the constraints on private-sector growth.

Appendix A
Inventories and the Output Decline of Early 1990

A number of researchers have looked at the behavior of finished goods inventories in early 1990. But they have reached surprisingly different conclusions. We first show that these differences come in part from issues of both measurement and timing. When properly interpreted, the evidence is one of finished goods inventory accumulation in industry in January 1990. We then turn to the cross-sectional evidence on the behavior of firms by branch in industry during the first quarter of 1990 and document a clear relation between sales decreases and inventory increases.

The Aggregate Evidence

There are two reasons why inventory data in 1990 are hard to interpret. The first is a standard measurement issue. Inventories are not valued at current but at historical cost. Thus, the level of inflation affects the reported value of inventories, and changes in inflation affect the reported value of inventory investment. And there were indeed large changes in inflation during 1989 and 1990. The second is a measurement issue specific to the transition. There has been a steady privatization of the trade sector. As inventory numbers cover only the state sector, part of the measured decrease in trade inventories is in fact a transfer to the private sector.

With these two points in mind, table 2A.1 reports finished goods inventories in trade and industry for December 1989 and January, March, and December 1990. It gives two numbers for each case. The first gives inventories deflated by the current producer price index. The second gives inventories deflated by the average producer price index over the current and previous months. Inventories in trade, industry, and total are normalized by sales in trade, industry, and total, respectively, for December 1989 (not by current sales, which were sharply lower in 1990). The last column gives unnormalized inventories for December 1990. Two basic conclusions emerge from the table.

The first is one of a decline in trade inventories throughout the year, with or without inflation adjustment. Available data on quantities validate the finding of a decline over the year but contradict the finding of a decline in January. In a monthly survey of nine state trade enterprises used to monitor developments

Table 2A.1   Finished Goods Inventories

	$I/(S_{Dec.1989})$				
	Dec. 1989	Jan. 1990	Mar. 1990	Dec. 1990	$I_{Dec.1990}$ Dec. 1990
Industry:					
$n = 1$	.16	.28	.26	.22	18.6
$n = 2$	.17	.36	.24	.22	18.9
Trade:					
$n = 1$	1.15	.72	.79	.78	31.8
$n = 2$	1.34	.97	.79	.79	34.6
Total:					
$n = 1$	.60	.53	.54	.50	50.4
$n = 2$	.70	.71	.54	.51	53.5

Note: The first four columns give inventories in a given month normalized by sales in December 1989. n refers to the method of deflation of inventories. $n = x$ indicates deflation by the average producer price index over the last current and last $n - 1$ months. The last column gives inventories in Zl trillions in December 1990.

in early 1990, stocks of televisions were up by 30 percent in January over December, refrigerators by 23 percent, and washing machines by 11 percent. The same survey also shows a large decumulation later in the year. By May, stocks were 27 percent, 27 percent, and 40 percent, respectively, below their December levels.[42]

The second is one of an increase in finished goods inventories in industry, with accumulation in January and partial decumulation later. We take the evidence of an initial accumulation of finished goods in an industry to be an indication that that industry was hit primarily by an adverse demand shock. We turn now to the cross-sectional evidence.

The Cross-Sectional Evidence: Sales and Inventories

We look at whether branches in industry that had larger declines in sales had, ceteris paribus, larger accumulation of finished goods inventories. We use data on sales and inventories of state firms for branches at the three-digit level, for the last quarter of 1989 and the first quarter of 1990. We specify the regression as

$$(A1) \quad (I_{it} - I_{it-1}) / S_{it-1} = aI_{it-1} / S_{it-1} + b(S_{it} - S_{it-1}) / S_{it-1} - \varepsilon_{it}.$$

I_{it} stands for inventories in branch i at the end of 1990:1 and S_{it} for sales during 1990:1, both deflated by the price of the output of branch i at the end of 1990:1. I_{it-1} and S_{it-1} stand for the same variables in 1989:4. The specification allows for two effects. The first is the desire by firms to decrease inventories from their previous level. We expect a to be negative. The second reflects the effects of sales on inventory accumulation. If firms were primarily affected by an adverse shift in demand, we expect a larger decrease in sales to lead to larger

42. Our source here is the Ministry of Domestic Markets.

accumulation and thus b to be negative. If firms were primarily affected by supply constraints, we expect tighter constraints to result in low sales and more decumulation and thus b to be positive. The results of estimation are given in table 2A.2.

The first regression in table 2A.2 establishes the basic cross-sectional fact about inventory and sales and offers support for the hypothesis that branches were primarily affected by an adverse shock in demand. It shows that larger sales declines were associated with inventory accumulation. The result holds across subsamples. A set of industries where supply disruptions appear to have played a role is food processing, where both sales and inventories decrease. The second regression, which excludes food processing, shows a more significant relation. Thus, the interpretation of the data is that, while firms wanted to decrease inventories (a is negative), the decline in sales was such as to lead, on net, to an increase. For the branches in our sample, the increase in real inventories from 1989:4 was equal on average to 12 percent of monthly sales, and more than 90 percent had an increase in inventories.

The Cross-Sectional Evidence: Sales, Inventories, and Credit

Within this framework, one can examine the effects of other variables on both sales and inventory behavior. In the remaining regressions, we take up the potential role of credit factors, along lines suggested by Calvo and Coricelli

Table 2A.2   **Sales, Inventories, and Credit**

	Dependent Variable: $(I_{it} - I_{it-1})/S_{it-1}$				
	Constant	I_{it-1}/S_{it-1}	$(S_{it} - S_{it-1})/S_{it-1}$	$(C_{it} - C_{it-1})/S_{it-1}$	R^2
OLS	.07	−.36	−.07		.14
	(5.0)	(−3.8)	(−1.6)		
OLS *	.05	−.03	−.10		.05
	(3.8)	(−.2)	(−2.4)		
OLS	.05	−.09	−.08	.31	.39
	(4.9)	(−1.0)	(−2.1)	(5.9)	
IV	.06	−.14	−.07	.26	.38
	(5.0)	(−1.4)	(−2.1)	(4.1)	
	Dependent Variable: $(S_{it} - S_{it-1})/S_{it-1}$				
IV	−.25			.21	.00
	(−15.4)			(1.3)	

Note: Sample for all regressions except regression *: branches in industry, excluding coal, fuel, and electric power, with rates of change in sales between −60 percent and +50 percent from 1989:4 to 1990:1, and sales in excess of Zl 100 billion. There are 85 observations. Regression * further excludes food processing and has 70 observations. The indices t and $t - 1$ refer to the quarters 1990:1 and 1989:4, respectively. S_{it} are sales for branch i for quarter t, deflated by the average price of output of branch i during the quarter. I_{it} and C_{it} are inventories of finished goods and the stock of "working credit" (bank credit not associated with an investment project) for branch i at the end of quarter t, deflated by the price of output of branch i at the end of quarter t. The IV regressions instrument the credit variable by the ratio of credit to sales at the end of 1989:4.

(1991), who have argued that part of the decline in output was due to firms being unable to borrow to pay for inputs, thus decreasing production and decumulating inventories to satisfy sales. From 1989:4 to 1990:1, 80 percent of branches in our sample in industry had a decrease in real working credit so defined, and the average decrease as a proportion of initial sales was 3 percent.

We thus construct a variable equal to the change in real working credit from 1989:4 to 1990:1, divided by sales in 1989:4. The next two regressions focus on the effects of working credit on inventories given sales. The first regresses changes in inventories on changes in sales and changes in working credit. The change in working credit may be partly endogenous, however; inventories may in part be used as collateral. Thus, the second regression instruments the change in credit by the initial credit-to-sales ratio in 1989:4. In both cases, the evidence is that inventory changes are still negatively correlated with sales but also positively correlated with the change in working credit. Our last, admittedly crude, regression looks for direct effects of working credit on sales and regresses the change in sales on the change in working credit, without other controls. It shows a positive, marginally significant relation between credit and sales. The effect is quantitatively small. The estimated coefficient implies that the 10 percent decline in working credit as a proportion of sales—the average for the sample of branches is 3 percent—leads to a 2 percent decrease in sales.

Appendix B
The Collapse of the CMEA and the Output Decline in 1991

How much of the decline in output in early 1991 can be attributed to the CMEA shock, and through which channels? Was it through the direct and indirect effects of the decrease in the value of exports to the CMEA, which was between 2 and 3 percent of GDP, or was it through disruptions due to the loss of crucial imports? Or were there other factors at work?

We look at the behavior of sales across branches in industry, first at the two-digit level because some of the variables that we want to use can be constructed only at that level, and then at the three-digit level. The results are reported in table 2B.1. Our basic specification is

(B1) $(S_{it} - S_{it-1}) / S_{it-1} = a(X_{it} - X_{it-1}) / S_{it-1} - \varepsilon_{it}.$

S_{it} stands for the average monthly value of sales in branch i during the first five months of 1991 and X_{it} for the average monthly value of ruble sales during 1991:1 (converted to zlotys at the official rate), both deflated by the average price index for output of branch i during the first two quarters of 1991. At the two-digit level, X_{it} includes both direct and indirect ruble sales, with indirect

Table 2B.1   **Sales and the CMEA Shock**

	Dependent Variable: $(S_{it} - S_{it-1})/S_{it-1}$			
	Constant	$(X_{it} - X_{it-1})/S_{it-1}$	(Q_{it-2}/S_{it-2})	R^2
2 digit:				
OLS	−.10	.46		.22
	(−5.0)	(2.5)		
OLS	−.09	.38	−.46	.20
	(−3.4)	(1.9)	(−.8)	
		(X_{it-1}/S_{it-1})	(Q_{it-2}/S_{it-2})	
OLS	−.07	−.71	−.24	.38
	(−2.9)	(−3.0)	(−.5)	
3-digit:				
OLS	−.06	−.42	−.97	.12
	(−2.7)	(−2.8)	(−1.7)	

Note: The sample for the first three regressions is two-digit branches in industry, excluding coal, fuel, and electric power. There are 20 observations. The sample for the last regression is three-digit branches in industry, excluding energy, coal, fuel, and power, with rates of change in sales between −60 percent and +50 percent from 1990 to the first half of 1991 and sales in excess of Zl 100 billion. There are 101 observations. t and $t-1$ refer to the average for 1990 and the average for the first 5 months of 1991, respectively. S_{it} and X_{it} are average total sales and average ruble sales—direct and indirect—respectively, for branch i, deflated by the average price of output of branch i during t. Q_{it-2}/S_{it-2} is the ratio of ruble imports to sales in branch i for 1989.

sales being computed using the 1987 input-output matrix.[43] S_{it-1} and X_{it-1} stand for the average monthly value of the same variables during all 1990.

The first line reports the results of this regression over the twenty two-digit branches. The coefficient on ruble sales is significantly different from zero and one. The adjusted R^2 is, however, a low 0.22. The second regression adds the ratio of CMEA intermediate imports to sales in 1989 (the latest year for which we have the required data). The coefficient on this import variable is negative, but not significant. Other things equal, an increase in the share of imports of 1 percent leads to an additional decline in sales of 0.4 percent. The third regression uses the share of ruble exports to sales in 1990. The results are of a strong negative effect of the export share and a weak negative effect of the import share.

The last regression reports results from estimation at the three-digit level. As ruble exports are not available at that level of disaggregation for 1991, we use instead the three-digit share of ruble exports in sales in 1990. Also, only direct exports are measured. For data availability reasons also, we use the two-digit- rather than the three-digit-level share of CMEA imports in sales for 1989. The results are consistent with those obtained at the two-digit level and

43. This extends work in Berg and Sachs (1992), which gives further details of construction.

show a strong effect of the export share, with a coefficient of -0.42, and a marginally significant effect of the import share, with a coefficient of -0.97.

In all four regressions, the constant term, which captures the decline of output for which we do not account with CMEA variables, is negative. It is equal to 75 percent of the total decline at the two-digit level and 50 percent at the three-digit level.

References

Banaszuk, M. 1992. Polish bankruptcy law in (in)action. Warsaw: Sachs & Associates. Mimeo.

Berg, A., and J. Sachs. 1992. Structural adjustment and international trade in Eastern Europe: The case of Poland. *Economic Policy,* no. 14 (April): 118–73.

Blanchard, O., and R. Layard. 1992. Post-stabilization inflation in Poland. Massachusetts Institute of Technology. Mimeo.

Bolton, P., and X. Roland. 1992. The economics of mass privatization: Czechoslovakia, East Germany, Hungary and Poland. Working Paper no. 375. Ecole Polytechnique, Laboratoire d'Econometrie.

Calvo, G., and F. Coricelli. 1991. Stagflationary effects of stabilization programs in reforming socialist countries: Supply side verses demand side factors. Washington, D.C.: International Monetary Fund. Mimeo.

Center for Research on Economic Tendency and Markets (CRETM). 1990. Business survey. Warsaw: Institute of Economic Development Central School of Planning and Statistics.

Commander, S., F. Coricelli, and K. Staehr. 1991. Wages and employment in the transition to a market economy. Washington, D.C.: World Bank. Mimeo.

Coricelli, F., and R. de Rezende Rocha. 1991. Stabilization programs in Eastern Europe: A comparative analysis of the Polish and Yugoslav programs of 1990. In *Reforming Central and Eastern European economies: Initial results and challenges,* ed. V. Corbo, F. Coricelli, and J. Bossak. Washington, D.C.: World Bank.

Dabrowski, M. 1992. The Polish stabilization, 1990–1991. *Journal of International and Comparative Economics* 1:295–324.

Dabrowski, J., M. Federowicz, and A. Levitas. 1991. Polish state enterprises and the properties of performance: Stabilization, marketization, privatization. *Politics and Society* 19, no. 4:403–37.

Dornbusch, R. 1991. Credibility and stabilization. *Quarterly Journal of Economics* 106, no. 3:837–51.

Frydman, R., and S. Wellisz. 1991. The ownership control structure and the behavior of Polish firms during the 1990 reforms: Macroeconomic measures and microeconomic responses. In *Reforming Central and Eastern European economies: Initial results and challenges,* ed. V. Corbo, F. Coricelli, and J. Bossak. Washington, D.C.: World Bank.

Gomulka, S. 1991. The causes of recession following stabilization. *Comparative Economic Studies* 32, no. 2:71–89.

———. 1992a. Economic, social and political problems in economic transformation: The case of Poland, 1989–1992. London School of Economics, March. Mimeo.

———. 1992b. Polish economic reform, 1990–91: Principles, policies and outcomes. *Cambridge Journal of Economics* 16 (September): 355–72.

Gorski, M., D. Jaszczynski, and E. Geryszewska. 1990. Rownowaga na rynkach wyrobow przemyslowych w Polsce (Equilibrium on the market for industrial goods in Poland). Report no. 1. Warsaw: East European Research Group.

Jackman, R., and A. Scott. 1992. Wages, prices and unemployment in Eastern Europe. London School of Economics, April. Mimeo.

Jorgensen, E., A. Gelb, and I. Singh. 1991. Life after the Polish "big bang": Representative episodes of enterprise behavior. In *Reforming Central and Eastern European economies: Initial results and challenges,* ed. V. Corbo, F. Coricelli, and J. Bossak. Washington, D.C.: World Bank.

Kornai, J. 1990. *The road to a free economy: Shifting from a socialist system: The case of Hungary.* New York: Norton.

Lane, T. 1991. Inflation stabilization and economic transformation in Poland: The first year. Working Paper no. 91/70. Washington, D.C.: International Monetary Fund.

Lipton, D., and J. Sachs. 1990. Creating a market economy in Eastern Europe: The case of Poland. *Brookings Papers on Economic Activity,* no. 1:75–133.

Rosati, D. 1990. Impact of replacing CMEA trade regime by a market trade regime. Warsaw: Foreign Trade Institute. Mimeo.

Schaffer, M. 1992a. Poland. In *National economies of Europe,* ed. David Dyker. London: Longman.

———. 1992b. The Polish state-owned enterprise sector and the recession of 1990. *Comparative Economic Studies* 34, no. 1 (Spring): 58–85.

World Bank. 1989. *Poland: Policies for trade promotion.* Washington, D.C.: World Bank, Trade Policy Division, Country Economics Department.

Comment   Mark E. Schaffer

The Berg and Blanchard paper concentrates mainly on two tasks: explaining the output drops of 1990 and 1991 and explaining the persistence of inflation following the stabilization program implemented in January 1990. The authors emphasize throughout the behavior of state-owned enterprises, seeing them as the key economic actors in the transition economy so far. I share with the authors their view of what the key issues are, I find their analysis both convincing and illuminating, and I am in wholehearted agreement with their basic conclusions.

If I were to limit myself simply to listing points of disagreement, my comments would be rather short. So what I will do first is present some additional evidence in support of one of Berg and Blanchard's main arguments, namely, that the output drops seen in Poland in early 1990 and in early 1991 are the result of demand shocks: the first associated with stabilization and the second with the Council for Mutual Economic Assistance (CMEA) trade collapse following dollarization at the beginning of 1991. The latter point is not controversial, but the first—that the contraction in early 1990 resulted from a demand shock—is not universally accepted.

The evidence comes from reconstructing enterprise financial data on a cash-flow basis. As the authors point out, inflation makes both standard enterprise profitability figures and nominal inventory data difficult to use. In particular, when inflation is rapid, historical cost profit is significantly biased upward by a large paper capital gain on inventories of materials. The bias results from the increase in the price level between the time at which inputs are purchased and the time at which the final products containing the inputs are sold. This is the main reason that reported profitability in Poland was so high in 1989 and 1990. Much more useful are enterprise finance data in terms of current revenues and expenditures, that is, in cash-flow terms.[1] The key figures are presented in table 2C.1; all quantities are expressed as a percentage of sales.

Column 1 gives expenditures on materials as a percentage of sales for the enterprise sector. This figure increases in the first quarter of 1990, following the stabilization. This suggests a demand shock: demand dropped all at once, but it took a few months for this to be fully reflected in lower purchases of materials, and in the meantime total inventories in real terms increased. The same thing happened with the second demand shock in early 1991.

This evidence also supports the authors' findings regarding the role of credit in the stabilization of early 1990. The Calvo-Coricelli "credit-crunch" hypothesis is that a decline in real credit meant that firms were unable to finance adequate purchases of inputs and so decreased their production. Berg and Blanchard look for but find no strong evidence that tight credit contributed much to the fall in sales in early 1990. The data presented above show that, in aggregate, expenditure on materials fell more slowly than sales. This too suggests that a lack of turnover credit was not the key factor in the output collapse.

For the remainder of my comments, I will return to the traditional discussant's role of stating points of disagreement, raising doubts, etc., although, as I said earlier, there is little in this paper with which I disagree or about which I am dubious.

The authors mention at various points the negative consequences of leaving state-owned enterprises under the control of workers but imply (and said so explicitly in their conference presentation) that this is not quite a disaster either. A further reason that this may not be a disaster is because industrial relations may be smoother in a worker-controlled state-owned firm than in a firm where the state takes an active role in, say, wage setting. In a sense, there is no one to strike against in a worker-controlled firm. This is especially important in Poland, the Polish labor force being so good at strikes that it brought down two Communist governments in a decade. Strikes have occurred in Polish state-owned firms over the past two years, but, except for the few attempts at nationwide general strikes, they have tended to be scattered and frequently petered out with no substantial concessions or actions by the government.

I like very much the detailed analysis of wage and price inflation. I think, however, that the effect of wage increases has been overstated by the authors

---

1. These are not available directly but are derived from historical cost data and accounting identities (for details, see Schaffer [1992a, 1992b]).

Table 2C.1   **Material Expenditures, Profits, and Wage Costs**

	ME/S in % (1)	π/S in % (2)	WC/S in % (3)
Year			
1989	43	34	21
1990	41	23	18
1991	40	7	22
Quarter			
1989:4	42	44	21
1990:1	46	28	15
1990:2	40	24	17
1990:3	40	22	19
1990:4	41	20	20
1991:1	43[a]	11	20
1991:2		7	22
1991:3	39[a]	7	22
1991:4		3	23

Note: Data cover the entire enterprise sector. S = sales of own production. ME = expenditure on materials. π = historical cost profit (*wynik finansowy*). WC = total wage costs (basic wage bill, wage tax, social security taxes).
[a]Half-year results.

in one respect, namely, in the effect on firm profits. It is true that, in 1991, historical cost profits collapsed and that product wages (but not consumption wages) and unit labor costs increased substantially. But profit as a percentage of sales plummeted from 23 percent in 1990 to 7 percent in 1991, while wage costs as a percentage of sales increased only from 18 to 22 percent (table 2C.1, cols. 2, 3). Had unit labor costs stayed at their 1990 level, then (ceteris paribus) profitability would still have dropped by 12 percent. The picture is about the same according to the profitability measure used by the authors, the markup.[2] Other causes of the fall in the markup were the increase in amortization allowances at the start of 1991 and a decrease in the inflation bias. This is of course still a big change in the division of revenue in favor of workers, but not as large as the profit drop might suggest.

A few trade-related points. I think that the authors underplay somewhat the effects of the appreciation of the zloty. They focus on the role of foreign competition in restraining firms from passing on cost increases to domestic customers, but it also seems likely that the appreciation hurt exporters directly. Since the start of 1990, the export price index has gone up much more slowly than the domestic price level and not a lot faster than the zloty/dollar rate; the hard

2. Measured on a consistent basis, the markup fell from 27 percent in 1990 to perhaps 12 percent in 1991. About one-third of the fall is the direct result of the increase in unit labor costs. Markups calculated directly from official figures (e.g., Berg and Blanchard's table 2.1) understate the fall because of changes in accounting definitions (notably those for interest charges).

currency export price index was virtually flat in 1990.[3] This is consistent with the view that firms exporting to the West have little or no market power and basically price in dollars. As the zloty appreciated, the real zloty price that these firms received for their goods fell. This is also part of the reason that the CPI increased more rapidly than the producer price index; the latter includes prices of exports.

At the end of the paper, the authors discuss the options for macro policy and conclude that, while there is in principle room for some reflation, there is a lack of tools with which to pursue it. I think, however, that they are too dismissive of the devaluation option. If other "nominal anchors" are available and are biting (incomes policy, monetary policy), we do not have to let the exchange rate do all the work in fighting inflation. Berg and Blanchard are doubtful that state firms would respond to a devaluation by increasing exports much, but I think that the remarkable increase in hard currency exports (40 percent in 1990!) following the devaluation at the start of the program suggests that they may be too pessimistic.

My last point is a general question for which I have no ready answer. Berg and Blanchard stress the aggregate demand side when analyzing why Polish output has fallen. Implicit in their analysis are the assumptions that output has indeed declined, that aggregate supply has either not fallen or fallen (much) less than aggregate demand, and that there is therefore some scope for reflation. There is by now a considerable amount of evidence, ranging from recalculations of Polish GDP (Berg and Sachs 1992) to product-level survey data, that the decline in economic activity has been substantial and widespread. And, in the Polish case, we do not have to look hard for sources of aggregate demand shocks. But the aggregate supply question needs more attention. If, for whatever reasons, aggregate supply (potential output) has also contracted substantially, reflation is not an option.

However, precisely why and how aggregate supply might have contracted is not at all clear. The authors discuss briefly, and dismiss, a couple of possibilities (e.g., supply constraints). I want to discuss, and dismiss, another possibility that has sometimes been mentioned, namely, the cessation of value-subtracting activity. A number of authors have argued that there may have been a substantial amount of such activity in prereform socialist economies. This suggests that, in the Polish case, aggregate supply may have fallen following price liberalization because, at the new free market prices, production of value-subtracting goods would cease. This is probably best classed as a supply shock, although one could put it in terms of demand: following the January 1990 price liberalization, producers asked prices for these goods that would have been high enough to make the goods value adding, and nobody bought them.

---

3. If we set January 1990 = 100, in December 1991 the export price index is 130, the zloty/dollar rate is 117, and the CPI is over 300. Separate monthly indexes for ruble and hard-currency trade were not published in 1991.

This argument does not appear to apply to the Polish case, however, for two reasons. First, as Berg and Blanchard point out, the decline in output was spread widely across the economy. Just to add to the evidence that they cite, industry-wide surveys indicate that both sales and production of 80–90 percent of all products fell in 1990. Second, the "value-subtracting" argument has implications for the behavior of quantity indexes. A Paasche (end-period weighted) value-added index would measure the change in Polish economic activity at the new liberalized prices. A decrease in activity that is value subtracting at the new prices would, ceteris paribus, cause a Paasche value-added index to increase, not decrease, following price liberalization (the less value is subtracted, the greater is value added). In fact, the official Polish quantity indexes (sales, gross output, and value added) are all Paasche—they all measure activity at liberalized prices—and all, such as they are, show large declines of similar magnitudes in 1990–91.[4]

Yet one is still left wondering whether there is a supply-side story to be told. Put another way, transition in all the countries of Eastern and Central Europe appears to be very costly. It seems unlikely (although I suppose possible) that output is falling everywhere by so much mostly because of a combination of the cost of stabilization and the cost of the CMEA trade collapse. If other factors were at work that resulted in large declines in aggregate supply elsewhere in the region, then maybe these factors were at work in Poland too. But, as to what these factors might be, I will not venture to speculate further.

References

Berg, Andrew, and Jeffrey D. Sachs. 1992. Structural adjustment and international trade in Eastern Europe: The case of Poland. *Economic Policy,* no. 14 (April): 117–73.

Schaffer, Mark E. 1992a. The enterprise sector and the emergence of the Polish fiscal crisis, 1990–91. Working Paper no. 180. London School of Economics, Centre for Economic Performance, August.

Schaffer, Mark E. 1992b. The Polish state-owned enterprise sector and the recession in 1990. *Comparative Economic Studies* 34. no. 1 (Spring): 58–85.

Discussion Summary

Jeffrey Sachs emphasized that the fall in Polish output did not follow the standard pattern for a market economy going through a demand-induced recession. Before liberalization, a large part of industrial output had not been connected to consumers' final demand for goods. This explains how Poland could experience a 25 percent decline in industrial production while real consumption standards were largely unchanged. Sachs said that a 25 percent decline in industrial

---

4. For more on this point, see Schaffer (1992b).

output in a Latin American country would wipe out the economy's service sector. In Poland, the service sector has boomed. Sachs also emphasized the important role of the private sector. He was optimistic that private enterprises would be able to generate growth even in the nonservice sectors. He noted that industrial firms account for 11,000 of the 46,000 large-scale private enterprises.

Saul Estrin had two suggestions for the authors. First, he noted that the analysis in the paper suggested that workers in the state-owned sector were capturing short-term rents at the expense of the long-term viability of the state-owned firms. Estrin said that it would be useful to verify that sectors with big wage hikes had low rates of investment. Second, Estrin pointed out that workers could capture rents only in industries that are not competitive. Hence, he proposed that the authors check to see if there has been a relation between market structure and wage gains.

Jan Winiecki agreed with the authors that the 1990 contraction was primarily due to an aggregate demand shock arising from the program of economic liberalization. He emphasized that the CMEA shock was only partially responsible for the contraction in 1991. Winiecki suggested that the authors pay more attention to monetary policy and particularly to the effect of the pegged exchange rate. He noted that, over a period of seventeen months, the exchange rate had remained fixed while prices shot up 330 percent.

Like Sachs, *Jacek Rostowski* felt that the authors had underestimated the role of the private sector in the transformation of industry. He noted that industrial production in the private sector increased by 50 percent in 1991, adding that the private sector now accounts for 20 percent of total industrial output. Rostowski also wondered whether Polish wages were too high since they were equal (after tax) to wages in Czechoslovakia.

Fabrizio Coricelli joined in the criticism of the aggregate demand analysis in the paper. Coricelli noted that Poland experienced excess aggregate demand before liberalization. He wondered whether liberalization and trade shocks could have generated a sharp enough drop in aggregate demand to explain the enormous fall in output. He noted that the authors' analysis assumes that Polish firms were quick to adjust to a purported decline in expected demand. This assumption conflicts with anecdotal evidence that these firms are more like "sluggish monsters."

Andrew Berg responded first. He presented several pieces of evidence that supported the aggregate demand analysis in the paper. He noted that there was relatively little heterogeneity in sales declines across state-run industrial firms at the two-digit level. In addition, he said that he did not see much evidence that import competition was playing an important role in the decline in output. Finally, he noted that quantity-based data on television and refrigerator inventories provide clear support for the claim that inventories rose sharply in January 1990. Berg concluded by addressing Coricelli's query about the speed of adjustment in Polish firms. At the start of 1990, firms suddenly began to generate huge inventories. This unprecedented phenomenon quickly alerted the firms to the existence of the demand shock.

Olivier Blanchard suggested that some of the disagreements that had been voiced by participants were largely differences in emphasis. He felt that most of the participants agreed with the general conclusion that the sharp declines in output had as their approximate causes demand rather than supply shocks.

3 Stabilization and Transition in Czechoslovakia

Karel Dyba and Jan Svejnar

3.1 A Historical Overview of Economic Performance

Unlike most other socialist countries, Czechoslovakia used to be a relatively developed economy that became underdeveloped as a result of an externally imposed system.[1] It is also a country that maintained relative macro stability and thus entered the economic transformation of the 1990s in a better position than the other socialist economies. Finally, both within the Soviet bloc and in comparison with all countries, Czechoslovakia displayed one of the most equal distributions of income (Yotopoulos and Nugent 1976; and Begg 1991). On the political side, Czechoslovakia is currently undertaking a peaceful partition along national lines that will result in the creation of independent Czech and Slovak republics in 1993.

Czechoslovakia was created out of the disintegrating Austro-Hungarian Empire as a single state composed of the Czech and Slovak lands. Before the Second World War, Czechoslovakia was a democracy, with GNP per capita similar to that of Austria.[2] However, owing to historical factors, Slovakia started as an economically less developed agricultural region, while the Czech lands were industrialized and economically advanced. As a result of targeted government policies, these differences diminished substantially over the following seven decades.

During the pre–World War II period, Czechoslovakia was a successful open

The opinions expressed in this paper are those of the authors. They do not represent official views of the Czech government. The authors would like to thank David Begg and other conference participants for useful comments on an earlier draft of the paper and Josef Kotrba for valuable research assistance. This paper was partially supported by grant 806–34 from the National Council for Soviet and East European Research.

1. For an account of Czechoslovak economic development, see, e.g., Begg (1991).

2. As Gelb and Grey (1991) indicate, in 1938 the GDP per capita in Austria and Czechoslovakia was $400 and $380, respectively.

economy, with about 30 percent foreign capital ownership and well-developed human capital. Its industries were technologically advanced, and its products were renowned worldwide for their workmanship.

By 1990, Czechoslovak GNP per capita was reported by the World Bank at $3,300, thus being in line with those of Venezuela and Yugoslavia, but amounting to only about 25 percent of that of Austria.[3] The discrepancy between the Czechoslovak and Western GNPs increased further in 1991 as the officially recorded Czechoslovak GNP declined by an estimated 16 percent (see table 3.1). The economy was closed and strictly regulated, and many Czechoslovak products were of mediocre quality, selling at a discount and with some difficulty in the West. Compared to Hungary and Poland, Czechoslovakia was more centralized and, according to some observers (see, e.g., Begg 1991), also falling behind in terms of economic growth.

This negative development occurred over four decades. During the post–World War II reconstruction of 1945–47, the country was still a market economy, although large industrial enterprises as well as banking and insurance companies were already nationalized. After the February 1948 Communist takeover, the Soviet system of central planning was introduced into the economy, the remaining private firms were nationalized,[4] and heavy industry was assigned priority in the development strategy. Czechoslovak foreign trade was forcefully reoriented from world markets toward the Soviet bloc countries.

The Czechoslovak government relied on central planning as the operating system throughout the 1950s. The economic slowdown in the early 1960s resulted in reforms, which culminated during the Prague Spring of 1968 with a partial program of price liberalization, an attempt at separating economic policy from political decision making, more enterprise autonomy, and workers' participation in enterprise management. However, the system of central planning was reimposed after the 1968 Soviet-led invasion, and it remained virtually intact until the late 1980s.

Czechoslovakia also had a long history of monetary and fiscal conservatism. Already in 1919, one year after the creation of the country, Czechoslovakia's finance minister, Alois Rasin, took effective measures to terminate within Czechoslovakia the hyperinflation that raged throughout the former Austro-Hungarian Empire. By temporarily closing the border, stamping the Austro-Hungarian currency that was in circulation in the Czechoslovak territory at the time, and recognizing the stamped currency as the only legal tender, he turned Czechoslovakia into an island of stability while hyperinflation continued in all the neighboring economies.[5] This initial conservatism was followed through-

---

3. The estimated GNP of Czechoslovakia naturally depends on the methodology used. Other studies generate higher estimates.
4. Private agriculture was collectivized or converted into state farms.
5. For details, see, e.g., Sargent (1986, chap. 3).

Table 3.1 Production, Employment, and Unemployment

	1985–89	1989	1990				1990	1991				1991	1992ª	
			1	2	3	4		1	2	3	4		1	2
Real NMP:														
Index:														
CSFR		100.0	91.8	99.4	96.0	108.6	99.0	87.5	81.8	71.8	77.3	76.9	70.0	69.7
% Δ:b														
CSFR	1.95	.7	…	…	…	…	−1.1	−4.6	−11.4	−16.0	−19.5	−19.5	−20.0	−17.5
CR	1.6	.9	…	…	…	…	−1.1	−4.9	−11.7	−16.0	−19.0	−19.0	−18.0	−15.0
SR	2.6	.2	…	…	…	…	−5.8	−5.2	−11.1	−16.0	−18.0	−18.0	…	…
Real GNP:														
Index:														
CSFR	…	100.0	94.5	100.2	97.6	106.1	99.6	91.7	87.4	76.6	79.3	83.8	78.2	77.6
% Δ:b														
CSFR	…	…	…	…	…	…	−.5	−3.0	−8.0	−12.5	−15.9	−15.9	−14.7	−13.0
CR	…	…	…	…	…	…	−1.1	−1.9	−10.0	−12.3	−14.1	−14.1	−17.4	−14.0
SR	…	…	…	…	…	…	…	…	−8.0	−13.0	−14.0	−14.0	−18.0	−15.0
Real ind. prod.:														
% Δ:b,c														
CSFR	2.4	.7	−2.9	−3.0	−3.7	−3.7	−3.7	…	−15.1	−19.8	−23.1	−23.1	−25.9	−18.9
CR	2.3	1.3	−2.9	−2.8	−3.7	−3.5	−3.5	−8.7	−14.4	−18.8	−22.5	−22.5	−22.7	−18.5
SR	2.6	−.8	−3.1	−3.6	−3.9	−4.1	−4.1	…	−16.7	−20.5	−24.9	−24.9	−25.5	−18.8

(*continued*)

Table 3.1 (continued)

	1985–89	1989	1990					1991					1992[a]	
			1	2	3	4	1990	1	2	3	4	1991	1	2
Real agri. prod.:														
% Δ:[d]														
CSFR	1.4	1.7	...	...	...	...	−3.9	...	...	...	...	−8.4	...	...
CR	1.0	2.3	...	...	...	...	−2.3	...	...	...	...	−8.9	...	...
SR	2.3	.6	...	...	...	...	−7.2	...	...	...	...	−7.4	...	...
Employment:														
% Δ:[b,e]														
CSFR	.7	.3	−.7	−1.3	−1.7	−2.5	−2.5	−8.4	−9.7	−11.1	−12.5	−12.5	−13.4	−12.2
CR	.6	.6	−.8	−1.3	−1.6	−2.5	−2.5	−8.4	−10.0	−11.2	−12.9	−12.9	−15.0	−13.8
SR	.9	−.2	−.7	−1.3	−1.9	−2.7	−2.7	−8.2	−9.1	−10.7	−11.7	−11.7	−12.3	−11.0
Unemployment														
rate (%):[f]														
CSFR	...	...	...	...	...	.8	.8	2.3	3.8	5.6	6.6	6.6	6.5	5.5
CR	...	...	...	...	...	.1	.1	1.7	2.6	3.8	4.1	4.1	3.7	2.7
SR	...	...	...	...	...	1.0	1.0	3.7	6.3	9.6	11.8	11.8	12.3	11.3

Source: Federal Statistical Office and Czech Statistical Office.

Note: CSFR = Czech and Slovak Federal Republic; CR = Czech Republic; SR = Slovak Republic.

[a]1992 data for the CSFR, CR, and SR are preliminary. Data for 1990–92 have not yet been made consistent across the CR, SR, and CSFR.

[b]Cumulative percentage change related to the period up to the same quarter in the preceding year.

[c]1991 and 1992 data include small and private enterprises.

[d]Percentage change related to preceding year. Data are not collected on a quarterly basis.

[e]Average number of employees in the state and private enterprises.

[f]End-of-quarter (year) data. Employment = average number of employees in the state and cooperative sectors.

out the two decades of democracy and also until the final phase of Communist rule.

The World Bank estimates of Czechoslovak GNP per capita are based on current exchange rates, and as such they are possibly downwardly biased. Nevertheless, the long-term decline in Czechoslovakia's welfare relative to advanced economies is self-evident. One thus has to accept the official and Western data on Czechoslovakia's long-term economic growth with caution. These data suggest that the most impressive rate of growth occurred during the First Five-Year Plan (1949–53), when the official measure of net material product (NMP) increased nearly 10 percent per annum. However, this rate of growth proved unsustainable. The first half of the 1960s witnessed virtual stagnation and resulted in the subsequent reform. The economy grew at about 7 percent a year during the reform period, 1965–70, and it registered almost 6 percent annual growth in the early to mid-1970s. A major slowdown in the rate of growth to 3.6 percent occurred between 1975 and 1980 as the first oil shock turned the terms of trade against Czechoslovakia within the Council for Mutual Economic Assistance (CMEA). This was also a period of poor agricultural performance.

The 1980s witnessed a further deceleration in economic growth. The world recession, rising input prices, and restrictive government policies resulted in a 1.8 percent growth rate in the first half of the 1980s. As can be seen from table 3.1, the situation did not improve markedly in the second half of the 1980s as the growth rate of NMP was only 1.9 percent a year in the period 1985–89. With economic observers noting that inflation was being underestimated, the 1980s may in fact be seen as a decade of economic stagnation (see, e.g., Dyba 1989).

Other indicators also signaled deterioration in economic performance and increasingly desperate attempts on the part of the Communist government to maintain a degree of public support. The ratio of net fixed investment to NMP fell from 20 percent in 1975 to a mere 13 percent in the late 1980s, and the share of consumption in NMP rose. Export growth slowed down in the 1980s, and exports to developing countries were accompanied to an increasing extent by trade credits. Czechoslovakia became a net creditor within the CMEA, especially vis-à-vis the Soviet Union and Poland. This was increasingly, albeit reluctantly, financed by borrowing in the West.

The long-term deterioration in economic performance was caused by a number of factors. The centralization of the economy after 1948 first created strong growth as the system rapidly mobilized existing resources. Another source of growth was the rapid increase in inputs, which temporarily resulted in a high growth rate. The shortcomings of the command system, which gradually became overwhelming, were the perverse incentives, limited innovation, inefficient allocation of resources, and rigidities. These latter factors became particularly important as demand patterns started to change, input growth could no longer be sustained at the high rates, and the quality of marginal inputs declined. Czechoslovakia also suffered from its isolation from world markets and its extreme reorientation toward trade within the CMEA. This reorientation increased the technological backwardness of Czechoslovak industry and its vulnerability to disruptions in the CMEA markets.

3.2   The Principal Measures during Stabilization and Transition

3.2.1   The Start of Economic Transformation, 1989–90

The November 1989 revolution brought in a liberally oriented transitional government and created expectations of a radical economic transformation from a command to a market economy. The new government immediately devalued the koruna (Kčs) vis-à-vis the convertible currencies, revalued it vis-à-vis the ruble, and tightened budgetary policies for 1990, setting itself the target of a 1–1.5 percent budget surplus. The government also declared that the introduction of a market economy and integration with the Western economies would be the key to reestablishing economic prosperity. Specific proposals for the strategy of economic transformation were quickly put forth (see, e.g., Svejnar 1989), but disagreement also emerged about both the direction of the economic transition and the nature and timing of specific measures. As a result, a government economic strategy reflecting the principles outlined above was not officially adopted until 24 May 1990.

The 8–9 June parliamentary elections brought in a coalition that broadly favored the market-oriented transformation.[6] The new government in principle adopted the 24 May economic resolution, but few significant economic measures were adopted in the immediate postelection period. The two important measures were the elimination of a negative turnover tax, which was accompanied by a Kčs 140 compensation for each citizen on 9 July 1990, and the gradual start of negotiations of new commercial policies with various market economies and organizations such as the EEC.

The main reason for delaying the economic transformation was the fact that other factors made rapid progress in designing and implementing an economic transition problematic. The most important of these factors were the inability to achieve consensus on the details of an economic program within the executive branch of the federal government, the desire of the new Parliament to play a major role in preparing economic laws and policies, the need to create a new set of economic laws,[7] and the start of difficult negotiations about the relative

6. The election brought about major personnel changes in the federal Parliament, with the broadly based Civic Forum and Public Against Violence parties together winning 170 of the 300 total seats, the Communist party retaining only forty-seven seats, and the Christian Democratic Alliance capturing forty seats. Less extensive personnel turnover took place in the executive branch since many of the ministers of the transitional government belonged to the newly formed coalition among the Civic Forum, Public Against Violence, and Christian Democrat parties.

7. An alternative would have been to adopt temporarily a modified set of Western (e.g., German or EEC) laws. However, in view of the voluminous nature of Western legal statutes and the paucity of skilled translators, it turned out to be simpler to create a new set of Czechoslovak laws.

jurisdictions of the federal and the two national (Czech and Slovak) governments.

On 1 September 1990, the government formally submitted to the Parliament a "scenario of economic reform." The document outlined economic and social principles, specific measures, and time parameters. It was also a political document that reflected the compromises that were hastily concluded among the major groups in the Parliament.

On the macroeconomic front, the scenario emphasized a strict anti-inflationary policy. All other macroeconomic goals (growth, employment, and balance of payments) were "within reasonable limits" subordinate. In order to realize the anti-inflationary policy, the government set as specific 1990 policy targets zero growth of money supply and a budget surplus of at least 1–1.5 percent.[8] Measures proposed for 1991 were a continuation of the earlier set of policies, but they were more far reaching in that they included a restrictive monetary policy, a 2–2.5 percent budget surplus, a convertible koruna for current account transactions, and a positive real interest rate.

The proposed micro policies aimed at inducing efficient allocation of resources, introducing new institutions, and minimizing the social costs of transition. The micro transformation was to be achieved through (a) a major tax reform emphasizing the introduction of a value-added tax, a personal income tax, and an "enterprise" tax, (b) a budgetary reform stressing independence of units and ensuring the transparency of budgetary allocations, (c) de-étatization and privatization of property, (d) price liberalization, (e) internal convertibility of the koruna, (f) reduction and retraining of redundant labor, (g) legalization of collective bargaining together with a high tax on wage growth exceeding limits set by government, and (h) restructuring of social security and health care systems and a gradual separation of their funding from the state budget.

The Parliament speedily approved the scenario, but it immediately faced the problem of how to draft and pass the large number of laws and decrees that needed to be put in place before the transformation would be launched on 1 January 1991. This indeed proved to be a major burden, and the resulting fatigue was increasingly visible. The introduction of some widely expected laws (e.g., those related to the privatization of small enterprises) was consequently delayed.

3.2.2 Transformation Measures Undertaken in 1991 and 1992

On 1 January 1991, the government launched a major set of reforms, consisting of liberalizing 85 percent of producer and consumer prices, devaluing the koruna and pegging it to a basket of five Western currencies, introducing internal convertibility of the koruna together with a 20 percent import surcharge, controlling the growth of wages, and activating a social safety net.

These radical measures were introduced in the context of a proclaimed determination to pursue restrictive macro policies, and they were supplemented

---

8. These goals were in fact pursued from the start of 1990.

by a strong push to speed up the privatization process, attract foreign capital, promote the growth of private firms, decrease government subsidies to firms as well as some other government expenditures (e.g., on arms), and generally reduce the role of the state in the economy. In many respects, the measures introduced by the Czechoslovak authorities in January 1991 resembled those launched by the Poles a year earlier.

The broad quantity targets declared by the government for 1991 were to limit inflation in terms of the GDP deflator to 30 percent, GDP decline to 5–10 percent, unemployment to a 4.5 percent annual average rate, and real wage decline to 10 percent. The target for the current account was a deficit of Kčs 2.5 billion.

For 1992, the government set itself the target of at least partially liberalizing the remaining controlled prices, especially in the area of apartment rents, transportation and communication, and water and sewage. Money supply was to increase 10–15 percent, while the exchange rate policy was to remain unchanged. Unemployment was expected to rise further, and the government intended to maintain an incomes policy for state enterprises with more than 150 employees. Privatization of small units was to continue,[9] and that of large firms was to be launched on a large scale, covering about twenty-five hundred out of a total of about six thousand state enterprises in the first privatization wave.

Additional likely measures were to include lower interest rates to stimulate investment, stronger indirect support for small- and medium-sized enterprises, regional policies, development of a more efficient banking sector through privatization and greater independence of commercial banks as well as increased competition, greater regulation of certain parts of the capital market (e.g., the investment privatization funds), gradual introduction of a new tax system together with superior tax collection and enforcement, restructuring (deétatization) of social security, and further liberalization of foreign trade.

The government generally persevered in pursuing the policies set for 1991 and 1992, but, as we will show presently, it did not reach all its targets. In terms of policy implementation, one can see from table 3.2 that bank credit to state enterprises and households was held in check, rising somewhat in nominal but falling significantly in real terms in 1991 and declining absolutely in 1992. In contrast, bank credit to private enterprises rose from almost zero in mid-1990 to Kčs 71.4 billion at the end of 1991 and Kčs 125.7 billion in mid-1992. Credit to private firms thus became equivalent to 12 percent of credit extended by banks to state enterprises at the end of 1991 and 22.3 percent in mid-1992. In 1991, the rise in this ratio reflected the growing emphasis on credit expansion for the newly forming private firms. In 1992, the increase also reflected the transformation of large state enterprises into private joint-stock companies.

---

9. Between January 1991 and June 1992, over 25,000 units were sold in auctions. Prices ranged from several hundred dollars to a record price exceeding $10 million.

Table 3.2   Credit to Enterprises and Households (Kčs billion)

	1985–89	1989	1990				1990	1991				1991	1992	
			1	2	3	4		1	2	3	4		1	2
Bank credit to state enterprises:[a]														
CSFR	524.3	530.9	524.4	532.9	540.3	529.8	529.8	558.4	586.6	599.9	575.3	575.3	574.0	564.9
CR	355.1	360.5	314.3	387.6	395.4	383.0	383.0	397.1	414.2	420.0	403.7	403.7	398.1	390.5
SR	169.2	170.4	210.1	145.3	144.9	146.8	146.8	161.3	172.4	179.9	171.6	171.6	175.9	174.4
Bank credit to private enterprises:[a]														
CSFR	…	…	…	.5	1.4	3.4	3.4	9.3	24.7	40.5	71.4	71.4	85.4	125.7
CR	…	…	…	.4	1.1	2.8	2.8	7.7	20.5	33.1	55.5	55.5	64.3	94.4
SR	…	…	…	.1	.3	.6	.6	1.6	4.2	7.4	15.9	15.9	21.1	31.3
Interenterprise debt (credit):[a,b]														
CSFR	25.0	7.2	10.6	13.8	27.8	53.6	53.6	76.4	56.8	…	…	…	…	…
CR	18.7	4.8	6.4	8.3	18.0	37.8	37.8	56.5	32.1	…	…	…	…	…
SR	6.3	2.4	4.2	5.5	9.8	15.8	15.8	19.9	24.7	…	…	…	…	…
Interenterprise debt (credit):[a,c]														
CSFR	…	…	…	…	…	…	44.9	78.6	123.4	147.1	145.4	145.4	143.3	123.7
CR	…	…	…	…	…	…	31.8	55.6	88.8	100.2	101.7	101.7	98.8	79.3
SR	…	…	…	…	…	…	13.1	23.0	34.6	46.9	43.7	43.7	44.5	44.4
Bank credit to households:[a]														
CSFR	42.1	46.9	44.5	47.1	47.2	50.0	50.0	51.2	51.6	52.7	55.4	55.4	56.3	55.7
CR	26.5	29.5	27.2	29.8	29.9	31.8	31.8	32.4	33.2	33.9	36.2	36.2	37.4	37.2
SR	15.6	17.4	17.3	17.3	17.3	18.2	18.2	18.8	18.4	18.8	19.2	19.2	18.9	18.5

Source: Federal Statistical Office, Czech Statistical Office, and the Czechoslovak State Bank.

Note: CSFR = Czech and Slovak Federal Republic; CR = Czech Republic; SR = Slovak Republic.

[a]End-of-quarter (year) data.

[b]Frozen payments due to insufficient balances in the bank accounts of debtor enterprises (bank data).

[c]Unpaid obligations past maturity data (enterprise accounts).

As can be seen from table 3.3, all three measures of money supply (M0, M1, and M2) grew at less than half the rate of inflation in both 1990 and 1991. The more expansive monetary policy, preannounced for 1992, is visible in the data as of the second quarter of 1992. The restrictive money supply policy of 1990–91 was accompanied by rising (not freely set until mid-1992) interest rates. The government also permitted the protected banking sector to establish a sizable spread between the interest rates on loans and deposits, thus allowing the banks to build up reserves. The official, unified exchange rate, established at the start of 1991, was set near the parallel market rate, and the differential between the two has remained quite small. Czechoslovakia's modest foreign debt increased from $8.1 billion at the end of 1990 to $9.4 billion by the end of 1991 as the country borrowed $2.135 billion in 1991.[10] However, the increased debt was fully reflected in increased foreign currency reserves, which rose from $1.2 billion in December 1990 to $3.3 billion in December 1991. The debt remained virtually unchanged in the first half of 1992, thus testifying to the country's ability to proceed with the economic transformation without incurring a major foreign debt burden.

As can be seen from table 3.4, fiscal policy was initially somewhat less successful. After finishing 1990 with a minor surplus, registering significant budget surpluses in the first six months of 1991, and still achieving small surpluses until October, the government ended 1991 with a Kčs 22.1 billion deficit. While this deficit constituted only 5 percent of budget expenditures, it reflected a potentially problematic dynamics. In particular, the early surpluses were brought about primarily by high enterprise income and profit taxes, which reflected the initial profitability after price liberalization,[11] and the still relatively low level of unemployment compensation and other expenditures. As enterprise profits declined and additional state expenditures on health and education were approved by republican Parliaments in October, government expenditures began to exceed revenues. It is interesting to note that, while unemployment rose dramatically during the year, the level of unemployment compensation expenditures did not reach the level of reserves allocated for this purpose. Rather, the achievement of zero inflation led to pressure to increase government expenditures, which were automatically processed by the banks. The initial success with inflation thus reduced fiscal coordination and resulted in reduced policy control.

For 1992, the government has agreed to decrease agricultural subsidies and improve the targeting of the social safety net. The goal is to reduce current and increase investment expenditures in real terms. As can be seen from table 3.4,

---

10. The loans were provided as follows: $1,313 million from the International Monetary Fund, $205 million from the World Bank, $248 million from the European Community, $89 million from the G-24, and $280 million from the financial sector.

11. The high profitability reflected both the fact that enterprises accumulated raw material inventories before price liberalization and the custom of paying income and profit taxes on the value of delivered rather than paid-for goods.

Table 3.3   Money Supply, Interest Rate, Exchange Rate, and External Debt

	1985–89	1989	1990				1990	1991				1991	1992	
			1	2	3	4		1	2	3	4		1	2
Money supply (% Δ):[a]														
M0	5.5	8.8	2.9	6.5	7.7	8.4	8.4	−1.1	3.4	9.5	20.0	20.0	−2.5	7.5
M1	4.0	.5	−7.4	−2.5	−5.3	−6.4	−6.4	−3.4	−1.1	9.8	28.8	28.8	−4.1	.8
M2	5.8	3.5	−2.3	−.2	−1.5	.5	.5	−.3	5.6	12.4	27.3	27.3	2.0	7.1
Nominal interest rate (%):[b]														
Loans	5.1	5.0	5.4	5.4	5.6	7.6	5.9	14.7	15.1	14.2	13.9	14.5	13.5	13.7
Deposits	3.1	3.2	2.6	2.7	2.8	3.3	2.8	7.6	8.2	8.6	8.0	8.1	8.7	6.9
Exchange rate (Kčs/$):[b]														
Commercial	15.1	15.1	16.5	16.6	16.0	22.7	18.0	…	…	…	…	…	…	…
Tourist	…	…	37.6	30.2	27.0	31.0	30.9	…	…	…	…	…	…	…
Auction	…	121.2	78.8	48.0	34.3	41.1	50.4	…	…	…	…	…	…	…
Parallel market	33.70	42.4	41.5	36.3	33.3	41.0	38.0	34.1	31.7	32.5	30.8	32.3	30.2	30.0
Official (unified)	…	…	…	…	…	…	…	27.9	30.3	30.5	29.2	29.5	28.8	28.8
External debt ($ billion)[c]	6.2	7.9	7.4	7.1	7.6	8.1	8.1	8.3	8.8	9.3	9.4	9.4	8.9	9.8

Source: The Czechoslovak State Bank.

[a]End-of-quarter (year) data reflecting changes relative to the end of the previous year. M0 = currency; M1 = M0 plus demand deposits; M2 = M1 plus time deposits and foreign currency deposits.

[b]Average rate in respective quarter (year).

[c]End-of-quarter (year) data.

Table 3.4   **Fiscal Budgets of the Czech and Slovak Federal Republic (billions of current Kčs)**

	1989	1990	1991	1992[a]
Revenue	306.7	339.9	460.9	307.5
Turnover tax	74.7	108.5	123.1	79.0
Income & profit tax	74.1	79.0	129.2	77.7
Payroll taxes	78.2	79.6	150.4	107.8
Other revenue	79.7	72.8	58.2	43.0
Expenditures	312.2	339.1	483.0	304.8
Subsidies to enterprises	51.4	48.7	59.4	24.7
Social security	91.6	95.8	123.8	90.7
Subsidies to local budgets	52.5	58.1	72.0	23.2
Other expenditures	116.7	136.5	233.8	166.2
Surplus (deficit)	(5.5)	.8	(22.1)	2.7

Source: Federal Ministry of Finance.
[a]January–August data.

the consolidated budget was maintained in surplus during the first eight months of 1992, with the Czech Republic running a slight surplus and the Slovak Republic running a deficit.

3.2.3   External Shocks

In assessing the effect of the Czechoslovak stabilization and transition policies, one must bear in mind that these policies were carried out in the context of the disintegration of the CMEA and the decline in economic activity among the traditional trading partners. The absorption of East Germany by West Germany in 1990 represented the first shock as East Germany was a major trading partner, accounting for approximately 10 percent of Czechoslovakia's foreign trade. Further shock came from the disintegration of the Soviet economy and the reduced demand from recession-stricken East European trading partners. Finally, the switch from CMEA trade to free trade based on world prices on 1 January 1991 resulted in a significant shift in the terms of trade against Czechoslovakia. Official calculations point to a 26 percent worsening of Czechoslovakia's terms of trade in the first quarter, 28 percent in the second quarter, and a cumulative 22 percent decline in the first three quarters of 1991.

3.3   Economic Developments in 1989–92

As can be seen from table 3.1 above, the slowdown in NMP growth to 0.7 percent in 1989 turned into a 1.1 percent decline in 1990 and a further 19.5 percent decline in 1991. The sizable decline in 1991 was accounted for primarily by a 23.1 percent fall in industrial production as agriculture declined by a more modest 8.4 percent. Slovakia experienced a somewhat greater decrease in industrial production (24.9 percent) than the Czech lands (22.5 percent) but also a shallower decline in agricultural production (7.4 vs. 8.9 percent, respectively). The Czechoslovak authorities started to calculate GNP in 1991, and their estimates suggest that this indicator of performance registered a 16 percent decline in 1991.

As the indices as well as the cumulative percentage change figures in table 3.1 indicate, the decline in officially measured NMP continued into the second quarter of 1992. In contrast, GNP has remained relatively stable since the third quarter of 1991, thus confirming the stronger performance of the service sector relative to the rest of the economy.

It is important to stress that there are several important deficiencies of the official data. First, price increases tend to be overestimated as a result of structural changes in reporting. In particular, data from stores indicate that there has been a lower decline in sales than is generally assumed, thus pointing to an overestimation of price increases for a given value of sales. Second, the official data underestimate the growth of the private (informal) sector, which escapes the official statistical and tax coverage. Hence, although table 3.1 is meant to cover all enterprises, it is not clear to what extent the attempt has been successful. Finally, foreign trade appears to be severely underestimated as mirror statistics from the OECD report higher levels of Czechoslovak exports and imports than appear in the Czechoslovak customs data (see table 3.5–3.7).

As is evident from table 3.1 above, the modest growth in employment over the mid- to late 1980s turned into a decline in 1990. With a 2.5 percent employment decrease in 1990, a 12.5 percent fall in 1991, and a 10 percent decline in the first half of 1992, enterprises clearly carried out sizable reductions in employment. This is further accentuated by the fact that average hours worked declined in most enterprises owing to the elimination of overtime and other measures. Nevertheless, through the end of 1991, employment declined in a less pronounced way than production. The data for the first two quarters of 1992 suggest that performance is improving, especially in construction.

The employment pattern that has emerged is that the initial labor force re-

Table 3.5   Czechoslovak Foreign Trade (billions of current Kčs, f.o.b.)

	1989	1990	1991	1992[a]
Exports	217.5	216.5	321.2	176.7
"Socialist" countries	132.3	106.7	126.3	43.5
Market economies	85.2	109.8	194.9	133.2
Imports	214.7	246.3	293.7	171.7
"Socialist" countries	133.8	125.7	125.9	62.7
Market economies	80.9	120.6	167.8	109.0
Surplus (deficit)	2.8	(29.8)	27.5	5.0

Source: Federal Statistical Office.

[a]January–July data.

Table 3.6   Czechoslovak Imports from OECD Countries in 1989–92 (all data are monthly averages, $million)

Country	1989	1990	1991				1991	1992:1
			1	2	3	4		
OECD	306.0	406.0	518.0	461.0	458.0	658.0	565.0	. . .
EEC	219.0	277.0	406.0	347.0	340.0	487.0	394.0	. . .
EFTA	68.2	106.3	86.3	92.1	98.3	138.7	103.4	. . .
United States	4.5	7.4	10.2	9.7	8.0	13.5	10.3	33.5
Japan	4.6	4.2	7.3	4.2	5.4	6.0	5.7	9.0
Austria	31.6	64.1	52.2	55.0	63.0	91.6	65.5	84.44
France	19.4	23.9	80.2	27.7	22.6	33.9	40.1	35.3
Germany	121.9	160.7	231.4	216.6	232.3	320.5	250.2	337.4
Italy	23.8	32.4	30.9	40.6	29.2	49.1	37.9	52.6
Netherlands	14.1	16.3	18.7	17.7	16.1	26.2	19.6	27.4
Spain	4.3	4.7	5.6	4.5	2.4	5.0	4.3	5.87
Sweden	9.0	12.2	11.0	9.8	10.0	15.61	11.63	19.15
Switzerland	18.1	20.8	19.0	19.4	18.9	23.7	19.8	19.75
United Kingdom	17.9	19.7	18.9	16.3	14.8	26.5	19.0	26.0
Yugoslavia	35.2	38.6	24.7	27.0	N.A.	N.A.	N.A.	N.A.

Source: OECD, monthly statistics of foreign trade.
Note: N.A. = not available. EFTA = European Free Trade Association.

Table 3.7   Czechoslovak Exports to OECD Countries in 1989–92 (all data are monthly averages, $million)

Country	1989	1990	1991				1991	1992:1
			1	2	3	4		
OECD	347.0	408.0	476.0	500.0	546.0	678.0	551.0	. . .
EEC	238.0	285.0	359.0	381.0	416.0	532.0	423.0	. . .
EFTA	76.2	84.3	80.7	77.5	83.0	100.9	85.5	. . .
United States	7.2	7.3	9.2	10.1	13.0	15.8	12.0	17.8
Japan	10.8	10.7	10.3	11.4	7.7	12.9	10.5	10.5
Austria	42.4	47.1	44.2	46.7	53.1	68.1	53.0	61.78
France	22.4	29.0	28.9	30.4	31.3	35.4	31.5	39.8
Germany	110.7	140.2	215.1	220.5	259.8	328.2	255.9	33.49
Italy	33.8	39.9	38.5	49.0	43.5	72.5	51.5	68.1
Netherlands	16.0	18.6	22.2	21.7	21.2	25.3	22.6	16.0
Spain	7.3	7.3	7.3	9.2	8.3	11.2	9.04	12.68
Sweden	9.6	10.4	10.9	9.8	9.8	10.67	10.29	12.86
Switzerland	10.4	9.9	9.9	10.3	8.9	10.77	9.96	10.39
United Kingdom	21.4	20.1	16.5	19.1	19.8	21.5	19.3	22.3
Yugoslavia	40.8	43.1	52.6	68.2	N.A.	N.A.	N.A.	N.A.

Source: OECD, monthly statistics of foreign trade.
Note: N.A. = not available. EFTA = European Free Trade Association.

ductions usually took the form of retirements and the termination of guest workers. This was followed by hiring freezes and, eventually, layoffs. Among the Czechoslovak workers, hardest hit at first were hence the labor force entrants (especially young people) as insiders in state enterprises temporarily insulated themselves from the effect of the external shock and the transition. Interestingly, as layoffs began to take place, the effect was inversely proportional to age, with the older (preretirement-age) workers suffering the lowest unemployment rate. However, as the transition entered its second full year in 1992, one began to observe significant layoffs among the workers of preretirement age as well.

As the unemployment data in table 3.1 indicate, unemployment was a virtually unknown phenomenon in Czechoslovakia until the second half of 1990. Unemployment became serious in 1991, the overall rate rising from less than 1 percent at the start of the year to 6.6 percent at year's end. The Czechoslovak government estimates that about one-third of reported unemployment in 1991 was fictitious, covering individuals who were gainfully employed but collecting unemployment benefits or those who did not actively look for work. The reduction of the unemployment benefits and the halving of the eligibility period from one year to six months at the start of 1992 contributed to the fall in the unemployment rate from 6.6 to 6.5 percent in the first quarter and 5.5 percent in the second quarter of 1992. Other factors that are cited by officials in the federal as well as the Czech and Slovak labor ministries as possibly contributing to this unexpected decline in the unemployment rate are the boom in the private sector of the economy, the active labor market policies of the government, and the unwillingness of directors of state enterprises to lay off workers and risk conflict before privatization.

There has been a remarkable asymmetry across the Czech and Slovak republics in unemployment dynamics. While employment declined by about 2.5 percent in 1990 and by 12–13 percent in 1991 in both republics, unemployment has risen much more rapidly in Slovakia. By the end of 1991, the unemployment rate was 4.1 percent in the Czech lands and 11.8 percent in Slovakia. Moreover, in the first quarter of 1992, the unemployment rate fell from 4.1 to 3.7 percent in the Czech Republic but increased from 11.8 to 12.3 percent in the Slovak Republic. The discrepancy in the unemployment rates of the two republics reflects a faster rise of the private sector in the Czech Republic, a more liberal application of unemployment compensation and severance pay policies in Slovakia, a stronger tendency for older workers to take (early) retirement in the Czech Republic, and the higher propensity of Czech workers to find employment in Austria and Germany. Interestingly, starting in the second quarter of 1992, one can observe a downward trend in the unemployment rate in Slovakia as well. Both republics registered a one-point decline in the unemployment rate in the second quarter, resulting in a 2.7 percent rate in the Czech lands and 11.3 percent in Slovakia. The preliminary data for October 1992

Table 3.8   Prices, Wages, and Consumption

			1990					1991					1992[a]	
	1985–89	1989	1	2	3	4	1990	1	2	3	4	1991	1	2
Consumer price index:[b]														
CSFR	1.0	1.4	2.4	3.1	13.6	18.4	18.4	40.9	49.2	49.5	53.6	53.6	1.8	3.0
CR	1.0	1.5	2.2	2.7	13.3	17.5	17.5	39.3	48.0	48.1	52.0	52.0	2.2	3.8
SR	.9	1.3	2.3	3.8	14.0	19.2	19.2	44.9	51.6	53.4	58.3	58.3	1.4	1.9
Producer price index for industry:[b]														
CSFR	.2	-.7	.3	.4	.5	16.6	16.6	48.1	53.7	53.0	54.8	54.8	2.9	5.2
CR	.4	.1	.5	.6	.7	15.6	15.6	48.7	54.2	54.5	56.6	56.6	3.2	6.0
SR	-.2	-2.7	-.2	-.1	.0	19.4	19.4	45.3	51.5	48.7	50.6	50.6	2.3	3.6
Nominal earnings (% Δ):[c]														
CSFR	2.0	2.4	3.6	2.7	2.8	3.6	3.6	6.0	10.5	12.2	16.4	16.4	21.2	22.1
CR	2.0	2.4	3.5	2.6	2.7	3.4	3.4	5.8	13.8	12.3	16.3	16.3	21.3	23.0
SR	2.1	2.6	3.7	2.9	3.0	3.9	3.9	6.1	10.8	12.2	16.6	16.6	20.5	19.7
Real personal consumption (% Δ):[b]														
CSFR	2.9	1.8	...	...	...	...	1.1	-26.0	-37.1	-34.3	-33.1	-33.1	-4.6	5.0
CR	2.8	1.6	...	...	...	...	1.7	-24.0	-29.0	-33.5	-29.0	-29.0	...	...
SR	3.3	2.1	...	...	...	...	.5	...	...	...	...	...	...	...

Source: Federal Statistical Office and Czech Statistical Office.

Note: CSFR = Czech and Slovak Federal Republic; CR = Czech Republic; SR = Slovak Republic.

[a]1992 data are preliminary.

[b]Refers to end-of-quarter (year) data, which are cumulative, reflecting changes relative to the end of the previous year.

[c]% change related to the same period in the preceding year.

suggest that the unemployment rate in the two republics stood at 2.6 and 11.2 percent, respectively.

After decades of seeming stability,[12] consumer prices registered an 18.4 percent increase in 1990, a major 53.6 percent jump in 1991, and a mere 3 percent rise in the first two quarters of 1992 (see table 3.8). The 1990 increase was brought about primarily by the removal of the negative turnover tax in July and the devaluation of the koruna in the fall. The 1991 and 1992 price increases, the dynamics of which are captured in detail in table 3.9, reflected the liberalization of 85 percent of all prices on 1 January 1991, followed by the liberalization of 10 percent of prices in the rest of 1991 and in the first half of 1992. As can be seen from table 3.9, the 1991 price liberalization resulted in a 26 percent jump in consumer prices in January and a gradual tapering off of inflation in the following five months. Indeed, consumer prices still increased by 7 percent in February and almost 5 percent in March, but the monthly rate of increase remained at or below 2 percent in the second quarter of 1991. The economy registered complete price stability from July to October, but then consumer prices rose again by 1.6 percent in November and 1.2 percent in December. Monthly inflation fell well below 1 percent in the first eight months of 1992 but jumped by 1.8 percent in September. The authorities expect a 10–12 percent inflation rate for all of 1992.

While the price rise associated with the July 1990 elimination of the negative turnover tax was accompanied by a compensating adjustment in incomes, other price increases and the price liberalization of 1991 were carried out in the presence of relatively tight controls on wages, at least through the first half of 1991. As can be seen from table 3.8 above, nominal earnings increased by a mere 3.6 percent in 1990 and 16.4 percent in 1991. Real earnings, measured as nominal earnings relative to the consumer price index, hence declined by 12.5 percent in 1990 and 24 percent in 1991. Personal consumption, which still registered a modest 1.1 percent increase in 1990, declined precipitously, falling 33 percent in 1991. The decline in the conventionally measured living standard has thus been considerable for an average consumer. At the same time, the rise of unemployment was stemmed and the success of the stabilization program undoubtedly aided by the ability of the authorities to keep the labor cost per worker down. It is worth noting that the situation appears to have changed in the first quarter of 1992 as real wages have surged ahead by about 8 percent.

There also appears to have been considerable widening of income differentials and stratification in social status. For many individuals, especially

---

12. As mentioned earlier, the long-term price stability under the Communist regime was in part generated at the expense of shortages. In addition, it also reflected data manipulation in the construction of the baskets of commodities for price indices.

Table 3.9   Consumer and Producer Prices in 1991 (% Δ relative to preceding month)

	Jan.	Feb.	Mar.	Apr.	May	Jun.	Jul.	Aug.	Sep.	Oct.	Nov.	Dec.
1991:												
Consumer prices:												
CSFR	25.8	7.0	4.7	2.0	1.9	1.8	−.1	.0	.3	−.1	1.6	1.2
CR	25.8	6.1	4.3	2.4	1.9	1.8	−.3	.0	.3	.2	1.4	1.1
SR	25.9	8.8	5.8	.8	1.9	1.8	.5	.5	.1	−.4	1.7	1.9
Producer prices in industry:												
CSFR	24.0	19.3	.1	2.9	1.7	−.8	−.5	.4	−.4	.0	.9	.6
CR	20.4	22.4	.9	3.0	1.5	−.8	−.1	.6	−.3	−.2	1.2	.4
SR	33.0	12.3	−2.7	2.6	2.2	−.6	−1.5	.2	−.5	.4	.1	.7
1992:												
Consumer prices:												
CSFR	1.0	.5	.4	.5	.4	.3	.8	.6	1.8	...	...	...
CR	.9	.7	.6	.6	.5	.4	.6	.6	1.9	...	...	...
SR	1.2	.2	.0	.1	.2	.2	−.2	.6	1.7	...	...	...
Producer prices in industry:												
CSFR	1.0	1.9	.1	.5	1.1	.6	.6	.0	.3	...	...	...
CR	1.0	2.0	.2	.8	1.3	.6	.7	.2	.5	...	...	...
SR	.9	1.7	−.3	−.1	.8	.6	.5	−.4	−.1	...	...	...

Source: Federal Statistical Office and Czech Statistical Office.
Note: CSFR = Czech and Slovak Federal Republic; CR = Czech Republic; SR = Slovak Republic.

those losing in relative terms, this has been hard to accept. The ability of the government to keep the social peace has thus been a remarkable achievement, and it remains to be seen if the situation will remain as peaceful in the future.

The restrictive economic policy, external shocks, and the nature of the transformation process also resulted in a major decline in investment activity. As can be seen from table 3.10, real net fixed investment rose by a mere 2.9 percent in 1990 and declined by a full 20 percent in 1991. Preliminary estimates indicate that the decline has continued in 1992. Given the low product demand, restrictive macro policies, and uncertainty over the transfer of property rights, enterprises have thus opted to cut down on investment.

The savings data, reported in tables 3.10 and 3.11 in nominal terms, imply a major decline in the propensity to save in koruny in 1990 and the first half of 1991. There was a more substantial increase in koruna savings in the second half of 1991 and the first two quarters of 1992, but the increase still fell short of the increase in nominal earnings of the population. Over the last two years,

Table 3.10   Investment and Savings

	1985–89	1989	1990					1991					1992[a]	
			1	2	3	4	1990	1	2	3	4	1991	1	2
Real net fixed investment (% Δ):														
CSFR	2.8	3.1	...	...	...	...	2.9	−10.0	−28.3	−22.0	−20.0	−20.0	...	...
CR	2.3	1.7	...	...	...	...	2.7	−12.0	−20.0	−15.0	−13.0	−13.0	...	...
SR	3.5	4.1	...	...	...	...	3.2	...	...	...	...	...	...	...
Savings of population in Kčs (% Δ):[b]														
CSFR	2.3	4.6	.8	1.2	.9	−2.6	−2.6	−1.2	.1	2.6	12.7	12.7	3.0	4.7
CR	5.8	4.0	.9	1.4	1.1	−2.0	−2.0	−.8	1.9	4.6	14.7	14.7	3.0	5.5
SR	4.4	5.8	.7	.9	.4	−3.9	−3.9	−2.3	−3.7	−1.8	8.5	8.5	3.1	3.0
Savings of enterprises in Kčs (% Δ):[b]														
CSFR	6.0	2.8	−18.7	−14.1	−15.4	−15.8	−15.8	−.0	7.4	11.3	34.9	34.9	2.8	4.7
CR	...	...	...	...	...	...	...	3.3	10.4	15.0	31.3	39.3	6.5	8.0
SR	...	...	...	...	...	...	...	−7.5	.6	2.9	25.3	25.3	−6.3	−3.6

Source: Federal Statistical Office, Czech Statistical Office and The Czechoslovak State Bank.

Note: CSFR = Czech and Slovak Federal Republic; CR = Czech Republic; SR = Slovak Republic.

[a]1992 data are preliminary.

[b]End-of-quarter (year) data reflecting changes relative to the end of the previous year.

Table 3.11   **Savings in Foreign Currencies (Kčs billion)**

	Jan.	Feb.	Mar.	Apr.	May	Jun.	Jul.	Aug.	Sep.	Oct.	Nov.	Dec.
1990:												
Enterprises	...	...	3.9	4.3	4.8	6.0	6.1	7.6	8.7	11.2	12.7	18.0
Households	2.1	2.3	2.8	1.8	2.0	3.7	3.9	4.2	3.2	7.1	6.5	10.2
1991:												
Enterprises	15.0	15.5	14.1	21.7	21.2	21.1	21.5	21.6	22.8	21.8	19.5	19.8
Households	11.3	12.6	14.0	15.4	16.7	18.2	19.2	21.1	22.3	23.2	24.4	26.6
1992:												
Enterprises	20.0	19.4	21.9	21.9	26.6	26.0	26.1					
Households	29.8	31.2	35.1	36.3	37.6	39.8	42.3					

Source: The Czechoslovak State Bank.
Note: End-of-month data.

there has also been a steady increase in the savings in foreign currencies. These figures, reported in billions of koruny in table 3.11, reflect not only the savings patterns but also the relative fluctuations of the major Western currencies over time.

As can be seen in table 3.2 above, a major response of enterprises to the restrictive monetary and fiscal policies has been an increasing reliance on inter-enterprise debt (credit). There are two data series that permit one to assess the extent of this phenomenon in Czechoslovakia. The first one—frozen bank payments due to insufficient balances in the bank accounts of debtor enter-prises—captures the extent of insolvency of firms as reflected in this one mea-sure. The series shows a major and continuous rise through the first quarter of 1991 in both republics, exceeding 10 percent of total bank credit to all enter-prises from the third quarter of 1990 on. The series reportedly registered a significant decline in the Czech Republic in the second quarter of 1991, the period when the banks decided to discontinue the collection of these data.[13]

The second data series refers to unpaid obligations of enterprises as shown in enterprise accounts. This series has been collected continuously since 1990, and it has the advantage that it also contains direct interenterprise debt that is not channeled through banks. The series depicts a major rise in interenterprise debt from Kčs 45 billion at the end of 1990 to Kčs 145 billion at the end of 1991. Hence, while the interenterprise debt was equal to 8.4 percent of the total bank credit to enterprises at the end of 1990, by the end of 1991 it had jumped to over 28 percent. This is a significant rise, one that potentially repre-sents an enormous problem for the government and the banks. It also in large

13. The decision to discontinue the collection of the data was related to the disintegration of the traditional monobank system and the reported difficulty in tracking frozen payments across the growing number of commercial banks.

part explains why virtually no state enterprises have gone bankrupt in the presence of the seemingly very restrictive macroeconomic policies and great external shocks. The government has been aware of the problem, and in the fall of 1991 it allocated Kčs 50 billion from its (future) privatization income to the banks for the purpose of increasing their capitalization and partially (selectively) reducing the bank debt of promising enterprises. The data on interenterprise debt show a major decline in the first half of 1992 to Kčs 123.7 billion. This is welcome news for the government, but the accuracy of this series for recent months needs to be checked.

As far as foreign trade is concerned, Czechoslovakia carried out a major structural transformation. After registering a significant trade deficit in 1990, Czechoslovakia appears to have achieved a surplus in 1991 (table 3.5 above). Other official data also indicate that trade with the (former) socialist economies accounted for more than 60 percent of the total trade in 1989 but that this share dropped to about 50 percent in 1990 and 40 percent in 1991. Trade in nonconvertible currency basically disappeared in 1991, and Germany replaced the Soviet Union as Czechoslovakia's main trading partner, accounting for almost one-quarter of Czechoslovakia's foreign trade.

A major controversy surrounds the question of whether trade contracted or expanded during the transition. Official estimates suggest that the physical volume of exports declined 30 percent and imports 31 percent in the first six months of 1991 and that a slight rebound in exports occurred thereafter. A relevant source of data in this context is the OECD. The OECD data, presented in tables 3.6 and 3.7 above, suggest that Czechoslovak exports to OECD countries have grown strongly and continuously between 1989 and the first quarter of 1992. These data also indicate that Czechoslovak imports from OECD countries grew until the first quarter of 1991, declined by about 10 percent in the second and third quarters of 1991, and rebounded strongly in the fourth quarter. The OECD data hence paint a much more optimistic picture of trade expansion than the official Czechoslovak data. Since the official Czechoslovak data are based on incomplete customs statistics, it appears that the OECD data may provide a better reflection of trade performance with the advanced countries.

3.3.1 Privatization

Privatization is the cornerstone of the transformation program, and arguably the success of the transition hinges on the ability of the government to transform the inefficient state-owned enterprises into efficient private ones. The privatization of small- and medium-sized enterprises and other economic units has been relatively successful. While perhaps proceeding more slowly than originally forecast, in 1991 the Czechoslovak government sold over 15,000 units, and by the third quarter of 1992 the figure was close to 30,000. An even more important means of privatizing small- and medium-sized properties has been the restitution of property to previous (pre-1948) owners or their heirs.

By mid-1992, over 120,000 units were restored through a process that also included housing, thus creating a precondition for the future establishment of a real estate market. The proceeds from the small-scale privatization have amounted to about Kčs 15 billion (about $500 million) in 1991. In comparison, the amount of foreign investment for 1991 was about $600 million.

The process of privatizing approximately 6,000 large firms is divided into two waves. The first wave covers 2,930 firms (2,210 of them in the Czech Republic), and it has been taking place since the spring of 1992. The firms being privatized are selected from among a number of competing projects proposed to the Czech and Slovak ministries of privatization as well as the federal Ministry of Finance. The projects can be prepared by any domestic or foreign individual or group, who can propose to follow any one or a combination of the permissible privatization methods, ranging from direct sale to an individual or a private domestic or foreign firm to distribution of virtually all shares to citizens at large through a system of vouchers.

In the first wave, 1,491 of the 2,930 firms have allocated part of their shares for the voucher privatization scheme, which consists of the following procedure. Each adult Czechoslovak citizen who is a permanent resident of Czechoslovakia is entitled to purchase a voucher book with 1,000 investment "points" for Kčs 1,000 (somewhat less than one-third of the average monthly wage). Some 8.56 million adults (i.e., most of the eligible individuals) have purchased these voucher books, and, during the first wave of privatization, they have used the points to bid for those shares of the 1,491 companies that have been allocated for voucher distribution. The voucher-book holders have voluntarily placed 72 percent of their points in the hands of forty-three privately formed investment privatization funds (IPFs), which bid for enterprise shares on behalf of the individual investors. As a result, 28 percent of the points are being invested directly by individuals.

The process of converting points into shares within the wave consists of rounds in which the bidders (individuals and IPFs) know the administratively set price of a share (in terms of points) of each enterprise and submit their written bids accordingly. In each round, shares are exchanged for points in those cases where the supply of shares exceeds the demand by individuals and IPFs, with the remaining shares being offered in the following round at a lower price. In those cases where demand exceeds supply by less than 25 percent and there is a "sufficient" demand for shares by the IPFs, the shares are first distributed to the bidding individuals, and the remainder are then rationed proportionately to the bidding IPFs. *Sufficient* demand of IPFs means that no IPF should receive less than 80 percent of its demand. In cases where demand exceeds supply by more than 25 percent or where the IPFs would have to be rationed by more than 20 percent of their bid, points are returned, no transaction takes place, and the price of shares is raised by the government for the next round.

As of November 1992, the process has gone through four rounds.[14] It was very successful in that a majority of points had already been exchanged for shares after the second round and an overwhelming majority of individuals and IPFs participated in each round. At the end of the fourth round, only 8 percent of points remained unallocated. Similarly, most shares slated for voucher privatization were thus placed. The problem with the scheme is that it generates few complete transactions and tends not to converge. Thus, in the first three rounds, less than 10 percent of all the firms participating in the first wave of the voucher privatization sold all their shares. Similarly, the price adjustments carried out by the authorities have sometimes been excessive, with the result that most firms have been switching between excess supply and demand between rounds. At present, the government expects to terminate the bidding process by force in round 5 before the end of 1992.

The Czechoslovak government launched the voucher privatization process in the expectation that a large number of state enterprises would rapidly improve their economic performance and stop relying on government subsidies. A major process of this kind of course also entails risks, and, as of November 1992, the Czech and Slovak governments were holding different views of the outcome. The Czech government sees the voucher privatization process as a major success and intends to use vouchers for privatizing most of the remaining large firms (including energy, mines, the mail system, and telecommunications) in the second wave in 1993. In contrast, the Slovak government sees the entire voucher scheme as slow and less efficient. As a result, it plans to rely more on traditional privatization means (e.g., direct sales, auctions, sealed bids, and employee stock ownership plans) in the second wave. With the partition of Czechoslovakia into the separate Czech and Slovak republics on 1 January 1993, one will hence observe two different privatization schemes being carried out in 1993.

Let us briefly discuss two potential problems that may appear in the future in connection with the Czechoslovak voucher scheme. The first potential problem is the lack of regulation of the IPFs. The IPFs have formed and until recently operated in a virtually unregulated environment. The precondition for starting a fund was the deposit of Kčs 100,000 (about $3,300), a proof of Kčs 1 million (about $33,000) in net worth somewhere in the world, and a signed declaration of behavior in conformity with a law regulating IPFs that would be drafted and passed in the future. The conditions were trivial, and a large number of IPFs quickly emerged, some being affiliated with reputable organizations (e.g., banks) and others representing fly-by-night organizations. IPFs immediately started competing for voucher books, and, at the start of January 1992, a number of IPFs formally offered to pay fixed multiples of the Kčs

14. For a detailed assessment of the first wave of voucher privatization, see Svejnar and Singer (1992).

1,000 purchase value of the voucher books. In particular, each of these IPFs promised to pay its clients in one year a guaranteed sum (usually Kčs 10,000–15,000) for the shares held for them by the IPF.

These offers were important because they stimulated most Czechoslovaks to buy voucher books. Within a matter of weeks, the number of individuals holding voucher books increased from 1.5 to 8.5 million. The mass purchase of voucher books increased the effective demand for shares, and, with the number of firms tentatively slated for privatization approximately given, it greatly reduced the value of each voucher book. The promise of the attractive payout by some IPFs after one year also spurred a large number of individuals to place their vouchers with these IPFs and created a significant danger of a run on the unregulated funds in one year's time. In the meantime, the funds realized that the value of each voucher book is considerably less than was expected with 1.5 million registrants, and some withdrew from the game. A law regulating the IPFs was eventually passed in 1992, but it does not require that funds promising fixed payouts be obliged to deposit these amounts ex ante with the government. The danger of a run on the funds, a rapid fall in share prices, and some funds becoming insolvent hence remains a possibility. This aspect of IPF operations may become regulated.

A related problem is the fact that the privatization ministries reacted to the growing number of voucher holders by attempting to increase the proportion of shares slated for voucher privatization in individual privatization projects. While motivated by the desire to increase the supply of shares for voucher privatization, the important side effect of this increased importance of voucher holders relative to other owners was a greater dispersion of future ownership among many firms. The problem of dispersed ownership and inadequate corporate governance, inherent in the voucher privatization method, was thus potentially exacerbated.

It is difficult to assess the seriousness of these potential problems arising in the context of the Czechoslovak privatization process. Yet it is important to realize that a process of this magnitude can hardly be designed without flaws. There is no doubt that, apart from the special case of East Germany, Czechoslovakia has embarked on the most ambitious project of large-scale privatization in Central and Eastern Europe.

3.4 Evaluation

By applying restrictive macroeconomic policies, the Czechoslovak government succeeded in rapidly extinguishing the inflationary pressures brought about by the sudden liberalization of about 85 percent of all prices on 1 January 1991. Containing the price explosion within a period of three to six months and maintaining price inflation at around 10 percent a year thereafter while gradually liberalizing the remaining prices has been an impressive accomplishment—one unparalleled elsewhere in Central and Eastern Europe. The economy has also adjusted remarkably in that the private sector has been developing rapidly in response to the removal of administrative restrictions, price liberalization, and provision of bank credit and exports have picked up after an initial period of major decline.

On the negative side, one observes an economy that has plunged into a more severe and prolonged recession than was officially expected. The recession has to a significant extent been caused by external shocks associated with the disintegration of the CMEA and the associated unfavorable shift in the terms of trade. Part of it is spurious and due to systematic errors in data collection, especially the underreporting of private activities.

In undertaking tough measures, the government greatly benefited from the willingness of the population to undergo a painful transition. Unlike the other transitional economies, Czechoslovakia has experienced virtually no strikes and social unrest. Part of the tolerance can be attributed to cultural values; however, a part is due to the government's resolve to move quickly and demonstrate results in such visible areas as privatization.

The ability to maintain social peace is of course only one measure of success. The imminent partitioning of Czechoslovakia into independent Czech and Slovak republics reflects not only cultural and social differences between the two nations but also the different views that the two governments have on how to proceed with economic policy. The Czech government intends to pursue relatively restrictive monetary and fiscal policies and complete the privatization process with the aid of the voucher system. The Slovak government seems to prefer a more expansive macroeconomic policy and to place priority on more traditional methods of privatization. The impressive aspect of the partitioning is the peaceful nature of the process and the concerned effort of the two governments to maintain to the greatest possible extent the existing economic links through a customs union and free mobility of all resources (including labor) and commodities.

A major problem facing both republics in 1993 and thereafter is the restructuring of the large state or newly privatized enterprises. These firms have to a large extent avoided the effect of the restrictive policies by relying to an increasing extent on interenterprise debt (credit). To some extent, the rise of interenterprise credits is to be expected in a newly established market economy. Yet the debt has risen too fast, and, despite the restrictive macroeconomic policies, not enough enterprises have been forced to close down so far. The impressive stabilization exercise has thus been accompanied by only limited enterprise restructuring. The expected remedy for this problem is large-scale privatization, the first wave of which is to be concluded at the end of 1992.

One of the most important questions is whether the large-scale transfer of ownership will result in rapid restructuring and improved efficiency of a great number of enterprises. Yet there was hardly any real alternative to the voucher system of privatization. Without it, new investment would hardly come in. And new investment is indispensable for medium- and long-run growth. Given the generally outdated technology, falling investment, and limited, although growing, extent of foreign investment ($600 million in 1991 and about $1 billion in 1992), the ability of the Czech and Slovak economies to expand and remain competitive as wages rise depends crucially on technological innovation and substantial productivity improvements.

References

Begg, David. 1991. Economic reform in Czechoslovakia: Should we believe in Santa Klaus? *Economic Policy,* no. 13:243–86.
Dyba, Karel. 1989. Czechoslovakia, 1970–1990: Growth, structural adjustment, and openness of the economy. *Europaische Rundschau* 3:49.
Gelb, Alan, and Cheryl W. Gray. 1991. The transformation of economies in Central and Eastern Europe. Policy Research Series, no. 17. Washington, D.C.: World Bank.
Sargent, Thomas J. 1986. *Rational expectations and inflation.* New York: Harper & Row.
Svejnar, Jan. 1989. A framework for the economic transformation of Czechoslovakia. *PlanEcon Report* 52 (29 December): 1–18.
Svejnar, Jan, and Miroslav Singer. 1992. The Czechoslovak voucher privatization: An assessment of results. University of Pittsburgh, Department of Economics, October. Typescript.
Yotopoulos, Pan, and Jeffrey Nugent. 1976. *Economic development.* New York: McGraw-Hill.

Comment   David Begg

As one would expect, Karel Dyba and Jan Svejnar have given us a balanced and informative account of developments within what, for the moment at least, remains the Czech and Slovak Federal Republic (CSFR). I agree with most of their analyses and judgments, and I welcome their effort to provide us with as up-to-date data as possible. In what follows, I focus on the areas in which my emphasis would have been different, and I try to indicate where I think the authors still leave questions unanswered.

I begin with bank credit and the related issue of the explosion of interenterprise debts. To my mind, the authors give too little attention to the first, too much to the second. It is hard to imagine a well-functioning market economy without a reasonably stable and well-run banking system. If credit contracts are not enforced, budget constraints do not bite, and prices do not allocate resources. Yet, in most of Central and Eastern Europe, this is precisely what is happening. State-owned enterprises (SOEs) began the transition to the market with bank debts from the past, an arbitrary endowment conveying little information about managerial efficiency or prospective profits under the new regime. The response of banks, still state owned, has been to allow most SOEs to ignore scheduled payments and to capitalize arrears. In itself, this may not be undesirable, precisely because the original debt endowments had little economic significance. Unfortunately, however, waiving scheduled payments and capitalization of arrears is quickly extended from original loans to new loans used to finance operating deficits of SOEs.

This latter channel has several very unhelpful effects. First, for a given monetary target, too much credit is automatically preempted by incumbent SOEs. Not only does this impede the allocation of credit to new private businesses—which in table 3.2 would have been larger but for this effect—but it also inhibits restructuring of the enterprise sector. Second, until budget constraints harden and bankruptcies are enforced, corporate governance will remain weak. Third, as the authors observe, the banking sector, worried about the soundness of its loan book, is likely to respond by pressing for wider spreads between lending and deposit interest rates. The authorities in the CSFR have allowed this to occur (although to a lesser extent than in some neighboring countries). But such financial repression is an inefficient method of recapitalizing banks, a lesson of the earlier experience in Latin America.

In such circumstances, the social return to swift recapitalization of banks (which in turn facilitates early privatization of banks and greater competition in this sector) is extremely high. Begg and Portes (1992) discuss how this should be undertaken and explode some common myths. For example, it is often alleged that the public finances, already strained, will not withstand the additional burden of bailing out banks by writing off SOE debts. Yet, properly measured, the public finances bore the cost at the instant that past loans to SOEs became nonperforming. Marking to market merely recognizes that reality. The CSFR has led the way in Central and Eastern Europe in making a (small) start on recapitalizing the banks. The larger amount still required *will* add to the budget deficit. One useful role that external lender-monitors such as the International Monetary Fund can play is to confirm that this better bookkeeping does not violate previous conditionality agreements, whose targets for the budget deficit should be correspondingly adjusted.

In contrast, although, like the authors, I have also lamented the explosion of interenterprise debt in the CSFR and elsewhere (Begg 1991), I now take the view that this problem is greatly exaggerated. First, as the authors are aware, most statistics are gross before any attempt to clear what A owes B, B owes C, and C owes A. Second, one should bear in mind that, in mature Western economies, such as the United States or the United Kingdom, the magnitude of interenterprise debts at any point in time is about the same as the outstanding stock of bank credit to companies. Table 3.2 indicates that, as elsewhere in Central and Eastern Europe, interenterprise debts are rising sharply but from a tiny base: even now, they remain much smaller in relation to bank credit than in the United States or the United Kingdom. Third, interenterprise credits are, to an important extent, the *symptom* of the failures in the bank credit market described above. Suppliers would press more readily for payment if they knew that, otherwise, their cash flow would suffer and could not automatically be replenished via further bank loans.

These remarks aside, I share the authors' judgments about the evolution of the CSFR economy, although in places I wished that their analysis had gone further. The degree of wage moderation during 1991 was spectacular, and I find it hard to assess the success, or, more accurately, the prospects for continuing success, of the stabilization policy without at least an implicit judgment as to the reasons why wages remained so low. Is social cohesion greater than in neighboring countries such as Poland, or was the threat of unemployment the principal explanation? The answer matters since it may prove hard to sustain social cohesion, whereas the threat of rising unemployment is likely to be present for many years to come. Since the authors offer us neither an analysis of the past nor even a guesstimate about the future, we are left intrigued but unsatisfied by their discussion of the labor market.

More generally, if the trailblazing Polish experience is anything to go by, there is at least the possibility that Dyba and Svejnar have taken their snapshot at the very time peculiarly favorable to reform: just before a wage explosion and just before the public finances get seriously out of control through inability to collect taxes, a shrinking tax base, and mounting pressures for public expenditure. Of course, these may not happen in the CSFR, and I am sure that we all hope that they will not. The authors mention some disquieting signals in passing, but I would have liked them to tackle this issue head on.

References

Begg, D. 1991. Economic reform in Czechoslovakia: Should we believe in Santa Klaus? *Economic Policy,* no. 13:243–86.
Begg, D. K. H., and R. D. Portes 1992. Enterprise debt and economic transformation: Financial restructuring of the state sector in Central and Eastern Europe. Discussion Paper no. 695. London: Center for Economic Policy Research.

Discussion Summary

Josef Zieleniec said that the government is not doing enough to encourage the formation of new start-up firms in the private sector. He noted that new private firms are disadvantaged because they cannot provide collateral when they apply for loans. As a result of this problem, and the general problem of undercapitalization in the banking sector, the banks have been unwilling to extend credit to the new firms.

Jan Winiecki warned that Czechoslovakia's current account surplus would not last. He noted that many of the East European economies have experienced short-lived trade surpluses just after reforms were implemented. At the time of price liberalization, firms held large stocks of inputs and finished goods. After these inputs are used up and the goods are sold, the trade balance deteriorates. This pattern of sales also generates temporarily high accounting profits and associated tax payments.

Kemal Derviş suggested that it may possible for the Czechoslovakian investment privatization funds (IPFs) to provide 1,000 percent returns. He emphasized that these returns are not related to the marginal product of capital. Instead, these returns reflect the peculiar features of Czechoslovakia's voucher scheme. Derviş noted that it is difficult to guess the ultimate market value of the privatized firms. In East Germany, the realized sale value of public assets has been zero or negative. However, public assets in Czechoslovakia might be more valuable because the profitability of East German firms was wiped out by the German exchange rate and wage policy. Derviş said that Czechoslovakia has one of the most competitive exchange rates in the region.

Michael Bruno questioned whether the large spread between deposit and lending rates is linked to tight monetary policy. He said that it is possible that the spread reflects weak balance sheets in the banking sector, notably a large proportion of bad loans. If this is the problem, a monetary expansion will not help. Rather, the banks need to be recapitalized. Bruno also warned that the current account will eventually deteriorate. Because Czechoslovakia is a relatively open economy, a rebound in output will produce a big increase in imports. Finally, Bruno speculated that the sharp rise in Slovakia's unemployment rate is related to the fact that the Slovaks were relatively more vulnerable to the CMEA (Council for Mutual Economic Assistance) shock than the Czechs.

Dani Rodrik criticized the accuracy of the official Czechoslovak trade statistics. He said that OECD data indicate that trade volume increased during the first quarter of 1991, contradicting the Czechoslovak data. Rodrik suggested that the rise in Czechoslovakia's reported trade volume levels during the second half of 1991 might be a reflection of an improvement in bookkeeping techniques. Rodrik also discussed the macroeconomic effect of the CMEA shock. He estimated that two-fifths of the 19 percent output decline in Czechoslovakia can be attributed to the CMEA collapse.

Jeffrey Sachs also questioned the reliability of some of the statistical data in the paper. Sachs was particularly critical of the consumption estimates in the Czechoslovak national accounts. In his work with Andrew Berg, Sachs found that Polish household consumption data did not support the consumption numbers in the Polish GNP accounts. Berg and Sachs discovered that the Polish national accounts focused overwhelmingly on the official sector, missing all consumption coming from the private sector, including the booming retail sector. With this in mind, Sachs questioned the accuracy of the reported 30 percent decline in Czechoslovak real personal consumption. In addition to these observations, Sachs suggested that the authors devote more analysis to the distinctions between Bohemia and Slovakia. Finally, he suggested that the authors should report on the development of new private-sector firms instead of focusing on the process of privatization of state-owned firms.

Karel Dyba made several comments. First, he agreed with Rodrik that the CMEA shock by itself could not account for the decline in output. Dyba said that, if Finland is used as a benchmark, then the CMEA shock explains half the Czechoslovak output decline. Second, he criticized the hypothesis that the banks were facing severe financial problems. He said that the banks tend to exaggerate their problems. Third, Dyba discussed the particular problems of Slovakia, notably that Slovakia has been more oriented toward the Soviet market and that Slovaks have less "economic education" than their Czech counterparts. Finally, he emphasized the need to push forward with reforms quickly. He said that Czechoslovaks have to move ahead and master problems as they arise. He concluded that inaction is much worse than action with possible mistakes.

4   Hungary—Partial Successes and Remaining Challenges: The Emergence of a "Gradualist" Success Story?

Kemal Derviş and Timothy Condon

To both the observant visitor and the analyst comparing indicators of economic performance and welfare, Hungary appears to have at least some degree of success in a region where the tremendous difficulties of systemic transition have in many cases taken on crisis proportions. Table 4.1 summarizes some indicators of the economic situation at the end of 1991 that demonstrate the point in comparison with other East European countries, leaving aside the Yugoslav republics.

Official statistical estimates can, of course, be quite misleading these days in Eastern Europe. For example, the average 1991 exchange rates, which are used to compute the U.S. dollar value of GDP, may not be close to their long-run equilibrium values. Czechoslovakia in particular has an extremely competitive exchange rate, although it is difficult to project how much real appreciation is likely and warranted over the next few years. The real size of the emerging, still informal private sector is also hard to estimate, and, in some countries, the contraction of output and real income is not as catastrophic as the statistics seem to indicate. More inclusive measures of economic activity, however, would make Hungary look even better. There are now data suggesting that it is in Hungary that the small-scale private sector has grown most rapidly. Initial findings of a World Bank–sponsored research project looking at the development of private manufacturing firms in Poland, Hungary, and Czechoslovakia reveal that Hungarian firms have shown dynamic growth. A sample of 120 Hungarian manufacturing firms surveyed in September 1991 found that production and employment were growing rapidly and that over half the firms

The opinions expressed in this paper are those of the authors and do not necessarily reflect the views of the World Bank.

The authors wish to thank Gérard Bélanger, Michael Bruno, András Horvai, Álmos Kovács, and Ernest Stern for comments on an earlier draft and Olivier Blanchard for helpful suggestions on revising the conference version of this paper.

Table 4.1   A Comparison of Macroeconomic Indicators in East European
                   Economies

	GDP per Capita, 1991 (U.S. dollars)	GDP Growth (%)		Unemployment Rate, Year-End 1991 (%)	Inflation, 1991 (%)[a]
		1990	1991		
Poland	1,800	−12	−8	12	76
CSFR	2,100	−3	−16	8	59[b]
Romania	740	−8	−14	4	220
Bulgaria	830	−12	−23	10	430
Albania	520	−10	−30	N.A.	80
Hungary	3,300	−4	−10	8	35

Source: World Bank staff estimates.

Note: CSFR = Czech and Slovak Federal Republic. N.A. = not available.

[a]Annual average change in the CPI.

[b]Reflects large once-and-for-all adjustments early in the year, with very low inflation in the second half of the year.

were exporting. Small-scale private-sector activity is also developing in Poland and Czechoslovakia, but in those countries it is still largely confined to services and trade. Informal observation confirms and reinforces the message, although the evidence can be only anecdotal. Serious problems remain, of course, particularly relating to fiscal balance and employment. However, Hungary appears to be getting some positive results in a part of the world that is facing the economic challenge of the century.

There is also little doubt that the path followed by the Hungarian systemic transformation has been very different from both the theory and the practice of the transition policies adopted by the other East European countries.[1] Not necessarily by grand design or as a result of some carefully planned social engineering of the type Vaclav Klaus (1991, 44) warns us against, but as a result of the particular political and historical circumstances prevailing, Hungary did not engage in any sudden shock therapy. There was no day zero of the reform with maxidevaluation, massive price and trade liberalization, and fixing of nominal anchors. Structural reforms in the enterprise and financial sectors have also proceeded gradually, although the "opening" to foreign private investment took place in 1988 and has been wholehearted. Table 4.2 summarizes some of the key events and policy actions characterizing the Hungarian systemic transformation, which most observers agree started in earnest in 1985. The table tries to capture some key quantitative aspects of this "gradualism" that, ex ante, would look so cautious and insufficient compared with many of the radical programs designed for other countries in recent years.

1. Economic reforms in Eastern Europe have been extensively described (see, e.g., Blanchard et al. 1991; Fischer and Gelb 1991; and Bruno, in this volume).

Table 4.2   Hungary: Indicators of Liberalization and Systemic Transformation

	1985	1987	1989	1990	1991
Private-sector share of GDP (%)	< 10	< 10	< 10	10–20	20–30
Share of imports liberalized (production weights) (%)	0	0	16	37	72
Maximum tariff in manufacturing (%)	50	50	50	50	50
Average tariff (simple average) (%)	18	16	16	16	13
CPI inflation (annual average) (%)	7	9	17	29	35
Real effective exchange rate index (1985 = 100)[a]	100	97	88	94	106
Share of consumer prices freed (%)	35	41	62	77	90
Share of subsidies in GDP (%)	15	16	13	9	7

Source: Data provided by the Hungarian authorities and World Bank staff estimates.

[a]Trade-weighted index using producer price indexes. An increase signifies an appreciation.

Again, it should be emphasized that the historical path described in table 4.2 was just that; it was *not* the implementation of a theoretical construct but the result of uneasy compromises between guardians of the old regime constantly loosing ground, "reform Communists" trying to improve the system and maintain control, more radical reformers trying to accelerate change, the Bretton Woods institutions trying to encourage moves toward freer markets, and, finally, since mid-1990, rather pragmatic center-right politicians seeking to accelerate the process of systemic transformation and integration with Europe while minimizing social hardship, with their political base more in the countryside and the small towns than with the intellectual elite in Budapest.[2]

In evaluating the Hungarian experience, it is, of course, important to remember that the reform process started very early with the adoption of the New Economic Mechanism in 1968 and was never fully reversed, as happened in post-1968 Czechoslovakia. Despite periods of recentralization, particularly in the mid-1970s, there is no doubt that Hungary has had much more time to develop practices and attitudes conducive to the functioning of markets than most other countries. While the journey toward private ownership, hard budget constraints, and free markets and prices started in earnest only in the mid-1980s, two decades of experiments with market socialism did prepare the ground.[3]

There is, however, more in the Hungarian "story" to think about than just the advantages of having started early. True, Hungary did not face the calamity of hyperinflation in the period that we are discussing and did not, therefore, have to administer stabilization shock therapy the way Poland *had* to in 1990

2. This difference between Hungary and Poland was recently emphasized by L. Balcerowicz in a luncheon address to the U.S.-Poland Action Commission, Chicago.

3. For an excellent description in English of the Hungarian reform process until the mid-1980s, see Kornai (1986). See also Balassa (1983) and Antal et al. (1987). Hare (1991), Boote and Somogyi (1991), and Erlich and Revesz (1991) describe the more recent reforms. Many good papers written by Hungarian economists are unfortunately not widely known outside Hungary.

and Russia has to today. There were, and are, however, real choices to be made regarding the speed of trade liberalization, the timing and form of fiscal reforms, exchange rate policy, and policies vis-à-vis the enterprise sector, including the tactics of privatization and the governance of enterprises remaining public. In these areas, Hungarian reforms followed a sequence and yielded certain results that we will describe in the paper.

The objective of this paper is *not* to take the years 1990 and 1991 and compare, using normative objectives, Hungarian performance with, say, Czechoslovak or Polish performance. Other authors in this volume and elsewhere attempt such a comparison. The recent phase of the Hungarian experience is, however, extremely interesting in itself, even if rooted in a particular historical and national setting, and even if it is not replicable by others at different times and is propelled by different political dynamics.

4.1 Balance of Payments and Debt: Success after Walking a Tightrope

By 1987, Hungary's total external debt had reached $20.5 billion, amounting to 75 percent of GDP and 312 percent of convertible-currency exports, putting Hungary into the group of the very highly indebted countries. Table 4.3 compares indicators of indebtedness for some of these countries, with Hungary appearing as one of the most difficult cases. Looking at the numbers in late 1987, many predicted that Hungary would go by the then familiar route of debt renegotiations, reschedulings, attempts at debt reduction, etc. Alone in this group, Hungary remained current and did not reschedule or ask for debt reduction. In 1991, an improvement can be perceived, at least in the ratios of debt and debt service to convertible-currency exports (which fell to 187 and 35 percent, respectively), and Hungary emerges in 1992 with a much strengthened balance of payments and good renewed access to international capital markets, a story worth telling, with some unusual features.

During 1987–90, with 1990 being the worst year, Hungary was walking a tightrope, always very close to a liquidity crisis, with the ratio of debt service to convertible-currency exports one of the highest in the world. Table 4.4, summarizing the evolution of Hungarian debt by type of creditor, shows how important the Bretton Woods institutions, with associated cofinancing from the Japanese Export-Import Bank, were in supporting Hungary's strategy of remaining current and avoiding rescheduling. In the four years from January 1987 to December 1991, the net exposure of private creditors was almost unchanged, while the net exposure of the Bretton Woods institutions, including cofinancing arranged with the Export-Import Bank of Japan, increased by $1.4 billion.[4] The International Monetary Fund (IMF) supported Hungary through two standby arrangements in 1988 and 1990 and a three-year extended arrange-

---

4. In special drawing rights (SDRs), private exposure declines, and the overall increase in debt is somewhat smaller.

Table 4.3   **Debt Indicators for Selected Highly Indebted Middle-Income Countries (%)**

	1985	1986	1987	1988	1989	1990
Argentina:						
Debt/GDP	77.4	66.6	72.6	62.6	107.2	58.1
Debt/exports of GS	493.2	593.3	695.4	517.0	537.9	405.6
Total debt service/exports of GS	58.9	76.2	74.3	44.5	36.2	34.1
Brazil:						
Debt/GDP	47.5	42.3	42.1	35.2	24.9	24.5
Debt/exports of GS	361.5	451.8	430.4	314.1	286.8	342.4
Total debt service/exports of GS	38.6	47.0	41.9	48.2	29.8	21.8
Hungary:						
Debt/GDP[a]	67.7	71.2	75.0	68.0	69.6	64.7
Debt/exports of GS[a]	284.6	328.3	312.2	285.7	257.6	269.0
Total debt service/exports of GS[a]	75.2	81.2	59.7	51.2	45.1	53.5
Mexico:[b]						
Debt/GDP	52.5	77.6	77.9	57.8	45.5	40.7
Debt/exports of GS	326.0	422.7	363.6	312.8	253.0	222.0
Total debt service/exports of GS	51.5	54.2	40.1	48.0	37.9	27.8
Philippines:[b]						
Debt/GDP	87.7	95.5	89.5	76.1	67.1	69.4
Debt/exports of GS	335.6	324.2	317.6	262.1	223.0	229.2
Total debt service/exports of GS	31.8	34.6	38.0	32.0	25.3	21.2
Poland:						
Debt/GDP[a]	47.0	49.6	66.7	61.2	52.3	77.7
Debt/exports of GS[a]	570.6	602.2	602.2	513.3	493.2	386.7
Total debt service/exports of GS[a]	35.0	29.8	29.1	21.5	17.7	7.5
Venezuela:						
Debt/GDP	57.0	56.7	72.2	57.9	74.6	69.0
Debt/exports of GS	335.6	324.2	317.6	262.1	223.0	229.2
Total debt service/exports of GS	25.0	45.3	37.8	43.8	24.5	20.9

Sources: World debt tables, 1991 World Bank database, and data provided by the Hungarian authorities.

Note: GS = goods and services.

[a]For Hungary and Poland, debt stock and service and export figures are in convertible currency only.

[b]Debt and debt service reduction agreements were concluded with Mexico and the Philippines in 1990.

ment in 1991, the latter for $1.5 billion. Cumulative World Bank support was even more substantial, with commitments of $1.8 billion, including three loans for balance-of-payments support for a total of $650 million.

In mid-1990, this substantial effort on the part of the Bretton Woods institutions was complemented by a three-year, $1 billion loan from the European Community (EC), linked to the performance criteria and policy commitments agreed on with the IMF and the World Bank. If the end result of this massive multilateral support had been merely a substitution of official for private debt, with no real breakthrough in underlying creditworthiness, one would be justi-

Table 4.4   **Composition and Evolution of Hungary's External Debt (U.S.$ millions)**

	1987	1988	1989	1990	1991[a]	Total Change, 1987–91
Total debt	20,530.9	20,184.8	20,751.0	21,505.9	22,812.1	2,281.2
World Bank and cofinancing	976.9	1,146.9	1,275.4	1,624.5	1,999.5	1,022.6
IMF	808.5	634.2	456.2	329.6	1,214.9	406.4
Bilateral and other multilateral	509.7	613.5	718.5	1,090.0	1,791.5	1,281.8
Commercial	17,289.2	17,207.7	17,940.2	18,271.8	17,652.2	363.0
Medium and long term	14,186.5	13,844.7	14,633.7	15,331.3	15,475.0	1,288.5
Short term	3,102.7	3,363.0	3,306.5	2,940.5	2,177.2	−928.5
Nonconvertible debt	946.6	582.5	360.7	235.0	154.0	−792.60

Source: Estimated data provided by the Hungarian authorities.
[a]Estimated.

fied in questioning the wisdom of the strategy supported by the Bretton Woods institutions. A convincing breakthrough did, however, come in 1991, notwithstanding the regional economic collapse affecting Eastern Europe and what was then the Soviet Union.

The breakthrough has two components, which are seen in the evolution of the balance of payments (table 4.5). Comparing the 1991 results with the 1987–89 averages, with 1990 viewed as a transition year, and treating 50 percent of private transfers as a form of portfolio investment,[5] there is a $1 billion improvement in the adjusted current account and a $1.9 billion turnaround in the extended capital account. These figures taken together represent $2.9 billion, about 10 percent of GDP.

The current account improvement was due to rapid export growth to Western markets, the improvement in the balance on the travel account, and the compression of import demand. Exports to convertible currency markets increased by 25 percent in volume in 1990–91. Several factors have contributed to the growth of exports. First, with the transformation in 1991 to world prices and convertible currencies as the basis for this trade, there was an 87 percent contraction in ruble exports in the first ten months of 1991 (table 4.6). The peculiar modalities of ruble exports, especially the operation of the prompt payment system that guaranteed payment in domestic currency as soon as documents were presented at the Central Bank that the goods had crossed the border, made ruble exports a main factor fueling the expansion of liquidity (with effects on the balance of payments in convertible currencies) in 1989. Policy anticipated the decline of ruble trade; in 1990, ruble export licenses were sharply curtailed

5. Private transfers in both 1990 and 1991 are in fact a mixture of misrecorded current account receipts (services, tourism, and small-scale exports) and portfolio investments, which increased rapidly following the liberalization of restrictions on resident holdings of foreign exchange deposits in 1989 and the passage of the Foreign Investment Act in 1988.

Table 4.5   Convertible-Currency Balance of Payments, Capital Flows, and Reserves (U.S.$ millions)

	1987	1988	1989	1990	1991
Adjusted current account	−981	−919	−1,563	−236	−163
Capital account	332	978	1,525	−177	2,883
Direct foreign investmentª	...	...	180	701	1,925
Net medium- and long-term borrowing	1,194	716	1,357	91	1,668
Net short-term capital	−778	288	−44	−893	−617
Net capital, not elsewhere included	−84	−26	32	−76	−83
Changes in net reservesᵇ	547	−174	−88	413	−2,720
Memorandum items					
Total international reserves	2,159.2	1,976.3	1,725.3	1,166.5	4,017.3
Reserves in months of importsᶜ	4.1	3.5	2.6	2.0	3.7
Net private transfers	102	115	126	727	866
Noninterest current account (% of GDP)	1.3	1.8	.6	5.5	5.9

Source: Data provided by the Hungarian authorities.
ªIncluding 50 percent of net private transfers in 1990 and 1991.
ᵇA minus sign indicates an increase.
ᶜImports of goods and services.

to halt the further buildup of accumulated ruble trade surpluses, giving producers a year to try to find new markets.

The end of the ruble trade, apart from filling some orders left over from 1990, created an "export or perish" mentality among Hungarian exporters. This led to an aggregate trade diversion from the Council for Mutual Economic Assistance (CMEA) toward the EC, as shown in table 4.7. Disaggregated Hungarian customs data show an even more pronounced decline in the former CMEA share (excluding the former East Germany). In industrial branches with a significant CMEA export orientation—mining and machinery—as well as in the agriculture sector, a large export shift to European markets occurred in 1991. However, the decline was not across the board, and nonruble exports to the countries of the former CMEA were equivalent to $1.2 billion in the first 10 months of 1991.

The expansion of new, export-oriented businesses also contributed to the strong export performance. This, in turn, was made possible by the liberalization of private-sector activity with the passage of the Company Act in 1988 and the near total liberalization of foreign trading rights in 1991. The growth in the number of economic organizations—from 10,000 at the beginning of 1989 to over 50,000 in 1991—and in the number of private entrepreneurs—from 225,000 to 340,000 during the same period—has swelled the number of individuals and organizations with foreign trading rights tenfold to 30,000 in 1991. Small exporters (those with fewer than fifty employees) accounted for 69 percent of the increase in the value of nonruble exports in 1991 as their

Table 4.6   **Growth of Exports (index with 1990 January–October = 100)**

	Ruble	Nonruble	Total	Share	Ruble	Nonruble	Total
Mining:							
CMEA	1	479	480	44	...	2,400	49
Europe[a] and others	0	614	614	56	...	212	206
Total	1	1,093	1,094	100	...	353	85
Electric energy:							
CMEA	...	...	...	...	...	...	...
Europe[a] and others	...	...	...	...	...	...	...
Total	...	...	...	...	...	...	...
Metallurgy:							
CMEA	169	11,034	11,203	20	5	606	223
Europe[a] and others	3	44,230	44,233	80	1	89	88
Total	172	55,264	55,436	100	5	107	100
Machinery:							
CMEA	9,947	28,329	38,276	25	18	1,180	65
Europe[a] and others	143	113,874	114,017	75	1	166	142
Total	10,090	142,203	152,293	100	15	201	110
Building materials:							
CMEA	111	754	865	6	30	271	152
Europe[a] and others	22	12,442	12,464	94	36	180	179
Total	133	13,196	13,329	100	31	186	177
Chemical industry:							
CMEA	610	12,930	13,540	14	4	648	78
Europe[a] and others	66	84,360	84,426	86	6	143	140
Total	676	97,290	97,966	100	4	159	126
Light industry:							
CMEA	1,867	4,055	5,922	7	22	757	67
Europe[a] and others	107	77,911	78,018	93	10	178	174
Total	1,974	81,966	83,940	100	21	185	156
Miscellaneous industry:							
CMEA	49	124	173	6	9	1,378	31
Europe[a] and others	16	2,612	2,628	94	19	87	86
Total	65	2,736	2,801	100	10	91	77
Food processing:							
CMEA	1,720	24,825	26,545	25	13	265	117
Europe[a] and others	...	81,752	81,752	75	...	144	141
Total	1,720	10,657	108,297	100	12	161	134
Construction:							
CMEA	10	836	846	61	3	154	156
Europe[a] and others	...	545	545	39	...	12	12
Total	10	1,381	1,391	100	2	28	26
Agriculture:							
CMEA	656	7,288	7,944	19	10	114	61
Europe[a] and others	11	33,268	33,279	81	1	175	172
Total	667	40,556	41,223	100	10	160	127
Forestry:							
CMEA	4	4	0	...	...	...	...
Europe[a] and others	...	5,373	5,373	100	...	153	153
Total	...	5,377	5,377	100	...	153	153

Table 4.6 (continued)

	Ruble	Nonruble	Total	Share	Ruble	Nonruble	Total
Total:							
CMEA	15,140	90,658	105,798	19	14	390	82
Europe[a] and others	386	456,981	457,367	81	2	144	138
Total	15,526	547,639	563,165	100	13	162	122

Source: Data provided by the Hungarian authorities.
[a]Including East Germany.

Table 4.7 **Direction of Exports**

	Shares of Total Exports (%)					Annual Change (%)[a]			
	1987	1988	1989	1990	1991[b]	1988	1989	1990	1991[c]
EC	19.8	22.5	24.7	33.5	40.3	18.1	6.7	34.5	42.0
CMEA	50.2	44.8	40.8	30.2	25.7	−7.1	−11.4	−26.7	−4.8
Other	30.0	37.7	34.5	36.3	34.0	13.4	2.7	4.5	12.7
Total	100.0	100.0	100.0	100.0	100.0	4.1	−2.7	−.8	16.0

Source: IMF direction of trade statistics.
[a]In U.S. dollar value.
[b]Through the third quarter.
[c]1991:3 compared with 1990:3.

share of total exports rose from only 3 percent of total nonruble exports in 1990 to 29 percent in 1991 (table 4.8). The growth of small exporters was particularly strong in the large exporting sectors, machinery, chemical industry, light industry, and food processing. Although enterprises with export proceeds of less than $0.5 million accounted for only 4 percent of total exports, incremental exports from this size group accounted for over 9 percent of the growth in total export proceeds between 1989 and 1991 (table 4.9).

Better international trading conditions should also be mentioned in discussing Hungary's export success. The trade protocol signed with the EC in 1988 lowered quantitative import restrictions on Hungarian products entering the EC, with some exceptions, including textiles and iron and steel products. And, in 1991, Hungary became an associate member of the EC, with full membership expected within five to ten years. Hungary's "Europe Agreement" provides for the establishment of a free trade area in industrial goods, enhanced access for agricultural products, and eventual free trade in services. Other countries, notably the United States, have concluded trade agreements and extended GSP (general system of preferences) and MFN (most-favored nation) status to Hungary.

While there has been a significant improvement in the current account, it

Table 4.8   **Structure and Growth of Exports, 1991 (millions of current forints)**

	Jan. 1991–Oct. 1991			Exports of Jan. 1990–Oct. 1990		
	Ruble	Nonruble	Total	Ruble	Nonruble	Total
Industry						
All enterprises	14,831	500,325	515,156	13	164	123
Large enterprises	7,932	364,167	372,099	7	23	92
Small enterprises	6,899	136,158	143,057	227	1,404	1,124
(% of total)	(47)	(27)	(28)			
Mining:						
All enterprises	1	1,093	1,094	. . .	353	85
Large enterprises	1	867	868	. . .	283	68
Small enterprises	. . .	226	226	. . .	5,650	5,650
(% of total)	(. . .)	(21)	(21)			
Electric energy:						
All enterprises	. . .	. . .	. . .	. . .	. . .	. . .
Large enterprises	. . .	. . .	. . .	. . .	. . .	. . .
Small enterprises	. . .	. . .	. . .	. . .	. . .	. . .
(% of total)	(. . .)	(. . .)	(. . .)			
Metallurgy:						
All enterprises	172	55,264	55,436	5	107	100
Large enterprises	138	43,994	44,132	4	88	82
Small enterprises	34	11,270	11,304	486	736	735
(% of total)	(20)	(20)	(20)			
Machinery:						
All enterprises	10,090	142,203	152,293	15	201	110
Large enterprises	5,022	107,365	112,387	8	158	84
Small enterprises	5,068	34,838	39,906	230	1,211	785
(% of total)	(50)	(24)	(26)			
Building materials:						
All enterprises	133	13,196	13,329	31	186	177
Large enterprises	66	8,345	8,411	16	127	120
Small enterprises	67	4,851	4,918	319	942	918
(% of total)	(50)	(37)	(37)			
Chemical industry:						
All enterprises	676	97,290	97,966	4	159	126
Large enterprises	474	68,734	69,208	3	114	90
Small enterprises	202	28,556	28,758	119	4,373	3,494
(% of total)	(30)	(29)	(29)			
Light industry:						
All enterprises	1,974	81,966	83,940	21	185	156
Large enterprises	878	55,017	55,895	9	130	109
Small enterprises	1,096	26,949	28,045	241	1,529	1,265
(% of total)	(56)	(33)	(33)			
Miscellaneous industry:						
All enterprises	65	2,736	2,801	10	91	77
Large enterprises	8	1,343	1,351	2	52	43
Small enterprises	57	1,393	1,450	124	345	322
(% of total)	(88)	(51)	(52)			
Food processing:						
All enterprises	1,720	106,577	108,297	12	161	134
Large enterprises	1,344	78,502	79,846	9	122	102

Table 4.8   (continued)

	Jan. 1991–Oct. 1991			Exports of Jan. 1990–Oct. 1990		
	Ruble	Nonruble	Total	Ruble	Nonruble	Total
Small enterprises	376	28,075	28,451	281	1,440	1,366
(% of total)	(22)	(26)	(26)			
Construction						
All enterprises	10	1,381	1,391	2	28	26
Large enterprises	1	133	134	...	3	3
Small enterprises	9	1,248	1,257	35	150	147
(% of total)	(90)	(90)	(90)			
Agriculture						
All enterprises	667	40,556	41,223	10	160	127
Large enterprises	461	21,088	21,549	7	96	76
Small enterprises	206	19,468	19,674	49	565	501
(% of total)	(31)	(48)	(48)			
Forestry						
All enterprises	...	5,388	5,388	...	153	153
Large enterprises	...	3,509	3,509	...	106	106
Small enterprises	...	1,879	1,879	...	943	943
(% of total)	(...)	(35)	(35)			
Total						
All enterprises	15,508	547,639	563,147	13	162	122
Large enterprises	8,394	388,897	397,291	7	120	90
Small enterprises	7,114	158,742	165,856	200	1,120	936
(% of total)	(46)	(29)	(29)			

Source: Szabo (1992).

Note: Small enterprises are those with fewer than 50 employees.

Table 4.9   **Distribution of Exporters by Value of Exports**

	1989		1991[a]		
Value of Exports	No. of Enterprises	Total Exports[b]	No. of Enterprises	Total Exports[b]	Contribution to Growth (%)
> $10 million	136	4,421,848	158	5,267,552	45.1
$5–$10 million	97	698,530	144	994,177	15.8
$4–$5 million	33	142,155	53	237,225	5.1
$3–$4 million	72	248,214	83	289,023	2.2
$2–$3 million	91	217,940	148	357,314	7.4
$1–$2 million	170	244,271	278	389,835	7.8
$.5–$1 million	205	148,476	409	287,279	7.4
< $.5 million	1,899	172,425	5,108	346,943	9.3
Total	2,703	6,293,859	6,381	8,169,348	100.0

Source: Kopint-Datorg, Budapest.

[a]Estimate.

[b]Thousands of U.S. dollars.

should be emphasized that the situation remains fragile. Import demand could respond vigorously to an overall upturn in economic activity, and only continued good export performance would allow the consolidation of the recent improvement in the current account in a context of sustained economic growth. In this context, we recommend a supportive and competitive exchange rate policy. Significant real appreciation would endanger continued good export performance and the resumption of growth.

The elements of the breakthrough emerging from the extended capital account were the increase in private transfers and foreign direct investment, both of which were negligible prior to 1990. Administrative restrictions on resident holdings of foreign exchange were eliminated in late 1989, and the resulting surge in private transfers in 1990 was partly fueled by residents shifting foreign exchange holdings from "under the mattress" into the banking system. However, the activity of the expanding private sector—especially the establishment of joint ventures with foreign partners—helped sustain private transfers in 1991. Even more important than these transfers, the growth of direct foreign investment in 1991 is one of the most encouraging signs of Hungary's breakthrough, and there are many reasons for it, including Hungary's hospitable business climate, privatization policies, and the longer history of greater openness toward the West (for a discussion of privatization, see sec. 4.3 below).

Overall, the strength of private transfers and the remarkable growth of foreign direct investment represent a vote of confidence in the sustainability of the turnaround in Hungary's external position and prospects in the internal market. The breakthrough in the balance of payments significantly strengthened the international reserve position and helped Hungary regain solid access to international commercial capital markets, a vindication of Hungary's debt strategy in the eyes of the rest of the world. It has also disarmed domestic criticism of the National Bank of Hungary (NBH) for its policy of punctual repayment of the debt. Such criticism started during the election campaign in 1990 and became sharp when the Polish debt write-off was announced in early 1991. The growth of convertible-currency exports mitigated the decline in real GDP, thus helping preserve social peace and political stability. Things were bad in 1991, but looking at their former CMEA partners, Hungarians could take comfort from the observation that they could have been much worse.

4.2   Industrial Performance and Internal Adjustment

As noted by Rodrik (in vol. 2), almost all Hungary's real GDP decline in 1991 could be attributed to the CMEA shock. Industrial production fell by 21.5 percent in 1991, with some of the largest declines in the sectors most dependent on the former CMEA market (table 4.10).

Enterprise adjustment has resulted in job losses and growing unemployment but also real wage declines. Employment in the industry sector declined by 13.4 percent in 1991. Total unemployment increased from 1 percent at the end

Table 4.10   **Industrial Production, 1991 (annual % change)**

	Industrial Production[a]	Employment	Average Gross Productivity	Real Wages[b]	Ruble Exports/ Value Added (%)[c] 1989	1990
Mining	−10.9	−15.9	6.0	10.5	3.5	2.1
Electricity	−8.0	−5.5	−2.9	3.9	1.1	.2
Metallurgy	−32.7	−18.4	−17.5	.2	17.9	12.8
Machinery	−34.9	−16.8	−21.7	−2.3	75.6	56.4
Building materials	−33.0	−12.8	−23.2	−8.1	6.3	3.1
Chemical industry	−18.5	−7.3	−12.1	−5.0	30.4	25.3
Light industry	−24.9	−13.5	−7.3	.4	26.8	15.3
Food industry	−9.7	−7.1	−2.8	4.6	36.6	25.5
Total industry	−21.5	−13.4	−9.4	−1.4	37.2	25.0

Source: Central Statistical Office, *Monthly Statistical Bulletin,* Ministry of Finance, and World Bank staff calculations.

[a]Covering enterprises with more than 50 employees. Including enterprises with fewer than 50 employees would result in a decline of 19.1 percent for "total industry" in 1991.

[b]Product wages.

[c]Current forints.

of 1990 to 8 percent in December 1991. Bankruptcies are also on the rise. Liquidation of 1,268 firms was begun in 1991, and the process was completed for 480 enterprises. The corresponding figures for 1990 were 630 and 206. Industry-wide real product wages declined by 1.4 percent (table 4.10), which stands in marked contrast with the Polish experience in 1991 (see Berg and Blanchard, in this volume). In 1990 and 1991, wage policy relied on a tax-based incomes policy, which taxed excessive wage increases at the enterprise profit rate (40 percent). However, such policies have failed in Hungary in the past, and we suspect that it was probably the tightening of enterprise cash constraints resulting from the CMEA shock that forced enterprises to limit wage increases.

Evidence of tighter cash constraints abounds. First, gross and net enterprise profits and retained earnings, all expressed in relation to GDP, deteriorated in 1991 following even larger declines in 1990 (table 4.11). Second, as in Poland and Czechoslovakia, enterprises have used financial maneuvers to cushion the real shock, such as the buildup of interenterprise credit and payment arrears, including to the government. The NBH reports that, in general, companies are far in arrears with their contributions to the Social Security Fund (see NBH 1991, 44), and, according to unofficial reports, interenterprise credit adjusted for expost producer price inflation, after falling slightly in 1990, increased by about 20 percent in 1991, although this increase was far less than that recorded in 1988 when financial policies began to be tightened in response to the nar-

Table 4.11   Enterprise Profits, 1986–91

	1986	1987	1988	1989	1990	1991[a]
Gross domestic product	1,088.8	1,226.4	1,409.5	1,730.4	2,080.9	2,494.0
Less gross labor income	515.4	561.2	676.4	792.2	974.1	1,268.0
Less indirect taxes[b]	364.8	415.7	524.0	649.9	759.5	819.1
Plus indirect subsidies[c]	219.2	238.8	217.2	201.5	178.2	142.3
Gross operating surplus of enterprises	427.8	488.2	426.3	489.8	525.5	549.2
Less other deductions[d]	53.1	50.1	46.4	36.5	66.7	70.4
Gross enterprise profits before taxes	374.6	438.1	379.9	453.3	458.8	478.8
Less depreciation[e]	103.9	111.0	118.4	151.7	160.8	178.3
Net enterprise profits before taxes	270.8	327.1	261.5	301.6	298.0	300.5
Less direct taxes on income[f]	221.3	267.1	155.5	186.6	192.0	186.0
Plus subsidies received after profit	7.4	8.2	2.9	3.0	2.4	1.1
Less profit sharing	15.3	16.3	21.4	22.4	32.7	27.5
Net retained earnings	41.6	51.9	87.5	95.6	75.7	88.1
Memorandum items						
Gross labor income	47.3	45.8	48.0	45.8	46.8	50.8
Indirect taxes	33.5	33.9	37.2	37.6	36.5	32.8
Indirect subsidies	20.1	19.5	15.4	11.6	8.6	5.7
Gross enterprise profits	34.4	35.7	27.0	26.2	22.0	19.2
Direct taxes	20.3	21.8	11.0	10.8	9.2	7.5
Net retained earnings	3.8	4.2	6.2	5.5	3.6	3.5

Sources: Central Statistical Office, *Statistical Yearbook;* and Ministry of Finance.

Note: Figures are given in terms of billions of forints, except for "memorandum items," which are given in terms of percentage of GDP.

[a]Estimate.

[b]Taxes on production and on factors of production.

[c]Consumer price subsidies paid by the state budget, local governments, and social security (for medicines).

[d]Including allocations to welfare and cultural funds and to voluntary funds for import price equalization.

[e]Excludes depreciation of state flats.

[f]Includes tax on profits, wage tax, tax on fixed assets, and investment tax.

rowing of Hungary's access to international commercial credit markets (fig. 4.1).

The NBH's blacklist of companies in a "permanent state of imminent insolvency" for which it refuses to discount bills of exchange grew from 281 enterprises at the end of 1990 to 716 by the end of 1991. It is also noteworthy that a market in financial information about enterprises has developed, presumably because this information can reduce transaction costs in privatization. A magazine that publishes the names of delinquent debtors and the amounts owed was

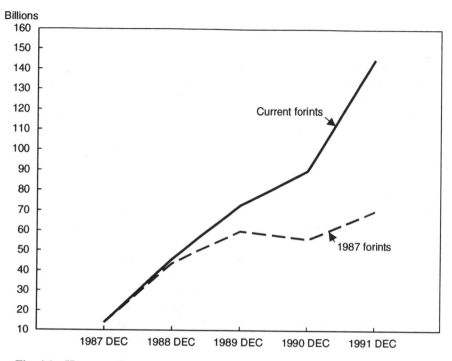

Fig. 4.1   Hungary: Interenterprise credit
Source: National Bank of Hungary.

started in 1991. An enterprise specializing in factoring has also been established.

The government has come under increasing pressure to take measures that help "manage" the transition. Some hard-hit branches of industry have been granted temporary one-year import protection. Tariffs were raised on imported televisions and cement, while a quota was introduced on steel imported from Czechoslovakia, Romania, and the former Soviet Union. Recognizing that the commercial banks will feel the crisis in the industrial sector, but unable to determine what the size of the problem has been, the government has undertaken to guarantee 50 percent (Ft 10 billion, or about $130 million) of the debts inherited by the banks when the two-tier banking system was created in 1987. Bad loans made after that will be provisioned out of taxable income over a three-year period. The NBH also opened a special credit facility in 1990 to provide additional short-term refinancing credit for commercial banks to help break closed circles of interenterprise arrears. Additional temporary credit facilities and selective government credit guarantees are under consideration to mitigate the adverse financial spillover effects on healthy enterprises of widespread enterprise liquidations.

4.3 Hungarian Enterprises and Systemic Reforms

Beyond the short-term measures designed to cope with the effects of the external shock lies the need to realize the systemic transformation of the Hungarian enterprise sector. It is success in the systemic transformation that can lead to an acceleration of growth essentially through much better total factor productivity performance. Just as the widening performance gap in total factor productivity between market and command economies brought about the demise of the latter, the expectation of a dramatic increase in productivity growth through systemic transformation justifies the painful transition and adjustment costs throughout Eastern Europe.

Despite a great deal of preparatory debate and the abolition of the pure command economy in the late 1960s, it was only in the mid-1980s that Hungary really became an economy regulated by "horizontal" rather than "vertical" relations between the majority of economic units. Until then, the fact that enterprise managers were appointed "from above" by bureaucratic superiors meant that vertical command relations still constituted the essence of the system, despite market contacts and relations between enterprises. In 1985, with new regulations instituting the election of top managers by the employees of most firms rather than their appointment by sectoral ministries, Hungary really made the qualitative leap to what one can call market socialism with self-managed enterprises.

On the positive side, market relations were strengthened by the 1985 reforms, and managers really did have a chance to determine most outcomes and rewards through market-oriented decisions rather than relations with ministerial bureaucracies. On the other hand, the incentive structure was not that of a Western, capitalist market economy. The 1985 reform led to a virtual elimination of the government's role as "owner," without establishing an alternative to exercise this role, thus eliminating any long-term interest in the preservation and appreciation of enterprise capital. This led to pressures for excessive wage increases, allowed various forms of decapitalization to become commonplace, and created insuperable obstacles for the kind of serious restructuring essential for long-term productivity growth and competitiveness.

Starting in 1988 and 1989, with the final disintegration of the Communist power structure in the entire region, Hungary launched the next phase of systemic transformation, this time with the building of a private ownership economy as the explicit objective.

Characteristically, the Hungarian approach has been pragmatic, ready to adjust policies rapidly to the lessons of experience and unwilling to embark on sudden and large-scale social engineering. The door to privatization was opened with the passage of the 1988 Company Act, which liberalized private business activities and permitted the establishment of company forms familiar in market economies. There ensued a quite vigorous process of partial self-privatization, with enterprises transferring some of their productive assets into newly formed joint ventures, leaving the less productive assets and most debt in the untransformed parent enterprises, which remained effectively without owners. This process did transform some state-owned assets into corporate form with mixed ownership, rapidly enlarging the private sector. It was open to much manipulation and easy profit, however, for those who happened to control enterprises at that particular time, many close to the old Communist power structure. It also compounded the problems of the old parent enterprises.

In the face of substantial public dissatisfaction with the distributional implications, the process of privatization was greatly centralized in 1990 with new laws attempting to protect state-owned assets and with the creation of the State Property Agency (SPA), which was given the responsibility of overseeing all privatization and which was also to take an active role promoting and organizing direct sales and public offerings to foreign and domestic investors. Hungary did not consider adopting free distribution or voucher schemes to accelerate the process of the transformation, but the central bank did put in place a subsidized credit line for domestic investors wanting to buy state assets, a measure presented to the Bretton Woods institutions, particularly allergic to subsidized credit schemes, as a limited form of voucher distribution à la Poland and Czechoslovakia. To attract foreign capital, foreign investors were offered favorable tax treatment, including five-year tax holidays for some investments.[6]

This second phase of the privatization process produced mixed results. The excesses associated with unsupervised spontaneous privatization diminished, but, despite laudable efforts, the SPA, facing tight budget, skill, and experience constraints, was unable to deliver rapid privatization through its own proactive programs. Inside and outside Hungary, the perception was that privatization had been slowed down by too much central control.

In the second half of 1991, the overall strategy was again readjusted, in consultation with the Bretton Woods institutions and as part of a program supported by a special adjustment loan from the World Bank. The attitude toward self-privatization and management buyouts, but with SPA oversight, again became more permissive, with the emphasis shifting from concerns about valuation and distribution to the need for accelerating the emergence of new entrepreneurial groups with ownership stakes. Privatization of smaller establishments in the service and retail sector was also accelerated. Finally, for medium-scale enterprises employing fewer than 300 workers, it was decided that privatization could be effected by advisers chosen from a preapproved list,

6. When the Foreign Investment Act was passed in 1988, 20 percent profit tax relief was available to any foreign investor contributing at least 20 percent of the capital to the joint venture or Ft 5 million (about $65,000). That incentive was eliminated in 1991. For capital contributions of at least Ft 25 million or 30 percent of the entity's total capital, the tax relief increased to 60 percent for the first five years and 40 percent thereafter. Finally, for activities of "special importance," 100 percent relief was granted for the first five years and 60 percent thereafter. In 1991, the law was changed to limit the maximum period for profit tax relief to ten years. There is also a reinvestment incentive available to foreign partners in joint ventures. These preferences will be phased out as of 1994.

subject only to selective expost review by the SPA, thus effectively decentralizing the process and freeing scarce SPA management and staff resources for efforts directed at the largest enterprises.

Another major component of the strategic readjustment that took place in 1991 has been the recognition of the need for clear ownership and governance rules for that part of the enterprise sector that would remain under state ownership in the near future. Toward that end, virtually all state enterprises will now be corporatized—reestablished under Hungary's general Company Act—and provided with the same governing organs—boards of directors—as privately owned companies. This will remove the present different legal treatment of public and private enterprises and also facilitate the subsequent privatization of many of these enterprises. Most of the corporatized state enterprises will be made available for privatization, without any differentiation between foreign and local investors. For these "to-be-privatized" enterprises, ownership will be vested with the State Property Agency. A limited number of enterprises will be kept under majority state control for the time being, with ownership to be exercised by the State Asset Management Corporation (SAMC), a separate organization reporting directly to the Council of Ministers, which is expected to play a different role than the State Property Agency for its much larger group of more transient state-owned corporations. All the economies in Eastern Europe face a difficult trade-off. On the one hand, they want to move as rapidly as possible to true private ownership of productive assets. The conviction of almost all decision makers, political parties, even labor leaders, is that private ownership is desirable and that "simulating" it by asking publicly owned entities to behave "as if" they were private does not really work. What is often not well understood by some critics of the privatization process in the transition economies is that the obstacle is *not* political—certainly not ideological—but *practical.* The experience of the last two years shows that even giveaway schemes, explicitly designed to achieve maximum speed for privatization, take time. One simply cannot establish effective forms of private ownership by decree overnight.

The trade-off arises because leaving large segments of these economies in a state of limbo, with managers and workers uncertain about their future and nobody responsible for the value of the productive assets, inflicts great damage. But building strong public ownership institutions, renationalizing, would also be a dangerous strategy. Why create bureaucracies only to dismantle them later when privatization takes place? Each country faces this trade-off, and there is no perfect solution. The approach that Hungary has chosen, after considerable debate and mixed initial results in the enterprise sector, is to have one agency, the SPA, with the overriding objective of rapidly privatizing 80 percent of existing assets. Its role as public owner will be minimal. The new State Asset Management Company, on the other hand, will have to fulfill a longer-term public ownership role for a list of assets that are judged difficult to privatize in the short run or for which privatization is not desired.

The advantage of this approach is that it dramatically reduces uncertainty for the enterprise and for potential investors. It also gives a clear role to both the privatization agency and the asset management corporation. It does not ask the same organization to behave as a long-term owner *and* to divest itself as quickly as possible with little regard for anything else.

It is too early to evaluate the results of these arrangements. Further readjustments in policies and regulations may well become desirable. A particular concern may well emerge if the share of foreign buyers remains as high as it has been so far. The tax holidays offered to foreign investors have been extremely and perhaps unnecessarily generous. The announcement that they will be phased out from 1994 onward is, in our view, appropriate. The overall results achieved by the end of 1991 by Hungary's privatization and private-sector development policies are, however, quite substantial. More than half of all foreign investment flows to Eastern Europe (excluding Germany) in the year 1991 went to Hungary, and close to 30 percent of "formal" GDP is in the private sector, compared with 10 percent in 1989. Efforts at counting the informal, unrecorded sector raise this percentage much higher. The next two years should also bring improved governance to enterprises remaining in the state sector, with full corporatization for almost all entities. If the reforms succeed, the systemic transformation of the enterprise sector from a mostly self-managed form of market socialism to a mixed market economy with a dominant private sector and also a large number of commercialized, wholly or majority state-owned corporations could be completed before 1995. A sensible design is there. The challenge is implementation.

4.4   Downsizing the Government and Restructuring the Budget

Commercialization and privatization in the enterprise sector is only one component of the overall systemic transformation in which Hungary and the other East European economies are engaged. In all these economies, the share of national income intermediated by the government remains very large. Under the old regime, low incomes and wages went hand in hand with an appropriation of profits by the state, which then transferred back parts of the "economic surplus" in the form of free or nearly free goods and services available to the entire population. Parallel to the systemic transformation in the enterprise sector is the need for systematic transformation of the role of government in society: an efficiently functioning market economy requires a "smaller" government. Public revenues should come from transparent and nondistorting taxes rather than from an appropriation of the profit wherever it appears, and public expenditures should be targeted to the provision of public goods—national defense, environmental cleanup, some public infrastructure—and to the support of the poorest and most vulnerable groups in society, instead of the entire population. Note that a *small* government does not at all mean an ineffective or unimportant government. On the contrary, as the scope of government activ-

Table 4.12   General Government Size (in % of market price GDP)

	Hungary	Turkey[a]	Chile	Korea[a]	Portugal	Germany	Austria	EC Avg.[b]
Revenues	61.3	18.4	30.3	18.2	37.1	45.7	46.9	43.6
Expenditures	63.8	22.8	30.6	16.7	45.3	46.6	44.5	46.5

Source: IMF, Government Finance Statistics Yearbook, 1990. Data are for 1989, except for Chile (1988).
[a]Central government only. For comparison, Hungary's central government revenues and expenditures were 54 percent of GDP and 56 percent, respectively.
[b]GDP-weighted average.

ities and responsibilities decreases, it should become more effective in fulfilling the important role of providing public goods and supporting the vulnerable. The reorientation of government activity is, of course, closely linked to fiscal policy and macroeconomic stability. Without this reorientation, it will not be possible to achieve a sustainable fiscal balance because the universal entitlements covering the entire population are inherently incompatible with the revenues that a modern tax system applied to a market economy can be expected to yield.

Table 4.12 compares the share of government revenues and expenditures in GDP in a selected group of advanced European countries, middle-income developing countries, and Hungary. The statistics are not strictly comparable. In Hungary, for example, there is considerable double-counting in the accounts because of failure to consolidate fully transactions between different levels of government. Nonetheless, the broad picture is clear: the share of government in Hungary is not only way above that in countries at similar levels of per capita GDP but even higher than in the advanced West European welfare states.

It is with the comparisons in table 4.12 as background and the conviction that an overall downsizing of the government is desirable that we look at fiscal policy over the next few years. First, what is likely to be the "financeable" deficit that is consistent with the macroeconomic targets for growth, inflation, seigniorage, and external debt?[7] What, then, is a reasonable medium-term projection for tax and other revenues as a share of GDP? The sum of the financeable deficit and of total revenues gives us the envelop for aggregate government expenditures. As we shall see, such calculations lead us to conclude that there is a need for quite drastic public expenditure reforms, as total expenditures must adjust to lower tax revenues and a reduced financeable deficit.

Stabilizing the rate of inflation at a considerably lower rate and limiting the growth of external debt impose limits on the sources available to the government for financing its deficits. For example, reducing inflation from 35 percent

7. Van Wijnbergen (1989) is an early example of the approach of using the concept of the financeable fiscal deficit to analyze consistent fiscal policy.

in 1991 to 10 percent in 1993 will result in a loss of seigniorage revenues equivalent to an estimated 2 percent of GDP, which must be factored into the calculation of the fiscal adjustment needed over the next few years.[8] The extent of the required fiscal adjustment is measured by the financeable deficit, which is the deficit consistent with the macroeconomic targets for growth, inflation, and external borrowing. The financeable deficit compatible with West European inflation levels and private-sector-led GDP growth in the 4–5 percent range is projected to average 1.5 percent of GDP in 1994–95 (table 4.13).

The analysis is explicitly medium term in nature. In any particular year, it may be possible to finance a larger deficit without triggering much higher inflation or reducing productive investment. This is, in fact, what appears to be in store for 1992–93. Medium-term consistency on an increasingly private investment-driven growth path does not, however, leave much room for government deficits in excess of 1.5 percent of GDP. It would be a disaster for Hungary if the fact that large deficits could be financed in 1992 and 1993 led to a belief that noninflationary recovery is possible without a major fiscal effort.

To translate the required adjustment into policy measures, the financeable deficit is split into its two components, central bank profits and the general government balance, net of receipts from and payments to the central bank. Real central bank profits or losses in Hungary can be approximated by the outflow of interest payments on net foreign liabilities, with real receipts on domestic credits approximately at zero.[9] Real NBH losses are projected to average 3.6 percent of GDP in 1994–95 compared with 4.6 percent in 1991, reflecting the real decrease in gross external debt and the real increase in international reserves. The consolidated state budget is the fiscal aggregate generally used in discussions of fiscal policy in Hungary, and the prescriptions for adjustment in the general government balance will, therefore, be directly translated into adjustments in the consolidated state budget.[10] Thus, the consolidated state budget primary deficit, which was an estimated 1.8 percent of GDP in 1991 (the overall deficit of 4.1 percent of GDP less estimated net transfers to NBH of 2.3 percent), should move to a surplus of about 2.0 percent in 1994–95, an adjustment equivalent to almost 4.0 percent of GDP.

At the same time, the authorities intend to reduce the tax burden on Hungarian businesses and citizens, and tax reforms planned for 1992–93 are expected

---

8. The detailed calculations are from World Bank (1991, chap. 2).

9. Real central bank losses arise from the burden of servicing the external debt (67 percent of GDP in 1991) and providing credit at below-market interest rates to the non-government sector. During 1990, the effective nominal interest rate on National Bank of Hungary refinancing credits to the nongovernment sector was 22 percent, while market rates ranged from 27 to 32 percent.

10. The balance of the general government is determined mainly by the balance of the consolidated state budget. It comprises the state budget, the Social Insurance Fund, the Housing Fund, and, beginning in 1991, the Employment and Solidarity funds. Levels of government excluded from the consolidated state budget—budgetary chapters and their institutes, extrabudgetary funds (except for those mentioned above), and local governments—have not contributed significantly to the general government deficit in the past.

Table 4.13   The Fiscal Adjustment Required for Macroeconomic Consistency
                    (share of GDP)

	1991	Average, 1994–95
1. Financeable deficit/surplus (compatible with noninflationary rapid recovery)[a]	−6.4[b]	−1.5
Minus		
2. Real interest payments on net foreign liabilities[c]	−4.6	−3.6
Equals		
3. Consolidated state budget primary deficit/surplus[a]	−1.8	2.1
4. Required fiscal adjustment[d]		3.9

Source: World Bank staff estimates.

[a]Minus sign indicates deficit.

[b]Actual deficit, given by the consolidated state budget primary deficit net of transfers from the central bank plus estimated losses of the National Bank of Hungary, proxied by interest payments on net foreign liabilities, expressed in relation to GDP; not derived from sustainable medium-term sources of financing.

[c]Minus sign indicates outflow.

[d]Plus sign indicates equal improvement.

to result in a reduction of revenues equivalent to about 2 percent of GDP, mainly from reforms to increase the neutrality of the enterprise profits tax. Thus, macroeconomic consistency and the revenue implications of planned tax reforms require an adjustment in expenditures equivalent to about 6 percent of GDP in the medium term. Expenditure reductions of this magnitude could be achieved by reducing subsidies, reforming income maintenance programs, and privatizing commercial activities currently performed by the public sector. The savings that could be achieved by these measures would likely be partially offset by higher outlays on priority spending programs. The expected changes in the size and composition of government spending underlying the more ambitious reform program are summarized in table 4.14. Estimating the effect of reforms on the overall size of government expenditures is complicated by the fact that the implications of a proper consolidation of accounts cannot be estimated with great accuracy. However, on the basis of a preliminary analysis of the government accounts, which identifies the functional categories where double-counting is likely to be a problem, and evidence from other countries about what level of expenditure in these categories would be reasonable, a reduction in general government outlays from 58 percent of GDP in 1991 to 40–42 percent by 1995 could be targeted. This would be closer to the average size of government in the EC. The expenditure reforms would also make the composition of government spending resemble the EC average more closely by shifting expenditures from broad income maintenance programs toward human and physical infrastructure, where a social consensus exists on the need for significant improvements (see Ministry of Finance 1991, 23–25).

Table 4.14   **Effect of Budget Reform Proposals (% of market price GDP)**

	1991	1995	Change
Expenditure adjustment, net			−7 to −8
Reductions, gross			−12
Subsidies	7	1	−6
Housing purchase	3	0	−3
Consumer price subsidies	1.5	.4	−1.1
Transport	.7	.4	−.3
Producer subsidies	2.5	.6	−1.9
Production	1.5	0	−1.5
Export	1.0	.6	−.4
Pensions	10.3	8	−2
Family allowances	3.2	2	−1
Sick pay	1.2	.2	−1
Maternity and child care benefits	.9	.8	−.1
Privatization of profit-oriented CBIs	1.7	0	−1.7
Increases, gross			4 to 5
Employment and solidarity funds	1.4	2.4	1
Other social assistance (cash)	1.0	2.1	1
Education	4.5	5 to 6	1
Health care	5.5	6 to 7	1
Transport infrastructure	.6	1.3	.5 to 1
Effect of 1992–93 tax reforms			−2
Revenues of profit-oriented CBIs	1.5	0	−1.5
Net budgetary savings	3 to 4		
Adjustment required for macroeconomic consistency			3.5 to 4
Memorandum items			
General government expenditures, 1991			58
Account consolidation[a]			9 to 11
Adjusted expenditures, 1989			47 to 49
Net expenditure reduction			7 to 8
General government expenditures after reform			39 to 42

Source: Ministry of Finance and World Bank staff estimates.

Note: CBI = central budgetary institution.

[a]Inadequate accounting of CBI expenditures results in large unclassified expenditure and possibly large double-counting of expenditure and revenue. Recorded general public services expenditures and other economic affairs and services expenditures are thought to be the most affected accounts. In the EC, the average shares of GDP devoted to expenditures on general public services and other economic affairs and services are 2.5 percent (ranging from 1.0 percent in Spain to 4.1 percent in Ireland) and 1.1 percent (ranging from 1.0 percent in Ireland to 1.6 percent in the Netherlands), respectively. In Hungary, they are 7.5 percent and 7.4 percent, respectively. Proper account consolidation should result in a decline in recorded expenditures (and revenues) in these categories to the levels found in the EC, which would imply a reduction equivalent to about 9–11 percent of GDP in the size of measured general government expenditures.

4.4.1   Subsidy Reductions

Subsidies have come down from 13 percent in 1989 to 7 percent in 1991. Continued progress in reducing subsidies should permit their elimination, except for urban public transport and, possibly, agricultural exports. The authorities intend to reduce subsidies to no more than 4 percent of GDP in 1993. Apart from those already mentioned, all other consumer subsidies, including those for housing purchases, production, and enterprise investments in the competitive sectors, could be eliminated. Provided that inflation can be significantly reduced as planned, it should be feasible to reduce subsidies to around 1 percent of GDP by 1995 (0.6 percent for export subsidies, 0.4 percent for passenger transport), which would imply a budgetary savings equivalent to 6 percent of GDP.

4.4.2   Reforming Income Maintenance Programs

Hungary's numerous, but in some cases poorly designed and administered, income maintenance programs are a legacy of the Communist system. The largest programs are the pension system (with expenditures equivalent to 10 percent of 1991 GDP), the health care system (5 percent), maternity and family benefits (a combined 4 percent), and unemployment and labor retraining benefits (1.4 percent—but, with unemployment expected to reach 13–15 percent in 1992–93, spending is expected to increase to about 2.5 percent of GDP). To address the shortcomings of the income maintenance programs and reduce their heavy burden on the budget requires a shift in their orientation. In the pension system, for example, reforms are needed to reduce benefits but also to protect benefit levels from inflationary erosion, which has been a problem, particularly for aged pensioners. In other areas, especially family allowances and maternity and child care benefits, a reorientation away from broad and untargeted support toward smaller programs where the benefits are more clearly tied to needy beneficiaries is called for. Finally, greater use of incentives for cost consciousness is needed; the reform of sick pay benefits to require employers rather than the government to pay for the first ten days of sick leave is an example. The potential savings from these measures are estimated at 4 percent of GDP.

In view of the difficult adjustment period facing Hungary, it is more likely that expenditures on income maintenance programs will rise sharply in the next two to three years before declining over the medium to longer term. The main factor underlying an increase in income maintenance expenditures is the expected increase in unemployment in the next two years as a consequence of the privatization of state enterprises and the need to restructure enterprises previously dependent on sales to the CMEA market. Higher than anticipated unemployment in 1991 caused expenditures on unemployment compensation to exceed the projected level. To cope with higher unemployment, the maximum period for which an individual can receive unemployment compensation has been reduced from two years to eighteen months, the maximum benefit has also been reduced, and the contribution for unemployment insurance has been increased from 2 percent of wages in 1991 to 7 percent in 1992, which should be sufficient to handle a year-end 1992 unemployment rate of 10 percent and a peak of 12 percent in 1993. Under such a scenario for unemployment, expenditures on job retraining and unemployment compensation could increase to the equivalent of nearly 4 percent of GDP in 1993 and then decline to 2–2.5 percent by 1995. If social assistance payments keep pace with the growth of unemployment compensation benefits, spending could also rise to over 3 percent of GDP in 1993 and decline to about 2 percent by 1995.

4.4.3   Privatization of Government Commercial Activities

The privatization of large numbers of government tasks, which has the potential to give a significant boost to the development of the private sector, has yet to begin in Hungary. Lack of progress in privatizing government function is partly due to lack of adequate budget information about the operations of the very complicated government structure. The government has little ability to monitor or control revenues and expenditures, and improved budgeting is a priority. The draft Act on Government Finances is designed to improve the reporting system at all levels of government and make it easier to monitor government expenditures.

Budgetary chapters (spending ministries) are responsible for two types of institutions, those formed initially in order to administer traditional public-sector responsibilities (e.g., education, health, social security, public administration, defense, police) and those formed to engage in quasi-commercial activities (e.g., water and road management). The former are described in the Hungarian system as "interested in the remainder" (surplus); the latter are "interested in the result" (profit).[11] Expenditures by commercially oriented institutions were the equivalent of 1.7 percent of GDP in 1990, revenues were 1.5 percent of GDP, the state budget transfer was 0.3 percent of GDP, and employment was 53,000, or 1 percent of the total labor force. These institutions should be privatized and government employment reduced by at least 50,000 workers.

Subsidy reductions, the reform of social welfare programs, and privatization of government operations could yield savings equivalent to approximately 12 percent of GDP by 1995, although higher spending on priority programs and the revenue effects of the 1992 tax reforms could reduce the net budgetary savings to 3–4 percent of GDP. This would accommodate the 3.5–4 percent of GDP adjustment required for macroeconomic consistency.

Expenditure management during the transition will be difficult because,

11. However, some of those from the first group have important commercial activities. For example, Hungarian television (known in Hungary as MTV) has significant advertising revenues.

while it will be easy to increase expenditures in high-priority areas, there is likely to be political opposition to the expenditure reductions. In part, this reflects the nature of many of Hungary's social welfare programs; nearly everyone is a beneficiary because targeting is almost nonexistent. The result, as confirmed by analysis undertaken in Hungary of the incidence of the social welfare programs,[12] is that middle- and upper-class households—wielders of political influence—are the largest beneficiaries of many income maintenance programs. Nevertheless, in order that budget reform be carried out in a fiscally prudent fashion, measures to reduce expenditures should be introduced prior to embarking on reforms that will raise expenditures. The government has targeted a reduction in subsidies equivalent to 3 percent of GDP in 1992–94. Additional reductions could be achieved in subsidies for post-1989 housing purchase loans, provided that inflation can be stabilized. If progress in the Uruguay Round of the GATT negotiations permits, a significant reduction in agricultural export subsidies could be made. The privatization of government activities, including the reduction in the government work force, should also be accelerated.

4.5 Conclusion

Hungary has been able to overcome the debt crisis of the late 1980s and the devastating shock of collapsing CMEA markets in 1991 without major macroeconomic instability and suffering a decline in output that has remained moderate when compared with the region as a whole. The turnaround in the balance of payments in 1991–92 has been impressive, with Hungary's performance in attracting direct foreign investment setting a new standard. Present fiscal difficulties should not lead one to forget these remarkable achievements, which were realized without foreign debt forgiveness. The country's systemic transformation is only half completed, however, and, for Hungary to emerge as a full success story, the transformation of the enterprise sector and the restructuring of the budget constitute the twin challenges requiring a huge effort in the immediate future. Provided that events unfold as in the programs and laws already adopted, after decades of debate, five years of serious reforms, and a detour through self-management, the new economic "system," close in essence to that of neighboring Austria, Italy, or France, could be in place in the near future. If the next round of reforms really takes hold, an unprecedented, deep transformation could be achieved with hardship and sacrifice, but without massive socioeconomic dislocation. Success seems within reach, provided perseverance, renewed courage on the fiscal front, and the ability to reach political compromise continue to accompany the cautious realism that has so far characterized Hungary's management of the systemic transition.

---

12. A team of Hungarian experts has analyzed the effect of taxes and social benefits in cash and kind on the distribution of income in Hungary (see Kupa and Fajth 1992).

References

Antal, L., L. Bokros, I. Csillag, L. Lengyel, and G. Matolcsy. 1987. Change and reform. *Acta Oeconomica* 38:3–4, 187–213.

Balassa, B. 1983. Reforming the New Economic Mechanism in Hungary. *Journal of Comparative Economics* 7, no. 3:253–76.

Blanchard, O., R. Dornbusch, P. Krugman, R. Layard, and L. Summers. 1991. *Reform in Eastern Europe.* Cambridge, Mass.: MIT Press.

Boote, A. R., and J. Somogyi. 1991. Economic reform in Hungary since 1968. Occasional Paper no. 83. Washington, D.C.: International Monetary Fund.

Erlich, E., and G. Revesz. 1991. Collapse and systemic change in Central-Eastern-Europe. Budapest: Hungarian Academy of Sciences.

Fischer, S., and A. Gelb. 1991. The process of socialist economic transformation. *Journal of Economic Perspectives* 5, no. 4:91–105.

Hare, P. G. 1991. "Hungary: In transition to a market economy. *Journal of Economic Perspectives* 5, no. 4:195–202.

Klaus, V. 1991. *Signals from the heart of Europe.* Frankfurt: Gablor-Gannex.

Kornai, J. 1986. The Hungarian reform process: Visions, hopes, and reality. *Journal of Economic Literature* 24, no. 4: 1687–1737.

Kupa, M., and G. Fajth. 1992. Hungary: Reform of social policy and expenditures. Report. Washington, D.C.: World Bank.

Ministry of Finance. 1991. *Governmental programme of conversion and development for the Hungarian economy.* Public Finance in Hungary, no. 82. Budapest.

National Bank of Hungary (NBH). 1991. *Quarterly Review* (March).

Szabo, L. 1992. Kulgazdasagunk uj adottsagai es tendenciai (Foreign trade: New trends). Budapest: Ministry of Finance and Institute for Economic Research and Information.

van Wijnbergen, S. 1989. External debt, inflation, and the public sector: Toward fiscal policy for sustainable growth. *World Bank Economic Review* 3, no. 3: 297–320.

World Bank. 1991. Hungary: Reform and decentralization of the public sector. Washington, D.C. Mimeo.

Comment   Kalman Mizsei

It is not easy to serve as a rapporteur to a paper with which one has such far-reaching and fundamental agreement as I have with that of Derviş and Condon. The authors' main message is that Hungary has a fair chance to become a *gradualist success story,* although obviously among some particular, historically established circumstances with all the limited lessons that this might have for the other transforming countries. I fully agree with this statement and also with the choice of the authors to pick it up as the main theme of the Hungarian story. They are also right when emphasizing that the recent policy style is *not* an outcome of any "grand design" or "implementation of a theoretical construct" but that it has emerged out of different considerations, interests, historical situations, etc.

Furthermore, I also think that the authors have rightly structured their paper around three crucial topics: foreign debt, privatization, and the public budget. I share their view that Hungarian debt management has been an incredible success so far, in spite of the fact that the story has obviously not yet ended. One might also add that the psychological implications of this strategy for society are also worth noticing: while the undoubtedly justified and right Polish debt strategy had the unpleasant side effect of "spoiling" the elites and teaching them that, whatever they do with the country, the West has an "inherent" duty to help them, in Hungary the public sense is that we have to help ourselves. This attitude in itself is an asset. (Again, I do not claim that the mentioned side effect would mean that the Poles should not have followed the applied debt strategy.)

The authors are somewhat too benign to the Hungarians when emphasizing the toughening of regulation on the ruble trade: during the first half of 1990, the policy was sufficiently tough, but this was not the case for the second half of the year, when a softer policy created a large trade surplus that was practically a form of implicit aid to the Soviet Union and that strained Hungary's monetary policy. Also, the authors are a bit too nice to the Hungarian policies when speaking about bankruptcy: especially the events of the first half of 1992 show that the institutional system of the country is still not ready to let the bankruptcy machinery function properly. Therefore, it will be necessary to readjust regulation soon; the courts are absolutely unable to cope with the filed cases, the chain of microeconomic financial crises is too long, etc. However, the other side of the coin is again that Hungary is the only country where this stop-and-go process has already achieved some significant progress. I also agree with the authors that, in order to support a revival of industrial growth, the policies of real appreciation of the currency cannot be maintained in the longer run.

It is very pleasant for me to be more critical than analysts of the Bretton Woods institutions on issues of Hungarian economic policy. In fact, I am more critical of the two remaining issues of the paper: privatization policy and public finance. First, for a minor correction, the authors overemphasize the stop-and-go nature of Hungarian spontaneous privatization. I completely agree with their general attitude toward decentralized privatization. (I can add that it is a small satisfaction for me personally to see that after almost three years the message about the necessity of decentralized privatization gets through in the Western analyses of East Central European economic transformation.) However, one should notice that, even right after the 1990 elections, the flow of "spontaneous" privatization cases has not stopped for a minute. We can speak only about a minor slowdown.

Where I really disagree with the authors is their endorsement of the formation of a "temporary" large holding company for firms that remain in state hands for a while. First, it would be good if only 20 percent of the state assets went to the new State Asset Management Corporation (SAMC). We do not have guarantees for that, and there are worrying signals that the share will be more. Certainly, there are a number of firms that will be incorporated into the "superholding" for which there is no good justification to remain state owned. I am also more worried than the authors that Hungary might repeat the Italian or Austrian case where this kind of solution quickly generates clientelist political structures. Then it will be extremely difficult to get rid of these assets even when the state can theoretically concentrate on the issue. So I appreciate the dilemma presented by the authors, but I would certainly not create those superstructures.

The authors argue that the establishment of the SAMC will divide clearly the role of State Property Agency ("divesting itself") and that of the long-term state owner. Again, this might provide the system with some additional certainty but at the costs of creating a large institution with a vested interest in maintaining state property in sectors like manufacturing where it obviously should not be the owner.

Nonetheless, I agree with the authors, who find the achievements of Hungarian privatization so far "quite substantial." In fact, this is the only privatization machinery in the post-Communist world that has been working steadily and with notable successes. The Czech-Slovak mixture might also become quite successful because of its pragmatic part (enterprise privatization plans) and if the voucher-scheme does not become a major failure.

Finally, on the budget, the authors' contribution both in this paper and in their World Bank analysis (World Bank 1991) to understanding the alternatives to the recent situation has been very substantial. I think that their reform proposal is basically realistic and politically feasible. Where I have some doubts is their subsidy reduction program: it would probably squeeze the rural sector so much that it might cause unbearable social costs because of the extremely distorted international markets in agricultural products. Therefore, the reduction in general government expenditure from 58 percent of GDP to somewhere around 40 percent in four years is also probably too ambitious. It would, in fact, be a real shock treatment, something the authors seem to prefer to avoid in general. It is also quite questionable whether the expectations of the authors on the level of savings on income maintenance programs could be realistic.

Unfortunately, however, the whole debate is rather theoretical because the government has shown already in 1992 that its direction of action is quite the opposite to what Derviş and Condon have prescribed in the paper. Revenues have fallen further, and no reforms have been started on the expenditure side. Therefore, the official budget deficit plan has become totally unrealistic. The recent revised plans almost double the deficit target to the range of 5 percent of GDP. This might be close to reality. The government lives with the illusion that, because high savings ratios make deficit financing possible, they do not really need to act until the next elections on the expenditure side; consequently, cosmetics will do.

However, because financial deepening is very modest in postsocialist Hungary, the crowding-out effect of the deficit is very strong. Interest rates cannot be cut along with the falling rate of inflation. Deficit financing, although quite possible, is also very costly because the public is, at the time being, cautious about buying government securities. So, the timetable outlined by the authors will certainly not be realized, and general government expenditures will be above 50 percent of GDP with an inflation rate much higher than the mentioned 10 percent in 1995. However, after the 1994 election, the new government will certainly be able to use the recent plans of deficit cuts and lower government spending. It is hoped that the macroeconomic situation will not deteriorate much so that the "economic miracle" of Hungary can continue beyond 1994.

Reference

World Bank. 1991. Hungary: Reform and decentralization of the public sector. Washington, D.C. Mimeo.

Discussion Summary

Michael Dooley warned that it is imperative that Hungary start to privatize the financial sector. He said that, until that happens, privatized nonfinancial firms will enjoy a soft budget constraint because they will have access to credits from excessively generous state-run banks.

Michael Bruno agreed with the authors that Hungary has had a relatively successful macroeconomic policy. He noted, however, that there is a gap between the objective success of the macroeconomic policy and a widely held negative public perception of that policy.

Olivier Blanchard said that the presentation of the authors gave the impression that Hungary's reform program has been much more successful than the reforms in Poland. Blanchard suggested that this was partially misleading, noting that foreign direct investment is the only category in which Hungary has done overwhelmingly better than Poland. Moreover, whatever success Hungary has had must be interpreted in light of the fact that Hungary had a substantial head start in the reform process.

Jeffrey Sachs also defended the performance of the Polish economy. Sachs noted that Poland's 1991 budget deficit was 2.7 percent of GNP, less than Hungary's deficit of 4 percent. Polish GNP fell by 8 percent in 1991, while Hungarian GNP fell by 10 percent. Poland has experienced faster growth in the private-sector share of GNP and faster growth in the volume of exports to the West. The Polish inflation rate fell in 1991, while the Hungarian inflation rate rose. Finally, Sachs noted that the Polish achievements are even more impressive when one remembers that Hungary started its reform program twenty years before the Poles did.

Andras Simon criticized the authors for overemphasizing the success of the gradualist approach. He agreed with other commentators that Hungary's purported success is explained by its early start.

Kemal Derviş's response covered several topics. First, he noted that the government is trying to improve the operations of the banking sector both by supervising and reforming the banks and by eventually privatizing them. Second, he emphasized the importance of the corporation program for the firms that will continue to be held under state ownership over the next few years. He praised the government for taking the ownership role away from the sectoral ministries and creating a new institution (the SAMC, or State Asset Management Corporation) to exercise that role. He noted that the existence of the SAMC reflected not ideological opposition to privatization but rather an awareness of the practical impossibility of successfully privatizing the entire state sector immediately. Third, Derviş addressed the gradualism debate. He said that shock therapy is clearly the right response to hyperinflation, but he said that gradualism may be a better approach to trade liberalization. He also noted that shock therapy runs the risk that a single shock may not be enough to stabilize the economy permanently and that multiple shocks may be more costly than a gradual reform program.

5 East German Economic Reconstruction

Rudiger Dornbusch and Holger C. Wolf

> In the last resort, labor productivity is the most important, the decisive factor for the victory of the new society.
>
> *V. I. Lenin*

In November 1989 the Wall came down. Less than a year later the former German Democratic Republic (GDR) had fully adopted the West German economic, legal, and institutional framework. In July 1990 the currency reform took place, and by October of that year the German Democratic Republic had ceased to exist. Monetary, social, and economic union was accomplished almost by the stroke of a pen. The radical transition sent a clear signal that the break with the past was both complete and irreversible, thus setting the basis for a rapid restructuring.

The immediate effect of unification on East Germany's economy was nothing short of radical. The five new states are now in the midst of a depression that economically, although not socially, dwarfs the Depression of the 1930s. GDP fell by almost 30 percent (see fig. 5.1), and industrial production stands at less than 50 percent of the 1989 level. Unemployment, including short time and public works programs, exceeds 30 percent of the labor force (see table 5.1). Eighteen months after unification, the output and employment decline appears to have been arrested; the first signs of recovery are visible. Yet the turnaround rests on massive transfers—DM 139 billion in 1991 and an estimated DM 180 billion in 1992.[1]

The challenge and the big question is how to move from here to a viable economy, with far higher productivity, far higher employment, and sharply reduced transfer payments. Nobody entertains an illusion that this can be accom-

The authors gratefully acknowledge financial support from the National Science Foundation and the Center for European Studies, Harvard University. Comments from participants at the conference—especially Olivier Blanchard, Stan Fischer, Larry Summers, and Janet Yellen—helped improve the paper. The weekly research and statistical reports of the Deutsches Institut für Wirtschaftsforschung in Berlin provided a valuable resource that deserves special recognition.

1. See Deutsche Bundesbank, *Monatsberichte* (March 1992).

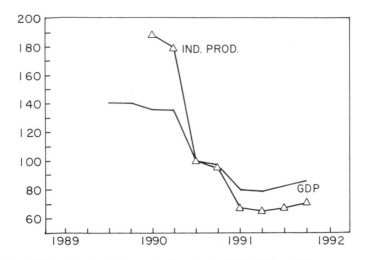

Fig. 5.1   GDP and industrial production (index 1990: 111 = 100)

Table 5.1   Key German Data, 1991

	West	East
GDP (billion DM)	2,502	193.1
Employment (millions)	29.0	7.3
GDP/employment	86,341	27,034
Annual wage (DM)	44,640	19,920
Consumption per capita (DM)	21,600	12,300
Unemployment (%)[a]	4.8	29.5
Transfers (% of GDP)	5.5	72.9

Source: DIW Wochenbericht, nos. 1–2 (1992); Sachverstandigenrat (1991).

[a]Including short work (50 percent), public work programs, retraining measures, and forced early retirement (in 1990 prices).

plished in a year or two, but can it be done in ten or fifteen? And, even if it can be done in ten or fifteen years, is that long a transition politically acceptable?

The interesting questions today lie in two directions. One set of queries concerns the transition and the policies that were used. The decline was to some degree inevitable: the bill for forty years of mismanagement, inefficient resource allocation, and environmental neglect came due overnight. Yet one may ask whether the one to one conversion and the acquiescence in massive wage increases following unification significantly worsened the collapse and, if so, whether there were plausible alternatives? The other set of problems concerns policy choices in the area of privatization, restructuring, and subsidies. Should policy focus on maintaining employment, or should it accelerate the transformation; is it more important to move companies into private hands at any price—in terms of revenues and of job losses—or should policy focus on getting deals that lock in restructuring.

This paper reviews the transition experience in East Germany and comments on the policy choices and results in four areas:

- The monetary reform and the conversion question
- The collapse of production
- The privatization debate and experience
- The migration issue

Before entering the detailed discussion, it is worth offering some perspective. The political decision by Chancellor Kohl to take a plunge—financially and economically—was dramatically bold. While there is, of course, an important purpose served in discussing how things were done and how they might have been done, the basic fact is that East Germany is experiencing a radical economic transformation that will make it viable in not too many years. The transformation costs a fortune, it is painful, it could not be done without the special intra-German relation, but it is working. One view is that it will take a generation; we believe, however, that most of the work will be done in fifteen years.

One wonders how, with far less external support, the other post-Communist societies can expect to make their transition. One possible answer is that they will not. The other is that they do not suffer the special German handicap of unification with wage parity in sight but with productivity far out of line.

5.1   The Conversion Issue

The conversion debate involves three separate questions.[2] The first deals with the sanitation of balance sheets of firms and banks at the time of the monetary reform, the second has to do with the appropriate rate of conversion for monetary assets of the public, and the third concerns the choice of a conversion rate for current payments, specifically wages.[3]

5.1.1   Balance Sheets

On the asset side, the national balance sheet of East Germany contains state-owned property ranging from real estate and forests to shops, pharmacies, and *Kombinate*. On the liability side are the monetary holdings of the public and external debts. It is apparent that, at this stage, *internal* debts did not represent a net liability of the public to the government. In the consolidation of banks and firms—both state owned—they simply canceled out. Moreover, since these debts bore no relation to the future earning capacity of the firms, and

2. For a comprehensive treatment of the monetary aspects of unification, see Nölling (1991).
3. For a detailed institutional discussion and an assessment, see Lipschitz and McDonald (1990).

since their cancelation would have most assuredly not have had any moral hazard connotations, they should simply have been written off.

The sale price of Treuhand enterprises could in principle be altered to reflect the debt holdings. But one cannot help gaining the impression that, had debts been canceled, banks and firms would now have cleaner balance sheets and debts would be no extra, unnecessary complication throughout the system. In the present setting, the Treuhand employs debts as a negotiating point, assuming debt sporadically to render enterprises more palatable to potential buyers. By this circuitous route, a sizable fraction of debt will eventually end up in the federal budget anyway, but in a manner that further obscures the role of the Treuhand and the responsibilities of managers.

5.1.2 Monetary Conversion

The second aspect concerns the conversion of monetary assets (see table 5.2). The reason that the conversion rate for monetary assets receives such central importance is, of course, that, for most East German households, money constituted the dominant part of overall asset holdings. Other financial instruments did not exist, nor, with few exceptions, did directly held real assets.

In the year prior to reform, the black market rate had reached seven ostmarks to the deutsche mark, falling off toward the conversion date in response to the public discussion of the likely conversion rates. The actual conversion rate—on average 1.6 ostmark per deutsche mark—resulted from a one to one rate of conversion for assets up to a certain level, with special provisions for certain groups, and a rate of two to one for the remaining assets. The argument for a favorable conversion rate here is primarily political: not to disappoint asset holders/savers on day one of the new money and the new market. Of course, the drastic reduction of money balances in the 1948 reforms did not prevent high saving rates in the 1950s, suggesting that political considerations were preponderant.

The monetary conversion did *not* involve a transfer from the West to the East. Rather, in the East, bank balances were simply redenominated from ostmarks into deutsche marks. Actual deutsche mark cash required to meet with-

Table 5.2   Balance Sheet of the Credit System (postconversion, billion DM)

Assets		Liabilities	
Domestic credit	180.7	Deposits	156.0
Foreign assets	36.3	Enterprises	27.8
Other	29.0	Foreign liabilities	55.6
Total	246.0	Currency	6.8
		Other liabilities	27.0
		Total	246.0

Source: Lipschitz and McDonald (1990).

drawals was obtained from the Bundesbank by borrowing at the discount rate. With this arrangement, the choice of the conversion rate involved a redistribution among various holders of monetary assets—rich and poor—and an intergenerational redistribution. Favorable rates of conversion for households, without a correspondingly burdensome conversion rate for debtors, redistribute wealth toward the current generation.[4] This implies a reduced incentive to save and an increased burden, at least in the short run, for the West, which underwrites the solvency of the system. While ultimately the burden might be paid out of net revenues from the operation and liquidation of state property, that prospect appears increasingly illusionary.

5.1.3   Wage Conversion

In the run up to monetary union, one of the hottest questions concerned the rate chosen for wage conversion. Interestingly, from the present perspective, it seems altogether a moot issue. Not moot, of course, is the question of how wage parity without matching productivity will work out for growth and productivity.

At the time of conversion, East German wages were roughly one-third those in the West (at a one to one exchange rate), and East German productivity was about one-third that of the West. Thus, a one to one conversion rate seemed broadly plausible. The black market rate, however, had been as high as seven, and the "shadow" exchange rate that priced the resource cost of one deutsche mark's worth of exports corresponded to an exchange rate of four ostmark per deutsche mark. The Bundesbank argued strongly against the one to one conversion: in their view, a far less favorable conversion—two to one—was essential to make East Germany competitive and hence to avoid an employment or a fiscal disaster.

As it turned out, the one to one conversion had no lasting effect on relative wages: since the conversion, wages in the East have increased steadily, and outright parity is the avowed objective of unions on both sides. Parity, in time, seems also to be accepted by politicians, for whom a two-part society is basically unacceptable. Of course, a two-part society cannot really be avoided: rather than having a sizable income gap dividing East and West, the line is now increasingly drawn between those who are and those who are not employed.

The push toward wage parity is the outcome of a game between unions aiming to minimize labor market competition and a government all but forced to generously underwrite unemployment, actual or hidden. The solution to that game is a high-wage strategy in the East, fatally driving toward wage parity at least in the organized sectors at the cost of large-scale unemployment (cf. Brauninger 1991; Burda and Funke 1991; and Franz 1991).

4. If households responded immediately to their new opportunities in goods or assets markets, the East German banking system would not have been viable. Public infusion of capital would have been required, financed by public borrowing.

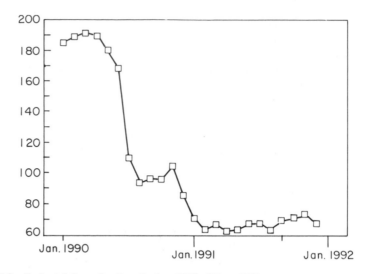

Fig. 5.2   Industrial production (index 1990: 111 = 100)

5.2   The Output Collapse

The rapid transition resulted in a severe initial decline in production.[5] Output in the manufacturing sector fell by half within a few months (see fig. 5.2). This section tries to determine why output dropped so sharply.

Before proceeding to details of the decline in activity and the range of explanations, it is interesting to put the output collapse in perspective, comparing East Germany with other transition economies. The striking difference is the dramatic extra decline in 1991, which comes on top of an already large fall in 1990 (see table 5.3).

The decline in production has been matched, with a lag, by a decline in employment. While the official unemployment figure remains relatively small, very sizable fractions of the economically active population have shifted into quasi unemployment in various forms, including short work,[6] retraining, early retirement, and public work programs, or have withdrawn from the East German labor force (see table 5.4).[7]

Total employment has fallen by more than 2 million; a further 1.6 million employment relationships are conditional on public support. In the aggregate,

5. For comprehensive treatment, see Burda (1990), Neumann (1991), Siebert (1990, 1991), and Sinn and Sinn (1991).
6. The short work regulation allows firms to retain workers while shifting the major part of wage costs to the unemployment insurance agency.
7. Prior to unification, East Germany boasted the world's highest female labor force participation ratio. After unification, the cutback in day-care centers forced a sizable reduction in the ratio. In addition to a reduction in the female labor force, some 450,000 economically active individuals moved to West Germany.

Table 5.3   **Output Collapse in Transition Economies (% changes)**

| | GDP | | Industrial Production | |
	1990	1991[a]	1990	1991[a]
Czechoslovakia	−3.1	−10.0	−4.0	−10.0
Hungary	−5.0	−5.0	−8.5	−8.0
Poland	−13.0	−6.0	−27.1	−12.0
East Germany	−13.3	−20.0	−53.9	−18.6

Sources: DIW Wochenbericht, nos. 1–2 (1992); Sachverstandigenrat (1991).
[a]1991 figures until fall.

Table 5.4   **The Labor Market: East Germany (thousands)**

	1989	1990	1991	1992[a]
Labor force	9,861	9,153	8,165	8,142
Employed	9,861	8,916	7,250	6,798
Dependent	9,678	8,597	6,735	
Independent	183	319	515	
Unemployed	0	237	915	1,343
Commuters	2	−89	−365	−500
Short work	0	758	1,640	520
Public works	0	3	185	393
Training	0	14	110	435

Sources: Sachverstandigenrat (1990, 1991); *DIW Wochenbericht,* nos. 5–6 (1992); BMWI (1992).
[a]January or last observation.

the active labor force has declined by more than 40 percent since 1989. A comprehensive measure of unemployment approaches one-third of the labor force.

The decline in employment is particularly acute in the industrial and the agricultural sectors. In industry, estimates of the medium-term labor force reduction center at 50–60 percent of initial employment. In contrast, employment in the service sector remained fairly constant, with substantial increases in the highly skilled professions.

While the decline in production dominated the decline in employment during the second half of 1990, the further reduction in employment during 1991 at fairly stable output levels resulted in an increase in measured productivity and turnover per employee. In the aggregate, turnover per employee remains, however, at a quarter of the West German level and thus substantially below relative production costs.

As a result of wage increases in excess of productivity increases and declines in producer prices, wage bills for a large fraction of the East German enterprises exceed net value added at factor costs. The net losses are covered by Treuhand liquidity loans and asset sell-offs.

5.2.1 Output and Spending

From the GDP accounts, it is immediately apparent that *all* individual components of real demand increased between 1989 and 1991 (see table 5.5). Thus, a fall in absorption cannot explain the decline in output. Second, the dramatic increases in imports—equal to half of 1989 real GDP—dominates by far any other development.

Additional information comes from the sectoral breakdown of GDP (table 5.6). The aggregate decline reflects primarily the sharp drop in industrial output. In other sectors, there was either expansion or at most a moderate drop. Sectors with high nontradable components, in particular construction, printing, and services, face high demand, while tradables sectors went into a steep decline. Thus, computer production virtually vanished, while printing expanded.

The data suggest two questions. First, what happened to the composition of demand? Second, with so much of a fall in industrial output, how could the demand for nontraded goods stay high?

The second question has, of course, an immediate answer in the massive transfers from the West that in various forms, including unemployment compensation and the financing of short work, sustained disposable income and hence kept up real aggregate demand (table 5.7). This explanation draws immediate attention to the problem of continuing transfers. Without transfers, disposable income would fall by 40 percent or more, and that would mean a collapse of demand for the entire domestic sector. Transfers are therefore bound to stay for a long time, although there is an important question of how best to target them.

As to the composition of demand, there is no surprise in the expansion of services and construction. The former did not substantially exist in the GDR and therefore will be built up increasingly over the years to come. The expan-

Table 5.5   **GDP Decline by Component (billion DM, constant 1990:2 prices)**

	1989	1991	Contribution to GDP Change (%)
GDP	281.2	196.0	−30.2
Consumption	155.1	181.5	9.4
Government	71.3	76.5	1.8
Fixed investment	51.4	63.0	4.1
Inventory investment	17.0	19.5	.9
Net exports	−13.5	−145.0	−46.7
Exports	49.9	61.0	3.9
Imports	63.4	206.0	−50.7

Source: DIW Wochenbericht, no. 33 (1991), nos. 1–2 (1992).

Table 5.6   **Value Added (billion DM, quarterly rates, not seasonally adjusted)**

	1990:1	1990:3	1991:1	1991:3
Agriculture	1.7	2.8	1.1	2.4
Industry	34.8	15.0	11.2	9.5
Handicrafts	4.2	5.0	4.5	5.5
Construction	4.2	4.8	3.8	6.1
Trade	3.5	3.3	2.2	2.2
Services	8.1	9.0	10.5	9.0
GDP	70.5	54.0	45.7	46.4

Source: DIW Wochenbericht, nos. 51–52 (1991).
Note: All data in prices of second half year 1990.

Table 5.7   **Income and Consumption (billion DM)**

	1990	1991	1992[a]
Disposable income	182.3	206.0	251.51
Net wages and salaries	116.3	102.0	116.0
Transfers	45.7	72.0	89.5
Distributed earnings	28.0	43.0	58.5
Deductions	7.7	10.5	12.0
Private consumption	175.2	201.5	232.0

Source: DIW Wochenbericht, nos. 1–2 (1992).
[a]Forecast.

sion of construction reflects the extraordinary state of disrepair of the housing stock, the availability of materials, and the need to create an infrastructure for the service sector. The relative ease of construction—in terms of skill requirements, lumpiness, credit, and planning—further helps understand the early expansion. Not surprisingly, construction is booming.

The remaining question then concerns the collapse of industrial output.

5.2.2   Industrial Output Decline

Complementary explanations for the dramatic fall in industrial output include the following: markets disappeared in the former CMEA (Council for Mutual Economic Assistance) trading partner countries; consumers shifted to Western goods because of availability or cost competitiveness; firms were caught in a cost-price bind where they could no longer profitably produce. Production might have declined because management was unable to cope with the breakdown of the traditional organization of input supply and output marketing, which gave way to a market economy.

The most immediate source of a decline in production has to do with firm closing by the Treuhand. A case in point involves the production of automobiles—the Trabant. But closing down of firms has so far not been pursued on a very wide scope, and thus important reasons for the fall in output must be looked for elsewhere.

The next reason for output decline has to do strictly with the supply side: firms faced a radically different set of relative prices. Wages increased, and so did materials prices, while many other inputs became freely available at much lower prices, requiring a radical behavioral change. At the same time, the shift to markets entailed a near complete depreciation of the organizational human capital of Eastern managers: the procurement abilities that characterize the successful manager under central planning are of little use in a market environment. The disruption of the status quo often translated into bottlenecks in material supplies or in an inability to maintain markets in the new environment.

On the demand side, the collapse of CMEA trade, shown in table 5.8, is an important part of the story. The decline is partly explained by the disruption and recession in the partner countries—CMEA trade in 1985–88 averaged 71 percent of East German exports. Substantial export credits and guarantees help sustain exports to Eastern Europe and especially to the former Soviet Union. Moreover, prices of exporting firms do not yet fully reflect costs. Liquidity credits and increasingly sales of productive assets still finance the discrepancy between costs and prices. The fall in demand from this region is not only explained by disruption but is also a reflection of the broader choice now available to the former partner economies and, of course, the exchange rate.

Although trade is an important element of the demand collapse, we should look mostly to domestic demand. A key factor in reducing demand was, however, surely the new and radical competition from the West. Overnight, all barriers to imports were eliminated, and Western goods, distributed by Western firms, became completely accessible. Thus, even though total consumption spending rose (in constant prices), the demand shifts toward Western goods far outweighed the increase in spending. Particularly in the initial opening, import penetration at the retail level reached in some areas as much as 90 percent (table 5.9). It is worth recording that those goods that did survive the initial test are now making a comeback. A case in point is a champagne with the brand name "Rotkappchen."

Interestingly, the import penetration is not focused exclusively on West German goods. For example, of 1991 new car registrations in the East, 56.6 percent were actually foreign, with only 6.3 percent coming from former CMEA partners (*Die Welt,* 2 February 1992).

Table 5.8   East German Merchandise Exports (billion DM)

	Total	CMEA	Other
1988	40.2	30.1	10.1
1989	41.1	29.8	11.3
1990	38.1	30.5	7.6
1991	17.9	12.1	5.8

Sources: Sachverstandigenrat (1991); Deutsche Bank (1992).

Table 5.9   **West German Goods on East German Shelves (West German goods as % of retail sales)**

Margarine	35	Fat	76
Cooking oil	41	Fruit yogurt	90
Detergent	53	Chocolate	96
Black tea	66		

Source: Die Zeit, 28 September 1990.

In judging the shift into imported goods, it would be a mistake to emphasize availability exclusively. Price clearly did matter—East German citizens bought cheaper cars than West German citizens. East Germany clearly did not have a substantial price advantage. With nominal wages rising in excess of productivity, prices were high, and firms lost output owing to reduced demand.

Interdependence effects must also have played a role. To the extent that the production decline occurred at the stage of final goods, there was a feedback to intermediate goods that were no longer demanded and hence, in the absence of alternative markets, no longer produced. The extreme inflexibility of the planned economy may have seriously aggravated the effect of final demand reductions throughout the production system.

5.2.3   An Assessment

Few observers would have predicted so dramatic a fall in production. The question arises why output in other East European economies declined so much less. Part of the answer lies clearly in the exchange rate or wage level: in East Germany, consumers could afford to buy Western goods, and they did splurge, more so because the prices were not at all out of line with the prices of similar (although "inferior") East German goods.

Poland had only moderate protection and thus offers a good comparison. The chief difference in the degree of import penetration comes from two sources. First, East Germans were already introduced to West German goods via the widely watched West German television. Second, in the case of East Germany, the West German firms organized the import and distribution of West German goods drawing on their experience and their resources. In the Polish case, this was done predominantly by small-scale Polish traders without scale and capital and thus with a far larger handicap. In addition, of course, the purchasing power of Polish wages in terms of foreign goods was minimal compared to that of West Germany after unification.

In the Czech and Slovak Federal Republic or Hungary, by comparison, trade restrictions continued at substantial levels up to the end of 1991 and in some measure even beyond. Moreover, even in the absence of trade restrictions, imports were forbiddingly expensive, and hence the demand shift was far less. The economies have in common, however, that much of industrial restructuring still lies ahead. In Germany, the availability of substantial transfers will cushion the blow, and investment will have to create high-wage jobs. In the other East

European economies, a supercompetitive exchange rate will have to be the chief mechanism for creating new employment as inefficient operations are streamlined.

In conclusion, there is no single explanation for the dramatic output decline. But, if a summary explanation is to be given, it has to be the combination of an overnight eradication of all trade barriers in a situation where product alternatives were known, products were made available instantly by the West, and wages were high enough to make large-scale import spending possible and optimal. That makes the East German case very special.

5.3   Privatization

The transition economies confront the dual problem of overall capital deficiency and misallocation of the existing resources. Ideally, the privatization process solves both problems by channeling resources to salvageable firms while freeing inefficiently allocated resources through the liquidation of nonviable enterprises. This section reviews the operation of the Treuhand and assesses its success and the prospective difficulties.[8]

5.3.1   Treuhand Organization

The hard-line stance of the Honecker government yielded an unexpected benefit to the East German privatization process: shunning partial reform, the socialist regime retained ownership of most productive assets under central control, eliminating the problem of "spontaneous privatization" and enabling the wholesale transfer of ownership to a newly founded agency, the Treuhand (THA).

At the time of its inception, the THA assumed ownership of approximately 95 percent of the enterprise sector, comprising some 9,000 industrial firms, 20,000 commercial enterprises, 7,500 hotels and restaurants, and 40 percent of the total land area, with a total employment of 3 million. The Treuhand is charged by law with privatizing the enterprises under its control, enforcing budgetary discipline, encouraging know-how transfers, fostering the creation of a competitive economic system, and stimulating capital inflows. Residual revenues from privatization are to be used as compensation for the losses incurred by the East German savers during monetary unification, thus implicitly obliging the Treuhand to extract substantial revenues form the privatization process (see table 5.10).

The THA provides liquidity assistance to enterprises, services debt, and can assume environmental liabilities and claims arising from ownership disputes. The Treuhand enjoys near complete authority over the enterprises under its control, including liquidation and separation into subunits. It is thus fairly unrestricted in the manner in which it can discharge its obligations, facing neither

---

8. For extended expositions of privatization, see Beirat (1991), Bos (1991), and Sinn (1991).

Table 5.10   Treuhand Budget, 1991 (billion DM)

Revenues	37.7	Expenditures	37.7
Privatizations	15.8	Interest and principal	13.8
Others	1.1	Restructuring of firms	12.9
Deficit	20.8	Cost of sales	4.8
		Other	6.2

Source: Bos (1991).

detailed de facto supervision nor binding deadlines for the completion of its tasks.

5.3.2   Treuhand Strategy

The wide leeway to customize notwithstanding, the Treuhand has implicitly adopted a set of policies.

Single Owners

The survival of many enterprises in the transition economies depends on their ability to attract a "foreign" investor willing to transfer process know-how, management, and marketing skills. The incentive for investors to become "active" depends positively on the stake held. Privatization plans consequently tend to include a role for majority shareholders (e.g., Blanchard et al. 1991; Lipton and Sachs 1990; and Tirole 1991). The Treuhand has pushed this consideration to the limit, concentrating on selling the entire object to a single buyer.

Most of the mammoth *Kombinate* cannot of course be sold as an entity. To obtain privatizable units, the Treuhand has begun to split enterprises into "core" and "noncore" businesses, to be sold separately. The breakup of *Kombinate* and even of smaller operations thus represents an important simplification.

Criteria

In deciding on a privatization proposal, the Treuhand places weight on investment and employment guarantees in addition to the price offered. Potential investors are required to submit a detailed restructuring plan, including proposed investment and employment levels. Both proposals are binding; violators incur a contractual penalty.

Liquidity Credits

With few exceptions, the Treuhand has presumed enterprises to be salvageable by default until balance sheets have been drawn up and approved, providing liquidity credits in the meantime.[9] After the completion of the balance

---

9. Some 80 percent of enterprises have received liquidity credits.

sheets, liquidity credits for the two lowest-ranked enterprise groups have been discontinued.

Debt

Enterprise debts in the postsocialist economies predominantly reflect arbitrary pricing decisions made under the former regime. By judging enterprise viability on the basis of ability to cover net of debt service outlays, the Treuhand has recognized the arbitrariness of the debt distribution across enterprises. Debts have been de facto consolidated, and enterprises contribute to debt service on the basis of their current and predicted cash flow.

5.3.3   A Case Study: Zeiss Jena

Before unification, Zeiss Jena employed 27,000 workers, predominantly in opticals. In March 1991, the Treuhand offered Zeiss Jena to its Western "sister" company, Zeiss Oberkochen. The THA took on the firm's accumulated debt of $812 million. Zeiss Jena was split into two subunits. Fifty-one percent of Carl Zeiss Jena GmbH was acquired by Zeiss Oberkochen for a price of DM 0.00. The Treuhand provided $375 million in start-up funds and loss compensation until 1995. The new firm employs 2,800 people.

The second unit, Jenoptik, was transferred to the state of Thuringia and retained 7,000 employees. The Treuhand provided $687 million in start-up funds and loss compensation until 1993. In total, some 17,000 jobs have been eliminated, with a per capita compensation of $13,750. Total Treuhand outlays are $812 million for debt, $1.06 billion for start-up funds and loss compensation, and $188 million for job loss compensation, in total $2.06 billion or $212,500 per job saved. Current forecasts view 1997 as the first profitable year for the restructured enterprises.

5.3.4   Outcome Today

After an extended period of preparation, privatization has begun in earnest, with around thirty sales per week. The impressive numbers—more than 5,200 privatizations to date out of an initial stock of 7,100 enterprises (see table 5.11)—are, however, somewhat misleading as the total number of enterprises has increased, reflecting the parceling strategy. Nevertheless, the Treuhand has made very rapid progress, ensuring employment for one-third of the original employees and obtaining some DM 114 billion in investment guarantees.

The overall picture hides substantial sectoral differences. Privatization of small- and medium-scale service enterprises is nearly completed. The transfer of utilities to the local authorities likewise has proceeded largely on schedule. In contrast, the privatization of the large industrial behemoths suffering from obsolete capital stocks, substantial overstaffing, environmental risks, and rapidly disappearing export markets remains sluggish. Privatization from below is proceeding rapidly. While a large fraction of nominal registrations are pres-

Table 5.11   **Privatization: Progress to Date**

	Jun. 91	Nov. 91	Feb. 92[a]
Cumulative sales (no.)	2,583	4,777	5,584
Employment guarantees (1,000s)	511	857	1,150
Investment guarantees (billion DM)	64	105	140
Total sales revenues (billion DM)	10	16	19
Closings	529	871	983
Management buyouts	. . .	808	894

Sources: Sachverstandigenrat (1991); BMWI (1992); *Financial Times,* 3 March 1992.
[a]February or latest.

ently inactive, it is estimated that the 435,000 new registrations imply some 175,000 effective enterprise foundations.

On the closure front, the Treuhand has been hesitant. While internal estimates apparently place the fraction of nonsalvageable enterprises at 30 percent and external estimates range considerably higher (Akerlof et al. 1991), as of December 1991 only 983 enterprises, less than 10 percent of existing firms, have been closed.

5.3.5   Problems and Issues

The availability of West German financial and personnel support, political stability, a hard currency, and EEC membership greatly facilitate the East German privatization process. While privatization has picked up, sales and particularly revenues fall short of the initial optimistic expectations.[10] In its annual member survey, the DIHT (Deutscher Industrie und Handelstag) identified concerns about environmental liabilities, a lack of infrastructure, a shortage of experienced local administrations, and legal uncertainty as the major obstacles perceived by potential investors (see table 5.12).

Increasingly, the THA faces three challenges: how much tailoring should go into the privatization process, how to deal with regional issues, and how to resist political pressures surrounding closings of large plants. We briefly comment on these.

Regional Policy

The extreme degree of industrial concentration frequently makes closing an enterprise commensurate with a decision to eliminate the industrial base of a town or an entire region, giving rise to conflicts between the microeconomically justified decision to liquidate a nonviable enterprise and regional policy objectives. For example, a quarter of Sachsen-Anhalt's labor force is employed

---

10. Detlev Rohwedder, the first chairman of the Treuhand, initially estimated revenues at DM 600 billion.

Table 5.12   **Perceived Investment Obstacles: A Survey**

	Legal Uncertainty	Administration	Infrastructure	Environmental Liabilities
Industry	37	25	24	14
Mining	13	0	4	83
Intermediate goods	34	28	17	21
Capital goods	41	24	26	9
Final goods	33	28	25	14
Construction	42	35	17	6
Trade	42	29	24	5
Services	39	30	26	5
Total	39	27	24	10

Source: Deutscher Industrie und Handelstag, Autumn Member Survey.

Note: Figures are given in terms of percentage of respondents answering affirmatively.

Table 5.13   **Workers per Firm**

Industry	FRG	GDR	Ratio	Industry	FRG	GDR	Ratio
Chemicals	296	1,419	4.8	Light industries	95	671	7.1
Metals	474	3,209	6.8	Textiles	169	1,301	7.7
Mechanical engineering	271	838	3.9	Food processing	125	480	3.8

Source: Schnabel (1990).

in the chemical industry (see table 5.13), estimated to have to shrink by two-thirds in the medium run (see "Man lasst uns nicht sterben" 1991). Privatization and regional policies should be strictly separated: if continuing support for economically nonviable enterprises is regarded as justified, the decision should reflect the political concern for regional balance and be funded outside the privatizing agency. A stronger regional differentiation of investment subsidies would be a promising start.

Auctions

Should the THA sell by auction rather than using customized sales? A criticism frequently levied at the THA holds that a shift to auctions with a sole emphasis on the bidding price would have shifted the valuation exercise to the individuals best informed about the potential of firms, the bidders, while avoiding excess windfall gains. The criticism fails to bite in several respects. First, the Treuhand did not inherit a salable portfolio but had to create privatizable units by recombining resources within the existing industrial behemoths.

Second, social and private valuations of enterprises are likely to differ substantially. In particular, East German firms capable of buying and closing a potential Eastern competitor would have valued the Eastern firm in relation to the market power rent. By insisting on investment and employment guarantees and hence on a restructuring strategy of the purchaser, the Treuhand reduced the scope for privately optimal but socially damaging asset transfers.

Restructuring and Liquidation

Much of the easily privatizable capital stock has by now changed hands. The Treuhand portfolio is thus becoming increasingly lemon-heavy: in an extensive survey of 1,500 Treuhand enterprises, the DIW concluded that 50–70 percent of the remaining enterprises cannot be privatized in their present state ("DIW Pladoyer für degressive Subvention" 1991),[11] requiring either liquidation or extensive restructuring.

The Treuhand's emphasis on restructuring has attracted widespread criticism. The critics argue that the Treuhand has neither the responsibility nor the ability to restructure: if an enterprise is viable after restructuring, then, surely, a private investor will be willing to undertake the job. The Treuhand, however, enjoys several advantages not available to private investors, in particular, the ability to internalize externalities relating to infrastructure, politics, and industrial structure and the ability to recombine existing assets to create a—roughly restructured—salable enterprise. Restructuring in this broad sense remains desirable.

The real danger over the next few years is the continued support of those enterprises without realistic hope for survival. By pursuing the policy of postponing the bankruptcy of a significant fraction of East Germany's industrial sector, the THA is allocating scarce resources to the stabilization of obsolete economic structures in preference to providing assistance to salvageable sectors. While the cushioning of the adjustment process is desirable, the social safety net must be directed toward mitigating the consequences of the necessary structural adjustment, not toward preventing the adjustment itself. Protecting people, not jobs, is the appropriate outlook. Rapid action on the liquidation front carries an additional political economy advantage: by imposing a front-end liquidation of the nonsalvageable enterprises, the unemployment rate jumps initially rather than increasing over an extended period. Front-loading of the adjustment cost focuses attention on increasing training and employment for displaced workers rather than on halting the rise of unemployment.

5.4 Migration

From the summer of 1989 to unification, some 540,000 East Germans moved to West Germany, followed by approximately 200,000 movers since. In

---

11. Enterprise managers are substantially more optimistic: while only 10 percent see their enterprises as currently competitive, some 30 percent believe that a competitive state will be reached within a year and a further 44 percent that successful restructuring will be concluded after two years (DIW survey).

addition, approximately 500,000 East German residents commute to work in the West, bringing the total labor force shift to more than 1 million.

The desire to halt migration from East to West Germany provided a major impetus to the course of economic unification. But is such migration really undesirable on purely economic grounds? Given time constraints in the construction of new plants, the alternative "employment in the East versus employment in the West" has not been relevant in the last two years and will remain irrelevant for a large fraction of the East German labor force for years to come. In the end, aggregate welfare arguments do not add up to a convincing case against migration. The concern with migration derives primarily from the distributional implications for wages and a fear that East Germany might be irreversibly hollowed out. Three questions arise. First, were the initial mass migration scenarios realistic? Second, has the policy of wage equalization backfired, inducing unemployment migration where wage migration might not have been a threat? Finally, does commuting obviate the migration threat?

The initial scenarios of mass migration lacked plausibility. Extrapolations based on the migration flows in the first few months following the collapse of the Wall confused stock adjustments with steady-state flows. After the initial wave, migration has amounted to barely 1 percent of the population per annum. Automatic stabilizers, in particular, rising rents and falling employment chances, further reduced migration pressures.

While the initial scenarios exaggerated the migration potential, the possibility of continued westward migration of the young, restless, and skilled, and thereby the transformation of East Germany into a permanently underindustrialized northern *mezzogiorno,* appeared real and was used to justify union claims for rapid wage equalization. Rightly so?

The gain from working in the West cannot be disputed: both the commuter and the migration households experienced real income gains far in excess of the gains achieved by households remaining in East Germany (see table 5.14). In line with initial expectations, the typical commuter/migrant tends to work in industry (26.4 percent), trade (15.9 percent), construction (14.6 percent), or

Table 5.14   Income Effects of Commuting and Migration

	All Households	Households with Commuters	Households Moving West
Disposable income:			
May 1990 (DM)	614	636	875
March 1991 (DM)	745	967	1,618
Average real increase (%)	12.1	41.1	79.5
Population fraction experiencing real increase (%)	60.3	81.7	. . .
Population (thousands)	15,751.9	1,073.9	. . .

Source: Krause, Headey, and Habich (1992).

Table 5.15   **Migration Plans (%)**

	Short Run	Medium Run
Total	4.6	47.9
Unsatisfied with household income	6.1	50.2
Expectation of own unemployment	14.0	54.2
Expectation of spouse's unemployment	10.1	43.3
University degree	3.0	51.6
Workers	4.5	47.5
Employee	4.8	60.0
Highly qualified employee	4.5	50.8
House owners	2.9	32.1
Dissatisfied with environment	8.3	52.9
East Berlin	6.0	51.8
South	6.0	48.2

Source: Based on a socioeconomic survey. Calculations reported in *DIW Wochenbericht,* nos. 5–6 (1992).

Note: Willingness of employed males aged younger than 49 years to migrate to West Germany.

services (14.0 percent), is fairly young (65 percent younger than thirty-six years; average age thirty-one), has concluded an apprenticeship (69 percent), and is presently employed as a skilled worker (43 percent).

Yet survey evidence on the migration behavior of economically active young males—the dominant migration group—suggests that the income gap was not the only or even the dominant incentive to migrate. As table 5.15, summarizing the responses of employed East Germans, suggests, the short-run mobility was furthermore quite small. Among the reasons given, unemployment dominates, followed by concerns about the environment, with income differentials ranking only third.

The responses also indicate a surprising homogeneity of answers with respect to educational background and current employment. In conjunction, migration responses may be more highly varied across regions than across qualifications. In particular, the industrial south, suffering from high unemployment and some of the worst environmental damage, appears to be headed for the largest population loss. In accordance with most empirical findings on migration patterns, house ownership significantly lowers willingness to migrate.

Table 5.16 extends the survey to all males in the age group. Again, unemployment significantly increases the willingness to migrate.

Surprisingly, individuals on short time, and hence realistically headed for unemployment, are least mobile in the short as well as in the medium run, possibly reflecting a perceived inability to find employment in West Germany. The survey rejects the hypothesis of an imminent mass migration in the spring of 1990. Job security rather than wage differentials appears to have been the main driving force behind migration. Indeed, rapid monetary union—with the entailed real appreciation—and rapid wage equalization may have on balance

Table 5.16   Willingness to Go West (%)

	Short Term	Medium Term
Total	4.9	50.2
Fully employed	4.6	47.9
Short time work	2.2	46.1
Unemployed	7.4	59.2
Commuters	9.3	61.9

Source: See table 5.15.

Note: Willingness of working-age males younger than 49 years.

increased rather than reduced the mobility of East German workers. The possibility becomes more plausible if the skill composition of the labor force is taken into account: (almost) wage equalization across the board may have driven older and unskilled workers with low probability of finding work in the West into long-term unemployment while failing to close the wage gap sufficiently for the most mobile highly skilled labor force groups.[12]

Outlook

The East German capital-to-labor ratio at present lies substantially below the West German ratio. With free factor mobility, equalization will occur over the medium run. Two possibilities arise: an eastward movement of capital (the miracle outcome) or a westward movement of labor (the *mezzogiorno* outcome). Some westward labor migration is unavoidable and even desirable. How far the economy shifts toward the *mezzogiorno* outcome depends on the wage and investment policies adopted. Low initial unit labor costs attract investment and favor the miracle outcome. The choice for rapid wage equalization contributed to the rapid rise in unemployment and on balance has likely increased rather than decreased migration, thus supporting the *mezzogiorno* solution.

In the remainder of this paper, we sketch three questions that no doubt will continue to be debated as developments in the East unfold over the next decade.

5.5 Unemployment or Status Quo Subsidies?

Unification has taken place, and it is too late to set the clock back on such key decisions as the conversion rate, the integrated labor market, and the open internal trade regime. A key question remaining for the coming years concerns

---

12. While 78.8 percent of individuals older than fifty-five years categorically ruled out westward migration, only 29.6 percent of the seventeen- to thirty-four-year-olds expressed the same sentiment (Scheremet and Schupp 1992).

the subsidy strategy. At present, the Treuhand runs an open-ended account for most firms in its portfolio,[13] subsidizing substantial losses. With the Treuhand holding the bag and unions pushing, there is no effective mechanism of wage restraint—parity in the express lane is virtually inevitable. But, even if parity is reached, should the policy be to maintain existing firms and employment, or should policy try to achieve a maximum of restructuring?

To some extent, the privatization process brings with it a restructuring, often agreed on in an explicit fashion, although one will have to see how these arguments fare if firms get into trouble. But the hard part of privatization has as yet not taken place—firm closing has been minimal even though a third of firms were thought to be unviable and another third of questionable staying power. In the meantime, employment is de facto subsidized and with it the status quo.

Wage increases have to date not been passed on to producer prices (see table 5.17), a reflection largely of the slim margin of price competitiveness enjoyed by East German products.

Relative wages in East Germany have increased significantly since unification, approaching 60–70 percent of the West German levels in the spring of 1992 (see table 5.18). While relative labor costs reflecting lower nonwage labor costs remain significantly lower at around 50 percent of the West German level, the still lower productivity ratio implies that unit labor costs in East Germany remain above the West German level. In consequence, wage bills for a large fraction of the East German enterprises exceed net value added at factor costs. The net losses are covered by Treuhand liquidity loans.

Two radically different policy options are open. One is the proposal by Akerlof et al. (1991) explicitly to subsidize wages so as to enhance profitability, competitiveness, and hence viability of employment in the East. The proposal has been formulated as well as one could hope to make the case, showing that, without a wage subsidy, East Germany is simply outpriced and hence largely unemployed. But there is something deeply unsatisfying in this approach: it basically takes as given that the existing firms and products are substantially viable and that it is only a question of bringing costs in line with prices at which output can be sold.

The proposal in no way obstructs the formation of new firms; on the contrary, it subsidizes employment and hence encourages the formation of new firms. But the weight of the proposal is to subsidize the currently existing employment patterns—simply to make it possible to keep doing what has been done in the past. But there is no reason to believe—and maybe danger in believing—that most or even half of the remaining firms are viable in anything resembling their current structure. A recent survey shows that Treuhand firms are systematically more optimistic about their economic prospects than private firms even though the reality, in market terms, is the other way round. The

---

13. Liquidity credits for the lowest two classifications of enterprises have been discontinued—at least for the time being.

Table 5.17   Prices (1989 = 100)

	Producer Prices	Cost of Living
Jul. 1990	64.2	98.0
Sep. 1991	63.2	115.4
Nov. 1991	63.2	127.6

Source: Deutsche Bundesbank, *Monthly Report* (various 1991 issues).

Table 5.18   Profitability of East German Firms

	Gross Wages (% of value added)	E. German Wage (% of W. German wage)
Textiles	213.7	67
Chemicals	210.9	33
Electrical	120.6	40
Machinery	102.4	40
Printing	74.5	59
Energy	30.0	40
Industry	138.3	50

Source: DIW Wochenbericht, no. 5 (1992).

alternative proposal, then, is to emphasize change and to subsidize that change aggressively. That means putting a firm end to the financing that will flow to all Treuhand firms—say after eight months—and forcing them at that point to borrow from commercial banks or to face automatic bankruptcy.

The accelerated termination of the current open-ended credits should have a counterpart in extended unemployment benefits, generous early separation payments, and a far better mechanism to finance small- and medium-sized firms. In the financing area, commercial banks do not do well in promoting the growth of small- and medium-sized businesses because collateral tends to be poor. As a result, retained earnings or family assets tend to finance the start-up, and these sources will be, of course, lacking in East Germany for years to come. Therefore, public participation funds (whether local, state, or federal) for any kind of small- and medium-sized businesses should be set up with extremely simple methods of securing and monitoring capital participations. These funds could play an initiating role in sponsoring new firms without even applying much of a subsidy, if any; their role is to act as intermediary in the capital market segment, where business formation is slowest and self-finance is the rule.

Because of the absence of self-finance, a strong case can be made for a public role. Of course, all this runs counter to the belief that markets do all the necessary work. But there cannot be any illusion: at present, East Germany is on welfare, and the current course of operations is to write blank checks. Deliberately creating a new business structure by closing down firms, confronting workers crassly with the need to put themselves in a new job, and facilitating the formation of a service and small enterprise sector promise better results than a massive status quo subsidy. Specifically, if workers were to go into training programs rather than continuing on short hours or absentee status in firms ultimately bound to go into liquidation, the restructuring of employment could be advanced by years.

5.6   Is East Germany Now Better Off?

Our next question is an almost surprisingly disingenuous one. Is East Germany now *economically* better off? The presumption surely was that the transition to a market economy would make the economy much better off—goods readily available, efficient production translating into low prices and high wages, a maximum of opportunity. If there were losers, it would surely be possible to compensate them. But there remains a doubt: mass unemployment and relative prices sharply different from what they were two years ago leave some room for a question mark. Is it possible, to stretch the point, that Czechoslovakia might be doing better even without a rich brother?

At first sight, East Germany is in fact better off. Real disposable income is up, and consumption has increased 17 percent, not even counting the welfare improvements that stem from increased variety and the far more convenient availability of goods.

But is that gain widely distributed, or does it fall mostly on those groups that directly participate in the West German economy or hold high-wage jobs? Do old people, for example, share in the benefits of transition? The question is appropriate because of the massive changes in relative prices. The abolition of consumer price subsidies resulted in significant increases in the consumer price index, concentrated in rent and transportation price hikes (see table 5.19).

A report of the DIW shows that 60 percent of households surveyed showed a gain in real disposable income, leaving 40 percent without such a gain and possibly with losses. No doubt, the losses would be even larger without the substantial leveling effects of taxes and transfers. In fact, so far taxes and transfers have kept the distribution substantially unchanged (see table 5.20).

Greater wage differentiation and a less complete system of transfers will likely worsen income distribution in the future. The question then is whether growth and migration are sufficient to enable everybody to get ahead. That is questionable; less questionable is where the East German economy would have

Table 5.19   **Prices in November 1991 (1989 = 100)**

Total	127.6	Food	126.4
Clothing	72.4	Rents, energy	375.8
Household items	85.0		

Source: Deutsche Bundesbank, *Monthly Report* (various 1991 issues).

Table 5.20   **Household Income Distribution by Quintile (% of income)**

	1990		1991	
	Bottom	Top	Bottom	Top
Gross income	6.7	35.8	3.9	39.8
Disposable income	14.1	29.9	14.7	31.2

Source: Krause, Headey, and Habich (1992).

headed with another ten years of mismanagement. Against that counterfactual there is bound to be an improvement.

But how about the comparison with Czechoslovakia? Clearly, the massive transfer payments and the large investment flows are rapidly transforming East Germany into an economy where the average standard of living will be 40 or 50 percent above that in Czechoslovakia. The current high unemployment is inevitable as an adjustment phenomenon and because of transfer payments does not fairly represent the level of consumption or welfare in East Germany.

5.7   *Wirtschaftswunder* or Welfare Albatross?

Our final question is what East Germany will look like in a decade. The answer is likely this: some regions will have a dramatic improvement in prosperity—border regions that are not environmentally damaged—and other regions, notably along the Polish border, will fall sharply behind. Regions that are environmentally hazardous will become deindustrialized and depopulated. In West Germany, there are today substantial regional variations in per capita income, and the same will be true in the East, with the high-income region of the East toward the bottom of the West German distribution. Migration will do a large part of the work, and massive investment, private and public, will have to do the rest.

After a lull in 1990, investment has increased substantially to a third of GNP and is expected to increase further in coming years (see table 5.21). Investment is further boosted by ambitious plans to modernize East Germany's telecommunications system, with a total price tag of DM 60 billion until 1997, as well as an overhaul of the transportation system, estimated at DM 700 billion over the next two decades.

Parallel to the high rate of investment, there is clear evidence of major revamping inside the firms. Table 5.22 shows the range of activities with which Treuhand firms try to make themselves attractive and profitable.

The relatively small size of East Germany has made it possible to move managers and administrators over on a scale that actually can create the required market culture in the East. The very short distances make commuting a real possibility—less than an hour for many, less than two in extreme cases. The small size also means that capital investment in infrastructure and business

Table 5.21   Investment in East Germany (billion DM)

	Equipment		Buildings			
	Private	Public	Private	Public	Residential Housing	Total
1989	17.0	2.7	14.4	5.5	10.5	50.1
1990	17.4	2.6	14.6	6.6	7.1	48.3
1991	33.4	3.5	14.9	9.4	6.8	68.0
1992	44.1	4.0	19.5	13.6	7.1	88.3

Source: DIW Wochenbericht, no. 41 (1991).

Table 5.22   Reform Measures of Treuhand Enterprises

	Firm Size: Employees		
	< 200	201–999	> 999
Outsourcing	15	21	44
Improvement of distribution:	64	77	85
In the East	54	57	57
In the West	31	47	62
New/improved products:	55	66	58
Own	33	50	50
Licensed	25	25	23
Rationalization	34	70	92
New machinery	43	42	40

Source: DIW and IfW (1991a, 1991b).
Note: Figures are given in terms of percentage of respondents having taken the action.

capital over the next decade can move the region substantially in the direction of West Germany.

What will East Germany do? It is unlikely that it will do exactly what the West is doing. More likely, activities will be somewhat less green, somewhat less customized, and substantially more focused on emerging markets in the East. But, of course, in manufacturing there will be competition with the low-wage transition economies. Just as the United States competes with Mexico in the production of entry-level cars, East Germany must now compete with Czechoslovakia. The sooner the new production structure is put in place, the better the chances to start competing.

There is no presumption whatsoever that income equalization will take place on a regional basis in a decade—that does not exist even in countries with many decades of regional policies.[14] In fact, within West Germany's states (excepting the city-*Lander*), the spread top to bottom of per capita income is 28

14. Near 80 percent equalization will put East Germany ahead of the United States in terms of labor costs.

percent. Once we look at partial equalization—say, 75 percent—and recognize the great scope for commuting, productivity improvements, and the externalities deriving from public capital, the investment effort may be radically smaller than the DM 1,000–DM 2,000 billion that have been produced by various models.

Barro (1991) has argued that East Germany will take generations—specifically, seventy years—not a decade to fifteen years as we argue, to move close to West German standards.[15] His view is based on research about catch-up and convergence among regions and countries over long periods of time. In these cross-sectional studies, catch-up is found to be slow and equal to only 2 percent of the gap each year.

What is different in the case of East Germany?[16] First, a set of essential prerequisites in the form of legal, economic, and administrative institutions were imported outright. It may take a moment for these to take hold and become second nature, but they are basically in place. Second, knowledge about markets, technology, and business is being imported on a massive scale far in excess of the rate that a peripheral country could handle under its own steam. Third, commuting and more generally minimal distances generate the maximum benefit in terms of exposure and interaction. Fourth, the supply of capital is ample and strictly without a regional risk premium. On the contrary, public finance strongly supports regional development. The wage strategy, whether the government intended this result or not, forces East Germany into the direction of a high capital-labor ratio. Politics support that move, and a safety net makes sure that it all adds up.

East Germany will not seem like a miracle. For that too much money is being spent. However, the turnaround in output and employment is now starting, and growth will pick up. But, for years to come, just as in the early 1950s, high unemployment rates will draw more attention than business formation or employment growth. A decade from now, it will suddenly be clear that differences have shrunk except in those places where extreme environmental damage makes it impossible to work and impossible to live. There may not be a *Wirtschaftswunder* because transfers and investment will be responsible for the rehabilitation. If there were to be a *Wunder* at all, it would most likely take the form of a dramatic increase in East German total factor productivity, which offers a powerful alternative to aid and capital investment.

15. The German government appears much more optimistic, arguing for a five-year convergence period ("Bonn Rejects Doubts" 1992).

16. For a further discussion of this point, see Dornbusch and Wolf (1992).

References

Akerlof, G., H. Hessenius, A. Rose, and J. Yellen. 1991. East Germany in from the cold. *Brookings Papers on Economic Activity,* no. 1:1–87.

Barro, R. 1991. Eastern Germany's long haul. *Wall Street Journal,* 3 May.

Beirat of the Bundeswirtschaftsministerium. 1991. Probleme der Privatisierung in den neuen Bundeslandern. *Studienreihe,* vol. 73. Bonn.

Blanchard, O., et al. 1991. *Reform in Eastern Europe.* Cambridge, Mass.: MIT Press.

"Bonn rejects doubts cast on economic prospects for East." 1992. *Financial Times,* 11 February.

Bos, D. 1991. Privatization in East Germany: A survey of current issues. Working Paper no. 92/8. Washington, D.C.: International Monetary Fund.

Brauninger, D. 1991. Wage and employment policy in Germany. *Deutsche Bank Bulletin* (July).

Bundesministerium für Wirtschaft (BMWI). 1992. Ausgewahlte Wirtschaftsdaten zur Lage in den neuen Bundeslandern. Bonn, 13 February. Mimeo.

Burda, M. 1990. The consequences of German economic and monetary union. Discussion Paper no. 449. London: Centre for Economic Policy Research.

Burda, M., and M. Funke. 1991. German trade unions after unification: Third degree wage discriminating monopolist? Discussion Paper no. 573. London: Centre for Economic Policy Research.

Deutsche Bank. 1992. *Focus Germany.* Washington, D.C.: Transatlantic Futures, March.

Deutsches Institut für Wirtschaftsforschung (DIW) and Institut für Wirtschaftsforschung. 1991a. Gesamtwirtschaftliche und unternehmerische Anpassungsprozesse in Ostdeutschland: Dritter Bericht. *DIW Wochenbericht,* nos. 39–40.

———. 1991b. Gesamtwirtschaftliche und unternehmerische Anpassung sprozesse in Ostdeutschland. *DIW Wochenbericht,* nos. 51–52.

DIW Pladoyer für degressive Subvention von Arbeit und Kapital in Ostdeutschland. 1991. *Handelsblatt,* 9 October.

Dornbusch, R., and H. Wolf. 1992. Economic transition in East Germany. *Brookings Papers on Economic Activity,* no. 1:235–61.

Franz, W. 1991. German labor markets after unification. University of Konstanz. Mimeo.

Krause, P., B. Headey, and R. Habich. 1992. Einkommensentwicklung der privaten Haushalte in Ostdeutschland. *DIW Wochenbericht,* no. 4.

Lipschitz, L., and D. McDonald. 1990. German unification: Economic issues. Occasional Paper no. 75. Washington, D.C.: International Monetary Fund.

Lipton, D., and J. Sachs. 1990. Privatization in Eastern Europe: The case of Poland. *Brookings Papers on Economic Activity,* no. 1:75–133.

Man lasst uns nicht sterben. 1991. *Der Spiegel,* no. 6 (February).

Neumann, M. 1991. German unification: Economic problems and consequences. Discussion Paper no. 584. London: Centre for Economic Policy Research.

Nölling, W. 1991. Geld und die deutsche Vereinigung. In *Hamburger Beitrage zur Wirtschafts- und Wahrungspolitik in Europa,* vol. 8. Hamburg.

Sachverstandigenrat. 1990. *Jahresgutachten 1990/91.* Bonn.

———. 1991. *Jahresgutachten 1991/92.* Bonn.

Scheremet, W., and J. Schupp. 1992. Pendler und Migranten-Zur Ar beitskraftemobilitat in Ostdeutschland. *DIW Wochenbericht* (March).

Schnabel, R. 1990. Structural adjustment and privatization of the East German economy. Mimeo.

Siebert, H. 1990. The economic integration of Germany. Institute for World Economics. Kieler Diskussionsbeitrage, no. 160.

————. 1991. Uniting Germany. *Economic Policy,* no. 13 (October): 289–340.

Sinn, H. 1991. Privatization in East Germany. University of Munich. Mimeo.

Sinn, G., and H. Sinn. 1991. *Kaltstart.* Tubingen: J. C. B. Mohr.

Tirole, J. 1991. Privatization in Eastern Europe. *NBER Macroeconomic Annual,* 221–58.

Comment   Janet L. Yellen

The authors are to be commended for their excellent survey of the progress of East German economic reconstruction since currency union in July 1990. I fully agree with their analysis of the relevant economic history and with their diagnosis of the current economic situation. In commenting on their paper, therefore, I will offer some additional reflections on two important issues raised in the paper: the likely length of the transition to Western productivity and employment levels and the Treuhand's privatization strategy.

The Length of the Transition

The authors ask of the East German economy the same question that the erstwhile mayor of New York, Ed Koch, continually asked of himself: "How am I doing?" Should the answer be accompanied by Koch's indomitable grin? The authors fail to answer this question, instead leaving the reader with two polar possibilities: East Germany may be another German *Wirtschaftswunder,* or it may be another Italian *mezzogiorno.*

Data in the paper allow calculation of how well East Germany is doing. The necessity in East Germany is to create a stock of new jobs, primarily in the tradable goods sector. At the current time, roughly 50 percent of the labor force is in underemployment, disguised unemployment, or full unemployment. These include the unemployed, those on short time, workers in ABMs (East Germany's public works program), workers in retraining programs, and many of the remaining workers in Treuhandanstalt firms, whose jobs will need to be phased out. The rest of the nonagricultural work force, which is in state and municipal governments, trade and transport, construction, self-employment, and a small nucleus in new private enterprises, are in jobs that are, in a long-run sense, viable. Thus, I will assume that new jobs are needed for roughly 50 percent of the work force.

New jobs require new capital stock. How long will it take to create enough capital to provide new jobs for 50 percent of the work force? One key number in this calculation is the rate at which new investment is occurring in East

This comment is based on joint research with George Akerlof and Helga Hessenius.

Germany. According to Deutsches Institut für Wirtschaftsforschung (DIW) estimates presented in the authors' table 5.21, gross private nonresidential investment in 1992 will total DM 63.6 billion. Assuming a civilian labor force of 7.7 million, this amounts to DM 8,260 per worker.[1] In West Germany, capital per worker, excluding residential housing, at the start of 1991 was DM 131,943.[2] Does the East German rate of capital formation entail a long or a short transition?

A variety of assumptions are necessary to see how long it will take before unemployment and disguised unemployment in the East German economy will disappear. The first assumption concerns the *average* capital-labor ratio of East German jobs. Since wages in East and West Germany are rapidly headed toward equality, it makes sense to assume, as a first approximation, that the average capital intensity of jobs in the East will be similar to that of those in the West. Three other assumptions are necessary in order to project the path of East German employment over time: (1) the *relative* capital intensities of the "old" sector (the sector of the economy now providing viable jobs) and the "new" sector; (2) the rates of depreciation of capital in the old and new sectors; and (3) the rate of migration.

Under the most optimistic assumptions, East Germany could experience a *Wirtschaftswunder*—a 6.9 year transition to full employment (defined as a 6 percent natural rate of unemployment)—if current gross investment levels are maintained. The optimistic assumptions are that the capital intensities of the old and new sectors are identical, that there is no depreciation of capital in either the old or the new sectors or the economy so that all investment is allocated to capital formation in the new sector, and that migration begins at 2.5 percent per year and falls linearly to zero as the economy reaches full employment.

But the transition could take much longer. The optimistic scenario ignores depreciation. With more realistic assumptions concerning depreciation of capital, the transition lengthens substantially. For example, with a 10 percent depreciation rate in the "old" sector and depreciation in the new sector of the one-horse shay type with a long lifetime so that replacement is not necessary in the period of calculation, the transition lengthens to twenty-five years.

The "optimistic" scenario further assumes that jobs in the old and new sectors of the East German economy are equally capital intensive. But, realistically, the "old" sector of the East German economy, now providing viable jobs, is heavily weighted with self-employment, state and local government, trade,

---

1. In contrast, estimated gross and net investment per worker in 1992 are DM 13,969 and DM 4,749, respectively, in West Germany.

2. This estimate is consistent with the predictions of the Solow model under the assumption that West Germany is in steady-state growth. Along a steady-state growth path, $k^* = i/(n + \lambda)$. Assuming population growth (n) of 1 percent and technological change (λ) of 2.5 percent, the implied steady-state capital intensity, k^*, corresponding to the 1992 estimated net investment per worker (i) of DM 4,749 is DM 135,685.

and services, all of which are relatively labor-intensive activities. We therefore ran an alternative simulation, otherwise identical to our "optimistic" case, in which the existing jobs in East Germany are assumed to be in relatively labor-intensive sectors while new jobs must be created in sectors that are relatively capital intensive. Specifically, we assumed that jobs in the old sector require (and currently possess) capital per worker that is 50 percent below the West German economy-wide average while jobs in the new sector require capital per worker that is 50 percent above the West German economy-wide average. With half the Eastern labor force in the old and new sectors, the average capital-labor ratios for the East and West German economies are identical. In this case, the transition lengthens from 6.9 to 10 years. For a reasonable range of parameter values concerning depreciation and relative capital intensities in the old and new sectors, the length of the transition is between seven and twenty-five years.

A final assumption underlying these computations is that the East German and West German capital-labor ratios are, *on average,* similar. If the average capital intensity of East German jobs turns out to be higher than that of those in the West, the transition may take substantially longer. This could occur if newly created jobs turn out to be highly capital intensive. For example, if the capital required to create a new job in East Germany is 50 percent higher than that assumed in the simulations described above, analogous computations yield full employment only after ten to thirty-three years of per capita capital accumulation of DM 8,260 instead of seven to twenty-five years. Unfortunately, there are two reasons to suspect that Eastern investment may be highly capital intensive.

First, the nature of German subsidies encourages capital intensive investments in the East. In order to stimulate investment, the federal government has set up a number of capital subsidy programs, which together cover about 50 percent of a firm's investment cost. In West Germany, the capital-labor ratio in industry is roughly DM 100,000 per worker. In contrast, the recent investments of Volkswagen and Opel involve capital-labor ratios of roughly DM 120,000–DM 135,000. And Siemens is reportedly building a plant in Brandenburg with 50 percent government subsidies and capital of DM 500,000 per employee—five times the industrial average in West Germany. We are not aware of any statistics that accurately portray the capital intensity of new investment in the East, but, since the length of time to full employment is roughly inversely proportional to the capital-labor ratio, it is important to discover whether the incentives for high capital intensity have resulted in significant bias. If there is such a bias, there is less room for optimism, and the German government should reevaluate its policies for investment subsidies.

A second reason for concern about the capital intensity of Eastern investment is that roughly half the DM 63.6 billion of "private" investment in East Germany that is forecast for 1992 (see table 5.21) consists of investment in telecommunications, transportation, and energy.[3] (Investment by West German firms in East Germany is expected to amount to about DM 35 billion according to an Ifo poll.) These sectors are enormously capital intensive: in West Germany, capital per worker in transport and telecommunications and in utilities is, respectively, twice and eight times the West German economy-wide average. Thus, our baseline calculations tend to overstate the amount of job creation associated with current investment levels.

The optimistic scenario described above also assumes that the rate of gross investment per worker will remain constant over time. Arguably, this is too pessimistic an assumption: perhaps, once more infrastructure investment has been completed, the pace of private investment may increase. However, investment could also decline if there is a recession in West Germany, as now seems likely. One of the motives for West German firms to invest in the East is that, following unification, they found themselves with extra demand and little spare capacity. A recession in the West would obviate the need for Western firms to expand capacity. In addition, higher interest rates due to tight Bundesbank policy would likewise discourage investment.

Finally, the optimistic scenario that I have described also assumes that public investment will continue and even expand. There is also the risk that such spending will need to be curtailed. This could occur for a number of reasons. First, a recession in the West will depress tax revenues and swell an already large budget deficit, reducing the ability of the German government to finance an ambitious infrastructure plan for the East. Second, the costs of unity to the German government will inexorably mount as the wage increases that have already been negotiated take effect over the next several years. If we assume that the German government will be unwilling to expand its budget deficit further, then the extra government spending necessitated by wage increases will translate dollar for dollar into reduced spending on public capital formation in the East and other government-supported activities. Consider the arithmetic. Of the roughly 7.7 million workers in the Eastern labor force, a large majority (perhaps as much as two-thirds) are directly or indirectly paid by the government. This includes state and local government workers, workers in transport, post, and telecommunications, workers in Treuhand firms, and workers on public construction projects. Any wage increases for these workers will be financed with government funds. In addition, the payments received by those who are unemployed, on short time, and in public works or retraining programs are indexed to the wages received by the Eastern work force. Retirement benefits also tend to rise with wage levels. Higher wages in the East will thus raise the expense of supporting the unemployed and underemployed as well. High wage settlements in the East are detrimental to Eastern recovery

---

3. "Private investment" includes the investment of government enterprises, which importantly include post and telecommunications, railways, and government-owned utilities.

through this spending channel as well as via their direct negative effects on the viability of existing jobs and the profitability of new investment.

Treuhand Policy

The authors have provided a very good overview of the policies being pursued by the Treuhandanstalt, the agency responsible for privatizing East German industry. The key questions are, Has the Treuhand pursued a wise privatization strategy? and, How should it deal with the money-losing firms that remain in its portfolio?

The authors outline two extreme options: unemployment or status quo subsidies. The Treuhand could liquidate any money-losing firms that it cannot quickly sell, throwing workers into the job market, an option that is not unthinkable given the generous level of unemployment compensation and the wide range of "public works" programs that are available. Or the Treuhand could continue subsidizing its money-losing properties to preserve jobs.

There is also a middle course. The middle course is what I perceive the Treuhand to be pursuing, and it is the course that I personally favor. The middle course is to agree to invest money—within limits—to save or preserve jobs in the course of privatizing firms and to close firms that cannot be privatized with a reasonable injection of government funds. If the Treuhand is permitted to pursue this strategy, most of the privatization work will be completed over the next several years, and the privatized firms that remain will be operating under hard budget constraints.

Why should the Treuhand spend money to save jobs? The logic is simple: it is both in the overall social interest and in the financial interest of the government. There is a major distortion in the East German economy: the current wage is far in excess of the market clearing level. With about one-third of the labor force unemployed or underemployed, the social cost of labor is low—far below the wage. As a result, there is too little employment. Arguably, high levels of unemployment speed economic restructuring by creating high motivation for workers to retrain and a pool of labor for new firms to hire. But unemployment is already above any level that could be deemed optimal for this purpose. The social gain from job creation exceeds the gain to potential employers. This justifies the Treuhand's policy from a social welfare standpoint. From a budgetary standpoint, the logic is equally simple: the budgetary gain from job creation is large and positive. A typical individual who leaves the unemployment rolls and finds work saves the German government 79.1 percent of his previous total compensation through lower unemployment benefits and higher income tax and social insurance receipts. This means that the German government saves money if it can create a job by spending less than 79 percent of worker compensation to do so. This provides a strong budgetary rationale for spending a significant amount of money to create new jobs or to save existing ones even if it requires selling firms at negative prices.

And this is precisely what the Treuhand has done, albeit haphazardly and without the transparency that the process should ideally have in the absence of political considerations. In selling the firms in its portfolio, the Treuhand has strongly favored investors who guarantee higher employment and future investment levels, not those offering the largest up-front bids. It has frequently "sold" firms for a token DM 1.00. The Treuhand has also accepted negative sales prices: this occurs when the Treuhand invests to "restructure" a firm prior to sale or when, as in the Zeiss Jena case described by the authors, the Treuhand provides "start-up funds" or "loss compensation." In other words, it is spending money to create jobs.

The economic logic that I have just outlined suggests that the Treuhand should establish an appropriate "shadow price" of employment to use in its evaluations of outside bids. Investors would receive a job creation "credit" based on the number of jobs saved and the number of future jobs guaranteed through promised investment. This credit would be added to the investor's (possibly negative) monetary bid in scoring proposals. In actuality, the Treuhand is pursuing a policy that may approximate the rule that I have outlined. Because the methodology employed is ad hoc, however, the Treuhand is probably spending too much money to save jobs in some instances and too little in others. In the case of Zeiss Jena, for example, the $212,500 per job that the Treuhand paid seems excessive since this amount probably exceeds the present discounted value of the budgetary savings even under the assumption that the workers would otherwise remain permanently unemployed. The second problem with the Treuhand's approach is that it is not transparent: potential investors are aware that the Treuhand cares about jobs but have no way of computing "how much" the Treuhand cares in preparing their bids.

Even with its heavy emphasis on employment, and even given its willingness to sell firms for a negative price, the Treuhand is appropriately following a middle course, making tough decisions to cut employment as privatization occurs. Consider the evidence. There were initially 3 million industrial jobs in Treuhand firms. Thus far, roughly 1 million jobs have been saved by the Treuhand, but about half are in service-sector establishments. A rough estimate is that a maximum of 500,000 jobs in industry have thus far been saved. Since, at present, there are about 1.9 million industrial jobs in Treuhand firms, at least 600,000 industrial jobs have been eliminated by the Treuhand in the course of privatization. A typical privatization involves employment reductions ranging up to 80 percent. Since many of the remaining Treuhand properties will be difficult to privatize and are likely to involve even smaller job savings, a reasonable forecast is that only 20–30 percent of the original industrial jobs will remain when privatization is complete. The German government has also shown backbone by ending special East German short-time arrangements on 1 January of this year, forcing many of the workers on these schemes into open employment or other social programs. The Treuhand is not just preserving the status quo. The Treuhand is appropriately spending money to save jobs, and, arguably, it is spending too little rather than too much. All in all, the Treuhand's policies seem reasonable.

There is further reason why the German government should be willing to pay limited amounts to subsidize privatization of Treuhand firms. The Treuhand's privatization strategy has succeeded in saving a large number of activities that may serve as the nuclei for successful further growth of jobs. In particular, the Treuhand has saved many of the core businesses of the former state-owned enterprises. The value of preserving an activity may be disproportionate to the number of jobs that are saved if the activity has the potential for future growth or if its survival makes other investments viable. As the authors note, investment decisions are highly interdependent, and multiplier effects are at work in East Germany.

Let me offer an example. In Eisenhüttenstadt, near the Polish border, there is a large steel factory—Eko Stahl—whose survival was problematic. In January 1992, the Treuhand finally announced that it would sell this company to the West German steelmaker Krupp. The sale involves substantial Treuhand subsidies. Had the plant been closed, Eisenhüttenstadt would have become a ghost town. Even under the privatization plan, employment at the firm will fall dramatically, from 11,300 prior to unification to about 2,800. However, since the plant will survive, so will numerous local independent metal-working enterprises and privatized firms that provide repair services to the steel plant. Major investments currently planned for the revived town include two shopping centers and a plant manufacturing advanced hydrofoils located next to the steel mill.

The authors argue that Treuhand firms should face hard budget constraints soon—within eight months' time—either by being forced to use commercial borrowing or, if unsuccessful, to face bankruptcy. I agree that hard budget constraints must be imposed. In fact, many people in Germany believe that a hard budget constraint has been imposed because Treuhandanstalt liquidity loans have been capped this year at a total of DM 30 billion. This constraint, however, has been quietly subverted by allowing Treuhand firms to engage in asset stripping by selling or mortgaging their considerable land holdings. As the authors' table 5.18 shows, in many sectors wage payments exceed value added. With a cap on its liquidity credits, the Treuhand is underwriting these losses by, in effect, selling off its remaining valuable assets. The Treuhand told us that firms were permitted to do this only if they were expected ultimately to survive.

Morals

Let me conclude by pointing to just one of the morals of the East German story for other times and other places. This concerns the importance of wages. The East German depression is so deep, indeed much deeper than that of its less fortunate Eastern neighbors, because real wages have risen so dramatically.

The warning to Eastern countries concerns the importance of keeping wages in line. Excess wages will make employment and investment unprofitable. In addition, they will throw government budgets out of balance. The consequences of high wages for East German recovery have been largely offset by massive transfers. But the German government has yet to face the consequences of future rises in East German wages, which, at a minimum, will affect the costs of state and local government, the cost of infrastructural investment, government make-work programs, unemployment insurance, and short time. The rising interest costs of the German debt may threaten the government with a loss of flexibility in expenditure, creating a dilemma similar to that now facing President Bush. I started by remembering Mayor Koch. In the end, it is appropriate to remember another New York mayor, John Lindsay, who granted large wage increases to city unions, subsequently leading to the bankruptcy of New York. The East German case yet again underscores the dangers of excessive wage increases in the absence of vigilant public watchfulness over the public purse.

Discussion Summary

Kalman Mizsei asked the authors how well the Treuhand was functioning from a bureaucratic perspective. He wondered whether corruption and inefficiency were problems. All of the other East European countries have chosen to create privatization institutions that are much smaller and less autonomous than the Treuhand. In response, *Rudiger Dornbusch* said that the institutional environment at the Treuhand "is a dream," with no reported scandals. He ascribed this success to the fact that the Treuhand is highly visible and is constantly under intense political scrutiny.

Larry Summers criticized the ad hoc industrial policy that he believes is being implemented by the Treuhand. He suggested that the Yellen plan (i.e., an explicit wage subsidy coupled with clean market-based privatization) looked much better than the current Treuhand policy. *Janet Yellen* appreciated Summers's support, but she noted that the Yellen plan had little chance of being implemented since it has previously been rejected by German policymakers.

Dani Rodrik noted that it is important to analyze the strategic behavior of unions when considering the effect of a wage subsidy. For example, if a government commits to full employment and uses a wage subsidy as its only instrument, then the unions can extract infinite rents. He believes that wage/employment subsidies will be successful only if the government gets trade unions "in on the process."

Barry Bosworth questioned Yellen's claim that "a typical individual who leaves the unemployment rolls and finds work saves the German government 79.1 percent of his previous total compensation." The calculation behind this number assumes that demand for the produced good is perfectly elastic. Bos-worth believes that it is more reasonable to assume that some jobs that are created by the government crowd out private employment. Yellen responded by emphasizing that most of the Treuhand firms that produce industrial output are in the tradables sector, where demand is highly elastic.

Dornbusch said that the Treuhand has been too cautious, and he felt that some participants were making the same mistake. Initially, the Treuhand had predicted that it would sell one-third of its firms, restructure another third, and close the remaining third. The Treuhand has done a good job in selling the viable firms, but it has not successfully dealt with the remaining two-thirds of firms that must be closed or restructured. He argued that Germany should not subsidize the status quo since this prevents the necessary structural changes from taking place.

Dornbusch concluded by emphasizing the important role that commuting will play for the economic prospects of East Germany. For example, mass commuting will drastically reduce the capital needs of East Germany. He said that all the capital requirement calculations have to be radically scaled down.

Holger Wolf emphasized that it is inappropriate to assume, as some of the participants had done, that East German and West German wages will quickly equilibrate. It may take as long as fifteen years for this convergence to occur. Wolf also noted that there are advantages to the fact that the Treuhand does not operate with an explicit shadow price for job creation. Having flexibility is helpful in designing idiosyncratic sales packages. Moreover, estimates of these prices can be imputed by looking at past deals.

6   Political Independence and Economic Reform in Slovenia

Boris Pleskovic and Jeffrey D. Sachs

With the dissolution of Yugoslavia and the Soviet Union, twenty new independent states have emerged where there were previously two. In each of these new states, there is an urgent agenda, including the creation of state institutions (fiscal authority, tax authority, central bank, border control, etc.), macroeconomic stabilization, and economic transformation from a socialist economy to a market economy. These momentous changes are generally being carried out under conditions of extreme political uncertainty, typically with legislative bodies that are only partially elected, or that were elected under the old regime, and with constitutions that are holdovers from the Communist period.

Of all the new countries, the one that has gone the furthest in economic reform is Slovenia. Slovene independence from Yugoslavia was achieved in steps during the period December 1990–October 1991 (see table 6.1). By the end of this process, on 8 October 1991, Slovenia introduced its own currency, the Slovene tolar, thereby becoming the first of the new states to achieve monetary independence.[1] As we shall stress, monetary independence has been highly effective in sparing Slovenia from the resurgence of hyperinflation in the rest of the former Yugoslavia in 1992.

Even with relative successes in the areas of macroeconomic stabilization and trade liberalization, Slovenia has proceeded far too slowly in the area of privatization. The delay in implementing privatization was not accidental but rather the result of intense political infighting of a sort that is being played out

Boris Pleskovic was chief economic adviser to Slovene Prime Minister Lojze Peterle during 1991 and the first part of 1992, until the change of government in May 1992. Jeffrey D. Sachs led a team of independent advisers, including David Lipton and Jaime Jaramillo-Vallejo, that provided macroeconomic advice to Prime Minister Peterle and that assisted in the drafting and implementation of the government's economic reform program.
1. The first state of the former Soviet Union to achieve monetary independence, Estonia, benefited by a careful examination of Slovenia's experience (Hanson and Sachs 1992).

Table 6.1	Timetable to Independence
26 December 1990	Referendum on independence passes with 90% approval. Slovene government appeals for loose confederation of Yugoslav republics, to be negotiated during the next 6 months
25 June 1991	Declaration of full independence and sovereignty, 6 months after referendum. Outbreak of war on 27 June 1991
7 July 1991	Brioni Accord, sponsored by the EC, calling for 3-month delay in implementation of full sovereignty, to pursue further negotiations
8 October 1991	Full independence and monetary reform, 3 months after Brioni Accord
15 January 1992	Recognition by the EC

throughout Eastern Europe and the former Soviet Union. On the one side are the non-Communist parties of the center and right that argue for a widespread distribution of shares to the general public; on the other side are lobbying groups of state managers and the new left-of-center parties that have succeeded the previously ruling Communist party who together are fighting for a transfer of ownership to the managers themselves. Similar political infighting has delayed several structural adjustment measures in Slovenia, including a much needed banking reform.

In this paper, we seek to explore Slovenia's progress in the triple tasks of state building, stabilization, and transition to a market economy. We begin with the political history of Slovene independence and then turn to the sequence of economic policy measures that accompanied the process of political independence, with special emphasis on monetary reform, macroeconomic stabilization, and the debate over privatization. We also examine the early evidence on Slovenia's trade prospects, related both to the breakdown of trade within Yugoslavia and to the shift of trade toward Western Europe. We conclude by outlining the priorities for the future, which include privatization and financial restructuring of commercial banks and enterprises.

6.1 Overview of Slovenia

Before 1991, Slovenia was most recently an independent country in the seventh century, when it was known as Carinthia. It was subsequently incorporated into the Frankish empire and later into the Hapsburg empire. In 1918, Slovenia joined Croatia and Serbia to establish Yugoslavia. When Yugoslavia became a Communist state under Marshall Tito's leadership following World War II, Slovenia became one of the six republics of the new socialist state. It became independent in 1991.

Yugoslavia, it is well known, chose a distinctive path of socialist development after Tito's break with Stalin in 1948. Industry was socialized, as in the rest of Eastern Europe and the Soviet Union, but was not subjected to central planning after 1965. Market forces were given more scope, and enterprises were left with significantly more autonomy than in the Stalinist states. Ownership was deemed to be "social" rather than "state," on the ostensible grounds that enterprises were managed by workers' councils rather than through centralized branch ministries. Yugoslavia also maintained a trade pattern that was distinctive among the socialist economies, in that the direction of trade remained heavily toward Western Europe rather than toward the other socialist states. Yugoslavia was never a member of the Council for Mutual Economic Assistance (CMEA) trading arrangements.

We will have occasion to discuss the ownership patterns in Slovenia later in the paper, but at this point it is worthwhile to clarify the distinctive features of the Yugoslav socialist model. While a vast economics literature emerged to describe Yugoslavia's "market socialism" and "workers' management system," the economic realities in the Yugoslav socialist economy were quite different from the idealizations in the academic literature. More important than the ownership and control structure itself was the fact that Yugoslav industrial enterprises were far more market oriented than their counterparts in Eastern Europe. These enterprises traded with Western customers, had considerable flexibility as to choice of inputs and outputs, and had some flexibility related to prices. In general, there was not a chronic shortage economy in the industrial sector or in the consumer markets, so that inputs were available on a fairly reliable basis. As a result of these factors, many Slovene companies were able to compete in name-brand markets, where quality and reputation are paramount, something unheard of among East European enterprises.[2] A good illustration is the Slovene ski manufacturer Elan, which successfully entered the Western ski market.

6.1.1 Economic Structure

Slovenia is the richest East European country. Its income per capita was over U.S.$6,100 in 1990, compared to an overall Yugoslav average of U.S.$3,060 and an average in the non-Slovene part of Yugoslavia of U.S.$2,800. While its income per capita is comparable to Greece and Portugal, and despite its relative openness, the industrial and employment structure of the Slovene economy has important similarities to other East European countries. As in other socialist economies, open unemployment was practically nonexistent in Slovenia until recently (Abraham and Vodopivec 1991).[3] Also, the Slovene economy, like others of Eastern Europe, is heavily concentrated in industry, compared with OECD countries, which have much larger service sectors (see table 6.2). In terms of employment and output, Slovenia is different from the rest of Yugoslavia, possessing a very small agricultural and a large industrial sector.

---

2. Some argue that the geographic location of Slovenia made its economy and its people even more exposed than those of the other Yugoslav republics to market forces.

3. There was, however, open unemployment in other parts of Yugoslavia, and the overall unemployment rate of Yugoslavia had reached 12.8 percent in 1990.

Table 6.2   Structure of GDP, 1988

	Agriculture	Industry	Services
Value added:			
Slovenia	4.5	51.5	44.0
OECD	2.8	33.0	64.1
Employment:			
Slovenia (1989)	9.9	50.9	39.2
OECD	9.4	30.0	60.6

Source: For the OECD, *The Economist Book of Vital World Statistics* (New York: Random House, 1990), 36. For Slovenia, *Development Issues of the Statistical System: Gross Domestic Product of Slovenia in 1987–1988,* no. 3 (Ljubljana: Statistical Office of the Republic of Slovenia, December 1991).

Other similarities between Slovenia and other East European countries include a very small privately owned sector, full employment with substantial excess demand for labor, and a relatively well-educated labor force. Slovenia also resembled other East European countries in the existence of a soft budget constraint for its enterprises, low labor mobility, and political intervention in enterprises in terms of investment and employment.

The Slovene economy is relatively open. Representing just 8 percent of the total Yugoslav population in 1990, Slovenia accounted for 20 percent of the gross domestic product (GDP) in the former Yugoslavia and 29 percent of total Yugoslav exports. In recent years, the volume of external trade (excluding the former Yugoslavia) amounted to U.S.$10 billion, equivalent to about 95 percent of the Slovene GDP, with exports exceeding imports by about 5 percent of GDP. In 1991, about 80 percent of merchandise trade was conducted with developed countries, 14 percent with East European countries, and about 6 percent with the developing countries. Major trading partners have been Germany (25 percent) and Italy (16 percent). As mentioned above, the former Yugoslavia was not a member country of the CMEA. Most of its trade with the former Soviet bloc was conducted in convertible currencies. In recent years, about 25 percent of the total sales by Slovene enterprises were exported to the markets of the former Yugoslavia. In 1992, trade with the rest of Yugoslavia has declined sharply, as we shall note below, and has shifted away from Serbia and toward Croatia because of the UN blockade of Serbia.

6.1.2 Political Developments

The first free elections in Slovenia were held in April 1990. The center-right coalition of six parties, called DEMOS, won the elections with a 52.9 percent majority. The opposition was represented by four parties on the left, combining political forces emerging from the now-divided Communist party. Legislative power is shared by three chambers in the Parliament. Every law has to be agreed on by each of the three chambers. The first two chambers were elected directly by the entire electorate. The third chamber, represented mainly by managers of social enterprises, was elected by the employees of enterprises only. Although a new constitution was adopted in December 1991, abolishing the third chamber, Slovenia will maintain its old institutions until the next elections, scheduled for the end of 1992.[4]

Despite a weak majority, DEMOS was able to avoid political instability at the beginning of its rule. Since most parties held the common goal of obtaining independence for Slovenia, there was more or less a nonpartisan spirit in the Parliament during the war and struggle for independence.

Following the recognition of Slovenia and the achievement of the main goal that had unified the parties, intense political infighting began. Political parties and interest groups had by then become better organized, and the economic reforms became increasingly politicized. The democratic parties argued for quick and transparent privatization of social enterprises and banks, including denationalization. On the other side, the opposition defended a gradualist reform process in order to prolong the life of the old system, under which it continues to hold major positions.

When it became clear that the two sides could not reach an agreement, the opposition started to block major legislation, including privatization, through the third chamber, where it had a majority. This resulted in a paralysis of the Parliament, which lasted for months. In April 1992, the government lost a motion of nonconfidence, and a new coalition of center and left parties formed a new government.

The experience of Slovenia seems to confirm recent cross-country research, which has shown that multiparty governments are especially prone to parliamentary paralysis (Sachs 1992). Some expected that the more developed and open Slovenia would pursue market reforms, including privatization, vigorously and serve as an example for the rest of Eastern Europe. These expectations were met to some extent since substantial progress was made in several areas of economic reform. An enormous task was accomplished, especially with respect to state building, monetary reform, and macroeconomic stabilization. On the other hand, Slovenia's relative prosperity may have reduced the sense of urgency regarding the major structural changes, including privatization and financial restructuring.

6.2   Economic Conditions before Independence

6.2.1   Yugoslav Hyperinflation

The Yugoslav economy was characterized by stagnation and unstable and rising inflation during the 1980s. Average output growth was 0.6 percent in the period 1981–89, as compared to 6.4 percent during 1974–80 (Estrin and Takla

---

4. After we wrote the paper, elections took place in December 1992.

1991). Open unemployment averaged 14 percent during the period 1981–89. Inflation started to accelerate in 1983, reaching about 70 percent in 1985, 90 percent in 1986, and 2,800 percent in 1989. The economy reached hyperinflationary rates of 50–60 percent per month at the end of 1989. At that time, Slovenia was still part of Yugoslavia and, as part of the dinar area, was subject to the same hyperinflation.

The hyperinflation was caused by chronic fiscal imbalances that resulted in a heavy debt structure, both of enterprises and foreign debt. The most interesting aspect of the Yugoslav hyperinflation, however, was that a significant component of the money in the economy was indexed money. This was a reflection of an acute case of currency substitution in the form of deutsche mark–denominated deposits within the banking system. Guest workers in Germany were encouraged to repatriate savings through the availability of deutsche mark–denominated accounts. These accounts were so popular, in view of the high and unpredictable inflation rate, that more than 80 percent of household monetary savings were in foreign-currency-denominated deposits by November 1989 (Banka Slovenije 1991). In addition, there was significant formal and informal indexation of wages and salaries.

This meant that there was little room for credit expansion without fueling inflation, as the ability to collect an inflation tax was almost nil. In addition, under the guidance of the International Monetary Fund (IMF), the key interest of which was maintaining Yugoslavia current on its external debt servicing, the Yugoslav authorities in 1988 and 1989 pursued an undervalued real exchange rate policy, in which the nominal exchange rate was steadily devalued in order to try to meet an undervalued real exchange rate target. Since each ratchet of the exchange rate was almost immediately matched by a rise in domestic prices and wages as well as in the dinar value of the domestic money supply, the devaluations were able to achieve the real exchange rate target only at the cost of rapidly accelerating inflation.[5]

An underlying cause of rising inflation throughout the 1980s was the inability of the federal authorities to exert any monetary control and to enforce financial discipline on enterprises. Enterprise losses increased from a measured 3 percent to 15 percent of GDP in the second half of the 1980s, although these data do not take sufficient care in distinguishing nominal from real interest costs of enterprises in measuring their true losses. These losses were accommodated by the banking system, within a system of soft budget constraints. And, despite its relative flexibility, the Yugoslav economy still suffered from political intervention at the enterprise level, with significant restrictions on free trade and partial control of prices. In 1987, only around 40 percent of prices were freely determined, and 48 percent of imports were subject to licenses.

---

5. This outcome of a real exchange rate rule for exchange rate policy has been observed extensively in Latin American countries, most notably in Brazil, the pioneer of the so-called crawling peg.

With a background of stagnation, poor financial discipline of enterprises, banks, and governments at all levels, and a drift toward hyperinflation, a systematic reform process began in the late 1980s, with a comprehensive stabilization package being introduced at the start of 1990. The government gradually liberalized most prices and imports between 1988 and 1989. As a result of this policy, the federal price office was abolished, and 87 percent of imports were liberalized by the end of 1989. At the same time, the government started enterprise and banking reforms.

6.2.2   The Markovic Program

In January 1990, the federal government under the leadership of Prime Minister Ante Markovic implemented an anti-inflation stabilization program. The program included current account convertibility of the dinar, an initial 20 percent step devaluation of the dinar at the start of the program, and tight fiscal and monetary policy. The policy of a crawling peg was abandoned, and a fixed exchange rate of seven dinars per deutsche mark was established to provide a nominal anchor to the system; it was held at that level throughout 1990. The government also froze nominal wages for six months at the start of the stabilization program. The program quickly brought down inflation to nearly 0 percent in April 1990.

Incomes and demand policies started to relax again in the summer of 1990 since the federal government was unable to implement the complementary structural reforms required of the program (including the bankruptcy of major loss-making enterprises) and thereby to maintain overall financial and wage discipline. The monthly rate of inflation increased to 2 percent in July and 8 percent in October, before falling to 3 percent in November and December 1990. Money in circulation rose by 138 percent in the ten months to the end of October, compared with an increase of retail prices of 110 percent, revealing a relaxed monetary policy (Estrin and Takla 1991). The breakdown of financial control and incomes policy was caused in part by the start of the centrifugal political process in the republics, which eventually led to the disintegration of Yugoslavia.

In the middle of 1990, a series of free elections started in the different republics, for the first time in forty-five years. Intent on garnering public support, political leaders in the republics began to chafe at the monetary and incomes restrictions of the Markovic Plan and began to seek ways to circumvent them. About the same time, Prime Minister Markovic began to run for office in a federal election foreseen at the end of the year. He formed a party and raised the wages of public-sector workers substantially as part of the election campaign. These events undermined the stabilization program and raised inflationary expectation in the public. Retail prices in Yugoslavia increased by 122 percent from December 1989 to December 1990.

The current account of the balance of payments deteriorated over the year. In the summer of 1990, exports fell sharply. To improve exports, the federal government devalued the currency, from seven to nine dinars per deutsche mark, on 28 December 1990. However, the prospect of stabilizing the economy further deteriorated after the central bank branch located in Serbia issued U.S.$1.3 billion of currency, in late December 1990 and early January 1991, that had not been authorized by the main office of the central bank.

At the beginning of 1991, the Yugoslav economy had a budget deficit of U.S.$2.6 billion, a 10.9 percent decline in industrial output, resulting in a 20 percent decline in GDP (for 1991 overall), and an unemployment rate of 18 percent (Chamber of Commerce 1991). The increasingly independent republics refused to pay taxes to the federal government, owing to political differences concerning the restructuring of the federation, and the National Bank of Yugoslavia relaxed monetary policy. A new inflationary cycle began; monthly price increases accelerated to double-digit levels in mid-1991, effectively marking the end of the economic reform program launched in 1990.

Although the stabilization program was successful in its first phase, it began to fail when monetary policy and financial policies were allowed to return to their previous laxness in the second half of 1990. What Yugoslavia's experience shows is that an effective stabilization program requires a determined and strong government to enforce a strict monetary and fiscal policy and financial discipline on enterprises and local government.

6.3   Slovene Independence

Under pressure from the Slovene public, as a result of growing political differences with the rest of Yugoslavia on the future direction of the federal state as well as the rapidly deteriorating economic situation, the Slovene Parliament voted to hold a referendum on independence on 26 December 1990 (see table 6.1 above). The referendum produced a 90 percent majority in favor of independence. After the referendum, Slovenia proposed a six-month period of negotiations with the other Yugoslav republics to form a loose confederation in the country. Six months later, and after no progress in the negotiations, on 25 June 1991 the Parliament of Slovenia declared full sovereignty. On 27 June, the Yugoslav armed forces attacked the country. Ten days later, the European Community (EC) helped bring about a cease-fire. An agreement, called the Brioni Accord, was reached in which Slovenia agreed to a three-month delay in implementation of full sovereignty in order to give time for further negotiations between Slovenia and the rest of Yugoslavia.

Three months after the Brioni Accord, and with no progress in the negotiations, the Parliament reactivated the implementation of independence laws. The drive toward independence was also spurred by the psychological effect of the attempted bombing of the Yugoslav prime minister by the Yugoslav air force during a visit by Markovic to Croatia and a rumor that the central bank in Belgrade intended to flood Slovenia with dinars. These events led to the early introduction of the national currency. The parliament called for the introduction of the Slovene tolar on 7 October 1991, and the government and monetary authorities undertook monetary reform the next day. On 15 January 1992, Slovenia was recognized by the European Community. Recognition by several other countries followed immediately and by the United Nations six months later.

6.3.1   Economic Steps toward Independence

In the spring of 1991, the government of Slovenia designed a macroeconomic program for the economic independence and restructuring of Slovenia (Assembly of the Republic of Slovenia 1991). The program, which was subsequently passed by the Parliament, had five elements: (i) monetary independence, (ii) macroeconomic stabilization, (iii) financial restructuring of loss-making enterprises, (iv) restructuring of commercial banks, and (v) privatization. There was also a wide range of legislation undertaken to establish the basic economic institutions of a sovereign state.

The macroeconomic program was designed as a comprehensive package of interrelated market reforms to be launched simultaneously with independence (Lipton and Sachs 1991). While the preparation started in all areas of the package at the same time, not all steps of the program were implemented in the order originally intended because of several unexpected turns of events. The declaration of independence did not lead to immediate sovereignty. War broke out, disrupting the work of the government and forcing the government to design and implement an emergency economic program instead of preparing long-term economic reforms. At the same time, under the Brioni Accord, the government agreed to three months of further negotiations, which again upstaged consideration of long-term reforms. When Slovene sovereignty was achieved, state-building activities, particularly issues of national defense, received most of the attention.

Among economic reforms, only the most urgent ones, monetary reform and macroeconomic stabilization, received wide political support. Under the circumstances, privatization and financial restructuring of enterprises and banks were not perceived as immediate priorities by the Parliament and the major political actors. Of the three closely related structural reform issues, privatization was considered as the most important. When privatization became a political issue, the other two reforms were put on a waiting list. Preparatory work continued on all three reforms, and the expectation was that, when privatization passed the Parliament, the others would follow immediately. As in the rest of Eastern Europe, however, privatization has proved harder than expected. Unfortunately, the delay of privatization slowed down the needed restructuring of banks and enterprises. In spite of this delay, enormous progress was achieved in most other areas of the economic program, especially monetary and fiscal reforms and institutional development, as discussed in the following sections.

6.3.2 Monetary Reform

In March 1991, the political leadership decided to make all the necessary preparations for the introduction of a new currency.[6] The new national currency, which was to be stable and convertible from the outset, was meant to isolate Slovenia from the inflationary chaos in the rest of Yugoslavia. The basic idea was straightforward. All bank accounts, domestic wages, prices, and other contractual relations were to be converted automatically from dinars to the new currency, the tolar. Currency in circulation was to be physically converted during a short period of time. The new currency was to be the sole legal tender after conversion and was to trade freely with international currencies on a convertible basis and also float freely vis-à-vis the Yugoslav dinar (Pleskovic and Sachs 1992).

To this end, actions were carried out on three fronts. First, steps were taken to create a central bank that was capable of carrying out credible and disciplined monetary and exchange rate policies. These steps included the drafting of a central bank law that assured its independence, the development of a policy design and control unit in the new central bank, and, perhaps more important, fiscal reforms to minimize the pressures for monetization of budget deficits. These steps resulted in the central bank law and the macroeconomic program adopted by the Council of Ministers in September 1991.

Second, to make the new currency convertible, legislation was adopted that established a unified market for foreign exchange, without the previous sharp socialist distinctions between households and firms. With a unified foreign exchange market, the central bank could intervene to carry out its exchange rate policy using a market-based approach.[7]

Third, the logistics of the conversion process required sufficient preparation to ensure a swift implementation that would minimize economic disruption and any chances of aggressive action by the federal government or by other republics. In the event, the conversion process was carried out in three days without halting the entire economy. However, the central bank board continued

---

6. Provisional notes were printed by the end of 1990 for emergency purposes, but there was no specific economic program for the monetary reform at the time. These notes were intended to be used in case the central bank in Belgrade stopped supplying Slovenia with dinar notes.

7. During the spring and summer of 1991, the National Bank of Yugoslavia maintained a substantially overvalued exchange rate that was harming the export-oriented republics of the north. As part of a strategy to minimize the effect in Slovenia of Belgrade's return to currency inconvertibility and overvaluation of the dinar in 1991, two foreign exchange markets were allowed in the Slovene territory prior to the introduction of a national currency. The first of these markets was a scheme (known as the EDP) that essentially allowed enterprises to operate at the free market rate of the dinar rather than the overvalued official rate. The second of these markets was meant to bring the black market into the financial system, allowing all individuals to trade foreign exchange within the system. The main trader in this market was the Ministry of Finance, which used the opportunity to build up some reserves for the government at the expense of running a fiscal surplus. The development of this market, just after the war, was instrumental in minimizing the effect of the uncertain political environment on tourism and border trade.

to convert dinars into tolars in special cases for several weeks after the initial deadline.

Several issues arose throughout the implementation of the process just described. Other monetary options were considered and discussed widely prior to the introduction of the new currency. These included the use of a currency board (in which the tolar to deutsche mark conversion rate would be irrevocably fixed and the currency would be fully backed by foreign exchange reserves) and the introduction of a parallel currency to circulate alongside the Yugoslav dinar, in which case both currencies would remain legal tender, at least for a while. The currency board was ruled out because Slovenia did not have foreign exchange reserves and external financial support could not be secured to allow the arrangement to succeed. The parallel currency alternative was dismissed from the beginning because it would only aggravate the existing currency substitution without isolating Slovenia from the ravages of Yugoslav hyperinflation (Pleskovic and Sachs 1993). The political leadership, under Prime Minister Lojze Peterle, stood firmly behind the concept of having a single national currency, designed to be stable and convertible from the start.

In addition, and as has already been mentioned, the introduction and management of the new currency was a fairly detailed process, and not all steps turned out as originally conceived (Jaramillo-Vallejo and Pleskovic 1991). The implementation started on 7 October 1991, when the Slovene monetary unit, the tolar, was declared by the Parliament as the sole legal tender in Slovenia, thus allowing the monetary reform to take place. The commercial banks, the Social Accounting Service, and the post offices were closed for most transactions during the three days starting 8 October 1991. The conversion of dinar banknotes into tolar banknotes was mostly accomplished in the first day and a half since Slovenia has a population of only 2 million and the amount of dinar cash in circulation was limited after several years of hyperinflation.

As planned, all bank accounts and all contracts were converted at a one-to-one ratio with the existing dinars. Dinar cash notes were converted into tolar notes, up to a limit of 20,000 dinars per person without restrictions. Dinars collected by the Bank of Slovenia (the central bank, hereafter BOS) during the conversion were deposited and frozen at the central bank, waiting for later negotiations with the rest of Yugoslavia.

The major motivation for the monetary reform was to protect the Slovene economy from hyperinflation, a fate expected for the Yugoslav dinar. As it turned out, these expectations were correct. Yugoslav inflation has grown very rapidly since October 1991, reaching 102 percent per month in July 1992. In contrast, in Slovenia, monthly inflation peaked at 21.5 percent in the month of conversion (resulting mainly from the depreciation of the tolar in the conversion process). Since then, the monthly inflation rate gradually fell to 5.1 percent in April 1992, to 2.0 percent in July 1992, and to 1.4 percent in August 1992. This deceleration in inflation took place without the use of price controls, although there was a temporary wages policy through February 1992. The monthly inflation rates of Slovenia and Yugoslavia are shown in table 6.3.

The differences in inflation also show up when comparing the free market exchange rate of the Slovene tolar and the black market rate of the Yugoslav dinar. As of 8 October 1991, the exchange rates were the same, as the tolar was substituted for the dinar on a one-to-one basis. Thereafter, the dinar has continued to depreciate rapidly vis-à-vis international currencies as well as against the tolar. By April 1992, the tolar purchased eight dinars (at the black market rate of the dinar). Exchange rate developments are shown in table 6.4. As described below, the tolar foreign exchange market was actually segmented, with the result that there were three relevant rates (by June 1992, the rates had largely converged). The free market rate is shown in table 6.4.

Slovenia started its monetary conversion without any foreign exchange reserves at the central bank. Foreign exchange reserves in commercial banks equaled $204 million at the end of September 1991. The improvement in the trade balance, due to the rapid recovery of exports and the compression of imports, together with a large amount of inflow of private capital, resulted in the banking system's having U.S.$1.0 billion in net foreign assets by August 1992. Private capital inflows were spurred by the new housing privatization program and by the introduction of capital account convertibility in the household market. At the same time, the BOS built up foreign exchange reserves from zero in October 1991 to about U.S.$660 million in August 1992. The positive trade balance reflected tight demand management, supported by an initial real devaluation of the tolar at the time of the monetary conversion, as well as the convertibility of the currency, which ended the antiexport bias of the overvalued dinar.

6.3.3 The Tolar Foreign Exchange Market

Immediately after the introduction of the new currency, the BOS organized the foreign exchange system in two separate markets. The government and enterprises were allowed to participate on the main market, while households had to carry out all their transactions on the parallel market. There were multiple exchange rates established for the main market: the official rate, the inter-enterprise rate, and the interbank rate. There were additional restrictions imposed on enterprises, as described below.

The initial foreign exchange policy was severely criticized by many observers, ourselves included. First, the critics pointed out that interbank meetings could not represent an appropriate vehicle for foreign exchange determination because of the monopolistic structure of commercial banking in Slovenia. Second, they emphasized that, in order to create an effective foreign exchange market, it is necessary to include all the players, including enterprises, banks, and households, and to remove restrictions on enterprises (Jaramillo-Vallejo 1991).

Reacting to political pressure, the BOS gradually relaxed some of the re-

Table 6.3   **Monthly Inflation Rates of Slovenia and Yugoslavia**

	Slovenia	Yugoslavia
1991:		
October	21.5	18.8
November	18.7	16.6
December	15.4	18.2
1992:		
January	15.2	26.1
February	11.0	42.2
March	11.5	43.2
April	5.1	72.2
May	6.5	80.8
June	5.9	102.2
July	2.0	62.0
August	1.4	42.4

Source: For Slovenia, Bank of Slovenia (1992); for Yugoslavia, communications from the Republican Statistical Office of Serbia; and various 1991 and 1992 issues of *Ekonomska Politika* (Belgrade).

Table 6.4   **Exchange Rate Developments in Slovenia and Yugoslavia**

	Tolar (free market)/DM	Dinar (black market)/DM	Dinar (black market)/ Tolar (free market)
1991:			
October	38.50	38.50	1.00
November	42.28	48.00	1.12
December	42.16	55.00	1.30
1992:			
January	45.75	85.00	1.86
February	52.31	125.00	2.40
March	52.70	220.00	4.17
April	56.15	450.00	8.01
May	53.02	580.00	10.93
June	51.17	1,300.00[a]	25.40
July	53.35	300.00[b]	5.60

Source: for Slovenia, Bank of Slovenia (1992); for Yugoslavia, various 1991 and 1992 issues of *Ekonomska Politika* (Belgrade).
[a]Effect of the UN blockade against Serbia and Montenegro.
[b]Denomination by 10.

strictions and changed its foreign exchange policy. It decided to implement a second-best policy, creating three foreign exchange markets that operate simultaneously: the interenterprise market, the official market, and the household market. The official market deals with the need for servicing foreign debt and making payments of essential imports through the budget and receiving payments of custom duties and taxes. The official exchange rate is used only in the official market. The interenterprise market deals with the need for current account transactions, while the household market serves individuals.

Exporters were initially required to surrender 30 percent of export proceeds for official purchases at the official exchange rate because of the BOS concern with the reserve buildup. In December 1991, when BOS felt more comfortable with its level of reserves, this requirement was repealed. In the interenterprise market, enterprises were allowed to sell and purchase foreign exchange among themselves or with commercial bank intermediation, at market-determined rates. Until mid-April 1992, enterprises were given only forty-eight hours to sell their foreign exchange earnings. After forty-eight hours, the individual enterprise had to sell its foreign exchange to the BOS at the official rate. To reduce the negative effect of this policy, the BOS started issuing foreign exchange–denominated CDs to exporters in January 1992. These CDs carry market interest rates and can be traded on the stock exchange.

The household market operates through a network of officially licensed foreign exchange offices. Until March 1992, the official exchange rate was between 10 and 49 percent lower than those in the other two markets. Since then, the differences among the rates have rapidly declined, and, by June 1992, all three rates had practically converged. In June 1993, the official exchange rate was 51.08, compared to the free market (interbank) rate of 51.17 (Bank of Slovenia 1992).

6.3.4   Fiscal Policy Reform

In order to achieve full economic independence from Yugoslavia through an independent and stable currency, Slovenia needed fiscal independence. In addition, the stabilization program required tight fiscal policies to control budget deficits. Slovenia has been quite successful in both modernizing the tax system and controlling budget deficits. However, much remains to be done, especially in reorienting public spending to better serve the needs of the restructured economy.

In the past two years, the government has undertaken significant reforms in taxation and fiscal consolidation. Under the self-management system, Slovenia had a very decentralized public sector. Public-sector agencies had independent authority to administer expenditures and set taxes. Most public services, such as health care and education, were financed through earmarking at various community levels. The republican government budget was responsible only for government administration and subsidies to the economy, accounting for less than 20 percent of total public-sector expenditures.

Tax reform started in 1990 and was implemented on 1 January 1991. The reform replaced old taxes and contributions with standard taxes on personal income and corporate profit and a simplified sales tax. Taxation on enterprise income was significantly reduced, while sales taxes were increased in 1992 to compensate for the loss of revenue. The reform also consolidated all the previous off-budget funds, with the exception of the pension and health fund, into the central government budget. So far the reform has been successful and is being continued, with preparatory work for introducing a value-added tax.

Under the Yugoslav system, Slovenia was not allowed to borrow in order to finance budget deficits. Thus, the government would adjust expenditures to match the revenues. For this reason, there was no need to make a drastic fiscal adjustment in 1991 since the republican budget had been traditionally balanced (Jaramillo-Vallejo 1991). This also means that the stabilization program in Slovenia did not require "shock" therapy, from the point of view of reducing a large fiscal deficit.

The overall public sector formally registered a surplus in 1991 amounting to 2.1 percent of GDP. In 1991, total expenditure of the public sector was reduced to 41 percent, compared to 49 percent of GDP in 1990. The reduction was possible because of lower transfers to the federal government. However, owing to arrears incurred by public utilities, the health care system, and local governments, the actual fiscal stance might have been more lax than reported.

An important accomplishment of the monetary reform in Slovenia was that the links between fiscal policy and money creation were severed by the government. Although the government might have accrued arrears in the budget, it has not financed its expenditures with loans from the BOS. This is an important change, compared with the previous policy of the federal government. Nevertheless, the Slovene government will need to continue to make efforts to balance the actual budget expenditures and improve financial discipline in the future.

In the 1992 budget, real increases are planned for administration, defense, agricultural subsidies, and investment programs in the infrastructure sector. Total public expenditures are projected to increase to 46 percent of GDP. A deficit of about 1.2 percent of GNP is projected. The deficit is expected to be financed mainly by borrowing from the domestic capital market.

The main weakness of the 1992 budget is that it puts too much emphasis on state security, for example, defense and police, while neglecting the need to restructure the economy. No financial resources are provided in the budget for bank and enterprise restructuring. The budget ignores increasing losses and indebtedness of enterprises and banks and the need for a comprehensive reform in these two sectors. A serious reform effort and future privatization will most likely result in increased unemployment, thus requiring additional resources for a social safety net. The 1992 and future budgets will need to take these issues into account in order to speed up the transition toward a market economy.

6.3.5   Institutional Reform

Compared to the East European countries, and similar to the new states that emerged out of the Soviet Union, Slovenia has faced enormous institutional challenges in the past two years (Lipton and Sachs 1992; Pleskovic 1993). One of the key aspects of independence is the need to create the legal and administrative basis of a sovereign state. It is an enormous institutional, legal, and administrative task to draft the laws. The new state must also quickly make a central bank, Ministry of Finance, and other institutions, largely taking existing institutions and turning them into self-sustaining actors. As a part of this process, the Slovene government drafted seventy-six laws, most of which are economic laws representing the legal cornerstone of independence.[8] The list of laws is shown in appendix table 6A.1.

A great deal of the macroeconomic events of the first year consisted of establishing the legal, administrative, and political base for state independence. Thus, Slovenia was faced with the task not only of reorienting its institutions to fit the needs of a market economy but also of building completely new institutions, sometimes from scratch, ranging from border controls and customs to the central bank.

In terms of economic institutions, the first priority of Slovenia was to establish its independent central bank and the necessary banking legislation. The task of creating a new central bank was facilitated to some extent because, in the former Yugoslavia, each republic had its own branch of the National Bank of Yugoslavia (NBY). The republican national banks, as they were called, together with the NBY, implemented monetary policy. While the Bank of Slovenia (formerly the National Bank of Slovenia) still needs upgrading and technical assistance to function as an independent modern central bank, substantial progress has been made in a short period of time.

To facilitate the privatization process, Slovenia established in March 1990 the Privatization Agency and the Development Fund. Both institutions were created as state-owned enterprises. The Privatization Agency's function is to monitor the privatization process, while the responsibilities of the Development Fund are limited to management and disposal of shares obtained from privatization. The role of the two agencies has been so far limited to the sale of a few enterprises to foreign owners, the evaluation of enterprises, and the preparation of legislation. As of the summer of 1992, no institutional arrangement has been made for restructuring chronic loss-making enterprises. However, there is growing pressure to deal with financial restructuring of poorly performing enterprises because of increasing losses.

Slovenia established the Bank Restructuring Agency in September 1991. An Enterprise Restructuring Agency is under consideration. The primary role of these two agencies will be to deal simultaneously with increasing debt, competition issues, and the poor financial performance of the banking sector and loss-making enterprises.

The government recognized the need to consolidate the existing twenty-three ministries into fourteen and has submitted the relevant legislation to the

---

8. There were other laws, e.g., for defense, police, and administration, that were important for achieving independence. Those are not included among the seventy-six laws, which focused primarily on economic legislation.

Parliament. The proposed legislation will, for example, abolish the Ministries of Planning and Industry. On the other hand, the role of the Ministry of Finance will be strengthened as part of the reorganization, which includes the establishment of a Treasury.

Slovenia has recognized that one of the most pressing needs is to design a legal framework for market activities. To that end, in the spring of 1991, the government conceived and started to draft sixty-one laws. The majority of these laws are related to economic reform. The list of the laws was submitted to the Parliament as part of the macroeconomic program in the fall of 1991 (see app. table 6A.1). The laws range from new auditing and accounting legislation to an antimonopoly law. The laws are at various stages of preparation, as seen in the table. Some of them (e.g., housing privatization, denationalization, pension, and health insurance laws) have already passed in the Parliament, while others (e.g., company, enterprise privatization, and bankruptcy laws) were submitted to the Parliament but have not yet been acted on.

6.4   Reform Agenda and Structural Adjustment

6.4.1   Current Economic Situation

Slovenia has been successful in carrying out the goals of political independence while at the same time achieving stabilization and carrying out fundamental economic reforms. Given difficult circumstances, including a civil war and a major loss of Yugoslav markets, Slovenia has performed relatively well during the last two years of transition from a socialist to a free market economy.

As in other East European countries, economic stabilization in Slovenia has been associated with a sharp initial decrease in output. Real GDP decreased by 2.7 percent in 1989, 3.4 percent in 1990, and 9.3 percent in 1991. Unemployment increased from 2.9 percent in 1989, to 4.7 percent in 1990, and 8.1 percent in 1991. On the demand side, the decline in output was caused by the reduction in exports to former CMEA countries, and especially to former Yugoslav markets, as well as by a drop in domestic consumption. While the decline in output was deep, it was less severe than in most other countries in Eastern Europe. Part of the reason for this is that Slovenia was more open and market oriented before the reform started and has therefore been able to shift production to Western markets more readily.

In the spring of 1992, there was an indication of economic recovery, particularly in the construction, transport, and tourism sectors. The decline in industrial output continues in 1992, but at a slower rate than in the last quarter of 1991. The unemployment rate has increased only marginally since the end of 1991, but it remains at 11 percent, the highest level in history (table 6.5). Merchandise exports increased in the first half of 1992 to U.S.$1,960 million from U.S.$1,890 million in the first half of 1991. Imports declined by

Table 6.5   Current Economic Indicators for Slovenia

	Industry, Monthly Growth Rate (deseasonalized)	Exports of Goods and Services[a]	Unemployment Rate (%)
1992:			
January	−1.69	275.6	10.5
February	−1.44	412.5	10.7
March	−1.46	503.7	10.7
April	−1.33	459.6	10.8
May	−1.50	406.3	10.8
June	−1.12	510.6	11.0

Source: Bank of Slovenia (1992).
[a]Millions of U.S. dollars.

U.S.$450 million during the same period. As a result of the decline in output, exports as a percentage of GDP increased from 39.5 percent in 1989 to 53.2 percent in 1991 (Ministry of Planning 1992).

The economy is expected to experience a recovery over the next few years. There are two fundamental problems that need to be addressed in the near future in order to speed up the recovery. First, trade will have to continue to be reoriented toward new Western and Eastern markets to compensate for the loss of former Yugoslav and CMEA markets, and, in many cases, enterprises will have to restructure internally in order to reorient to the new markets. As we have noted, the shift to Western markets is already occurring. Second, both the enterprise and the banking sectors are burdened with structural and financial problems, which impede a quick economic recovery. An appropriate solution to these problems will require faster progress in passing and implementing legislation on privatization and restructuring of enterprises and banks.

6.4.2   Trade Reorientation

From the macroeconomic point of view, the notable aspect of independence, besides monetary reform, was the internal shock caused by the civil war. The war cut Slovenia off physically from the markets in the rest of the country. These markets accounted for about 25 percent of total sales of Slovene enterprises in recent years. The civil war and economic problems in the former Yugoslavia nearly destroyed these markets and the financial system. In 1991, these problems caused a 38 percent reduction in exports to the other Yugoslav republics.

Slovenia did not suffer a major CMEA shock since, in the recent past, less than 20 percent of total trade was with Eastern Europe and the former Soviet Union. However, owing to the decline in economic activity in Eastern Europe, trade with these countries declined by over 20 percent and with the former Soviet Union more than 40 percent in 1991.

The adjustment of Slovenia's trade has been quite remarkable, despite the war and loss of markets in the former Yugoslavia and Eastern Europe. This was possible because of Slovenia's Western orientation in trade. In 1989, 68 percent of Slovenia's external trade (not counting the Yugoslav market) was with developed industrial countries, and 8 percent was with developing countries. In 1991, trade with the West increased to 80 percent of the total. Merchandise exports (machinery and transport equipment and various consumer products) to the West increased by U.S.$68 million to U.S.$3,074 million in 1991. The companies with the fastest supply response have been in transport equipment and electrical machinery, which are the largest exporters to the Western markets.

Despite the unfavorable circumstances in Eastern Europe and the Soviet Union, total Slovene exports of goods to non-Yugoslav markets in current prices declined by only 6.3 percent in 1991. This decline was on the East European and Soviet markets. Exports of nonfactor services declined by 38 percent, owing to tourism and cross-country transportation, the two sectors most affected by the civil war. The current account of the balance of payments had a surplus of U.S.$225 million in 1991 and U.S.$330 million in the first quarter of 1992. Decreased imports and increased exports to the West resulted in a trade (goods and nonfactor service) surplus of U.S.$351 million in 1991 and U.S.$366 million in the first quarter of 1992.

In the medium term, Slovenia will have to integrate itself more closely with Western Europe. The primary short-term goal of Slovenia should also be to continue reorienting its trade from the former Yugoslav and CMEA markets to new Western and Eastern markets. To achieve this goal, Slovenia will need to continue pursuing the goal of having a convertible and stable currency that does not become an obstacle for competitiveness. To this end, Slovenia should move to a unified foreign exchange market, where the exchange rate is determined mainly by market forces (Jaramillo-Vallejo 1991). Recent convergence in the parallel and official exchange rates for the Slovene tolar opens the way for an early merging of the current three foreign exchange markets.

While it will be difficult to recover trade markets with the former Yugoslavia, an effort should be made to simplify transactions with those markets. Under the current arrangements between Slovenia and Croatia, exporters from one republic are allowed to set up a nonresident account in the other and use the balance in that account to pay for their own imports. The bilateral nature of this arrangement has made it ineffective, highlighting the need for the establishment of a free market for exchange between the tolar and other currencies in the former Yugoslavia.

Slovenia inherited the Yugoslav system of foreign trade. With the recent removal of quantitative restrictions in most sectors (except agriculture and textiles), the trade regime has become relatively liberal. Tariffs are imposed on most imported items, with rates ranging between 0 and 25 percent. In addition, a special import duty, imposed on all imports, was recently lowered from 13 to 6.5 percent. The new customs law intends to abolish the special import duty. It is proposed that import duty rates should be between 5 and 25 percent (Chamber of Commerce 1991).

6.4.3   Privatization Strategy

A political decision to privatize commercial enterprises was part of the election campaign of the winning DEMOS coalition in 1990. The privatization strategy has been focused on the start-up of new private firms and the privatization of the existing social sector enterprises. Although several laws were drafted and submitted to the Parliament, only limited success has been achieved so far.

Slovenia inherited the "social" ownership pattern of enterprises from Yugoslavia. While, in the past, enterprises in Yugoslavia were "self-managed," the system was drastically changed with the 1988 Enterprise Law and the 1989 Law on Social Capital (Milanovic 1991). These two laws limited the self-management rights of workers and allowed firms to be transformed into joint-stock companies. The laws permitted internal and spontaneous privatization and have been restricted in Slovenia because of abuses. At present, enterprises in Slovenia are neither state owned nor self-managed: property rights are undetermined. Managers, workers, and the state all have some de jure decision-making powers. However, in practice, most of these enterprises are controlled by managers, who have, de facto, almost absolute decision-making power over them.

While existing small enterprises are being privatized rapidly in Poland, Czechoslovakia, and Hungary (Gelb and Gray 1991), this type of privatization was delayed in Slovenia. Some parliamentary parties were concerned that separate privatization of small enterprises would delay the privatization of large enterprises. In addition, most retail trade and services are part of large monopolies, which are difficult to break up without a comprehensive privatization law.

New private enterprises expanded rapidly during the last two years. However, official statistics on this phenomenon are scarce, as the official data still focus on the public sector. There were 4,000 registered commercial companies in 1989, about 8,000 in 1990, and 12,000 in 1991 (Ministry of Planning 1991). Of these, about 2,600 are social enterprises. While employment in the public sector declined by 8.2 percent, private-sector employment increased by 4.0 percent and self-employment by 8.1 percent in 1991. In the same year, 16 percent of the labor force, including agriculture, was registered in private business.

The Slovene economy is still dominated by socially owned enterprises. They account for over 80 percent of value added and for 84 percent of total employment and produce nearly all statistically recorded nonagricultural output. There are about 2,600 social enterprises to be privatized, representing about 58 percent of the value of social capital (the remaining 42 percent of social capital is in infrastructure, public utilities, and the like, which generally will not be privatized in the near future). Of these, about 150 are large enterprises with over 500 employees, 750 are medium sized with employment between 125 and 500, and the rest are small.

The first debate on privatization in Slovenia focused on the issue of whether "socially" owned enterprises should be first renationalized and then privatized or whether the intermediate stage should be skipped. The issue was resolved in favor of direct privatization. Since the elections, three drafts of the privatization law have been submitted to the Parliament.

In December 1990, the government submitted to the Parliament the first draft privatization law. This law was based on the evaluation of enterprises by registered professionals. According to the draft law, enterprise managers[9] would have been allowed to gain 100 percent control over the enterprise by purchasing 10 percent of the shares at a discount, provided that they buy additional shares over the next years. The other 90 percent of the shares would have been nonvoting "preferred shares" held by the government. The managers would have had the right to purchase these shares over time. The preferred shares would have paid a dividend yield of only 2 percent. Essentially, the managers would have had ownership rights to the enterprises using the very small amount of their own money as a down payment and would have been allowed to buy the rest of the shares by reinvesting enterprise profits over five to ten years. The general public would have received only a 2 percent return on equity in the interim and no share ownership in the end.

The draft law was widely discussed, strongly supported by the existing managers, and severely criticized within the democratic coalition (DEMOS). Several weaknesses were pointed out. First, many believed that accurate evaluation is virtually impossible given the absence of capital markets. Second, the proposed law was considered to be open to speculation and unfair, benefiting a small group of existing managers. Third, taking into account the low level of domestic financial savings, the proposal was considered especially inappropriate for large, capital intensive, and expensive enterprises. For these reasons, the proposed law lost the support of the ruling coalition.

The government, under the direction of new economic ministers, designed a second draft law on privatization. This draft was based on worker-management buyouts for small- and medium-sized firms and mutual funds and other institutional investors for large enterprises with over 500 employees. For large enterprises, 35 percent of shares would be distributed to adult citizens for free, 20 percent to pension funds, and 15 percent to a special "compensation fund," the shares of which would have been distributed to individuals meriting compensation as a result of the confiscation of private property in the course of Yugoslav

---

9. The draft law stated that managers and workers would buy the shares. However, with an average salary of approximately U.S.$200.00 per month, workers would hardly be in a position to buy them.

nationalizations of the late 1940s and early 1950s. Ten percent of shares would be distributed to workers free of charge, and 20 percent would be bought by workers and managers at book value.

In the fall of 1991, the second draft law passed the two democratic chambers of the Slovene Parliament, but then it was blocked in the third chamber. The third chamber (the chamber of "associate labor") represents socialist managers under the old Communist constitution. The managers filibustered for months, despite the clear majority political support for the broadly based mass privatization approach.

To avoid the blockade, the government, together with representatives of the major parliamentary parties, designed a third compromise draft privatization law. In this draft, the role of mutual funds was slightly scaled back, and the possibility of manager buyouts was enhanced, but under clear, transparent, and fair procedures. According to this proposal, 20 percent of shares would be distributed to workers and managers in their enterprises for free. Forty percent of the shares would be reserved for institutional investors. Of these, 20 percent would be distributed free to all citizens via five to ten mutual funds, 10 percent to the pension fund, and 10 percent to the compensation fund. The workers and managers would be allowed to choose between receiving free shares in their enterprises or in mutual funds. The remaining 40 percent of the shares would be sold to workers and managers or outside investors.

The compromise draft privatization law gained the support of a majority of the parliamentary parties. After intense debates in the Parliament, the concept of free distribution of shares received substantial support from the general public. A recent survey shows that 55–65 percent of the population support free distribution of shares (Tos 1992). The opposition to this concept from the third chamber of the Parliament weakened, after several of the managers-deputies started their own private enterprises. The compromise privatization law was passed by the Parliament in November 1992.

6.4.4   Financial Restructuring

Financial restructuring of commercial banks and enterprises was considered a high priority of the macroeconomic program of the government. The main goals of the program were to restore competition in both the banking and the enterprise sectors, to rehabilitate troubled banks and enterprises, and to change the ownership structure.

Slovenia inherited from the former Yugoslavia a banking sector that suffers from serious deficiencies, which impede the development of an efficient financial system. First, the banking system is heavily dominated by one bank, Ljubljanska Banka, which with thirteen associated regional banks controls over 90 percent of the banking business in Slovenia. Second, this bank and others in Slovenia are owned by social enterprises, which in turn are also major debtors and have their representatives sitting on the bank boards. Third, there is a large share of nonperforming loans in the banks' portfolios (30–40 percent) and an inadequate capital structure. Fourth, there is low confidence in the banking system, stemming from limitations on the withdrawals of households' foreign currency deposits (DM 1.8 billion) as a result of insufficient foreign exchange reserves to back the deposits.[10] Fifth, many banks are currently charging very high real interest rates for corporate loans, ranging between 20 and 30 percent per annum, apparently as the result of the existing monopolistic structure of the banking system and the poor quality of its portfolio. Sixth, traditionally, there have been very close ties between the central bank and the commercial banking system, causing problems with the effectiveness of monetary policies and banking supervision.

These issues have been widely discussed by the government and the Parliament. Eight months after the 1990 election, the situation initially worsened, when the two largest Slovene commercial banks were merged into a monopoly. Substantial progress has been made since then in improving the banking structure. Modern laws governing the central bank and commercial banking, prudential regulations, and the rehabilitation of banks have changed the banking system. Banks have been audited for the second time, and the Bank Restructuring Agency was established in the fall of 1991.

In the spring of 1992, the government prepared a partial bank restructuring program dealing separately with the problem of frozen foreign exchange deposits. The program consisted of a law to issue public bonds to cover DM 1.8 billion of frozen foreign exchange deposits of households. Because the law did not address bank restructuring and privatization, it was rejected by the Parliament.

Since then, the agency has prepared a bank restructuring program, which is currently under consideration and which draws on the independence program of the spring of 1991. Major objectives of the program are to restore the balance sheet of the banks to a healthy position, improve competition, change the ownership structure through privatization, and improve the structure and regulation of the banking system. An important aspect of the problem, still not properly addressed, is related to the financial restructuring of heavily indebted enterprises.

Although significant progress was made in revising the legal framework for enterprise activities, Slovenia has not advanced far with enterprise restructuring. Some firms have taken the initiative themselves, mainly through joint ven-

---

10. During the 1970s and 1980s, households were allowed to deposit foreign currency into foreign-denominated bank accounts (mostly deutsche mark denominated). This was used widely, for example, by families of Yugoslav guest workers in Germany as well as by the local domestic population. Deposits in each of the republics were credited to households, while the foreign exchange was routinely and mandatorily transferred to the National Bank of Yugoslavia in Belgrade. The central bank did not maintain these reserves in order to back the deposits in the banking system. Rather, the reserves were spent in debt servicing or in foreign exchange market intervention. Thus, the Slovene banks (mainly the Ljubljanska Banka) have foreign-denominated liabilities but insufficient foreign exchange assets, and Slovenia as a whole lacks the official reserves to provide to the commercial banks in the event of a major withdrawal of deposits. Starting in 1991, severe restrictions were placed on the withdrawal of these funds.

tures with foreign partners. Owing to the lack of privatization and bank restructuring, a vast majority of social enterprises have not made the adjustments that are needed to deal with the shift of markets and increased competition. This has resulted in the increase of enterprise losses, defaults on debts to the banking sector, and a rise in interenterprise arrears. In this pattern, Slovenia matches the experience of almost all other socialist economies in the transition to a market economy.

The financial position of Slovene enterprises has worsened since 1987. In 1991, the reported losses reached 31.4 billion tolars, or about 8.7 percent of GDP. About 100 large industrial enterprises account for two-thirds of total enterprise losses. The rest of the losses are concentrated in the public utility and infrastructure sectors. The lack of financial discipline, excessive employment, and past wasteful investments have been the main causes of the poor performance of Slovene enterprises. Past price controls also caused losses in some sectors. The losses are currently financed more or less automatically by interenterprise credits and arrears, bank loans, and, in a few cases, government subsidies, including tax exemptions.

As in other East European economies, bankruptcy has rarely been resorted to in Slovenia, mainly because the existing legislation is difficult to apply, banks are owned by social enterprises, the collateral system is underdeveloped, and there is a lack of professional experience with the process. In 1990, about 119 bankruptcy cases were initiated. In 1991, 571 enterprises qualified as bankrupt under the current legislation, but only 200 cases were initiated, as the current bankruptcy law has effectively been suspended with respect to social enterprises owing to the unusual circumstances of 1991 (the declaration of independence, the Yugoslav invasion). A new bankruptcy law is being considered by the Parliament, one along the lines of the American "Chapter 11."

One of the main factors influencing the adjustment process of enterprises is the weakness of the ownership structure in social enterprises and banks. Social enterprises in Slovenia are major owners of the banks. They have restricted the autonomy of the banks for credit allocation, thus limiting the bank's capacity to exert adequate financial discipline and worsening their portfolio of bad debts. In addition, the absence of ownership or clear control rights in the enterprises gave an incentive to managers and workers to decapitalize enterprises and increase the enterprises' debts. As a result, many viable enterprises are unable to service their rapidly accumulating debts, and many banks are close to insolvency. Therefore, a full recovery of the enterprise sector is conditional on faster progress on restructuring and privatization of banks and social enterprises simultaneously.

These facts were recognized by the government macroeconomic program in 1991. The program of financial restructuring of commercial enterprises and banks included, as the key element, generalized debt equity swaps between banks and heavily indebted enterprises, which could reduce the cash flow devoted to debt service payments. In addition, the program suggested that money-losing enterprises should be divided into three categories: (i) manufacturing enterprises to be financially restructured; (ii) manufacturing firms to be closed down; and (iii) public utilities, infrastructure, and state enterprises to be regulated. For the first category (i.e., heavily indebted enterprises), it was suggested that the debts of the enterprises needed to be reduced prior to or as part of privatization. For the second category, the restructuring was to include a clear timetable for closure and explicit subsidies to reduce employment gradually when outright closure was not feasible because of social or economic implications. For the third category (i.e., state enterprises), it was suggested that the government should establish a system for governance, regulation, and restructuring of these enterprises into commercial public services.

For the banking sector, the program of financial restructuring included breaking up the monopoly, a change in ownership structure and privatization, implementing prudential regulation, and establishing new institutions (e.g., deposit insurance, an export bank) and new banking legislation, including anti-monopoly, accounting, and auditing legislation.

6.5 Conclusion

Of all the new countries, Slovenia has gone furthest in economic reform during the last two years. During this time, Slovenia achieved political independence, stabilized its economy, introduced its own currency, and carried out fundamental economic reforms. Slovenia has made significant progress in its transition from a socialist to a market economy, despite difficult circumstances, including civil war and a loss of major markets.

Slovenia was more developed than other countries of Eastern Europe before the transition. Its economy was more open, prices and imports were relatively free, and the budget was more or less balanced. Nevertheless, it suffered from high inflation and a lack of monetary and fiscal discipline, especially at the federal level. By accomplishing successful monetary and fiscal reforms and macroeconomic stabilization with sharply reduced inflation, Slovenia has proved that it can manage its macroeconomic affairs better than the former Yugoslavia.

Slovenia is much richer and more open to the West than any other East European country. It is well ahead in terms of income per capita. But the gap is narrowing with respect to structural reforms and progress toward a market economy. Some countries of Eastern Europe, like Poland and Czechoslovakia have been quite successful in stabilizing and liberalizing their economies in a relatively short time. Poland, Czechoslovakia, and Hungary have made better progress in terms of privatization, especially of small- and medium-sized enterprises, and the rapid growth of the new private sector.

After accomplishing a successful stabilization and monetary and institutional reforms, the weaknesses of the socialist legacy of "social" ownership are becoming more clear in Slovenia. These weaknesses are reflected in an inefficient banking system and increasing losses and debts of social enterprises and banks. To overcome these problems, Slovenia has to turn its attention to the medium- and long-term problems of privatization and the restructuring of enterprises and banks. These problems deserve priority if Slovenia wants to retain a competitive edge in exports and become more efficient in its domestic markets. Restructuring of the economy will require reorientation of resources from heavy toward light industry, housing construction, and services. The social sector has to be substantially reduced and made more efficient through privatization and restructuring to reduce its heavy burden on the budget. Without privatization, enterprises will be left without incentives and the tools to restructure. While Slovenia needs to continue the stabilization policies and continue building free market institutions and legislation, privatization and restructuring are the most important issues left on the reform agenda.

Slovenia has an excellent opportunity to develop a full-fledged market economy and become integrated with Europe if it speeds up the reform process. It has all the conditions necessary to reach this goal in a relatively short time. The challenge ahead is to reach a consensus and implement the rest of the reforms needed for a well-functioning free market economy.

Appendix

Table 6A.1   A List of 76 Laws—the Legal Cornerstone of Independence

Ratified laws
 1. Law on the Bank of Slovenia
 2. Law on Banks and Savings Banks
 3. Law on Pre-Rehabilitation, Rehabilitation, Bankruptcy, and Liquidation of Banks and Savings Banks
 4. Law on Foreign Currency Transactions
 5. Law on Credit Transactions with Foreign Countries
 6. Law on Pricing
 7. Law on the Agency Guaranteeing Bank Deposits and Savings
 8. Law on Denationalization
 9. Law on the Agency for Privatization
10. Law on the Development Fund
11. Law on Cooperatives
12. Law on Registration of Businesses
13. Law on Bank Restructuring Agency
14. Law on Customs Service
15. Law on External Affairs

Proposed laws[a]
16. Law on the Ownership Transformation of Enterprises
17. Law on Economic Public Services
18. Law on Mutual Funds and Investment Companies
19. Law on the Compensation Fund
20. Law on Capital and Personal Enterprises
21. Law on Involuntary Settlement and Bankruptcy

Table 6A.1   (continued)

22. Law on Co-Management of Employees
23. Law on the Representation of Labor Unions
24. Law on the Protection of Competition
25. Law on Commerce
26. Law on the Protection of Consumers
27. Law on the Protection of Industrial Property
28. Law on Small-Scale Business
29. Law on Commercial Tax
30. Law on Customs
31. Law on Customs and Tariffs
32. Law on Free Trade Zones
33. Law on Accounting
34. Law on Financial Auditing
35. Law on Financial Transactions
36. Law on the Stock Exchange
37. Law on Securities
38. Law on Public Debt
39. Law on Institutions for the Stimulation of Exports
40. Law on Foreign Investment
41. Law on Public Servants
42. Law on Real Estate and on Real Estate Rights of Foreigners
43. Law on Railways
44. Law on Longshore Activities
45. Law on Airports
46. Law on Postal and Telecommunication Services
47. Law on Telecommunications
48. Law on Postal Services
49. Law on Roads
50. Law on Road Transportation
51. Law on Energy
52. Law on Rational Use of Energy
53. Law on Goods Reserves
54. Law on Innovation
55. Law on Employment of Foreigners
56. Law on Insurance
57. Law on Special Taxes for Import of Agricultural Products
58. Law on the Stimulation of Tourism
59. Law on Standardization and Technical Regulations
60. Law on Meteorology
61. Law on Public Notaries

Other ratified laws
62. Law on financing public expenditure
63. Law on income tax
64. Law on taxes on the profit of legal entities
65. Laws on income taxes
66. Law on amendments to the law on working relations
67. Law on taxes on citizens
68. Law on employment and unemployment insurance
69. Law on amendments of pension and disability insurance
70. Law on prices
(*continued*)

Table 6A.1   (continued)

71. Law on foreign credit transactions
72. Law on the monetary unit of the Republic of Slovenia
73. Laws on the use of the monetary unit in Slovenia
74. Law on housing
75. Law on research activities
76. Law on the partial reimbursement of damages caused by military aggression on the Republic of Slovenia in 1991

Note: The first 61 laws were submitted to the Parliament as part of the macroeconomic program for the independence of Slovenia. The rest of the list represents other laws ratified during the last two years.

ªSome of the proposed laws may have been ratified.

References

Abraham, Katharine, and Milan Vodopivec. 1991. Labor market dynamic during the transition of a socialist economy. Research proposal. Washington, D.C.: World Bank.

Assembly of the Republic of Slovenia. Executive Council. 1991. *Program for structural adjustment and economic policy in 1992*. Ljubljana, November.

Bank of Slovenia. 1992. *Monthly Bulletin*. Ljubljana, November.

Banka Slovenije. 1991. *Denarna in devizna gibanja* (Monetary and foreign exchange developments). Ljubljana: Analitsko Raziskovalni Center, June.

Chamber of Commerce. 1991. *Business opportunities in Slovenia*. Ljubljana.

Estrin, Saul, and Lina Takla. 1991. *Reform in Yugoslavia: The retreat from self-management*. Washington, D.C.: World Bank, Socialist Economies Reform Unit.

Gelb, H. Alan, and Cheryl W. Gray. 1991. The transformation of economies in Central and Eastern Europe. Policy Research Series no. 17. Washington, D.C.: World Bank.

Hanson, Ardo, and Jeffrey D. Sachs. 1992. Crowning the Estonian kroon. *Transition* 3, no. 9 (October): 1–3.

Jaramillo-Vallejo, Jaime. 1991. Contribution to the conference in Bled. *Slovenska Ekonomska Revija* 42, no. 6 (December): 425–32.

Jaramillo-Vallejo, Jaime, and Boris Pleskovic. 1991. Introduction of the Slovene currency. Washington, D.C.: Sachs & Associates. Mimeo.

Lipton, David, and Jeffrey D. Sachs. 1991. A program for economic sovereignty and restructuring of Slovenia. Washington, D.C.: Sachs & Associates. Mimeo.

———. 1992. Prospects for Russia's economic reforms. *Brookings Papers on Economic Activity*, no. 2:213–83.

Milanovic, Branko. 1991. Privatization in post-Communist societies. *Communist Economies and Economic Transformation* 3, no. 1:5–40.

Ministry of Planning. 1991. *Economic trends and policies in the Republic of Slovenia in 1991*. Ljubljana: Institute for Macroeconomic Analysis and Development.

———. 1992. *Slovenia in 1991–1992: Report on economic developments*. Ljubljana: Institute for Macroeconomic Analysis and Development.

Pleskovic, Boris. 1993. Regional development and transition in the former Soviet Union: A comment. *International Regional Science Review* 15, no. 3:297–305.

Pleskovic, Boris, and Jeffrey Sachs. 1992. Currency reform in Slovenia: The tolar standing tall. *Transition* 3, no. 8 (September): 6–8.

———. 1993. Author's response: We still take great pride. *Transition* 4, no. 1:11–12.

Sachs, Jeffrey D. 1992. Accelerating privatization in Eastern Europe. In *Proceedings of the World Bank's Annual Conference on Development Economics 1991,* ed. L. H. Summers and S. Shah. Washington, D.C.: World Bank.

Tos, Niko. 1992. *Public opinion in Eastern countries.* Ljubljana: Center za Raziskave Javnega Mnenja na Fakulteti za Druzbene Vede, June.

Discussion Summary

Saul Estrin made three points. First, he noted that, in comparison to the rest of Eastern Europe, Slovenia began the reform process with relatively favorable initial conditions. He emphasized Slovenia's long-standing experience with markets, high income per capita, extensive past success in exporting to the West, and limited exposure to the CMEA shock. However, he did note that Slovenia was hard hit by the breakdown of trade among the newly independent Yugoslav republics. Second, Estrin discussed the particular problems that Slovenia faces because of its legacy of worker-managed firms. Estrin suggested that workers and managers have a strong vested interest in the privatization process since these groups have heretofore controlled the firms in which they work. Moreover, because these control rights are vaguely defined, the privatization process may generate substantial conflict among the principal actors. Third, Estrin noted that the new states in what was once the Soviet Union and Yugoslavia face special challenges created by the transition to statehood. He observed that these hurdles would be relatively less problematic in Slovenia because its population is ethnically homogeneous and government legitimacy is not substantially questioned.

Simon Johnson asked the authors to evaluate the development of the private sector. *Boris Pleskovic* responded that the private sector has grown very rapidly but that its progress has been impeded because the legislature has not passed the Law on Small-Scale Business.

Jacek Rostowski asked why Slovene inflation continued at a rate of over 10 percent per month one quarter after the macroeconomic stabilization program was initiated. *Jeffrey Sachs* observed that the continuing high rate of inflation could be blamed on an expansionary monetary policy that violated the planned program of tight credit. Rostowski also asked to whom the enterprise managers are responsible since the workers' councils have been disempowered. Pleskovic answered that the managers are often not responsible to anyone. He said that the primary way to exert control over them is to cut off their access to subsidies.

Jan Svejnar asked for an elaboration on the political situation in Slovenia. Sachs responded that the Slovene political system is very complicated and currently prone to deadlock: Slovenia has three parliamentary chambers, ten political parties represented in Parliament, and a president and prime minister from different political factions. Sachs noted that the large number of elected political parties is a consequence of Slovenia's system of proportional representation with a minimum threshold.

Sachs concluded the session with a response to Estrin's comments. Sachs noted that the system of worker management was largely symbolic; managers were effectively in charge even before the current reform process. Sachs said that the current political phase is not just a clean discussion about the efficacy of different models of privatization but rather a struggle over who is going to end up owning/controlling Slovenia's assets at the end of the day.

Sachs also wanted to add to Estrin's list of the peculiar features of the Slovene initial conditions. Sachs noted that the Slovene banking system is particularly problematic because the banks are owned by the same enterprises to which the banks made many of their loans. On top of this problem, the banks have hitherto been largely unregulated.

7   Russia and the Soviet Union Then and Now

Stanley Fischer

As the republics of the former Soviet Union struggle to find a way out of the chaos of the unprecedented peacetime collapse of a superpower, attention inevitably centers on the pressing problems of reform. But those problems arise within the historical context of Russian and Soviet economic development.

The main focus of this paper is on the reform process. But I start with four historical questions that bear on the current situation. How advanced was Russia in 1913? What relevance, if any, does the New Economic Policy of the 1920s, or NEP, have for the current situation? Why did economic growth in the Soviet Union slow in the 1970s and 1980s? What role did Gorbachev's policies play in bringing about the final collapse of the Soviet Union?

7.1   Russia in 1913

In 1913, Russia was a rapidly developing country whose enormous territory and population made it an economic and military force to be reckoned with. By some estimates (Gregory 1982), its national income was at about the same level as that of the United Kingdom, slightly below that of Germany, and 21 percent of the U.S. level; Maddison, whose estimates are presented in table 7.1, ranks Russian GNP somewhat higher.[1] The data in table 7.1 show Russia well behind Europe and the United States in industrial, although not agricultural, production.

The author is grateful to Olivier Blanchard, William Easterly, Jacek Rostowski, Lawrence Summers, and Peter Temin for comments, to Ruth Judson for research assistance, and to the National Science Foundation for financial support.

1. By Maddison's estimates, per capita Russian GDP in 1913 was at about the same level as in Cote d'Ivoire in 1988; his estimate for U.S. GDP in 1913 puts it at a level between Mexico and Taiwan in 1988. These comparisons are made assuming that the data in table 7.1 refer to International Comparisons Project (ICP)–type estimates and using the data reported in Summers and Heston (1991).

Table 7.1   **Comparative Economic Performance, 1913**

	Soviet Union	United Kingdom	United States
Per capita GDP[a]	973	3,065	3,772
Population (millions)	158.4	42.6	97.6
Industrial production (index U.S. = 100):			
	Russia		
Electricity	7.8	18.2	100
Coal	5.6	56.4	100
Oil	30.3	. . .	100
Iron and steel	13.4	28.9	100
Cotton textiles	33.3	129.8	100
Agricultural production (average 1910–13, index U.S. = 100):			
Total cereals:	61	4	100
Wheat	118	9	100
Other cereals[b]	51	3	100
Potatoes	293	30	100
Cattle	57	12	100
Horses	112	8	100

Sources: Nove (1989) for industrial production; Mitchell (1976) for European agricultural production; *Historical Statistics of the United States* (1975) for U.S. agricultural production; Maddison (1989) for GDP and population.

[a]In international 1980 dollars; for 1987, Maddison shows the United States at $13,550 and the Soviet Union at $5,950.

[b]For Russia: rye, barley, oats, corn; for the United Kingdom: barley, oats; for the United States: barley, oats, corn.

The population in 1913 was predominantly rural, as rural as France had been in 1789, and agriculture still accounted for more than half the national product. When serfdom was abolished in 1861, the land was given to peasants in communal, not individual, ownership. Although private peasant ownership grew over the next half century, less than a third of peasant land was private in 1913.

Russia had industrialized rapidly (table 7.2), especially in the last two decades of the nineteenth century, even by comparison with Germany, and in those particular decades more rapidly than the United States.[2] Although the structure of land tenure inhibited the permanent movement of labor into the cities, it did not stop it; other resources for industrialization came out of the agricultural sector, through direct and indirect taxes, through tariffs on imports

2. Of course, these growth rates pale by comparison with present-day rates in the newly industrializing countries (NICs); Korean industrial production grew at an average rate of 15 percent from 1965 to 1988.

Table 7.2   **The Growth of Industrial Production, 1860–1913** (% per year)

	1860–70	1870–80	1880–90	1890–1900	1900–1910	1910–13
Russia	2.1	5.1	6.0	7.0	3.5	5.0
Germany	3.9	2.7	4.4	4.3	3.5	5.2
United States	4.6	5.7	5.6	3.8	5.4	5.4

Sources: Nove (1989) for Russia (Goldsmith data); Mitchell (1976) for Germany; *Long-Term Economic Growth, 1860–1970* (Washington, D.C.: Department of Commerce, 1973), for the United States (Nutter data).

destined for the rural sector, and through policies that encouraged the growth of agricultural exports.

Industrial growth from 1890 took place behind import barriers[3] and with the assistance of government investment in education and physical infrastructure. Gerschenkron (1962) emphasizes the importance of access to Western, increasingly German and American, technology.

Russia went on the gold standard in 1897 and stayed there until World War I. The state bank was required at the margin to hold 100 percent gold reserves against its note issue, with reserves in fact exceeding these amounts.[4] The country's dependence on external financing to support industrialization is well known. The foreign capital inflow at the end of the czarist period is estimated to have averaged about 2 percent of NNP, accounting for 40 percent of industrial investment and 15–20 percent of total investment (Gregory and Stuart 1986, 43). The gross foreign debt to GNP ratio in 1913 was about 40 percent, and the net debt to exports ratio was above 400 percent.[5] Foreign capital was dominant in mining, especially the oil industry, and owned over 40 percent of the metals industry.

7.2   War, Revolution, and the NEP

World War I, the Revolution, and the Civil War wreaked havoc on the economy. A Supreme Council of National Economy, VSNKh, was set up in December 1917 to run the economy. By February 1918, workers' control over factories had been established, land and the banks nationalized, and the foreign debt repudiated. Although decrees came from the center, actions were taken locally; the peasants redistributed land; this was a period of "elemental-chaotic proletarian nationalization from below."[6] Referring to the VSNKh, Nove (1989, 44) states that its leaders were young intellectuals, with little grip on the realities

3. The average tariff on manufactured goods in 1904 was 130 percent (Maddison 1969, 91).
4. Yurovsky (1925) provides an overview of monetary arrangements before World War I.
5. Calculation based on Maddison's (1969, 91) estimate that the gross foreign debt in 1913 was 8 billion rubles and the net debt 6.5 billion.
6. Nove (1989, 44), quoting a 1924 article by L. Kritsman.

of administration and that, "in any case, much of Russia was outside the authority of the government."

The problem of extracting resources from the country, to feed the towns and cities and to finance industrialization, is a recurring theme of Russian and early Soviet history. In mid-1918, all large factories were nationalized, as war communism began. In addition to nationalization of large firms, war communism involved a ban on private trade, forced appropriation by the Cheka and local officials of the rich and middle peasants' surplus production (as defined by the government), and partial attempts to move to a moneyless society by rationing some goods, such as food, and making others, such as the mails and the trolleys, free.[7] Agricultural production and especially the amount available to the government declined, with famine—leading to "uncounted millions" (Nove 1989, 76) of deaths—widespread in 1920 and 1921.

These Bolshevik policies succeeded well enough to win the Civil War, but by 1921 the country had seen a phenomenal decline of output, especially in industry (table 7.3), and was suffering from famine.[8] A rapid inflation was under way, with prices rising on average 1,000 percent per year between 1917 and 1921. With the Civil War won, but barely in control of its territory, with an economy in shambles, facing peasant uprisings and the revolt of the Kronstadt garrison, the government was forced early in 1921 to beat a tactical retreat to the New Economic Policy.

The NEP legalized private trade, liberalized prices, reduced the role of central planning, and in 1924 stabilized the currency. The Bolshevik government saw its key policy problems in agriculture and in distribution. Not enough food was coming out of the countryside to support the urban population, and not enough resources were coming out of agriculture to finance industrialization. Nove (1989, 70) quotes an ex-Menshevik taking part in a 1923 discussion (at a time when free discussion was still possible) on the lessons of the early postrevolutionary years: "The experience of the Russian revolution shows that the nationalization of petty trade should be the last phase of the revolution, and not the first."

Under the NEP, state requisition of agricultural output was replaced by a progressive tax, rising from 5 to 17 percent. Private trade was legalized, and peasants were allowed to sell their output to any purchaser. Large-scale industry, responsible for 75 percent of industrial output, remained nationalized, as did transportation, banking, and foreign trade. Foreign capital was invited in; however, despite well-known exceptions, there was very little response, with less than 1 percent of industrial output being produced in foreign-owned firms by 1928.

---

7. For a review of the debate over whether war communism was a set of improvised measures, responding to events, or rather an ideologically motivated attempt to move rapidly to socialism, see Gregory and Stuart (1986, 52).

8. According to Nove (1989, 57), the urban population halved between 1918 and 1920, and the number of (urban) workers declined from 2.6 million in 1917 to 1.2 million in 1920.

Table 7.3   The Effect of War and Revolution

	1913	1921
Gross industrial output:	100	31
Coal (million tons)	29	9
Oil (million tons)	9.2	3.8
Iron and steel (million tons)	8.5	.3
Agricultural output	100	60
Imports	100	15.1
Exports	100	1.3

Source: Nove (1989, 58).

Strategic nationalized industries[9] remained within the centralized planning system, but the bulk of nationalized firms were decentralized and ordered to operate commercially. They formed themselves into large trusts. Some nationalized firms were leased to individuals and cooperatives, and smaller enterprises were denationalized. Small-scale industry was dominated by the private sector. So too was distribution, within the industrial sector (including the distribution of goods produced by state-owned firms) and between city and country, including agriculture.

These structural reforms took place against a background of rising inflation.[10] The state bank was set up in 1921, and a new currency, the *chervonets,* backed by gold, was introduced in 1922. However, the Soviet ruble (*sovznak*) remained as legal tender, and its inflation continued as the Treasury issued notes to cover its deficit.[11] For at least two years, parallel paper currencies— the *chervonets* and *sovznak*—were circulating.[12] Cagan (1956) shows the quantity of currency rising on average at 49 percent per month between December 1921 and January 1924, with prices rising at 57 percent on average and 213 percent in the final month of the hyperinflation. Stabilization took place in March 1924, based in part on an improving fiscal performance. The budget for fiscal year 1924 (starting the previous October 1) was close to balance, with the assistance of excise, income, wealth, and a variety of other taxes, and the budget was in surplus in the next fiscal year.[13] In April 1924, the ruble exchange

9. Including war industries, fuel, banking, foreign trade, and transportation.
10. The Russian hyperinflation is one of the seven classic cases studied by Cagan (1956).
11. Rostowski and Shapiro (1992) analyze the Soviet hyperinflation and stabilization, arguing that the dual currency approach was skillfully used in the Soviet Union to stabilize at a negligible output cost.
12. As is well known, Gresham's law does not apply when the exchange rate between the good and the bad monies can adjust.
13. Rostowski and Shapiro (1992) emphasize that the budget was unbalanced when stabilization took place in March 1924 but do not present data on the budget deficit as a share of GNP. In the last quarter of 1923, seigniorage amounted to less than 25 percent of total tax revenues and less than 10 percent of total government revenues, indicating a budget in much better condition than

rate was restored to its prewar parity against the dollar, although the ruble was not made convertible into gold or foreign exchange.

The NEP led to a recovery of output, with national income and industrial and agricultural output in 1928 estimated at more than 10 percent above their 1913 levels. However, both for ideological reasons (sheer dislike of the activities of middlemen) and because they doubted the government's ability to extract sufficient resources for industrialization from the agricultural sector under the NEP, the Bolsheviks were moving away from the mixed economy after 1925.

Looking back to the NEP from 1992, the emphasis on private entry into the distribution sector, the restoration of agriculture, price liberalization, the leasing of state-owned enterprises, orders to larger state enterprises to behave commercially, the role of the dual currency, and the gradual approach to the stabilization of inflation all resonate in current policy debates.

7.3   The Soviet Growth Slowdown

The protracted debate over economic policy that took place between 1924 and 1927 ended with the adoption of the first five-year industrialization plan in 1928.[14] The private sector declined rapidly, reflecting not only the disappearance of the Nepmen but also the collectivization of agriculture, which had not been part of the first five-year plan.[15] Between 1930 and 1936, virtually all agriculture was collectivized. The state succeeded in procuring more food from the farm sector, even though grain production did not rise and the livestock population declined by half as peasants preferred eating them to giving them to the collectives.[16] The consequences of collectivization were devastating. Millions died in the famine of 1933; Nove (1989, chap. 7) provides some support for Conquest's estimate that up to 6 million peasants may have died as a result of the collectivization.[17] At the same time, industrial output was increasing by more than 10 percent a year.

The analysis of Soviet economic development between 1928 and 1985 de-

---

in the other hyperinflation countries. Katzenellenbaum (1925, 148) suggests that the Tanzi effect compensated for the loss of seigniorage revenue but does not provide data. Under the terms of the financial stabilization, the Treasury was allowed to sell silver coin, the production cost of which was about half its face value. The inflation stabilization and rapid economic growth allowed for considerable reliquification.

14. Nove (1989, 112–23) and Gregory and Stuart (1986, chap. 4) both present accounts of the Soviet growth strategy debate. Bukharin argued that the NEP alliance with the peasants should continue, allowing the peasants and the economy to grow into socialism; Preobrazhensky argued for a far more aggressive policy against the peasants. Stalin initially appeared to side with the gradualists and did not reveal (or perhaps reach) his final position until 1928.

15. The Nepmen were those who profited under the NEP through their private-sector activities, especially retailers and traders.

16. The livestock decline reduced the demand for rural grain consumption.

17. Gregory and Stuart (1986, 111) quote Swianiewicz's estimate that 3.5 million peasants were sent to the gulags, 3.5 million were resettled, and 3.5 million died during forced collectivization.

pends heavily on the reliability of Western data. There is no question that the official Soviet data vastly exaggerate growth performance, partly because higher prices enter the data as quality improvements, and partly because of incentives to report the achievement of production targets.[18] These problems have of course been carefully considered and, with respect to prices, taken into account by the authors of the classic Western studies, such as Bergson (1961). Their estimates and methodology form the basis for much of the Western analysis of the Soviet economy, including that presented in readily accessible form by Ofer (1987). A basic assumption is that physical quantities as presented in the official data are not systematically misreported. Thus, the fundamental difference between Bergson's estimate that Soviet GNP increased between 1928 and 1985 by 4.3 percent per annum and the official estimate of 8.8 percent (table 7.4) results from pricing corrections. The classic Western estimates generally assume that Soviet investment and capital data are more accurate than output data.[19]

Ericson's reports (1990a, 1990b) on Khanin's data question the basic assumption that reported quantities are not systematically biased, especially for non-standardized goods. Khanin estimates that GDP grew at 3.3 percent per annum between 1928 and 1985. These data, and especially the claim that investment and capital stock data are systematically overstated, would, if correct, necessitate a reconsideration of the extensive Soviet production function literature (e.g., Weitzman 1970, 1983; Desai 1985; Bergson 1987a), to be discussed shortly, and possibly of some accepted conclusions on the causes of the Soviet economic decline.[20]

The central planning system operated relatively well in the heat of World War II, when the goals of economic activity were as clear as they ever can be. Half of GNP was used for the war effort. Per capita consumption was cut by nearly a third between 1940 and 1944, with food consumption being reduced by half. The Soviet Union suffered immense losses, including about 20 million people and 30 percent of the capital stock.

Postwar recovery, helped to some extent by resource transfers from Germany and Eastern Europe, was very rapid, with output by 1950 about 20 percent above the 1940 level.[21] Per capita consumption had risen slightly less and in 1950 was only 10 percent above its 1928 level. This implies that, by 1950, per capita consumption had risen at only about 0.5 percent per year since 1913,

18. Ericson (1990a, 66–72) provides a summary critique of the official data. Bergson (1991) sharply questions the basis for some of the criticisms offered by Ericson and by Aslund (1990).

19. For a detailed justification of this view, see, e.g., Bergson (1987b). It had earlier been disputed by, among others, Wiles (1982).

20. Since Khanin's estimates lower both the growth rate and the rate of capital accumulation, it is possible that the estimated production function may not change much.

21. Ofer (1987), using Bergson's estimates, states that output during the war years was constant and grew at about 3.6 percent per annum from 1944 to 1950. Maddison (1969) shows a significant decline during the war followed by extremely rapid growth to 1950. The decadal growth rates implied by these two sources are very similar.

Table 7.4   **Soviet Growth Data, 1928–85 (% per annum)**

	Khanin	Bergson/CIA	TsSU[a]
National income (GNP):			
1928–85	3.3	4.3	8.8
1928–41	2.9	5.8[b]	13.9
1950s	6.9	6.0	10.1
1960s	4.2	5.2[c]	7.1
1970s	2.0	3.7	5.3
1980–85	.6	2.0	3.2
Capital growth:			
1928–66	4.5	7.4	7.2
1960–81	4.1	7.6	8.1

Source: Ericson (1990a, tables 2.1, 2.4).
[a]The former official statistical agency.
[b]Estimate for 1928–40, from Ofer (1987).
[c]From Ofer (1987).

although with significant improvements in education and literacy. In 1947, there was a currency reform to deal with the postwar liquidity overhang: cash (held disproportionately in agriculture) was exchanged at one to ten; savings accounts below 3,000 rubles were exchanged at one to one; and government bonds were devalued in the ratio one to three.

The Soviet Union rejected participation in the Bretton Woods institutions in 1945 and in the Marshall Plan in 1947, preferring to move away from the wartime alliance toward the establishment of a socialist bloc. By 1948, the East European satellite governments were set up, and, in 1949, China joined the socialist bloc. The Council for Mutual Economic Assistance (CMEA) was established in 1949 but remained moribund during Stalin's lifetime, as the Soviet government preferred to make bilateral rather than multilateral arrangements with other socialist governments.

The decade of the 1950s marks the high point of the Soviet system: GNP growth exceeded 6 percent per annum;[22] per capita consumption rose more than 4 percent; agricultural output increased sharply; Sputnik was launched; and Khrushchev warned that the Soviet Union would bury the United States. At the time, the threat seemed real.

All three data sources in table 7.4 agree that Soviet output growth declined substantially from the 1950s to 1985. By the 1970s, it was clear that the Soviet system was running into severe difficulties, as both Western and Khanin's data show (table 7.5). If the Khanin data in table 7.5 are correct, per capita output has been declining for fifteen years. In addition, the consumption growth rates in table 7.5 would be exaggerated.[23]

22. Growth was also very rapid in this decade in Germany and Japan.
23. Aslund (1990) argues that both the rate of growth and the level of consumption are exaggerated and suggests that consumption in the Soviet Union was about 20–25 percent of the U.S. level

Table 7.5   **Soviet Growth and Allocation Data, 1960–85**

	1960–70	1970–75	1975–80	1980–85
Growth rates (% per year):				
GNP	5.2	3.7	2.6	2.0
(Khanin)	(4.2)	(3.2)	(1.0)	(.6)
Labor (manhours)	1.7	1.7	1.2	.7
Employment	2.1	1.5	1.2	.7
Population	1.3	.9	.8	.9
Capital	8.0	7.9	6.8	6.3
TFP[a]	1.5	.0	−.4	−.5
Consumption	4.5	3.7	2.7	2.0

	1960	1970	1980
Share of GNP (%):			
Current prices:			
Fixed investment	27	29	28
Inventory change	3	4	3
Consumption[b]	59	55	55
Defense	12	13	16
1970 prices:			
Fixed investment	24	28	33

Source: Ofer (1987, tables 1, 3). (Khanin data from Aslund [1990] and Ericson [1990a].)

[a]TFP is total factor productivity growth, calculated by assuming a Cobb-Douglas production function with weights of 0.62 for labor hours, 0.33 for capital, and 0.05 for farmland.

[b]Includes collective consumption, primarily health and education.

Table 7.5 includes data on the much-studied question of the share of defense spending in GNP. The 1980 estimate of 16 percent in table 7.5 is within the range of most recent estimates, slightly on the low side.[24] This is about three times the U.S. burden, which is higher than that of most of the other members of NATO and the OECD.

Why did Soviet growth slow down? It has first to be noted that the pattern in table 7.5 is not markedly different from that in the West, except that the West recovered in the first half of the 1980s and that productivity growth continued to be positive in the West.

The simplest explanation for the Soviet growth slowdown is that the Soviet extensive growth model had reached its natural limits by the end of the 1960s. Soviet growth was based on the rapid accumulation of capital, the increasing use of labor, and increasing exploitation of natural resources. Capital accumulation at the rate of 7–9 percent per annum meant a steady deepening of capital

at the end of the 1980s. Bergson (1991) makes the case that, in 1985, Soviet per capita consumption was 28.5 percent of the U.S. level, specifically criticizing the basis for Aslund's lower estimate.

24. Several of the papers in Rowen and Wolf (1990) discuss the Soviet defense burden, concluding variously that it is between 15 and 25 percent of GNP.

that must have reduced the return to further capital accumulation. The participation rate of labor increased rapidly from 1928; by 1980, there was virtually full participation of labor, 86.6 percent of the relevant age group, compared with 70.9 percent in the United States. Given essentially full participation, the rate of population growth, which was below 1 percent after 1970 (table 7.5), limited the rate of increase of the raw labor input.[25] Even so, with the agricultural sector still accounting for 20 percent of employment in 1980, there should have been room for continuing increases in output from the transfer of formerly agricultural labor in the nonagricultural sectors; however, there has been little evidence of this classic Lewis-type mechanism at work in the Soviet Union. The Soviet Union invested heavily in natural resources, especially energy, in the 1970s and 1980s, but these areas too appeared to be hitting diminishing returns in the middle and late 1980s.

Weitzman (1970) estimated aggregate production functions for Soviet industry. His results suggested a low elasticity of substitution in Soviet industry and that the returns to further capital accumulation would diminish rapidly.[26] Alternative estimates use a Cobb-Douglas production function with decreasing rate of productivity growth (e.g., Desai [1985], who works with individual industry–level data). Bergson (1983), imposing both CES and Cobb-Douglas functions,[27] finds generally slowing productivity growth between 1950 and 1975, with especially slow growth in 1970–75. There is little doubt that productivity growth has been slowing, and it is quite possible that, as shown in table 7.5, it has been negative for fifteen years.

The production function debate describes but does not explain the decline in Soviet growth. If we adopt the Cobb-Douglas assumption, it remains necessary to account for the decline in productivity growth at the economy-wide level of 2 percentage points per annum since the mid-1960s (table 7.5).[28] However, this cannot be the whole story. The problem is not only that Soviet productivity growth declined but that it did so at output levels well inside the world technology frontier. Put differently, the question is why the Soviet Union stopped catching up, given the advantages of backwardness as emphasized by Gerschenkron (1962) or the convergence hypothesis of modern growth theory.

Educational levels and attainment in the former Soviet Union (FSU) are rea-

25. The rate of population growth was higher in the lower-income Central Asian republics than elsewhere in the Soviet Union, implying a shift in the location of either capital or labor to use this labor.

26. Data presented in Weitzman (1983) show the capital output ratio in Soviet *industry* rising by 98 percent over the period 1951–78; Ofer's (1987) data imply that the capital output ratio in the *economy* increased by 175 percent over the period 1950–80. Bergson (1983) dismisses the CES production function because it would have implied rates of return on capital of more than 40 percent in 1950.

27. Weitzman (1983) suggests that the data lack sufficient power to distinguish between the CES with constant rate of technical progress and Cobb-Douglas with decreasing rate of technical change.

28. If the CES assumption were correct, it would still be necessary to explain what technological choices in the Soviet Union made for a CES production function with sharply diminishing returns to capital when other countries appear to have avoided this difficulty.

sonably high by international standards, with literacy officially claimed to be complete. Educational attainment (table 7.6) appears to match that of Italy, although comparability of data is not guaranteed. In different versions, recent growth theories emphasize either the level of human capital or its accumulation as important factors in growth. The level of human capital is treated as an index of the ability to absorb new technology; by this criterion, the Soviet Union should have been well equipped to absorb both domestic and foreign technology. The accumulation of human capital serves to offset, or with some production functions entirely avoid, diminishing returns to capital accumulation. The data show that, between 1970 and 1989, as productivity growth was declining, the share of the labor force with secondary and higher education rose from 65 to 92 percent (JSSE 1991, 2:213). Thus, at least at first glance, the decline in Soviet productivity growth cannot be easily traced to the low level or low rate of change of human capital.

Bergson (1983) undertakes a full Denison-style decomposition of Soviet productivity. Even after adjusting for educational achievement and possible increasing returns, he finds a sharp decline in productivity growth, which he seeks to explain by examining the correlates of technical progress.[29] The scale of Soviet research and development (R&D) was massive and growing through the period of declining productivity growth, so it is not an obvious candidate, although Soviet R&D has been heavily directed toward the military. Bergson points to Sutton's (1973) work, which shows the Soviet Union unusually dependent on imported technology, therefore questioning the effectiveness of its own R&D effort. He also places considerable emphasis on the lack of adequate incentives for innovation. However, as he emphasizes, there are no clear factors responsible for slowing as well as low productivity growth.

The causes of the productivity growth slowdown have to be sought in the combination of the nature of the economic system and its incentives, with changing external conditions. This perspective is taken by Winiecki (1986), who examines the prospects for socialist economies. Among the causes of decline that he lists are the increase in the price of energy in the 1970s and 1980s, more significant for these highly energy-intensive economies than others; the growing complexity of production processes, with the centrally planned economies less well able to deal with complexity;[30] in particular, the fact that the Soviet-style economies had reached the range of GNP in which the service sector expands but did not have the technology to expand services; and the argument that the industries of the 1970s and 1980s required different skills, such as innovation, flexibility, and risk taking, than the heavy industries that had been the engine of growth before.[31]

Other factors should be added. Ofer (1987) emphasizes the system's "haste,"

---

29. Kontorovich (1986) uses Soviet data on innovations to conclude that there was a significant decline in innovation and its effect over the 1970s and into the early 1980s.

30. This argument provides one application for Kremer's (1993) O-ring theory of production.

31. This argument has been made about the relative decline of the United States by Piore and Sabel (1984).

Table 7.6   Soviet Human Capital in International Perspective

	Mean Years of Schooling (1980)	Scientists & Technicians (per 1,000 people)[a]	Tertiary Graduate Ratio (% of age group)	Science Graduates (% of total graduates)
Soviet Union	7.6	128	5.8	48
Japan	10.4	317	11.5	25
United States	12.2	55	15.5	30
Italy	6.4	83	3.2	50
Industrial countries	9.1	139	9.1	35
Developing countries	3.5	9	1.1	31

Source: Human Development Report (New York: Oxford University Press, for the UN Development Programme, 1991).

[a]As specified in source; should probably be per 1,000 labor force participants.

its emphasis on rapid and visible growth, leading it to neglect the long run, for instance, in infrastructure, maintenance of the capital stock, and the environment. The war in Afghanistan and the U.S. military buildup in the 1980s imposed an added burden on an already creaking system. The declining rate of growth and level of consumption after the 1970s must have reduced work incentives but, more important, increased the demand for reform, particularly when the communications revolution was making the improvement in living standards in Europe so clearly visible. The need to invest in agriculture, growing unsold inventories of goods and unfinished construction projects, low quality of output, and all the other inefficiencies that had been visible and talked about for years must have taken a cumulative toll.

7.4   The Gorbachev Era

The system that Mikhail Gorbachev inherited in March 1985 seemed to the outside world to be in serious, but not terminal, difficulties. Whether he could have prevented the collapse of the Soviet Union is a good question, on a par with whether Kerenksy could have prevented the Bolshevik coup. The question cannot of course be answered, but speculation on it would start from the incoherence of the policies pursued in his nearly seven years in power and from the decision to implement glasnost before perestroika.

The economics of the story through 1990 has been comprehensively told in the Joint Study of the Soviet Economy (JSSE 1991).[32] Gorbachev came to power recognizing, under the slogan of "acceleration," the need to reverse the growth slowdown and stagnation of the previous decade. The twelfth five-year plan, that for 1986–90, included a major retooling of industry, based on the desire to move from extensive to intensive growth. In addition, the plan included campaigns to improve quality control and reduce the use of alcohol, personnel changes in the party and management, and clarification of the (restrictive) conditions under which individuals could engage in private economic activity.

The antialcohol campaign did well in reducing official sales but less well in its objective of reducing consumption and absenteeism from work. The decline in vodka sales also had a significant effect on the budget, costing about 2 percent of GNP.[33] The other campaigns showed mixed success.

In 1986 and 1987, macroeconomic management was affected by the decline in the world price of oil. To compensate for lower export prices, the volume of

---

32. In addition to drawing in this section on JSSE, I use the accounts of recent developments in Aslund (1991a, 1991b), Ericson (1990b), Ofer (1990), and Shelton (1989).

33. Gorbachev was probably unaware that he was repeating history. Pipes (1990, 234–35) describes the effect of the prohibition of the manufacture and sale of alcohol imposed on the outbreak of World War I: "Prohibition, however, had little effect on alcohol consumption . . . [leading rather] to a rise in the output of moonshine. . . . But while alcoholism did not decline, the Treasury's income from alcohol taxes did, and these had formerly accounted for one-fourth of its revenues."

exports to the convertible currency area was raised by 22 percent, while the volume of imports from those countries was cut by 17 percent between 1985 and 1987. In addition, gold exports were increased. The capital account with the convertible area went into deficit, as the Soviet Union found it difficult to borrow.

As a result of the campaigns and reduced government revenues from fuel exports as well as higher spending to cover increased investment and food subsidies, the budget deficit rose rapidly between 1985 and 1987. As a counterpart to the budget deficit, bank lending to the government increased sharply, while credit to enterprises was cut back. On the other side of the banks' balance sheet, money growth increased (table 7.7).

A potentially decisive change in the planning system was introduced in the July 1987 Law on State Enterprises. Enterprises were to be given more freedom to choose output levels and even, within centrally set parameters, to choose prices. State orders were to be confined to direct purchases of goods for the state. It turned out, however, that enterprises preferred knowing where their inputs were to come from and requested the continuation of state orders, which in 1988 still accounted for 90 percent of industrial production. State orders covered a smaller share of output in 1989, with part of the remainder being traded on interenterprise wholesale markets.

The 1987 law allowed firms more freedom in setting not only prices and output but also wages and bonuses. The rate of wage inflation increased markedly in 1988 and 1989 (table 7.7), adding inflationary pressure to the system. During this period, there was a rapid increase in the number of cooperatives; by the end of 1990, cooperatives employed nearly 4 percent of the work force.

Agricultural distribution was severely affected by the reforms. Despite a rise in grain production in 1989, the share sold to state procurement agencies was

Table 7.7   **Soviet Macroeconomic Performance, 1985–91**

	1985	1986	1987	1988	1989	1990	1991
GNP growth[a]	.8	4.1	1.3	2.1	1.5	−4.0	−13.0
Gross investment growth	3.0	8.4	5.6	6.2	4.7	−2.5	−6.0
Budget deficit/GDP (%)	2.4	6.2	8.8	11.0	9.5	8.3	20
Retail price index[b]	3.5	4.4	4.5	6	8	20	100
M2 growth	N.A.	8.5	14.7	14.1	14.8	20.2	75
Nominal wage increase	2.9	2.9	3.7	8.3	9.4	12.3	70
Real wage[b]	−.5	−1.5	−.5	2	1	−6	−15

Source: JSSE, for budget deficit through 1990; *PlanEcon Report* 7, nos. 43–44 (9 December 1991), for other data; budget deficit for 1991 based on news reports; other 1991 data are forecasts based on first three quarters.

Note: N.A. = not available.

[a]CIA estimates.

[b]These are *PlanEcon*'s "realistic" estimates.

the lowest in thirty years. With the cities more dependent on state distribution than the countryside, these changes had uneven effects on the population.

By 1989, it was clear that Gorbachev's piecemeal approach to economic reform had not succeeded in restoring growth. Many were convinced that more systematic and thoroughgoing reforms would be needed and that the Soviet Union would have to move decisively to a market system. Over the next two years, Soviet researchers and policymakers came forward with several comprehensive economic reform plans, the best known of which was the Shatalin 500-Day Plan.

The Shatalin Plan differs from the reform plans that have been implemented in Eastern Europe and from Western reform plans for the FSU, such as the Joint (IMF, IBRD, OECD, EBRD) Plan, in several key respects. Obviously, the 500-day timing is extraordinarily ambitious—and unrealistic. The sequencing is also different, attempting to start with privatization and deferring price liberalization. The authors of the plan believed that privatization revenues could help balance the budget and absorb the money overhang, thereby reducing the danger of an inflationary spurt at the time of price liberalization. The Shatalin Plan places much less weight on the need for early convertibility than would most Western plans. At that time, it also did not emphasize the need for external assistance, believing that the Soviet Union could manage largely on its own. With respect to the macroeconomic essentials, the Shatalin group was completely orthodox, stressing the need for budget balance and monetary control.

President Gorbachev could not bring himself to adopt the Shatalin Plan. Doing so would have meant a clean break with the planning system, with the essential elements of communism, and with his prime minister. In July 1991, he was given another chance, after the work on the Grand Bargain (Allison and Yavlinsky 1991) had brought him to the G-7 summit in London.[34] At this point, the presentation of a coherent reform plan would have strengthened Western support. Instead, he sent the West a long and complicated letter, which was interpreted as implying either an unwillingness to move to a market system or a lack of understanding of what that meant. Time ran out on Gorbachev after the August coup attempt, even though interrepublican economic reform committees continued working on the economic constitution of a new union up to its dissolution.

The economic decline of the Soviet Union continued through 1991. An unusually inept currency reform in February, unaccompanied by any stabilization measures, had no effect on inflation. A price reform in April raised but did not decontrol prices. Reported exports collapsed, and it became increasingly clear that the Soviet Union could not service its debt. Late in the year, the republics

---

34. A *Washington Post* article by Jeffrey Sachs in May 1991 was also influential in putting the issue of economic assistance to the Soviet Union back in the headlines.

signed an agreement with the G-7 to be jointly and individually responsible for the servicing of the debt. However, by this stage, the republics were signing many agreements, and it was not clear which of them would be adhered to.

As the center's power dissipated, republics stopped paying taxes to the union government, which increasingly covered its spending by printing money. Gradually, the Russian government took over many of the responsibilities of the union government, including the payment of its bills. The estimated budget deficit for the last quarter of 1991 was 22 percent of GNP.

On Christmas Day 1991, President Gorbachev resigned, and the Soviet Union expired. While the death may have been inevitable, its timing surely owes much both to Gorbachev's early decision to open up the system and to his later inability to pursue a clear-cut economic reform strategy.

7.5   Reform in Russia and the FSU

The former Soviet republics are in many respects typical of reforming socialist countries.[35] However, they face formidable difficulties even beyond those confronting other reforming socialist economies. First, because their economies used to be run from Moscow, they lack a policy-making apparatus. Russia is best off in this respect, but, even so, the incoming economic reformers in Russia faced the task of dismantling the Soviet economic policy system and building up their own policy machinery at the same time as they were planning their reforms. Second, trading and currency relations among the republics are in a state of flux: the republics of the new commonwealth have, for instance, agreed in principle to continue using the ruble for two years, but there is no doubt that Ukraine is already implicitly introducing a separate currency through its coupon system and little doubt that it and at least Estonia will explicitly introduce a separate currency later this year. Third, the entire range of political and economic issues following the breakup of the Soviet Union, including the disposition of the armed forces and the ownership of assets and liabilities, has to be dealt with. Finally, the new states were not yet members of the international financial institutions when they became independent, so that there were inevitably delays in providing and coordinating external assistance to them. The international community was able to move exceptionally rapidly by admitting the republics to the IMF and the World Bank at the end of April 1992.

With respect to internal reforms, the new republics have to deal both with their short-run macroeconomic crises, manifested in a large budget deficit (Table 7.7),[36] high inflation, and balance-of-payments difficulties, and with

35. In the remainder of the paper, I draw freely on Fischer (1992b) and Fischer and Frenkel (1992).

36. There appear to be wide differences among budget situations in the different republics, with several republics claiming to have much smaller deficits than Russia. However, there are no published data on estimated 1992 republic-level budget deficits.

their long-term growth crises. The standard reform prescription (see, e.g., Fischer and Gelb 1991; JSSE 1990; Lipton and Sachs 1990) is for a five-point strategy, moving as fast as possible on all fronts: macroeconomic stabilization, requiring both a budget that is close to balance and tight control over credit; liberalization of the prices of most goods; current account convertibility of the currency; privatization; and the creation of a social safety net. At the same time, the government would be putting in place the legal framework for a market economy.

Obvious problems with the standard strategy derive from the difficulty of doing everything at once. For instance, liberalizing prices before the ownership of firms is clarified is problematic, for managers of state-owned enterprises are unlikely to be pure profit maximizers. But privatization before prices are liberalized is also problematic, for it will be impossible to value firms for sale when current prices and profits provide little guide to future performance.

The Russian approach differs from that of Eastern Europe in some key respects: in the ordering of price liberalization and macroeconomic stabilization; in the very clear linkage that the political process has revealed between industrial restructuring and macroeconomic stabilization; and in the importance of interrepublic economic relations.

7.5.1   Price Liberalization in Russia

The normal prescription is first (or simultaneously) to establish macroeconomic control and then to liberalize prices. In the event, the Russian government started its reforms by liberalizing prices well before it had any assurance that fiscal and monetary policy were consistent with macroeconomic stability.

The standard sequencing applies to countries where most resources are allocated through functioning markets and where price liberalization means removing incomplete price controls and reducing tariffs. That was not the situation in Russia. There the choice was either to liberalize prices and risk hyperinflation or to maintain price controls with the consequence of growing shortages. In weighing its decision, the government no doubt took into account the fact that a growing proportion of transactions were in any case being conducted in black markets, so that the effective choice was to a considerable extent between hidden and open inflation. It must also have taken into account the unavailability at the end of 1991 of external resources to help finance the budget and stabilize the currency. And, by taking a radical and virtually reversible step, it signaled that it meant what it said about radical reform.

Analysts of the Soviet economy have in the last few years focused on the existence of a monetary overhang. One of the benefits of starting with price liberalization is that the monetary overhang has probably disappeared. But the current confused inflationary situation is one that brings great risks of social and political discontent. The economic policymakers are not likely to remain in office if hyperinflation continues.

7.5.2   Macroeconomic Stabilization

In the spring of 1992, much needs to be done if macroeconomic stabilization is to be secured in Russia. The two essentials are fiscal consolidation and a tightening of monetary and credit policy. The Russian government was able to reduce the budget deficit by over 5 percent of GDP by cutting subsidies, defense, and investment spending. But its efforts to collect taxes have been less successful. The first-quarter budget deficit on an accruals basis was probably around 15 percent of GDP, while the deficit on a cash basis was much smaller, perhaps around 7–8 percent of GDP. The difference is accounted for partly by unpaid interest on external debt obligations.

The Soviet tax system relied primarily on profits and turnover taxes, the former collected mostly at the union level, the latter more at the republic level. On the expenditure side, subsidies, provided mostly at the republic level, took up about 20 percent of the budget and 10 percent of GDP. In their initial attempt at macroeconomic stabilization, the Russian government cut subsidies and relied on a generalized 28 percent sales (or value-added) tax to close the budget gap. The sales tax should have been collectible through the same channels as before, and profits and export taxes should also have been paid to the Russian government. However, revenues have fallen short of projections, partly because of the decline in exports, partly because the Parliament exempted food from taxation, and also because of poor tax compliance.

In the short run, fiscal stabilization will require further cuts in spending and increased revenues. The key to budget balance lies in the taxation of oil exports. The budget deficit would be closed if a planned 40 percent export tax can be collected, especially if recent declines in oil production can be reversed. Over the longer run, structural fiscal reform is needed to move away from the fiscal structure inherited from the Soviet Union. Given the inevitable weakness of tax administration at the early stages of reform, simplicity and collectibility are key criteria.[37] Unless the penalties for tax evasion are strengthened, Russia risks descending into the former Latin American trap, where no one pays taxes, no one is punished, the budget is chronically in deficit, and inflation is a perennial problem.

The issue of monetary or credit policy in Russia is mired in a dispute between the Central Bank of Russia (CBR) and the Finance Ministry over the need for tight credit. The CBR, with the support of Parliament, has argued that tightening credit now will merely lead to unemployment and bankruptcies without achieving any positive results. The Finance Ministry wants the CBR to tighten credit as part of the stabilization program.

This dispute extends beyond the usual sniping between the Finance Ministry and the CBR to the crucial issue of the relation between monetary and credit policy and restructuring policy. Budgetary stabilization alone cannot stop in-

---

37. Largely on these grounds, McLure (1991) argues for a consumption-based tax; see also Kopits (1991).

flation if the central bank continues to expand the stock of credit by lending to the private sector. Both the quantity and the cost of central bank credit matter: the CBR has so far been lending at a very negative real rate, which is not surprising when a price *level* change is taking place; however, there is no sign that it is willing to move the real interest rate to a positive level even when and if inflation recedes.

The key issue arises in the central bank's argument (and that of the parliamentary supporters of the central bank and industry) that it is essential not to starve existing firms of finance because enforcement of tight credit constraints could lead to the closing of enterprises. In the current distorted price and financial systems, the wrong firms might close. Further, given the geographic concentration of industry, even if such closings were justified on economic grounds, they could devastate the economies of entire regions, as, for instance, in the shipbuilding regions of the former East Germany. The standard prescription, to formulate a regional policy and finance it through the budget, is unrealistic given the government's inability to raise revenues. The provision of cheap credit then is a substitute for an articulated and financed restructuring and regional policy or a holding operation while an explicit restructuring policy is formulated and implemented.[38]

This argument is not in principle incorrect. It certainly increases the urgency of moving ahead on economic restructuring, primarily privatization, and the formulation of regional policies. However, there is no doubt that credit policy could be tightened now (April 1992) without precipitating massive bankruptcies. Prices have been liberalized, and firms need to begin to face a financial bottom line. This would encourage normal supply responses, including the disgorging of inventories, a process that would help reverse expectations of rising prices and move goods into distribution channels. The argument that a tightening of credit policies will lead to massive unemployment may become relevant within a year if no industrial restructuring takes place, but the fact is that few firms in the reforming East European countries have been closed and unemployment has increased only slowly.

The extension of interfirm credits presents another major problem for monetary and credit policy. Firms are simply not paying their bills to each other, and the resulting credits and debts have apparently increased from a very low level to around 20 percent of GDP within six months. Credit policy will have to find a mechanism to rein in these credits if monetary policy is to have any effect on the economy.

In the near term, monetary policy will need to support the stabilization effort if stabilization is to succeed and to attract Western financial assistance. There are several possibilities. First, the CBR may already be tightening credit— there are some reports that credit growth was slow in February. Second, an explicit monetary policy rule, such as a limit on domestic credit creation or the

---

38. I return below to the issue of restructuring and privatization.

maintenance of a fixed exchange rate, could be embodied in the expected IMF agreement. Third, the interest rate may be raised to positive real levels—although this is not a sufficient policy unless accompanied by central bank refusal to roll over debts. If nonetheless the policy conflict continues, then the situation can be resolved by President Yeltsin's intervention.

7.5.3   Incomes Policy

Taxes on excess wage increases have been used in Poland. One argument for such tax-incentive policies (TIPs) advanced in the 1970s is that these taxes mitigate an externality in the wage-setting process (Seidman 1978). A stronger argument in reforming socialist economies is that, so long as the ownership of enterprises is ambiguous, firms will tend to pay out excessive amounts to workers and other stakeholders. The requirement in Poland that firms pay dividends to the government also responds to this concern but would not by itself prevent decapitalization of the firm. An equally powerful argument derives from the potential dynamic inconsistency of anti-inflationary policy. The anti-inflationary government should not accommodate wage-cost pressures on prices. However, if wages do rise, the nonaccommodating government has to create unemployment, which it is loath to do. Rather than allow itself to be put in that position, the government seeks to prevent it by taxing excess wage increases.

There are two arguments against the use of tax-based incomes policy in Russia. First, opponents argue that market forces should be left to determine wages. But wage setting in government-owned firms is not a market process. As in Poland, the tax need not apply to firms in the private sector—thereby also providing an incentive to privatize. Second, it is argued that, since real wages have already fallen very low, there is no need to tax nominal wage increases, which would only be catching up for past declines. Data are not currently available to assess the level of real wages. Even if they are very low, the wage tax could become effective only on wage increases in excess of some base rate, which could be set so as to allow some real wage catch-up. There are thus arguments in favor of the use of a tax on excess wage increases in Russia.[39]

7.6   Enterprise Reform and Privatization

Debates in the Russian Congress in April 1992 drove home the close links between credit and industrial restructuring policy. Restructuring starts from the industrial structure left by the Soviet system. Soviet industrial enterprises were

---

39. Blanchard and Layard (1991) discuss some difficulties in the implementation of the Polish excess wage tax, particularly that it allowed a period of slower than permitted wage increases to be followed by a catch-up, in which wages could increase temporarily at more than the target inflation rate. This difficulty could be handled by rebasing the reference wage each month. (I am grateful to Olivier Blanchard for discussion of this issue.)

Table 7.8   Size Distribution of Industrial Enterprises (share of employees)

	1–99	100–499	500–999	1,000+	Of the 1,000+: 5,000–10,000	10,000+
Soviet Union (1988)	1.8	13.2	11.7	73.3	15.6	21.5
United States (1985)	27.6	33.8	12.7	25.8		
Poland (1986)	10	25	15	51		

Sources: Soviet Union, JSSE (1991, 2:37); United States, *Statistical Abstract of the United States* (1988, p. 499) (for manufacturing); Poland, Lipton and Sachs (1990, 84).

very large (table 7.8), and industry was correspondingly monopolized.[40] In 1988, there were 47,000 industrial enterprises in the Soviet Union. In the first half of 1990, republic- and local authority–owned enterprises accounted for 35 percent of value added.[41] The private sector in the Soviet Union was minuscule. Nearly 90 percent of employment was in state enterprises, 8 percent on collective farms, and less than 4 percent in private activity (including cooperatives). The number of cooperatives surged at the end of the Soviet period, exceeding 250,000 (with nearly 40 percent in construction) in the middle of 1991, employing over 6 million people and accounting perhaps for as much as 5 percent of GDP. However, 80 percent of these cooperatives were operating within existing enterprises (Johnson and Kroll 1991)—a process that can be viewed either as the beginning of industrial restructuring through the spinning off of viable components of firms or simply as the ripping off of state assets.

In Eastern Europe, the stated preference has been for rapid privatization. In practice, East European progress in privatization has been disappointing, especially in Poland, where sophisticated schemes for mass privatization have yet to be implemented (Berg, in vol. 2). There has been considerable success in small-scale privatization, the privatization of small, primarily retail, firms the purchase or lease of which is often financed by the selling governmental agency. Privatization of medium- and large-scale firms has been less successful, although the Czechoslovak voucher scheme could soon result in privatization of much of industry—and perhaps shortly thereafter also in widespread disillusionment with the promises of financial operators. Hungary, which has avoided grandiose schemes and encourages current management and workers to pursue the sale of their firms subject to approval by the State Property Agency, appears to be making some progress with privatization of larger firms (Fischer 1992a).

40. JSSE (1991, 2:40) provides a list of products for which industrial concentration by producer is high. They include sewing machines (100 percent), hydraulic turbines (100 percent), steam turbines (95 percent) (with hydraulic and steam turbines being produced by the same company), freezers (100 percent), and many more.
41. Data are from JSSE (1991, 2:15–40), which provides a succinct description of the enterprise sector and reform strategies.

Enterprise reform is bound to be gradualistic: privatization of large firms will take time, perhaps up to a decade until most of the largest firms have been mostly privatized. It will also take years—not months—to implement a strategy in which the state will be responsible for a significant—but diminishing—part of industry.

Such a strategy would look much like that being carried out in practice, although not in rhetoric, in Eastern Europe and that is starting in Russia. The first Russian auctions of small firms took place at the beginning of April, but local authorities are not showing much enthusiasm about the sales (Shleifer and Vishny, in vol. 2). Small-scale privatization would provide both a precedent and a signal that privatization is under way; it is also needed because the distribution sector in which such firms operate is vastly underdeveloped in Russia. The precedent of the NEP is relevant here: much of the success of the NEP in the 1920s was a result of its permitting private enterprise in the distribution sector; the activities of the Nepmen brought the then predominant rural sector bank into the economy in an active way. The growth of the distribution sector would play a similar role in developing a market economy in Russia. Growth in the distribution sector is likely eventually to come from new firms, but opening up the sector requires the privatization of the existing local authority–owned firms. As emphasized by Shleifer and Vishny (in vol. 2), existing stakeholders will have to be given incentives to obtain their support for privatization. If rapid progress cannot be made in this easiest area of privatization, the entire privatization and reform program would be severely set back.

Stories about the spontaneous or *nomenklatura* privatization of larger firms abound. Johnson and Kroll's (1991) case study evidence is that firms' managers have generally strengthened their control and their residual property rights during the period since 1988 but that they have not obtained de jure ownership of firms. Johnson and Kroll emphasize the part played by management and downplay the role of the *nomenklatura*. Newspaper and other reports of corruption in the transfer of property tend to emphasize the role of the bureaucracy. It is not inconsistent with Johnson and Kroll's evidence to argue that, in many cities and regions, property rights are being (insecurely) passed from the state sector to others, to the benefit of the *nomenklatura*.

Both existing management and existing workers will have to support privatizations of larger firms if they are to be moved quickly into the private sector. Thus, privatization schemes that give existing workers and management significant shares of the privatized firm are more likely to succeed than those that ignore the current distribution of implicit property rights (Shleifer and Vishny, in vol. 2). Shleifer and Vishny suggest that the shares be given in a way that directly encourages management and workers to privatize, for instance, by allowing shareowners to receive dividends only after privatization.

In dealing with larger firms, it is generally recommended to start with corporatization, moving the firms out of bureaucratic control and into the control of corporate boards. These boards would include worker representation; inevitably, their composition will have to compromise between the need for knowledgeable members and the objective of keeping out the *nomenklatura*.

Experience in Hungary suggests that the pace of privatization can be increased by encouraging self-privatization by existing firms, subject to state approval. This process can take place at any time while other privatization schemes are being developed and implemented.

A possible privatization strategy following corporatization starts with each board—for tractability, say boards of firms with more than 2,500 employees—presenting a restructuring plan to the privatization agency. All firms whose boards present a plausible restructuring scheme that does not involve large externalities for a given region or city will go into a privatization pool. Ownership rights for the firms in the privatization pool would be distributed to citizens as well as workers and managers through a voucher scheme, perhaps one that gives individuals ownership in holding companies rather than individual firms. Smaller firms could be privatized through vouchers in the same or a separate scheme.

During the restructuring process, it will be necessary for the state to decide how to deal with existing financial assets and liabilities in firm balance sheets. There is some advantage to a widespread write-down or even write-off of debts and corresponding assets, an action that would have to involve the banks. The banks could be compensated by being given claims on a diversified portfolio of firm equity and by being given government bonds as reserve assets.

The large size of the enterprises and the concentration of industries creates both advantages and problems for boards considering restructuring. On the benefit side, the large firms are too vertically integrated (each provides its own complete range of ancillary services, such as catering, machine tool shops for the manufacture of spare parts, haircuts, etc.), and restructuring can begin by peeling off viable parts of firms. Similarly, because the firms are in many cases monopolies with most of the country's technical knowledge in the production of that commodity, it is likely that some part of them will survive in the new regime.

The prime disadvantage of largeness is that rapidly closing down a giant firm that dominates the economy of a city or region will not be politically possible. These are the firms that will not go into the privatization pool and for which Russia will have to develop regional and restructuring policies. To state the point clearly, this borders on industrial policy. But there is no point in assuming that the Russian government will be able to do what most other governments—most obviously the German government[42]—cannot, which is to leave such restructurings to the market, particularly the market for corporate restructuring, which does not yet exist. To put the point succinctly, *privatization is not an adequate restructuring policy*. Pretending that restructuring will take

---

42. On the active role of the Treuhandanstalt in managing the industrial transition in East Germany, see Carlin and Mayer (in vol. 2).

place if left to the market would only delay actual restructuring. An agency, operated with external financial and expert support, could be set up to deal with those firms that do not go into the privatization pool, to develop restructuring (if necessary, phased shutdown) plans.

Within a few years, the Russian private sector will grow more through the creation of new firms than through privatization. Thus, an essential element of the enterprise reform strategy consists of the development of a legal and financial infrastructure and an educational system to support new enterprises.

East European governments have been concerned that, at the current overdevalued exchange rates, foreigners could buy up too much of their countries at too low a price. A similar concern seems to have arisen in Russia in the recent negotiations over a potential Chevron investment in the oil sector, which revealed a Groucho Marx–like fear on the Russian side of accepting any deal to which the other side agreed. Despite such concerns, foreign direct investment, which brings not only finance but also management expertise and technology, is being actively sought by the Russian government. Russia has hired foreign advisers to help develop and appraise potential foreign investments; this is an area in which the international agencies, which are presumably able to operate more as honest brokers, might play an active role. While foreign investors are obviously extremely interested in Russia, foreign direct investment will not flow on a substantial scale, such as the scale on which it is now flowing to Hungary (over 3 percent of GNP), until some sense of stability returns.

Foreign expertise can of course be obtained without foreign investment. There is no reason why foreign management should not be imported on contract even if foreign firms do not want to invest directly.

7.6.1   The Financial Sector

The creation of a viable private sector depends on the availability of financing for both the purchase of existing firms and the creation of new firms. Financing for privatization can come to some extent from the state sector—for example, in small-scale privatization through the leasing rather than the immediate sale of firms—and by setting the prices of firms low enough, through voucher schemes. The development of new firms depends more on the development of the banking system, through restructuring of existing balance sheets and the creation of new banks or units within existing banks. The possibility of canceling existing debts between firms and banks, and replacing them with bank claims on a diversified range of firms, has already been noted. Implicit or explicit state guarantees would be needed to ensure that banks do not go under if firms fail on a large scale. Financial sector reforms have lagged in Eastern Europe, except in Hungary. Many new and specialized banks have been set up in Russia, but the existing banks have not yet been reformed.

7.7   New Currencies, Interrepublic Trade, and Economic Coordination

The dissolution of the Soviet Union will lead to both a decline—at least in the near term—of interrepublic trade and the introduction of independent currencies in some republics of the FSU. Would the republics be better off staying in the ruble zone or introducing their own currencies? If Russia continues to move ahead on price liberalization, stabilization, and convertibility, there would be advantages for the other republics in staying in the ruble zone and automatically acquiring a more stable and convertible money. In addition, interrepublic trade would probably hold up better if the ruble zone is maintained.[43] Offsetting these advantages is the certainty that there will have to be major changes in relative wages among republics; these would be easier to attain if exchange rates among the republics' currencies could be adjusted. Republics with less developed tax systems may want to use seigniorage more than others; this too requires an independent currency. Of course, operating an independent currency will require improvements in the quality of central bank management.

By virtue of its size and relative wealth, Russia would be less affected by the breakdown of interrepublic trade and the ruble area than would the other republics. At the first stage of its reform program, Russia was able to force price liberalization on the others because they were not prepared to introduce their own currencies and manage their own economies. Russia's progress to macroeconomic stabilization has put pressure on other republics by reducing the availability of rubles to cover their budget deficits and meet payrolls. Russia hopes to tighten fiscal and monetary policies and move toward convertibility within a few months. The other republics will have either to stabilize at the same time or to introduce independent currencies. Beyond this defensive motive, an independent currency is seen as a necessary attribute of sovereignty in some of the republics.

In any case, Ukraine and perhaps the Baltics are planning to introduce their own currencies later this year, and other western republics are likely to follow. Presumably, these republics would want their currencies to be convertible as soon as possible, but, because reforms have been slow, convertibility will be delayed. The Central Asian republics will probably want to stay in the ruble area as long as they continue to receive transfers from Russia. Those transfers could be made explicitly through budgetary transfers or trade credits or by pricing Russian exports at internal Russian prices (i.e., net of export taxes). For 1992, Russia will not levy export taxes on oil sent to other republics. It is thus seeking at least temporarily to maintain the wider trading zone. In the

---

43. This argument is not analytically clear cut. If a country had an independent currency and was trying to maintain free trade, it would have one more instrument, exchange rate changes, with which to attain its free trade goal. However, countries more often introduce trade restrictions to protect the value of the currency.

longer run, the Russian decision on whether to provide transfers must be mainly political.

New currencies can be introduced cooperatively, by retiring an equivalent volume of rubles within the geographic territory or by retiring rubles owned by citizens of the republic, or in a confrontational way, by ignoring the existing stock of rubles. There is a mutual interest in avoiding a confrontation on this issue, so that new currencies are likely to be introduced cooperatively.

Republics other than Russia lag in the reform effort not only because they are not yet committed to moving toward a market system but also because they lack the qualified personnel needed to manage a reform program. Even Ukraine, which is politically committed to genuine independence and there-fore has to develop an independent economic policy management ability, is only now beginning to pull an economic team together—and Ukraine has a large population, financial resources, and a diaspora on which to draw. Eco-nomic management will be a real problem for other republics, even with the assistance of the international agencies.

7.7.1 Interrepublic Trade

The breakup of the ruble zone would speed the decline of interrepublic trade, especially if currencies are not convertible. It is often said that the repub-lics of the FSU were extremely closely integrated, more than market econo-mies are likely to be. The (unweighted) average 1988 export ratio (exports/ NMP [net material product]) in interrepublic trade exceeded 50 percent. For the USSR, the GDP/NMP ratio was 1.34, so the average interrepublic exports/ GDP ratio for the smaller republics would be about 40 percent (JSSE 1991, 1:225).[44] This is about the same as the dependence of the smaller European economies on intra-European trade. But, because of the extreme specialization of production in the FSU, the republics must be more mutually dependent for vital production inputs than they will be after economic reform.

The massive changes in relative prices that have to occur will disrupt produc-tion all over the FSU. They will also impose huge adverse balance-of-payments shocks on many of the republics, particularly the energy importers. Table 7.9 presents estimates of the balance-of-payments shift caused by moving to world prices for the five largest republics and for Lithuania, one of the worst hit.[45] These effects are being cushioned by Russia's agreement to maintain a rela-tively (to world prices) low price of oil for interrepublic trade for 1992 but are an indication of the macroeconomic adjustments that have to be made over the next few years.

The republics appear to be moving toward a series of bilateral trade deals for 1992. These agreements avert the worst outcome, a complete collapse of

---

44. In making this calculation, I assume that the services that are responsible for the gap be-tween NMP and GDP are not traded.

45. Similar data are presented in *PlanEcon Report* 8, nos. 9–10 (13 March 1992).

Table 7.9   Interrepublican and Foreign Trade Balances, 1987 (% of NMP)

	At Domestic Prices			At World Prices		
	Interrepublic	Abroad	Total	Interrepublic	Abroad	Total
Russia	.9	−8.3	−7.4	7.4	3.3	10.7
Ukraine	1.6	−7.7	−6.2	−3.9	−1.5	−5.4
Uzbekistan	−20.6	−.5	−21.1	−23.6	−.5	−23.1
Khazakstan	−20.0	−7.8	−27.8	−24.4	−4.1	−28.5
Belarus	11.8	−7.6	4.2	−8.3	−.8	−9.5
Lithuania	−4.5	−7.9	−12.3	−37.0	−2.2	−39.2

Source: JSSE (1991, 1:226–27).

trade, but pose the danger of a sharp reduction of the volume of trade as bilateral balancing—requiring the double coincidence of wants—replaces the multilateral trade that took place in the FSU. In a simple calculation, using a matrix of interrepublic trade, I assumed that, with bilateral clearing, trade between each pair of countries would settle at the lower of imports or exports in 1988. The volume of trade would decline to 44 percent of its previous value under this constraint, a huge shock with potentially dangerously disruptive effects on trade.

There is no question that trade patterns within the FSU have to change drastically over the next few years. It is therefore tempting to argue that whatever decline in trade takes place is part of a process of creative destruction, which will lead more rapidly to an efficient pattern of output. This is wrong as a matter of both theory and political economy. As a matter of theory, trade that has ultimately to disappear may nonetheless be desirable in a second-best situation. As a matter of political economy, a very rapid decline in production—even production that has ultimately to disappear—may stop a reform program in its tracks. The recent experience of Eastern Europe provides suggestive evidence that trade-related shocks can produce a too rapid decline in output.

7.7.2   The IRPM

What can the republics do to mitigate and smooth these shocks? They have much to gain by collaborating on questions of macroeconomic reform, if necessary in introducing currencies, and on trade—and therefore also on questions of interrepublic payments. At present, they lack a framework of collaboration. The case for the introduction of a mechanism like the European Payments Union (EPU) has been made by Dornbusch (1991) and Gros (1991), among others. The case for includes the need for a framework in which to collaborate, the potential gains from multilateral rather than bilateral clearing of trade, and the fear that, without such a mechanism, trade could spiral downward as each republic imposes restrictions on other republics that it fears cannot pay. The case against views a payments union as a mechanism that will

maintain central planning of trade and quantitative restrictions rather than promote rapid convertibility—a charge given some plausibility by the fact that
current account convertibility was attained in Western Europe only in 1958.

Much of the controversy over a payments union and the apparent Russian
opposition to it stem from the emphasis on the EPU precedent. The EPU board
did play a major role in managing trade and payments among its members, in
many respects taking the place of the IMF (Kaplan and Schleiminger, 1989).
That is not needed in the FSU, where the IMF and the World Bank are already
active, nor is the necessary experience available in the FSU. Rather, the need
is for a more modest organization, the IRPM (Interrepublic Payments Mechanism), which would have three tasks: (i) to operate as a technical organization
to clear payments now operating through the CBR; (ii) to provide a mechanism
for the extension of credit among republics and to economize on reserves; and
(iii) to provide a convenient focus for broader interrepublic cooperation.

The issue is usually posed as convertibility versus a payments union. But
parts of an IRPM would be needed even with convertibility. The banking systems in the republics of the FSU are underdeveloped, and explicit arrangements for improving interrepublic payments, and for dealing with payments
when independent currencies are introduced, will need to be worked out. The
arrangements would involve relations among the central banks of the republics
as well as among the nascent private banking systems and could be developed
with the assistance of external agencies. Here is the first necessary function of
an IRPM. Second, credit could be extended among the republics to try to prevent credit constraints from in effect imposing bilateral balancing on trade.
The central banks of the republics will have to agree on mutual credit limits,
to be administered through the IRPM, with—as in the case of the EPU—increasingly onerous settlement provisions as imbalances increase, and with up-
per bounds on imbalances. Convertibility is not a full substitute for such arrangements because the republics will be short of reserves. An IRPM can be
viewed as a means of economizing on hard-currency reserves, setting up an
alternative means of financing temporary imbalances among the republics,
even after convertibility is attained.

The IRPM should be thought of as providing transactions balances to finance current transactions, not long-term financing. Given the adjustments that
they have to make, some republics will run current account deficits for some
years. Financing plans for those deficits will involve agreement with the IMF
and may include separate intergovernmental agreements in the FSU for the
extension of longer-term credit. Those agreements could be negotiated at
IRPM meetings, but they are not an inherent part of an IRPM.

Some framework for continuing interrepublic collaboration and economic
relations is clearly needed. The republics need to collaborate not only in developing payments mechanisms and providing the associated credits but also to
prevent potentially destructive trade and currency reforms. To this point, they
have collaborated on an ad hoc basis, including the negotiation of bilateral

trade agreements. A more permanent multilateral arrangement, in the context of the IRPM, possibly with external technical assistance, would be constructive. It is not inherent in the creation of an IRPM that it slows progress to a market system; the inclusion of international agencies would help ensure that it moves in the right direction.

There is one other potential role for an IRPM. It could be seen as a mechanism through which external assistance is funneled to the republics and conditionality for such assistance is imposed. There might be a case for using the IRPM in this way if the republics were not about to join the IMF and the World Bank. But, since they will join, bilateral assistance can be provided through cofinancing of IMF and World Bank programs, with conditionality agreed on in direct negotiations between the agencies and the republics. The need for donor coordination remains (Fischer 1992).

In the area of interrepublic coordination and payments, as in privatization, the best is the enemy of the good, and the transition has to be managed. The best in this case would be full convertibility, with adequate reserves, for all currencies in the FSU. The current structure of interrepublic trade has to be destroyed. But convertibility with adequate reserves will not happen anytime soon, and trade can be destroyed too rapidly if nothing is developing in its place. That is the case for an IRPM that goes beyond the necessary minimum of a technical organization to manage the payments mechanism.

7.8 Concluding Comments

Although history does not repeat itself, there are interesting similarities between the situation that led to the adoption of the NEP and the current situation. The situation that now confronts Russia and the other republics is far less precarious than that of 1921. Output has not fallen to the extent it did then, there has been no war, and there has been very little bloodshed. Then the new Soviet government faced the hostility of the entire world and many of its own people; it was trying to create a new economic system, of which no one had any experience. The present governments have the technical assistance and goodwill of most of the rest of the world, they have been promised Western financial assistance, they have been admitted to the international financial institutions, and they are trying to return to a system that is well understood in the rest of the world.

Faced with a collapsing economy, the Bolshevik government reintroduced private enterprise. It privatized small firms and encouraged private production in agriculture and distribution; the revival of agriculture and the revival of distribution are two of the prime needs of the present government. The Bolshevik government did not privatize large firms, but it did change the ground rules under which they worked and ordered them to operate commercially. It took three years after the start of the NEP for stabilization to occur, a change that took place only after the tax system had been improved.

The pragmatism of the Bolsheviks is remarkable. Despite their ideology, they were willing for a long time to live with a mixed system. Similar pragmatism will be needed in the present reforms, for the large state sector cannot be privatized rapidly. While the privatization is being organized, it will be necessary to work on policies both to make the large-scale government firms operate as efficiently as is possible in the evolving market environment and to restructure them. It is also quite possible that macroeconomic stabilization will be delayed, as it was in the 1920s. Looking back, it is striking that the transition to the Soviet system took as long as it did—nearly eight years. A lengthy transition process has to be envisaged in the reverse direction as well.

There is one crucial respect in which the present reforms are completely different from those of the 1920s. Government then was in political control, willing to use terror to maintain itself. The Russian government, and most of the other governments of the FSU, plans to carry out its reforms democratically. That is certainly one of the reasons that the West has been willing to support this reform effort with technical and financial assistance.

References

Allison, Graham, and Grigory Yavlinsky. 1991. *Window of opportunity.* Cambridge, Mass.: Kennedy School of Government, Harvard University.

Aslund, Anders. 1990. How small is Soviet national income? In *The impoverished superpower,* ed. H. S. Rowen and C. Wolf, Jr. San Francisco: ICS.

———. 1991a. *Gorbachev's struggle for economic reform.* Updated and expanded ed. London: Pinter.

———. 1991b. Prospects for economic reform in the USSR. Paper presented at the World Bank Annual Conference on Development Economics, April.

Bergson, Abram. 1961. *The real national income of Soviet Russia since 1928.* Cambridge, Mass.: Harvard University Press.

———. 1983. Technological progress. In *The Soviet economy: Toward the year 2000,* ed. A. Bergson and H. S. Levine. London: Allen & Unwin.

———. 1987a. Comparative productivity: The USSR, Eastern Europe, and the West. *American Economic Review* 77, no. 3 (June): 342–57.

———. 1987b. On Soviet real investment growth. *Soviet Studies* 39, no. 3 (July): 406–24.

———. 1991. The USSR before the fall: How poor and why. *Journal of Economic Perspectives* 5, no. 4 (Fall): 29–44.

Blanchard, Olivier J., and Richard Layard. 1991. Post-stabilization inflation in Poland. Massachusetts Institute of Technology, Economics Department, May. Mimeo.

Cagan, Phillip. 1956. The monetary dynamics of hyperinflation. In *Studies in the quantity theory of money,* ed. Milton Friedman. Chicago: University of Chicago Press.

Desai, Padma. 1985. Total factor productivity in postwar Soviet industry and its branches. *Journal of Comparative Economics* 9:1–23.

Dornbusch, Rudiger. 1991. A payments mechanism for the Soviet Union and Eastern Europe. Massachusetts Institute of Technology, November. Mimeo.

Ericson, Richard E. 1990a. The Soviet statistical debate: Khanin vs. TsSU. In *The impoverished superpower,* ed. H. S. Rowen and C. Wolf, Jr. San Francisco: ICS.
————. 1990b. *The Soviet Union, 1979–1990.* International Center for Economic Growth, Country Study no. 7. San Francisco: ICS.
Fischer, Stanley. 1992a. Privatization in East European transformation. In *The emergence of market economics in Eastern Europe,* ed. C. Clague and G. C. Rausser. New York: Blackwell.
————. 1992b. Stabilization and economic reform in Russia. *Brookings Papers on Economic Activity,* no. 1:77–112.
Fischer, Stanley, and Jacob A. Frenkel. 1992. Macroeconomic issues of Soviet reform. *American Economic Review* 82, no. 2 (May): 37–42.
Fischer, Stanley, and Alan Gelb. 1991. The process of Socialist economic transformation. *Journal of Economic Perspectives* 5 (Fall): 91–106.
Gerschenkron, Alexander. 1962. *Economic backwardness in historical perspective.* Cambridge, Mass.: Harvard University Press.
Gregory, Paul R. 1982. *Russian national income, 1885–1913.* Cambridge: Cambridge University Press.
Gregory, Paul R., and Robert C. Stuart. 1986. *Soviet economic structure and performance.* 3d ed. New York: Harper & Row.
Gros, Daniel. 1991. A Soviet payments union? Brussels: Centre for European Policy Studies, November. Mimeo.
IMF, IBRD, OECD, EBRD. 1990. *The economy of the USSR: Summary and recommendations.* Washington, D.C.: World Bank. (Referred to as JSSE [1990].)
————. 1991. *A Study of the Soviet Economy.* 3 vols. Paris: OECD. (Referred to as JSSE [1991].)
Johnson, Simon, and Heidi Kroll. 1991. Managerial strategies for spontaneous privatization. *Soviet Economy* 7, no. 4:281–316.
Joint Study of the Soviet Economy (JSSE). 1990. *See* IMF et al. (1990).
————. 1991. *See* IMF et al. (1991).
Kaplan, Jacob J., and Gunther Schleiminger. 1989. *The European Payments Union.* Oxford: Clarendon.
Katzenellenbaum, S. S. 1925. *Russian currency and banking, 1914–1924.* London: P. S. King & Son.
Kontorovich, Vladimir. 1986. Soviet growth slowdown: Econometric vs. direct evidence. *American Economic Review* 76, no. 2 (May): 181–85.
Kopits, George. 1991. Fiscal reforms in the European economies in transition. In *The transition to a market economy,* 2 vols. ed. P. Marer and S. Zecchini. Paris: OECD.
Kremer, Michael. 1993. An O-ring theory of economic growth. *Quarterly Journal of Economics* 108, 3 (August): 551–76.
Lipton, David, and Jeffrey Sachs. 1990. Creating a market economy in Eastern Europe: The case of Poland. *Brookings Papers on Economic Activity,* no. 1:75–133.
McLure, Charles E., Jr. 1991. A consumption-based direct tax for countries in transition from socialism. Working Paper no. 751. Washington, D.C.: World Bank, August.
Maddison, Angus. 1969. *Economic growth in Japan and the USSR.* London: Allen & Unwin.
————. 1989. *The world economy in the 20th century.* Paris: OECD.
Mitchell, B. R. 1976. *European historical statistics, 1750–1970.* New York: Columbia University Press.
Nove, Alec. 1989. *An economic history of the U.S.S.R.* London: Pelican.
Ofer, Gur. 1987. Soviet economic growth: 1928–1985. *Journal of Economic Literature* 25, no. 4 (December): 1767–1833.
————. 1990. Macroeconomic issues of Soviet reforms. *NBER Macroeconomics Annual,* 297–339.

Piore, Michael, and Charles Sabel. 1984. *The second industrial divide*. New York: Basic.

Pipes, Richard. 1990. *The Russian Revolution*. New York: Knopf.

Rostowski, Jacek, and Judith Shapiro. 1992. Secondary currencies in the Russian hyperinflation and stabilization of 1921–24. Centre for Economic Performance, London School of Economics, January. Mimeo.

Rowen, Henry S., and Charles Wolf, Jr., eds. 1990. *The impoverished superpower.* San Francisco: ICS.

Seidman, Laurence S. 1978. Tax-based incomes policies. *Brookings Papers on Economic Activity,* no. 2:301–48.

Shelton, Judy. 1989. *The coming Soviet crash.* New York: Free Press.

Summers, Robert, and Alan Heston. 1991. The Penn world table (mark 5): An expanded set of international comparisons, 1950–1980. *Quarterly Journal of Economics* 106, no. 2 (May): 327–68.

Sutton, Antony C. 1973. *Western technology and Soviet economic development, 1945 to 1965.* Stanford, Calif.: Hoover Institution.

Weitzman, Martin L. 1970. Soviet postwar economic growth and capital-labor substitution. *American Economic Review* 60, no. 5 (December): 676–92.

———. 1983. Industrial production. In *The Soviet economy: Toward the year 2000,* ed. A. Bergson and H. S. Levine. London: Allen & Unwin.

Wiles, Peter. 1982. Soviet consumption and investment prices and the meaningfulness of real investment. *Soviet Studies* 34, no. 2 (April): 289–95.

Winiecki, Jan. 1986. Are Soviet-type economies entering an era of long-term decline? *Soviet Studies* 38, no. 3 (July): 325–48.

Yurovsky, L. N. 1925. *Currency problems and policy of the Soviet Union.* London: Leonard Parsons.

Comment   Lawrence H. Summers

Stanley Fischer's thorough paper does an excellent job of articulating what might be labeled the "economists' consensus" view of the situation in the former Soviet Union. Despite economists' reputation for never being able to agree on anything, there is a striking degree of unanimity in the advice that has been provided to the nations of Eastern Europe and the former Soviet Union (FSU). The legions of economists who have descended on the formerly Communist economies have provided advice very similar, if less nuanced, than the advice provided in this paper.

The consensus view of the transition problem articulated by Fischer consists of five propositions:

1. The situation in the formerly Communist economies is unlike anything the world has ever encountered before.
2. Simply addressing stabilization is insufficient to solving this problem as it is profoundly structural in nature.
3. The multitudinous problems faced by formerly Communist economies are all connected. Examples of newly privatized enterprises subtracting value

by buying oil at a nickel a gallon, or of privatization attempts foundering because of the difficulty of valuing enterprises when oil is selling for a nickel a barrel, abound.

4. The three "-ations"—privatization, stabilization, and liberalization—must all be completed as soon as possible. Maintaining the momentum of reform is a crucial political problem. An adequate set of transfer programs to support the unemployed is essential, as is a safety net for other losers in the reform process.

5. Western support cannot hurt the prospects for reform and has a prospect of helping both politically and economically. Given the enormous worldwide stake in the countries of the FSU making a successful transition to a democratic market system, more assistance is better than less.

I suspect that these are statements with which most economists who have thought about the FSU would agree. And they are consistent with the position that the International Monetary Fund (IMF) and the World Bank are taking as they negotiate with the nations of Eastern Europe and the FSU. So I have little to quarrel with in Fischer's paper. I just want to comment in a little more detail on several of the issues he takes up. Many of my comments are amplifications rather than qualifications or criticisms of Fischer's analysis.

First, there is a real issue as to whether reform in the FSU is being adequately financed. According to the Fischer paper (similar estimates are available elsewhere), imports into Russia were $82.9 billion in 1990 and only $45.6 billion in 1991. While the exact use to which the vaunted $24 billion aid package will be put is not clear, it is clear that it will not be nearly large enough to offset the dramatic import compression that the Russians are now suffering. It is unlikely that imports will rise to even two-thirds of their historic level in the next few years even if the whole scheduled aid package is disbursed. And the situation is considerably bleaker in the fourteen non-Russian republics.

It is instructive to compare the situations of the FSU and Eastern Europe. The nations of the FSU surely face far greater problems. They are further from the West geographically, systematically, and in terms of past contacts. The FSU economy is far more distorted in both a financial and a real sense than were any of the Communist economies of Eastern Europe. And it is facing the challenges of dissolution. Even without taking account of the breakdown of internal trade, import compression in the FSU is likely to be several times as serious as import compression in Poland and other parts of Eastern Europe.

Second, where should the exchange rate be pegged? Thinking just of Russia, Fischer suggests that the exchange rate be pegged in such a way that, when average wages are converted into dollars, they come out to about $100 a month. At current exchange rates, wages are in the $10.00–$20.00 range, so this implies a very substantial real appreciation. I suspect that it is unrealistic to expect (or try) to contrive a real appreciation of such a large magnitude.

For all the reasons that were given as to why Russia is in more dire straits than Poland, it seems to me that there is a case for setting the wage at a lower dollar level in Russia than it was set at in Poland, where it was close to $75.00 following stabilization. Considerations beyond the low productivity of Russian enterprise pointing in this direction include protection of those enterprises that need protection and the fiscal consequences of oil export taxes, which are more favorable at a lower than at a higher exchange rate, a consideration that is not present in Poland. On balance, I suspect that $50.00 a month is a more plausible short-run target than $100 a month. Of course, any kind of fixed exchange rate is not a viable option until some control over macroeconomic fundamentals is achieved.

Third, the energy sector should be a crucial locus of reform. The potential gains in export revenues from increasing the efficiency of petroleum production and increasing efficiency in energy use probably exceed $100 billion by the end of the 1990s. Right now, energy intensity per unit of GNP is more than five times the corresponding figure in Europe, and there are easy repairs that could raise drilling and shipping productivity substantially. Investments in the energy sector are probably the most levered investments that the West can make in raising the flow of hard currency to the FSU.

Russia and several other republics have potentially valuable oil properties. I am reminded of the statistic that, while in 1983 the value of Mexico's oil reserves was twenty times the value of its outstanding debt, yet Mexico had a debt crisis. I cannot help but wonder whether some part of financial engineering with respect to the FSU problem does not involve arranging for the transfer of hard currency to Russia and other republics with petroleum resources in return for claims on its oil reserves, perhaps claims guaranteed in some way by the Western governments who are seeking to help the FSU.

Fourth, I think that Fischer devotes too little attention to the issue of what to do about the Gordian knot of the financial sector. The bank's principal asset is loans to the state sector. Since most of the enterprises are under water, the banks are as well. It is pointless to fix up the banks if the enterprises are still in trouble. And, without viable banks, enterprises, restructuring, and liquidation are difficult to arrange. It is tempting to say that the right answer is to leave existing institutions aside and set up new banks to loan to new enterprises. That is happening on a large scale right now. The problem is that it is mostly Ponzi finance with less lending to new enterprises than to bankers' brothers-in-law. Supervision surely must be improved. But, given the magnitude of the supervision failures in the OECD, it would be unrealistic to rely on supervision as the complete solution to financial sector problems.

Fifth, it seems to me that the Fischer paper is entirely correct in emphasizing the problems with the Polish model of nonenterprise reform, which is to pound your fist on the table and insist that there be privatization or nothing else. But listening to his description of what should be done leaves one understanding why that advice is given in Poland. The prospect of the Russian government organizing to have a board that is going to assess the proposed restructuring plans enterprise by enterprise, perhaps in conjunction with the banks to whom the enterprise is in debt, is not encouraging. The confusion engendered by efforts to handle Canary Wharf in the West just points up the difficulty.

In addition to underscoring the importance of privatization, I would emphasize the importance of mass corporatization. This is highly desirable because of the importance of giving incumbent workers and managers in current firms a claim that will ultimately be sold. This provides an incentive to maximize enterprise value even in advance of privatization.

Sixth, the Fischer paper makes light of what is a very important part of the Russian balance-of-payments protection—the projection of substantial balance-of-payments improvement from raising prices on sales to other republics. There are two separate problems here. There is a real problem of the large subsidies that the Russian Republic has been giving to the other republics by selling commodities, principally oil, at very low prices. This is not a problem that any amount of payments mechanism is going to circumvent but a real structural difficulty; by accepting it in making arrangements with the Russian Republic, one raises the aid requirement or, alternatively, reduces the prospects for the remaining republics.

Seventh, there is the question of whether a payments union or some similar institution should be set up when and if republics introduce their own currencies. Here I think it is important to distinguish between the payments mechanism and the extension of credit. I believe that there is a clear case for multilateral clearing that will conserve on what will inevitably be scarce hard currency reserves. There is a much weaker case for the extension of long-term credits from one republic to another or from the West to some kind of interrepublic payments mechanism. There is Fischer's point that the IMF is probably better at doing some of what the European payments mechanism did than any Russian bureaucracy is likely to be anytime soon. And there is the additional point that the people with the least responsible macroeconomic policies will have the largest trade deficits and will, therefore, have the greatest access to finance. So for the West to finance its support for the republics through such a mechanism would be to give up important opportunities to apply conditionally on the basis of the pursuit of specific policies at the republic level.

Eighth, I wonder if the Fischer paper does not somewhat overstate the case for infrastructure investments? It is hard to deny that infrastructure investment is good, and it is hard to say that having a good infrastructure is not important, and there is much that is wrong with the infrastructure in the FSU. But I doubt that it is too bad relative to the infrastructure in other equally poor countries. And the available aid flows are trivial relative to the cost of modernizing the infrastructure of the FSU. It may well be that support for consumption to maintain the political momentum for reform is actually a higher priority than support for new infrastructure investment.

Discussion Summary

Geoffrey Carliner said that Summers's advice for Gorbachev sounded like China's post-1978 economic reform program. Carliner noted that China's leaders have proceeded gradually with their economic reforms and that they have had remarkable success. He wondered what relevance the Chinese example has for the current debate about gradualism in Eastern Europe.

Andrei Shleifer supported the Russian government's decision to liberalize prices before achieving macroeconomic stability (i.e., controlling the budget). He said that, before the reforms, the most important cost of fixed and distorted prices had been the incentive to withhold goods. This collapse in deliveries is being reversed by price liberalization. Shleifer noted that "open inflation with more or less correct relative prices is infinitely preferable to repressed inflation of the sort that Russia had before reform."

Shleifer also spoke about the difficulties involved in privatization, even privatization of small-scale firms. He noted that almost all local governments in Russia have their own small-scale privatization programs, most of which are inconsistent with Russian law. Shleifer also emphasized the danger of becoming complacent about continued state ownership of large companies. He said that "state ownership" currently involves almost no true control rights for the state. Control has de facto reverted to managers, local governments, and to some extent workers.

Olivier Blanchard asked whether there were lessons to be drawn from the historical analysis in Fischer's paper. Blanchard was particularly interested in the New Economic Policy (NEP), which was characterized by both rapid structural changes and experimentation with a mix of market forces and central planning. Blanchard also asked about the existing structure of control in Russia. He wondered whether it was still possible for policymakers in Moscow to implement decisions nationally.

Jeffrey Sachs responded to Blanchard's question about control. Sachs felt that, in order for small-scale privatization to work rapidly, the center will have to cooperate with local governments. Sachs also developed Blanchard's point about historical precedents. Sachs drew attention to an episode in 1918, when price controls led to a breakdown in food shipments to the cities. Instead of liberalizing prices, Kerensky tried to solve the problem by arranging barter transactions. This turned out to be a fiasco. Sachs stressed the parallels between this experience and the recent collapse in food shipments. Guaranteeing that the cities would be provisioned was one reason that the current reforms had to be implemented quickly.

Sachs criticized Carliner's suggestion that Chinese gradualism might be successfully implemented in Russia. Sachs emphasized that the Chinese have relied on state repression for the effective management of large enterprises. In reference to Summers's point that most economists in the 1960s were overoptimistic about the Soviet Union's prospects, Sachs cited Keynes's *Essays in Per-*

suasion. Keynes foresaw that the Soviet system would end in an economic disaster.

Stanley Fischer also responded to Summers's remark about the optimistic 1960s forecasts. Fischer noted that these forecasts were not obviously wrong until recently. He believes that the Soviet Union could have gone the Chinese route.

Fischer addressed the issue of rapid privatization raised by Shleifer. He agreed that it was important to establish rights and privatize as quickly as possible. However, he warned that this will take at least two years, and maybe much longer. Fischer emphasized that keeping things running in the meantime is also a priority.

In response to Blanchard, Fischer said that the NEP experience highlighted the need for pragmatism and the value of getting the private sector to take over agricultural production and the distribution system. Finally, Fischer reminded Sachs that, even though Keynes thought that the Bolsheviks had nothing to teach the West, Keynes still believed that, had he been Russian, he would have been on the side of the Revolution.

Biographies (Volume 1 and Volume 2)

Philippe Aghion is official fellow at Nuffield College, Oxford, and senior economist at the European Bank for Reconstruction and Development.

Anders Aslund is director of the Stockholm Institute for Soviet and East European Economics at the Stockholm School of Economics.

David Begg is professor of economics at Birkbeck College, University of London.

Andrew Berg is an economist in the research department of the International Monetary Fund.

Olivier Jean Blanchard is professor of economics at the Massachusetts Institute of Technology and a research associate of the National Bureau of Economic Research.

Barry Bosworth is a senior fellow in the Economic Studies Division of the Brookings Institution.

Michael Bruno is professor of economics at Hebrew University and a research associate of the National Bureau of Economic Research.

Wendy Carlin is lecturer in economics at University College, London.

Geoffrey Carliner is executive director of the National Bureau of Economic Research.

Susan M. Collins is associate professor of economics at Georgetown University, a senior fellow of the Brookings Institution, and a research associate of the National Bureau of Economic Research.

Timothy Condon is an economist in the Central Europe Department of the World Bank.

Fabrizio Coricelli is an economist in the Country Economics Department of the World Bank.

Alain de Crombrugghe is assistant professor of economics at the University of Namur, Belgium.

Kemal Derviş is director of the Central Europe Department of the World Bank.

Peter Diamond is the Paul A. Samuelson Professor of Economics at the Massachusetts Institute of Technology and a research associate of the National Bureau of Economic Research.

Michael P. Dooley is professor of economics at the University of California, Santa Cruz, and a research associate of the National Bureau of Economic Research.

Rudiger Dornbusch is the Ford International Professor of Economics at the Massachusetts Institute of Technology and a research associate of the National Bureau of Economic Research.

Karel Dyba is the minister of economy of the Czech Republic.

Saul Estrin is associate professor of economics at the London Business School.

Stanley Fischer is the Elizabeth and James Killian Professor and director of the World Economy Laboratory in the Department of Economics at the Massachusetts Institute of Technology and a research associate of the National Bureau of Economic Research.

Richard B. Freeman is professor of economics at Harvard University and a research associate of the National Bureau of Economic Research.

Lev Freinkman is an economist in the Moscow office of the World Bank.

Kenneth A. Froot is professor of business administration at the Graduate School of Business, Harvard University, and a research associate of the National Bureau of Economic Research.

Roger H. Gordon is professor of economics at the University of Michigan and a research associate of the National Bureau of Economic Research.

Oliver Hart is professor of economics at Harvard University.

Simon Johnson is assistant professor of economics at the Fuqua School of Business, Duke University.

Tom Kolaja is an industry specialist in the Ministry of Ownership Changes of the Polish Government.

George Kopits is senior resident representative in Hungary of the International Monetary Fund.

Pentti Kouri is director of Kouri Capital in Greenwich, Connecticut.

Richard Layard is professor of economics and director of the Centre for Economic Performance at the London School of Economics.

Anthony Levitas is a Ph.D. candidate in political science at the Massachusetts Institute of Technology and a research fellow at the Center for European Studies, Harvard University.

David Lipton is a fellow at the Woodrow Wilson Center for Scholars.

Colin Mayer is professor of economics and finance at City University Business School, London.

Kalman Mizsei is director of the Economic Focus Area and the Pew Economist in Residence at the Institute for EastWest Studies.

John Moore is professor of economics at the London School of Economics.

Wilhelm Nölling is president of the Landeszentralbank in der Freien und Hansestadt Hamburg, a member of the Central Bank Policy Council of the Deutsche Bundesbank, Frankfurt, and editor of *Hamburger Beiträge zur Wirtschafts und Währungspolitik in Europa*.

Boris Pleskovic is senior economist and deputy administrator, Research Advisory Staff, at the World Bank.

Dani Rodrik is professor of economics and international affairs at Columbia University, a research fellow of the Centre for Economic Policy Research, and a research associate of the National Bureau of Economic Research.

Jacek Rostowski is lecturer in Russian and East European economics at the School of Slavonic and East European Studies at London University, deputy director of the Centre for Research into Communist Economies, and an associate of the Centre for Economic Performance, London.

Jeffrey D. Sachs is the Galen L. Stone Professor of International Trade at Harvard University and a research associate of the National Bureau of Economic Research.

Mark E. Schaffer is a research fellow at the Centre for Economic Performance, London School of Economics.

Andrei Shleifer is professor of economics at Harvard University and a faculty research fellow of the National Bureau of Economic Research.

András Simon is professor of economics at the Budapest University of Economics.

Inderjit Singh is lead economist for the Transition and Macro-Adjustment Division of the Country Economics Department of the World Bank.

Jeremy C. Stein is associate professor of finance at the Sloan School of Management, the Massachusetts Institute of Technology, and a research associate of the National Bureau of Economic Research.

Lawrence H. Summers is undersecretary for international affairs in the Department of the Treasury.

Jan Svejnar is professor of economics at the University of Pittsburgh and CERGE, Charles University.

Sweder van Wijnberger is senior adviser in the Central Europe Department of the World Bank.

Dmitri Vasiliev is deputy minister of Privatization for the Russian government.

Robert W. Vishny is professor of finance at the University of Chicago and a program director at the National Bureau of Economic Research.

Jan Winiecki is executive director of the European Bank for Reconstruction and Development.

Holger C. Wolf is assistant professor of economics and international business at the Stern School of Business, New York University, and a faculty research fellow of the National Bureau of Economic Research.

Janet L. Yellen is the Bernard T. Rocca, Jr., Professor of International Business and Trade at the Walter A. Haas School of Business at the University of California, Berkeley.

Josef Zieleniec is a research associate of CERGE, Prague.

Contributors (Volume 1 and Volume 2)

Philippe Aghion
European Bank for Reconstruction and
    Development
6 Broadgate
London EC2M 2QS, United Kingdom

Anders Aslund
Stockholm Institute for Soviet and East
    European Economics
Stockholm School of Economics
Stockholm, Sweden

David Begg
Birkbeck College
University of London
7/15 Gresse Street
London W1P 1PA,
United Kingdom

Andrew Berg
Harvard Institute for International
    Development
1 Eliot Street
Cambridge, MA 02138

Olivier Jean Blanchard
Department of Economics
Massachusetts Institute of Technology
50 Memorial Drive
Cambridge, MA 02139

Barry Bosworth
The Brookings Institution
1775 Massachusetts Avenue, N.W.
Washington, DC 20036

Michael Bruno
Department of Economics
Hebrew University
Jerusalem, Israel

Wendy Carlin
Department of Economics
University College London
Gower Street
London WC1E 6BT, United Kingdom

Geoffrey Carliner
National Bureau of Economic
    Research
1050 Massachusetts Avenue
Cambridge, MA 02138

Susan M. Collins
The Brookings Institution
1775 Massachusetts Avenue, N.W.
Washington, DC 20036

Timothy Condon
Central Europe Department
The World Bank
1818 H Street, N.W.
Washington, DC 20433

Fabrizio Coricelli
Country Economics Department
The World Bank
1818 H Street, N.W.
Washington, DC 20433

Alain de Crombrugghe
Faculté des Sciences Economiques et
    Sociales
Namur University
Rampart de la Vierge, 8
B-5000 Namur
Belgium

Kemal Derviş
Central Europe Department
The World Bank
1818 H. Street, N.W.
Washington, DC 20433

Peter Diamond
Department of Economics
Room E52–344
Massachusetts Institute of Technology
Cambridge, MA 02139

Michael P. Dooley
Department of Economics
University of California, Santa Cruz
Crown College, Room 236
Santa Cruz, CA 95064

Rudiger Dornbusch
Department of Economics
Room E52–357
Massachusetts Institute of Technology
Cambridge, MA 02139

Karel Dyba
Ministry of Economic Policy and
    Development of the Czech Republic
CS-101 60 Praha 10
Czechoslovakia

Saul Estrin
Faculty of Economics
London Business School
Sussex Place, Regents Park
London NW1 4SA
United Kingdom

Stanley Fischer
Department of Economics
Room E52–274
Massachusetts Institute of Technology
Cambridge, MA 02139

Richard B. Freeman
National Bureau of Economic Research
1050 Massachusetts Avenue
Cambridge, MA 02138

Lev Freinkman
The World Bank
Ilyinka, 23, Entrance 10
Moscow 103132
Russia

Kenneth A. Froot
Dillon 23
Graduate School of Business
Harvard University
Soldiers Field
Boston, MA 02163

Roger H. Gordon
Department of Economics
University of Michigan
Ann Arbor, MI 48109

Oliver Hart
Littauer 220
Department of Economics
Harvard University
Cambridge, MA 02138

Simon Johnson
The Fuqua School of Business
Duke University
Durham, NC 27706

Thomas Kolaja
Ministry of Ownership Changes
ul. Krucza 36
00–525 Warsaw
Poland

George Kopits
Office of the Resident Representative in
    Hungary
National Bank of Hungary, Room 210
1850 Budapest, Szabadság tér 8-9
Hungary

Pentti Kouri
Kouri Capital
19 Benedict Place
Greenwich, CT 06830

Richard Layard
Centre for Economic Performance
London School of Economics
Houghton Street
London WC2A 2AE
United Kingdom

Anthony Levitas
Center for European Studies
Harvard University
27 Kirkland Street
Cambridge, MA 02138

David Lipton
Woodrow Wilson Center
1000 Jefferson Drive, S.W.
Washington, DC 20560

Colin Mayer
City University Business School
Frobisher Crescent, Barbican Centre
London EC4
United Kingdom

Kalman Mizsei
Institute for East West Studies
360 Lexington Avenue
New York, NY 10017

John Moore
Department of Economics
London School of Economics
Houghton Street
London WC2A 2AE
United Kingdom

Wilhelm Nölling
Landeszentralbank
Ost-West Strasse 73
2000 Hamburg 11
Germany

Boris Pleskovic
Research Advisory Staff
The World Bank
1818 H Street, N.W.
Washington, DC 20433

Dani Rodrik
Department of Economics
Columbia University
420 W. 118th Street, 1312
New York, NY 10027

Jacek Rostowski
School of Slavonic and East European
   Studies
University of London
London W1P 1PA
United Kingdom

Jeffrey D. Sachs
Department of Economics
Harvard University
Littauer Center M-14
Cambridge, MA 02138

Mark E. Schaffer
Centre for Economic Performance
London School of Economics
Houghton Street, Aldwych
London WC2 2AE
United Kingdom

Andrei Shleifer
Department of Economics
Harvard University
Littauer Center 315
Cambridge, MA 02138

András Simon
Department of International Economics
Budapest University of Economics
H-1093 Budapest
Fövám tér 8
Hungary

Inderjit Singh
Transition and Macro-Adjustment
   Division
Country Economics Department
The World Bank
1818 H Street, N.W.
Washington, DC 20433

Jeremy C. Stein
Sloan School of Management
E52–448
Massachusetts Institute of Technology
Cambridge, MA 02139

Lawrence H. Summers
Department of the Treasury
1500 Pennsylvania Ave,
N. W., Room 3432
Washington, DC 20220

Jan Svejnar
Department of Economics
4M30 Forbes Quadrangle
University of Pittsburgh
Pittsburgh, PA 15260

Sweder van Wijnbergen
Central Europe Department
The World Bank
1818 H Street, N.W.
Washington, DC 20433

Dmitri Vasiliev
Ministry of Privatization
Moscow
Russia

Robert W. Vishny
Graduate School of Business
University of Chicago
1101 East 58th Street
Chicago, IL 60637

Jan Winiecki
Executive Director
European Bank of Reconstruction and
    Development
One Exchange Square
London EC2A 2EH
United Kingdom

Holger C. Wolf
Management Education Center
New York University
44 W. 44th Street, Suite 7–78
New York, NY 10012

Janet L. Yellen
Walter A. Hass School of Business
350 Barrows Hall
University of California
Berkeley, CA 94720

Josef Zieleniec
CERGE
FSV UK
Prague
Czechoslovakia

Author Index

Subject Index

Agricultural sector: former East Germany, 161; Poland, 22; Russia, 241; Slovenia, 193

Austria, 107

Balance of payments: Czech and Slovak Federal Republic (CSFR), 120–21; Hungary, 128–29, 148; Poland, 76–77; Slovenia, 8

Balcerowicz Plan (1990), Poland, 1

Banking systems: Czech and Slovak Federal Republic (CSFR), 100, 102, 118–19, 120; Eastern European countries, 5, 20; former Soviet Union, 248, 254; Hungary, 22, 137; Poland, 67–68, 76–78; Russia, 244; Slovenia, 202, 212–16, 220

Bank Restructuring Agency, Slovenia, 206, 213

Bankruptcy: new procedures, 16; risk of, 65, 66; Slovenia, 214

Brioni Accord (1991), 198, 199

Budget deficit: Czechoslovakia, 102; financing of, 41–42; former East Germany, 185; Hungary, 142–43, 151–52; Poland, 1, 76, 152; Russia, 238; Slovenia, 205; Soviet Union (1991), 236

Budget levels: Eastern Europe: with fiscal reform, 38–39; Poland: with economic reform, 52, 53

Bulgaria: heterodox stabilization plan, 27; monetary policy, 23–26; radical reform with independence, 2; before and during reform, 24

Central Bank of Russia (CBR): credit policy of, 8, 238–40; payments operation of, 248

Central banks: Eastern European countries, 20; Poland, 67; Slovenia, 200–202, 206

CMEA. *See* Council for Mutual Economic Assistance (CMEA)

Company Act (1988), Hungary, 129, 138, 140

Corporatization: proposal in Russia for, 242–43; of state enterprises in Hungary, 140–41

Council for Mutual Economic Assistance (CMEA): collapse of, 4, 21; effect in Eastern Europe of collapse, 36–37; effect of collapse on Poland, 55–56, 60–61, 82–84, 85. *See also* Payments union; Ruble zone

Credit policy: Czech and Slovak Federal Republic (CSFR), 100–101, 112–13, 119–20; Eastern European countries, 42–44; Hungary, 135–37, 139; Poland, 52, 62, 77, 86; Russia, 238–40

Currency: Czech and Slovak Federal Republic (CSFR), 98, 99; Eastern European countries, 4; Poland, 52, 53, 87–88; Russia, 245–59; Slovenia, 191, 198–202; Soviet Union (1991), 235. *See also* Payments union; Ruble zone

Czech and Slovak Federal Republic (CSFR): economic reform, 98–104; employment, 105, 107, 109; fiscal policy, 99, 102, 110–12, 119–20; heterodox stabilization